PATRICK J. MCNAMARA

Sons of the Sierra

Juárez, Díaz, and the People of Ixtlán, Oaxaca, 1855–1920

The University of North Carolina Press

CHAPEL HILL

Designed by Heidi Perov

Set in Arnhem Blond by Tseng Information Systems, Inc.

Manufactured in the United States of America

This book was published with the assistance of the Anniversary Endowment Fund of the University of North Carolina Press.

The paper in this book meets the guidelines for permanence and durability of the Committee on Production Guidelines for Book Longevity of the Council on Library Resources.

Library of Congress Cataloging-in-Publication Data

McNamara, Patrick J.

Sons of the Sierra : Juárez, Díaz, and the people of Ixtlán, Oaxaca, 1855–1920 / Patrick J. McNamara.

p. cm.

Includes bibliographical references and index.

ISBN-13: 978-0-8078-3078-9 (cloth : alk. paper)

ISBN-13: 978-0-8078-5787-8 (pbk. : alk. paper)

1. Zapotec Indians—Wars—Mexico—Ixtlán. 2. Zapotec Indians—Mexico—Ixtlán—Politics and government. 3. Zapotec Indians—Mexico—Ixtlán—Government relations. 4. Peasant uprisings—Mexico—Ixtlán. 5. Díaz, Porfirio, 1830–1915—Relations with Zapotec Indians. 6. Juárez, Benito, 1806–1872—Relations with Zapotec Indians. 7. Mexico—History—Revolution, 1910–1920. 8. Ixtlán (Mexico)—Politics and government. 9. Ixtlán (Mexico)—History—20th century. I. Title.

F1221.Z3M375 2007

972'.74059768—dc22

2006048556

cloth   11 10 09 08 07   5 4 3 2 1

paper   11 10 09 08 07   5 4 3 2 1

THIS BOOK WAS DIGITALLY PRINTED.

To Charles A. Hale

Contents

Table, Map, and Illustrations

Acknowledgments

As I began the research for this book, I made an appointment with a prominent Mexican historian to introduce myself and seek any advice she might offer. When we met in her Mexico City office, I handed her some letters of introduction from historians she knew in the United States, and then I started to explain my interest in Zapotec communities in Oaxaca. As soon as I said Oaxaca, she interrupted and said in English (and in a rather loud voice as I remember), "Don't you people know we have other states in this country besides Oaxaca?" I don't remember the rest of our brief meeting. I have thought often of that encounter as I continued to research and write, and I am thinking of it again as this book is going to press. At first I thought she was just tired of meeting another scholar from abroad who had "discovered" one of the best places to work and live in Mexico. Later I realized that by mentioning Oaxaca as my starting point, it was easy for her to assume that I saw Mexico in somewhat clichéd terms—as the combination of indigenous and Spanish cultures that is omnipresent in Oaxaca, or, as I describe it more fully in the book, as a living museum where tourists travel to experience Mexico's lost past. Eventually, however, I came to appreciate her comment as a challenge to write a more unexpected history, to see Oaxaca's place in national history in a new light. Ironically, if I have succeeded at all, it is due to the exceptional work of many other scholars in and outside of Mexico who have written about Oaxaca before me.

Francie Chassen-López is at the top of that list of scholars whose work has helped me understand the complexity of Oaxaca. In addition to sharing her long list of publications in both English and Spanish, Francie has read this manuscript at least twice and has generously offered extensive advice. She has tried to keep me from making errors, and those that remain are despite her best efforts. More than anyone I know, Francie unites the community of scholars working inside and outside of Oaxaca. I was introduced to her by Howard "Manny" Campbell, another Oaxacan specialist, who has continued to inspire me by his dedication to working and living in Mexico. I am grateful to Manny for several times picking me up at the airport in Ciudad Juárez, sharing a few beers on the border, and then delivering me to the airport in El Paso for connecting flights. Francie and Manny introduced me to the close-knit group of historians working in Oaxaca. Professors Anselmo Arellanes Meixueiro, Héctor Gerardo Martínez Medina, Víctor Raúl Martínez Vásquez, Francisco José Ruiz Cervantes, and Carlos Sánchez Silva have provided help at various points in this project. These individuals have rewritten Oaxacan history and in the process organized archives throughout the state that have helped so many other scholars. I benefited directly from these efforts during my time at the Archivo General del Estado de Oaxaca in Oaxaca City. The archivists there were incredibly patient with my requests and generously allowed me to work at a desk closer to the stacks so that I could occasionally dig for documents on my own. Also in Oaxaca City, Itandehui Gutiérrez Yañiz at the Biblioteca Pública de Oaxaca, Sala de Genaro Vásquez, provided helpful guidance through the manuscripts of Manuel Martínez Gracida.

I am most grateful for help I received from numerous people throughout the Sierra Zapoteca. Most important were Víctor Ramírez Hernández and his family, who welcomed me into their home, invited me to family gatherings, and told me stories about their community of Ixtlán. I would also like to thank Luvia Mendoza Bautista of the Biblioteca Pública de Guelatao, Jaime Luna of the "Trova de Guelatao," Arrón Cruz Luna from the Museo Comunitaria Minereo de Natividad, and the entire Ixtlán town council, which gave me permission to work in its municipal archive in 2001.

As much as I would have liked to work full-time in Oaxaca, most of my archival research was carried out in Mexico City. By far, the most important place for me was the Colección Porfirio Díaz (CPD) at Universidad Iberoamericana. The archivists and staff at the CPD, especially María Eugenia Patricia Ponce Alocer, made the long journey to get there worthwhile and comfortable. They allowed me to work with the original documents and hired a student full-time to make photocopies at my request. I cannot think of working at the CPD without also thinking of Glen Kuecker, who worked on the other side of the table, found half of the documents I used in this book, asked me hard questions during our breaks, and made the long hours in Santa Fe enjoyable. I am grateful for his friendship and advice.

Over the years I had the pleasure of working in Mexico surrounded by a group of exciting (and now not so young) scholars. Jane Erickson, Jeremy Baskes, and I shared long conversations about Oaxacan and Mexican history from the vantage point of the Bar Jardín on the Zocalo in Oaxaca City. Matthew Gutmann, Susie Porter, Eric Zolov, Paul Hart, and Glen Kuecker transformed the world's largest city into a familiar circle of friends. Linda Arnold shared her unsurpassed expertise in the archives at both the Archivo General de la Nación and the Archivo Histórico de la Defensa Nacional. In particular, the documents came much faster after the soldiers/archivists at Defensa saw that Linda was helping me.

Archivists in Mexico City graciously allowed me to work with documents that truly represent Mexico's rich national treasure. Individuals at the Archivo General de la Nación, the Biblioteca Nacional, and the Centro de Estudios de Historia de México greeted my requests with professional courtesy and polite cooperation. Research funding has come from a Grant-in-Aid of Research at the University of Minnesota, a McKnight Summer Fellowship for the Humanities, a Faculty Summer Research Fellowship of the University of Minnesota, a Fulbright-Hays Training Grant from the U.S. Department of Education, and a Latin American and Iberian Studies Program Field Research Grant from the University of Wisconsin–Madison.

My colleagues at the University of Minnesota have provided generous encouragement over the years. I am particularly grateful for conversations I have had with Sarah Chambers, Christopher Isett, Erika Lee, M. J. Maynes, Bob McCaa, Jean O'Brien-Kehoe, Jeffrey Pilcher, JB Shank, Ajay Skaria, Rafael Tarrago, and Thomas Wolfe. I have also benefited from research assistance from Rodolfo Gutierrez and Ann-Marie Wolf. Mark B. Lindberg and Jonathan Schroeder of the University of Minnesota Cartography Lab created the map of Ixtlán District. Colleagues at other universities have also helped in making this book better, particularly Peter Guardino, Donna Guy, and Mark Wasserman.

Before coming to Minnesota I had the privilege of learning about Latin American history from historians and friends at the University of Wisconsin–Madison. Professors Florencia E. Mallon, Francisco Scarano, and Steve J. Stern created an intellectually rich and exciting environment that continues to shape how I think about Latin American history. As will be clear in the reading of this book, Florencia Mallon provided especially important help through her own engagement with Mexican history. Friends that used to be together in Madison have now scattered around the country, but they continue to provide support in professional and personal ways. Old and more recent conversations with Nancy Appelbaum, Anne Macpherson, Rene Reeves, Karin Rosemblatt, and Sinclair Thomson have contributed to this book. Most recently, I am grateful for advice from Elaine Maisner at the University of North Carolina Press; her professional and calm guidance has made the experience of publishing this book enjoyable. Other representatives of the University of North Carolina Press, especially Ron Maner and Bethany Johnson, have provided exceptional help in bringing this book to publication. I would also like to thank my family, especially Brenda, Frankie, and Benay, for patiently giving me the time and space to write this book.

Finally, I would like to acknowledge the many years of guidance, support, and friendship of Professor Charles A. Hale. As an undergraduate at the University of Iowa, Professor Hale invited me to take his graduate seminar on Latin American *pensadores*. His invitation to study the world of Latin American social and political ideas opened a door for me that I never would have found on my own. He became and remains a mentor in the truest sense of the word. This book is dedicated to him.

The Road to Ixtlán

*Plains, valleys, mountains: the accidents of terrain become
meaningful as soon as they enter history.*
Octavio Paz (1969)

In the fall of 1855, four hundred Zapotec men strapped single-shot rifles over their shoulders, clasped machetes to their belts, and marched from the rural mountain town of Ixtlán to the outskirts of Oaxaca City. A moderate liberal governor had collaborated with a conservative-led coup d'état, and the Zapotecs intended to restore a liberal leader they could trust. Their forty-mile journey through the dry and dusty peaks of the Sierra Zapoteca turned their white cotton pants and shirts a dingy gray. Some of them walked in tattered leather sandals; others simply went barefoot. They smelled of sweat, of dirt, of living, sleeping, and walking outdoors for several days. As they came over the last mountain pass, the valley of Oaxaca opened before them; but as they prepared for the final descent, their young commander, Porfirio Díaz, decided the men should rest one more night before they went into battle. These soldiers had been trained, but they had not been tested in real combat. Gathered in small groups around campfires, the soldiers tried desperately to fend off the chilly mountain air. Some of them, perhaps all of them, must have worried about the next day. Would they die on the battlefield? Would they ever see their families again? Would their sacrifices hold any meaning? They could see the city beneath them and the stars above them, and they did what soldiers do with most of their time—they waited.[1]

For the people living in Oaxaca City, the flickering orange glow that lit up the night sky threatened the calm and civility of urban life. Valley elites had grown accustomed to negotiating political disputes on their own terms, and the introduction of armed Indian peasants added a new and unpredictable dynamic into the political mix. Fearful of the Indian element that could overtake the city, the governor switched sides once again. He promised that liberals would continue to control the state government if the Zapotec troops returned to the Sierra. Rather than risk the unknown, the valley elite surrendered to the Zapotec army of Ixtlán district. Without firing a shot these soldiers had swayed the political process; and although no one knew it in 1855, the Zapotecs of Ixtlán district and their leaders would influence directly and indirectly the course of statewide and national politics for the next two generations.[2]

The years 1855 to 1867 represented a monumental period for Zapotecs from the Sierra, a time when their own ethnic identity would be redefined in a national context. In short, this blending of local and national interests became possible through the formation of a National Guard battalion in the district of Ixtlán. Zapotec men received arms from liberal leaders and then defended their homes and nation against foreign and domestic enemies. Zapotec women encouraged their male relatives to serve in the National Guard, but women also fed troops, carried supplies, spied on enemies, and buried the dead. Unlike economic or political changes, which happened slowly and unevenly in nineteenth-century rural Mexico, the introduction of a new military structure and the recognition of a new role for Zapotec men and women became the catalyst for a rapid and fundamental transformation in the ways in which these people thought of themselves in terms of the nation. For the first time since the European encounter, the people from the Sierra Zapoteca began to think of themselves as a part of—not apart from—the ruling regime in Mexico City.

The fact that Benito Juárez, a Zapotec Indian from the rural mountain town of Guelatao in Ixtlán district, served as Mexico's liberal president from 1858 to 1872 contributed to the political and cultural transformation that took place in the Sierra Zapoteca. Similarly, Porfirio Díaz began his political and military career in Ixtlán district at the age of twenty-five. He maintained familiar relationships with the people of this region even after he became president in 1876. Thus, men with direct ties to the Sierra Zapoteca dominated national politics for two full generations, more or less from 1858 to 1911. Still, Zapotecs decided for their own reasons to risk their lives for the nation. Led by men who sought prominent positions in local, state, and national affairs, Zapotec soldiers and their families found new opportunities to assert their own interests in political disputes as loyal citizens of the nation. These people would eventually argue that citizenship rights were not granted and guaranteed by the state or a political ally in high office. Rather, the rights of citizenship were defined and defended by communal participation in struggles over national defense. Armed and willing to assume a partisan role in the series of wars that engulfed Mexico in the 1850s, 1860s, and 1870s, the Zapotecs of Oaxaca's central highlands began to assert their influence more directly on political and economic decisions affecting the region. And because Juárez and Díaz had strong ties to the district of Ixtlán, these decisions would eventually shape the course of national history as well.

I begin by retelling the history of the civil wars of the mid-nineteenth century, although the primary purpose of this book is to examine how the memories and histories of those wars came to define rural political culture during the Porfiriato (1876–1911). I am not so interested in pointing out where memories diverted from lived experiences, for that would lead to the rather obvious conclusion that history is written in the present. Instead, I focus on how those memories formed the basis of a distinct political culture, a celebration of "heroic patriarchy," initially within Zapotec communities and then later more broadly. After years of fighting for Juárez and under the leadership of Díaz, Zapotec men and women had their own explanations for why they went to battle and what they should expect as a result of their sacrifices. They looked to the past, at first recent and then over the course of the Porfiriato increasingly distant, to forge a pact with Díaz and his local representatives in Oaxaca. In exchange for their service and loyalty, Zapotecs expected certain privileges, which they deemed as "rights" guaranteed by the 1857 Constitution. Significantly, their expectations were rather modest: the freedom to choose their own political leaders, the trust to maintain their weapons, the privilege to have land disputes adjudicated fairly, and the opportunity to work in the region's mines. From the perspective of Zapotec veterans and their families, the legitimacy of federal, state, and local officials depended on recognizing these rights achieved in struggles of the past. For that reason, "history" itself, as understood by people who had fought in the wars and by people who had only heard the stories of those battles, became a contested arena, a justification for both cooperation and conflict during the Porfiriato.

Though it is tempting to write a political biography of Juárez and Díaz that highlights their common origins, my focus is on the Zapotec people who supported them, confronted them, and still remember them today.[3] I am most interested in understanding the experiences, ideas, and perspectives of rural

Mexicans who had a personal stake in the lives and political careers of both Juárez and Díaz. By reconnecting Zapotec men and women to episodes of local, regional, and national history, we can see how socially marginalized individuals, in this case rural, poor, and ethnically distinct people, came to identify with the nation, and the associated repercussions of that relationship on the national political process. Like the narrow dirt road that connects Ixtlán to Oaxaca City, the road traveled by the Zapotec army in 1855, the interaction between local and national history in Mexico has always moved in two directions.

Sons of the Sierra

For more than five hundred years, travelers going to and from the Sierra Zapoteca have used the same passageway leading from the valley of Oaxaca through the mountains of the Sierra Madre Oriental and into the district of Ixtlán. I first traveled this route in the summer of 1991, and heard stories from people throughout the district about the ways in which this road has led to both war and peace.[4] Within Zapotec oral history, the road itself exists as a metaphor for the interaction of ideas, people, and economic resources that have moved in and out of the region. The actual distance between Ixtlán and Oaxaca City is not so great, and the relative ease with which Zapotec armies could threaten the capital city was not lost on politicians in the nineteenth century. Yet the road into the mountains also posed an obstacle for travelers who had to negotiate the narrow passes that cut through incredibly steep mountain slopes. There is and has been, in effect, a single route into the Sierra Zapoteca that regulates contact between people in this region and outsiders. The importance of this road reaches as far back in Zapotec oral traditions as 1468, the year an invading Mexica army marched into the mountains in a failed attempt to conquer the Sierra. According to one Zapotec account of the invasion, *Yvetzi ya rela*, the Mexica army encountered fierce resistance outside the town of Ixtepeji and was forced to retreat to the central valley. This victory was short-lived, however, for *Yvetzi ya rela* also recounts the trauma and hardship of war itself. The Zapotec commander, Juppa, lost his life because of a poisonous arrow, and the Zapotecs had to endure the political challenges of a changing world without their rightful leader. This encounter with the Mexica had a lasting influence on the region. In fact, the word "Zapotec" comes from the Nahuatl name given to the inhabitants of this part of the state: Zapotecatl.[5]

A half century later, when word reached the Sierra that Hernán Cortes

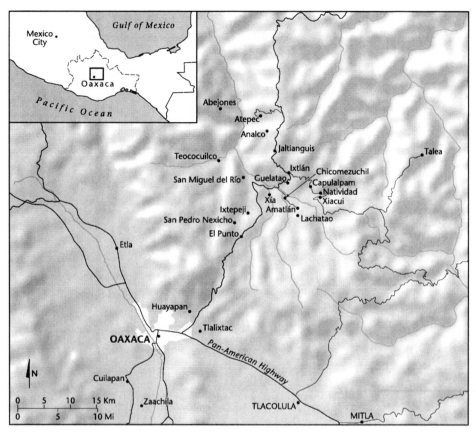

Ixtlán District, Oaxaca, ca. 2000.
Created by the University of Minnesota Cartography Lab.

sought allies to attack the Mexica capital of Tenochitlán, the Zapotec *cacique* (indigenous leader) Coquelay sent two hundred men from Ixtepeji to join with the Spaniards; tragically, only twenty returned to their village.[6] Worse, their alliance with the Spanish did not last long. Within a generation of fighting as allies in central Mexico, the Spaniards sought to colonize Oaxaca, including the Sierra Zapoteca. Just as before, the outsiders' attempt to control the Sierra met intense Zapotec resistance along the road to Ixtlán. Historical anthropologist John Chance describes the Spanish invasion of the Sierra as "one of the most brutal and protracted episodes in sixteenth-century Mexico."[7] The struggle lasted more than three decades, resulting finally in the demilitarization of Zapotec communities and the loss of Zapotec political autonomy. A small but influential population of Spanish and mestizo families eventually settled in the region. In general, these settlers held administrative political offices, traded with Zapotec households for cochineal dye and handwoven cotton textiles, and owned, managed, and worked in the region's gold and silver mines.[8]

The Spanish invasion ushered in other changes for Zapotec communities. Zapotec families largely survived by the complex network of *campesino* relationships within a particular community. *"Campesino"* typically gets translated as "peasant" in English, though the full meaning of the term in Spanish and in practice encompassed economic experiences beyond subsistence farming.[9] Zapotec communities held title to farmlands collectively. Within communities, agrarian committees assigned each male head of household particular plots of land to farm. These decisions were made in annual meetings, though they tended to follow custom so that a family might farm a particular plot for several generations. Within families, men and boys planted, watered, weeded, and harvested corn, beans, and squash. Women and girls also worked in fields at key times of the year and prepared food, gathered water for drinking and cleaning, collected firewood, and cared for small children. And everyone, men, women, and children, worked in the apple and sapote fruit orchards maintained by some communities. Still, family agricultural production fell short of providing an adequate food supply for the entire population of the district. People needed access to a cash economy in order to buy some basic foodstuffs like corn, wheat, and meat. They also needed money to pay for clothes, tools, and though they hated to pay them, taxes.[10]

For these reasons, even though most Zapotec families maintained access to farmland throughout the period examined in this study, Zapotec men and women pursued other economic activities as well. Men and women harvested cochineal insects and wove broadcloth textiles in their homes for trade with the Spaniards. Some also earned money as local politicians, miners, ore processors, textile factory workers, foresters, and soldiers. During much of the colonial era, the road to Ixtlán was used primarily as a trade route for goods moving into and out of the region. Remarkably, commodities traded along this road traveled far into the global marketplace. The cochineal dye from the Sierra Zapoteca turned British military uniforms a distinctive red, which gave the soldiers who wore them an intimidating appearance as the guardians of British colonialism.

If Zapotec families endured Spanish colonialism in similar ways, this common history did not lead to a sense of regional solidarity. As in other parts of indigenous Mexico, colonial administrators exacerbated tensions between communities and encouraged a deeper sense of belonging to a single town rather than a broader ethnic affiliation. Catholic missionaries bolstered this sort of localism, and towns that had always been known by Zapotec place-names added the prefixes of Catholic saints to identify specific hometowns. Every town adopted a different saint and blended these new Spanish names with their own Zapoteco references to trees, plants, rivers, and mountain peaks. Ixtlán, for example, refers to the *ixtli* fiber extracted from the maguey plant and used for tribute to the Mexica; under Catholic influence the town became Santo Tomás Ixtlán. Chicomezuchil comes from the name for the Zapotec flower god; it became San Juan Chicomezuchil. And Guelatao, or Yelatoo in Zapoteco, means "little lake," which described the small lake in the town center. In the new schema it became San Pablo Guelatao.[11] These hybrid Spanish-Zapoteco place-names that dotted the landscape fostered distinctions between villages, contributing even today to competitions on the annual feast days of each town's saint.

Still, some of these same Catholic missionaries contributed more directly to the preservation and codification of the Zapotec language in the region. As in other indigenous parts of the Americas, priests learned the local vernacular in order to preach to native people. In Oaxaca numerous priests became proficient Zapoteco speakers, and several became expert enough to publish dictionaries and grammars that explained the structure and syntax of some thirteen different Zapoteco dialects. Remarkably (because they were trying to end pre-Christian ideas and practices), these priests came to appreciate Zapoteco's beauty and complexity. Juan de Córdoba, for example, wrote that Zapoteco "has many more verbs than our language, which are used for the many moods of the Indians who speak it." These dictionaries survived the colonial period, and several were reprinted during the late nineteenth century. Zapotecs in Ixtlán district spoke their own dialect, which provided a certain degree of cohesiveness, particularly when they encountered outsiders. Like the new names for their towns, Zapotecs invented a new word for "outsiders," *Ven-ne stila*, which playfully described all foreigners as people who spoke Spanish (Castilla).[12]

A turning point for both Zapotec local history and Mexican national history took place in the early nineteenth century when, as a young boy, Benito Juárez walked the Ixtlán road from his birthplace in Guelatao to Oaxaca City. The epic story of the man who became Mexico's most celebrated national hero began with this humble journey. Against tremendous odds, Juárez earned a law degree, became state governor, and eventually president of the republic. From the perspective of the people Juárez left behind, his accomplishments were theirs. For them he was always *Goo Beguu*, little father.[13] When given the opportunity to defend Juárez's government, the communities of the region

General Porfirio Díaz, 1867. Courtesy of the Bancroft Library,
University of California, Berkeley.

Benito Juárez. Courtesy of the Bancroft Library,
University of California, Berkeley.

Soldiers from Ixtepeji, 1910. Reproduced from Michael Kearney, *The Winds of Ixtepeji: World View and Society in a Zapotec Town* (New York: Holt, Rinehart and Winston, 1972), p. 35.

formed a National Guard battalion in 1855 under the direction of a young district administrator, Porfirio Díaz. This battalion repelled conservative and French assaults on the Sierra, and several times Zapotec soldiers marched down the road to occupy Oaxaca City in order to turn the political process. Years of fighting for the liberal cause and Juárez's government forged a permanent bond between the people of Ixtlán district and Porfirio Díaz, a relationship that lasted throughout Díaz's own presidency (1876–1911). This study examines those relationships—the imagined and reconstructed ties to Benito Juárez and the collective and individual memories of Porfirio Díaz.

This book is about *"los Hijos de la Sierra,"* the Zapotec people of Oaxaca's central highlands. Originally, the men who fought in the Ixtlán National Guard called themselves "the Sons of the Sierra." As "sons," they expected to inherit the ancestral, patriarchal responsibilities of self-determination and communal authority. As Zapotecs of the Sierra, they asserted the importance of culture, place, and history for defining who they were in the world. In a broader and more enduring way, however, the sense of identity as expressed by the phrase *"los Hijos de la Sierra"* extended to all Zapotec people in the region.[14] The name implied legitimate political actors and loyal citizens of the nation. Significantly, Zapotec women argued that they, too, had contributed to the accomplishments of their male relatives by providing crucial moral and logistical support during war efforts. An awareness of sacrifice, obligation, and entitlement extended to both men and women. In addition, after the fighting had ended, the children and grandchildren of veterans assumed the rights and responsibilities of citizenship, calling themselves by the same name: the Sons of the Sierra. The people of the Sierra recounted the achievements of previous generations who had, according to Zapotec notions of history, shaped their own lives.[15]

A series of questions about the nature of Díaz's government brings together the local history of the Sierra Zapoteca with national political events. How did Díaz come to power in 1876, and what role did ordinary Mexicans play in his bid for the presidency? Once in office, did Díaz rule primarily by force, coercing reluctant populations to pay higher taxes, elect corrupt officials, and concede to industrial capitalism? Or did people somehow support the regime, negotiating a middle ground between their own local and national interests? Finally, what was the nature of Porfirian political culture, which might help us understand not why the regime fell in 1911, but why it lasted as long as it did? French historian Lynn Hunt has described political culture as the logic that justified political actions and ideas, a complex set of references that people shared, debated, created, and changed over time.[16] Hunt emphasizes the importance of language for understanding political culture, since the words used to describe symbols, ideas, and people provide evidence for when, why, and how political culture changed. I, too, want to highlight the use of language, for in many ways Porfirian political culture became a conversation between citizens and representatives of the state. At the heart of this conversation was a discussion about the rights of individuals within peasant communities and the responsibilities of the government. Still, this conversation was as much about the past as it was the present. Zapotecs, regional elites, and Porfirian officials in Mexico City used historical references to frame their conversations, to establish a shared sense of purpose, to create imaginary ties of kinship, and to justify the legitimacy of petitions and requests for assistance.

Díaz often used the people of the Sierra Zapoteca as a barometer for his own sense of being a leader "of the people." He corresponded with Zapotec men and women throughout his long political career, exchanging letters about the past, about old battles, dead soldiers, and former officers, and about the new policies of the federal and state governments. The past and the present were often linked, as both the president and his Zapotec interlocutors saw the politics of Porfirian Mexico as the product of a shared historical journey. Although Díaz responded to letters written by peasants and workers throughout the nation, the people of the Sierra Zapoteca represented for him his first and most important base of popular support. When they did not endorse his rebellion against Juárez in 1871, Díaz lost. And when they challenged him in 1910 because they did not like his candidate for governor, he threatened them with military repression. In response, they initially refused to organize a militia to defend his regime against rebels in the north. Before they would act, Zapotecs wanted to recreate a reciprocal agreement between themselves and the president, one that was more like the pact their grandfathers and fathers had formed with him years earlier. By 1911, however, Díaz could not forestall wider challenges to his government from rebels mobilizing throughout the country. He did not form any new agreements, or military alliances; he simply resigned, fled to Europe with his family, and eventually died in exile.

To set aside for the moment the official interpretation of the Díaz regime as an illegitimate and brutal dictatorship is to run the risk of being labeled a counterrevolutionary (i.e., counter-Revolutionary), a conservative, or worse yet, an apologist for antidemocratic, repressive, and elitist government. My purpose, however, is not to soften the sharp edges of a dictator. John Kenneth Turner's *Barbarous Mexico* (1910) still well characterizes the corruption and abuse suffered by countless Mexicans. The repressive apparatus brought to bear on the Flores Magón brothers and striking workers at Cananea, Sonora, and Río Blanco, Veracruz, still represents the degree to which Díaz and his cohorts were willing to go to enforce their limited sense of order and progress.[17] My goal is to place these events in a longer historical context, to seek the causes that led to such brutal manifestations, and to acknowledge the everyday ways in which men and women confronted *and* cooperated with Porfirio Díaz from the beginning to the end, from 1876 to 1911. In that sense, I hope to resituate the Porfirian regime in a way similar to Jeffrey Gould's pathbreaking study of the origins of the Sandinista revolution in Nicaragua. Most revolutionary studies, as Gould points out, concentrate on the final destruction of oligarchic regimes, on the social, political, and economic factors that immediately precede armed revolt. Gould examines instead the long process of constructing a revolutionary front through the origins, failures, and successes of various opposition movements. In the course of his research, Gould had to come to terms with "Somocista populism," the fact that rural workers initially supported Anastasio Somoza and the reformist proposals of his early administration. I have studied the construction of a dictatorial regime itself— its strengths and weaknesses, its successes and failures, its legitimacy and degeneracy. But like Gould's, my study uses the particular experiences of people in a place relatively distant from the nation's capital to explain the interaction between local and national history.[18]

The Sierra Zapoteca: The Importance of Place

In order to see the profound influence of a particular locale on national history, I want to explore the social geography of Porfirian Mexico from the perspective of the Sierra Zapoteca. Octavio Paz has written, "Geographies too, are symbolic: physical spaces turn into geometric archetypes that are emissive forms of symbols. Plains, valleys, mountains: the accidents of terrain become meaningful as soon as they enter history."[19] Historians of Mexico have long emphasized these accidents of terrain, concluding that the nation's divisive mountain ranges, arid deserts, and tropical rain forests separated populations and contributed to the profound resilience of local cultures, local actors, and local economies. The republic was born fractured in 1810 by political conflict and geographic isolation. In 1910, when the veil of national unity was torn away by revolution, rural Mexicans turned away from the center, gazed on the interests of their own communities, and only reluctantly, with "recalcitrance," came to accept the de facto control of the Revolutionary nation-state.[20] In general, this view of rural isolation has been described over the years as "many Mexicos," "closed corporate communities," "the *patria chica*" (the small fatherland), and most recently as *"campanilismo"* (the view from the church bell tower).[21] Although each of these ideas has its own set of definitions and subtle distinctions, they all describe a wide ideological gulf between rural populations and the nation-state. In effect, these concepts assume that rural Mexicans were too poor, too uneducated, too Catholic, and too far from Mexico City to care about political goals, opportunities, or ideas of national consequence. Although I disagree with the general notion of rural isolation, these studies usefully focus our attention on the importance of place in shaping social relationships and on the idea that rural people, a majority of the population until the mid-twentieth century, thought about different things and acted for different reasons than their urban counterparts.

I agree more with the perspective of other historians who have explained the surprising ways in which the lives of local populations intersected with regional, national, and international events.[22] I want to contribute my own "grain of sand" to this conversation, by suggesting that we should try to see beyond geographic barriers, like mountain ranges, and look deeper into the ways in which geography or more generally "space" is actually shaped by popular consciousness. In effect, the multiple meanings of belonging to a particular region were themselves bounded by the sense of belonging to a particular nation; regions were not fixed landmarks around which history turned.[23] In that sense, Octavio Paz was only partially correct, for geographies actually enter and reenter historical consciousness at different times and under different circumstances.

The proposition that "space" represents a separate category of historical and social analysis is fundamentally a well-established idea. Beginning in the 1940s, the French intellectual Henri Lefebvre argued that capitalism had created a "bureaucratic society of controlled consumption," organized in terms of state-dominated "spatial planning."[24] The French Annales tradition also emphasized geographic relations, where regions like the Mediterranean were transformed through long-term historical processes.[25] In more recent years, social geographers have advanced a critique of historical materialism by reexamining the ways in which capitalism reproduces power relations in recognizable patterns with spatial dimensions. A leading proponent of this view, Edward Soja, argues that "space," like race, class, and gender, is a socially constructed category that changes in material and ideological ways over time. Social space is produced through struggles and contradictions that seek to transform both the physical/material environment and the representation/meaning of that space in time. Thus *spatialité*, or spatiality, creates and is in turn recreated by a "second nature," the dynamic product of both human history and human geography. The stability of this second nature is constantly challenged by day-to-day human intervention and by long-term historical processes.[26]

Although I borrow this concept of spatiality from social geography to reconsider the interrelated processes of economic restructuring and cultural meaning, an emphasis on place and landscape is consistent with Zapotec notions of identity and history as well. I am interested in the creation of a "second nature" in Oaxaca's Sierra Zapoteca, which included not only the reorganization of natural resources for economic purposes but also the reconceptualization of regional and ethnic identity for political and cultural purposes. Economic transformations in the Sierra Zapoteca contributed to and were in turn affected by ideologies of ethnic, regional, and national identity. The Sierra was "recreated" during the liberal-conservative civil wars and then during the Porfiriato in terms of the way space was organized by capitalism and in the way the region was conceived in popular political culture. Thus, we can see how regionalism itself is fundamentally a study of spatial relationships, an analysis of the interconnectedness of one place to another. For this reason, regional history creates new possibilities for understanding issues of political consciousness and power.[27] Regions existed, and exist still, in discursive fields of identity. To be from one village as opposed to another, to be from one particular state, to be Mexican, these held meaning only in relationship to other villages, other states, other nations. During the Porfiriato, people from the Sierra Zapoteca maintained these oppositional identities as a result of their participation in defending national sovereignty. A further transformation took place after 1920, when Zapotec armies signed a peace accord with the Constitutionalist government in Mexico City. In fact, Oaxaca's current relationship to the nation, its "place" in Mexico's political, cultural, and economic life in the early twenty-first century, comes from this later transformation of regional and national space and not from some pre-Columbian preservation of an imagined indigenous world that refused to change.

Today Oaxaca has become a living museum of Indian communities, where Mexican and foreign tourists travel to get a glimpse of the country's pre-Columbian origins. Spectacular ruins at Monte Albán and Mitla, along with native dance festivals, woodcarvings, rugs, jewelry, pottery, and a unique cuisine, all suggest that the state is somehow tied more to the ancient past than it is to the present. Related to this image of the past, Oaxacan poverty is explained as a product of centuries-long neglect and static cultural resistance. In fact, poverty becomes a part of the tourist landscape; to be Indian in Mexico is to be poor, and no state is as "Indian" as Oaxaca.[28] In reality, the marketing of Oaxacan "Indianness" is relatively new, an economic sphere created primarily during the 1930s and 1940s when Mexican state officials pursued a national policy of *indigenismo*. During the late nineteenth century, Oaxaca was considered the Mexican "Land of Tomorrow," the future site of capitalist agricultural and industrial development.[29] Investors were encouraged to take advantage of the region's excellent growing conditions, its powerful mountain rivers (for irrigation and hydraulic power), its rich mineral resources, and its abundant supply of inexpensive labor. Not surprisingly, foreign investors responded to these opportunities, giving Oaxaca the fifth-highest rate of foreign investment in the country in 1910.[30] Clearly, the expectations for Oaxaca's economic potential were tied to the influence of powerful politicians living in Mexico City, and Presidents Juárez and Díaz surrounded themselves with trusted advisors from their native state. Nevertheless, the historical importance of Oaxaca, as the birthplace of presidents who ruled Mexico for nearly half a century and as a potential region of significant industrial expansion, has been buried under the ruins of Revolutionary rhetoric.

By weaving together a regional history of the Sierra Zapoteca with Díaz's military and political career, I explore the nature of grassroots expectations toward, support for, and alienation from the Porfirian regime itself. Rather than finding a monolithic, unwavering, brutal dictatorship, I identify important junctures and discontinuities within the thirty-five years of Porfirian rule. Three distinct periods of economic and political transformation characterize Porfirian history within the Sierra Zapoteca specifically and Oaxaca more generally. First, from 1876 to 1890, peasant communities expected and received compensation for their years of service in the form of basic infrastructural improvements and new industrial jobs for the region. The generation of men and women who had fought alongside Díaz, the "Reform generation," knew Díaz and his mestizo allies personally, and they used those personal relationships to their advantage.[31] A second period began in 1890, when a generation of men who had not fought in Mexico's civil wars began to direct the region's economic and political fortunes. Significantly, 1890 was also the point at which Díaz and members of a "Porfirian generation" began to systematically organize public celebrations of Mexican heroes, in particular of Benito Juárez. Although this was a time of relative economic prosperity, led by an expansion in the mining industry, conflicts over tax increases, land disputes, gubernatorial elections, and industrial development threatened the stability of the region. By 1906, Zapotecs had begun to feel abandoned by Díaz and betrayed by his local representatives. Finally, from 1906 to 1911, the local political establishment, along with the Porfirian regime in Mexico City, came under increasing criticism. An economic downturn, combined with antidemocratic and repressive measures, ended the period of consensual politics that Díaz had established as far back as 1876. By 1910, the earlier cooperation had given way to a deeper sense of betrayal. Mexicans were suffering under Díaz, but their pain was relatively recent. As they turned toward revolution, middle-class businessmen, industrial workers, and rural men and women—a "revolutionary generation"—were indignant and angry, not because they had been abused for so many years, but because they sensed that the rights and benefits won by previous generations were under attack by the regime.

Using the Sierra Zapoteca as a long-term reference point, I argue that rural popular classes largely supported Díaz during most of his presidency, personally identifying with the patriarchal imagery and paternalistic policies of his administration. Support for the government, however, did not come freely or easily. Oftentimes challenging and constantly negotiating with the president and his local representatives, Zapotec peasants were driven by their own sense of rights and responsibilities as loyal citizens of the nation. In effect, the persuasive power of Porfirio Díaz as "strong man" was constructed from below, in a dialogic way, through discourses of legitimacy and historical memory written and shared in particular regions and local communities. This sense of negotiation contributed to the origin, transformation, and ultimate failure of something we might call "Porfirian hegemony." My use of hegemony as a concept does not preclude conflict, or indicate the complete acquiescence of the powerless to the powerful. On the contrary, borrowing from Florencia Mallon, hegemony implies conflict and contestation, including the process of negotiating, cajoling, consenting, and resisting. As Mallon argues, hegemony is as much about the process of constructing power as it is about the product of that power itself.[32] In the Sierra Zapoteca this process took multiple forms. Peasants did not lose their land to encroaching haciendas or expanding mining operations, though land and labor disputes were a constant source of unrest in the region. They did not surrender to capitalism or perceive the mines as a threat to their way of life, though they insisted that the natural resources of the region ultimately belonged to the original inhabitants. They did not see the government that they had helped install as an encroaching enemy, though they demanded local political autonomy. They saw Porfirio Díaz as a former comrade, a Oaxacan, a potential patriarch with whom they could negotiate. They challenged mestizo caudillos to protect their jobs, their land, and their military pensions, and they confronted those men when there were disagreements. Finally, they saw beyond the *patria chica*, locating themselves in terms of national historical events and as notable historical actors.[33]

Storytelling as History:
The Challenge of Indigenous Nationalism

The tentative pact between ruling elites and Zapotec peasants was constructed and maintained primarily through memories and storytelling. By recalling their own memories of Benito Juárez, their own experiences with war, and their own interpretations of national independence, Zapotec men and women defined a particular set of political and social rights. Although Díaz and the Mexican political elite encouraged popular participation in patriotic celebrations, they were surprised at times by the ways in which ordinary citizens reinterpreted and reimagined their own memories of participating in national history. In the case of the Sierra Zapoteca, we see just how far people went beyond the limits of official nationalist ideologies, how carefully they refit their own memories into the nationalist narrative. Outside of Mexico City, memories of Juárez, memories of war, and memories of national independence were situated in cognitive spaces that emphasized the role of local communities in national history.

As Zapotec peasants constructed and maintained their own ideological attachments to the nation, they blended history and memory in several ways. First, individuals who had actively participated in the various wars of the mid-nineteenth century held personal memories of having fought in a certain place, at a specific time, and for a particular cause. For Zapotec men and women, the heroic tales of individual military service reinforced a deep sense of belonging to the nation. In many ways, these memories were supported and shaped by official documents that registered the participation of each male veteran. Still, with time the actual details of what had happened at a particular point in the past became less important than the multiple ways in which a specific event was remembered to have happened. Zapotec peasants shared these memories with public officials in correspondence, petitions, speeches, poems, songs, and personal encounters. Thus, the personal memories of individuals, the process of imagining and reimagining key events of the past, represented a crucial part of Zapotec national identity.

A second form of memory took shape as veterans of the mid-nineteenth century grew older and commemorative events around national holidays became more public. Through communal acts of publicly recognizing the accomplishments of living and dead relatives, a collective memory of having served the nation in its hour of need developed in the Sierra Zapoteca. Local rituals honoring veterans on Benito Juárez's birthday (March 21), Cinco de Mayo (May 5), and Independence Day (September 16) fostered a collective sense of attachment to the nation. Veterans and schoolchildren marched in parades, local leaders delivered speeches, families gathered for food and games, and everyone came out at night to watch fireworks and listen to the local philharmonic corps play national hymns. It was through these rituals, more widely practiced after 1890, that people who had not witnessed the tragedies and glories of war came to share a collective memory. Paul Connerton describes this process as the ways in which "a community is reminded of its identity as represented by and told in a master narrative . . . a making sense of the past as a kind of collective autobiography, with some explicitly cognitive components."[34] The origins or "invention of tradition" behind these public rituals reveal only a small part of their importance for Zapotec communities. Much more significant was the fact of their persistence and the performance going on within the rituals themselves. People who had been too young to experience war firsthand incorporated these memories into their own histories through the performative repetition of patriotic communal rituals.[35]

Finally, the people of Ixtlán district used "sites of memory" to forge and maintain a sense of common history and purpose with the nation. Sites of memory or "*lieux de memoire*," according to French historian Pierre Nora, are places, causes, or associations that attach memories of the past to meanings in the present. For Nora, interactions between history and memory create complex and contradictory phenomena that attempt "to stop time, to inhibit forgetting, to fix a state of things, to immortalize death, and to materialize the immaterial." Significantly, sites of memory are not timeless and unchanging. Rather, they "thrive only because of their capacity for change, their ability to resurrect old meanings and generate new ones along with new and unforeseeable connections (that is what makes them exciting)."[36] Ixtlán district itself was full of places where the mere mentioning of a certain village, river, or mountain could evoke specific historical references with multiple implications in the present. Guelatao, Benito Juárez's birthplace, was only the most obvious site of memory that held profound meanings for Zapotec peasants during the Porfiriato. In fact, the entire Sierra Zapoteca itself was renamed the Sierra Juárez in order to extend Benito Juárez's symbolic connection beyond his hometown.[37] Veterans and their families also referred to the series of political and military disputes simply by a place-name—Soyaltepec, Juchitán, Miahuatlán, Carbonera, La Noria, Tuxtepec, and especially Puebla. But the *lieux de memoire* in the Sierra Zapoteca included more than battle sites. Veterans' associations, philharmonic corps, and electoral clubs were also "places" where Zapotecs could go to draw deeper connections between the individual, the community, and the nation. Zapotec men and women used these sites of memory, along with personal and collective memories, to create their own interpretations of national history. The purpose of these popular histories, however, was not somehow to get the "facts" right about what had happened at a particular time or place in the past. The underlying purpose of Zapotec stories was to accentuate and celebrate the place of the living in the present.

The people of the Sierra Zapoteca used these memories and popular histories to imagine themselves as a part of the Mexican national community. In that sense, Benedict Anderson's view of the nation as an "imagined community" offers a useful way to begin talking about nationalism in Mexico. In another sense, however, Anderson's emphasis on the middle-class origins and orientation of nationalism presents a problem. In the revised and expanded edition of *Imagined Communities* (1991), Anderson expresses dismay that despite his initial emphasis on the New World origins of nationalism, a "Eurocentric provincialism remained quite undisturbed."[38] Creole pioneers, Anderson claims, were the first to imagine sovereign political communities. They were the first to use print capitalism to define a new political order that found its legitimacy in an imagined historical experience, shaped by "a common language (and common religion and common culture)" with the metropole.[39] But aside from locating the first nationalist revolts in the Americas, Anderson remains faithful to a Eurocentric concept of nationalism itself. Nationalism is an elite project for Anderson, in part because leaders of nationalist movements must use print technology to subvert the previous order, to reimagine and rebuild the new nation. As Partha Chatterjee notes in his critique of Anderson, there is nothing new here; we are still left with an essentialist model of Western "sociological determinism."[40]

I have an additional concern about Anderson's notion of "imagined community": his failure to problematize the "community." Anderson makes a false distinction between the "real" community inhabited by people and the "imagined" community inhabited by their nationalist devotions. By assuming that nationalism flattens hierarchies, Anderson ignores the ways in which communal tensions actually find expression in discourses of national identity. According to Anderson, the nation "is imagined as a community, because, regardless of the actual inequality and exploitation that may prevail in each, the nation is *always* conceived as a deep, horizontal comradeship. Ultimately it is this fraternity that makes it possible, over the past two centuries, for so many millions of people, not so much to kill, as willingly to die for such limited imaginings."[41] In Oaxaca's Sierra Zapoteca, conditions of inequality and exploitation within and between communities significantly shaped the imagination as well. Rather than a single community based on horizontal comradeship, Zapotecs during the Porfiriato imagined the nation as a confederation of multiple communities, each formed through vertical tensions around racial, class, gender, and generational identities. This ideal, they argued, emerged during the years of liberal/conservative civil wars, grew more powerful during the French Intervention (1862–67), and culminated with the triumph of Díaz's Tuxtepec Rebellion (1876). In effect, they had been willing to die not because they imagined themselves as individuals within a "horizontal comradeship" but because they imagined themselves as members of distinct communities allied in defense of local autonomy and national sovereignty. To borrow a phrase from the Germany historian Alon Confino, Zapotecs perceived the nation as a local metaphor.[42]

The structure of the Ixtlán National Guard reflected this image of how to organize the nation as well. As I explain more fully in chapter 1, the Ixtlán National Guard took into account preexisting hierarchies within and across Zapotec communities, effectively negotiating gender, generational, class, and ethnic tensions within the region. Mestizo men held ranked positions above Zapotec men; elder Zapotec men commanded their younger neighbors in community-based regiments; and women were excluded from any formal position or recognition within the war effort. In effect, merit and performance on the battlefield mattered little toward promotion in the National Guard units since preexisting factors determined where one entered the system. This model of "indigenous nationalism" did not offer a more democratic, bottom-up opportunity for organizing the nation. On the contrary, based on the practices and limitations of heroic patriarchy, elder men and political leaders could rely on the duty-bound obligations of neighbors within their communities. The plurality of communities mattered because it implied difference, multiplicity, and hierarchy. Ultimately, it was the patriarchal demands of duty and reciprocity, rather than equality, that motivated soldiers to go into battle or, in Anderson's words, to be willing to die.

My understanding of Zapotec notions of the rights and responsibilities of citizenship comes primarily from the stories told by people from Ixtlán district. In personal correspondence, community petitions, official complaints, speeches, songs, and fables, Zapotec peasants offered their own interpretations of national history and of their role in shaping that history. Although the vast majority of Zapotec peasants could not personally read or write, hundreds of individuals from dozens of communities wrote to Porfirio Díaz, various state governors, and local representatives of the regime. Zapotecs relied on what I call "communal literacy" to articulate their views to political leaders and to interpret the letters, laws, and reports sent by public officials.[43] Public scribes on town councils and professional scribes who sold their skills in Oaxaca City provided crucial assistance for some letter-writers. In addition, rural schoolteachers, children, or even a barely literate neighbor could help an individual draft a letter to an official or read a letter returned to that individual. Many Zapotec households maintained their own small collections of documents, including letters of military service, handbills distributed by military leaders, laws exempting them from tax obligations, and personal letters sent by political officials. Even for people who could not individually read or write, that is, for people who primarily used oral history as a lens on the past, written words on sheets of paper mattered. In fact, Zapotecs used a special word to describe people who wrote, *Guadiaa*, which was the same word they used to describe the artist-writers of ancient glyphs.[44]

Many of the letters Zapotecs sent to officials can now be found in archives across the country, though few historians have made systematic use of them. These documents provide a detailed account of changing attitudes about, expectations of, and correspondence with government officials in Mexico City. While local archives offered crucial details about Zapotec communities, the most important records I found came from the vast collection of personal letters and official correspondence gathered at the Universidad Iberoamericana in the Colección Porfirio Díaz. Only one-quarter of the nearly 500,000 documents amassed in the "Cartas" collection has been cataloged for researchers. I reviewed the remaining uncataloged collection, looking specifically for letters from Ixtlán district and from military veterans throughout the country. Thus, I base the argument for this book on new documentation that has been generally overlooked by previous accounts. Obviously, these documents require careful reading and cautious interpretation given their "official" or "onstage" quality, but they also provide a rare opportunity to more fully consider popular consciousness.[45] In these letters Zapotec writers challenged the president and his allies to honor promises that had been made to previous generations. At times they openly contradicted state officials, publicly endorsing alternative development strategies and opposition political candidates. At other times they expressed support. This spectrum of attitudes and actions, common to all reasonable people, including Zapotecs living in Oaxaca in the late nineteenth century, reflects both the limitations and latitudes of subaltern agency.[46]

I will rarely use the term "subaltern" again in this study, though I have found the body of theoretical and case studies written over the last two decades known broadly as "subaltern studies" crucial for thinking about the ways in which power is constructed within communities and between communities and the state. An added feature of these studies has been a debate among some scholars on the implications of borrowing references describing colonial and postcolonial relationships in one part of the world (India) and applying them to another (Latin America).[47] My decision to talk about Zapotecs or even "peasants" instead of "subalterns" suggests only that I want to focus on the intellectual insights offered by scholars and not get bogged down in terminology. Like other theoretical ideas, I took the questions raised by subaltern studies into the archives, and then used these ideas to help me organize a retelling that might be understood by other readers. Thus, my emphasis, much like Shahid Amin's in *Event, Metaphor, Memory* (1995), has been on writing a narrative informed by theory. I would like to think this approach is one that Zapotecs might appreciate as well, for in the letters and petitions they sent to state officials they mostly told stories. By their own accounts, they claimed to have fought in defense of the 1857 Constitution and, in particular, for the principle of *Libertad*. However, as will become clear, their notion of *Libertad* emphasized the rights of the community rather than the individual. I have tried to remain attentive to their emphasis on storytelling by including numerous examples of popular versions of local and national history. In effect, Zapotecs argued by experience and, later, by sharing the memories of that experience with officials. Zapotec men and women were not victims; they were not acted upon. They challenged local and federal officials to live up to specific promises, to honor previous agreements, and to acknowledge the role of ordinary Mexicans in national history.

The historian's reliance on written records is not without controversy. John Beverly, a professor of Spanish American literature and social theory, has criticized historians for relying on written texts to explain peasant ideologies of resistance and popular liberalism. Citing the 1995 Zapatista rebellion in Chiapas, Mexico, Beverly argues that peasants want to destroy archives and burn down the buildings that contain records "of their legal conditions of propertylessness and exploitation."[48] But this one-dimensional view of peasants against the state ignores the fact that, at times, peasants also exerted tremendous efforts to maintain official documents. In fact, the original Zapatistas of the 1910 Revolution rebelled in order to reclaim land that they knew belonged to the community because previous generations had protected crucial maps and documents. In Morelos as in Oaxaca peasants used official records to their advantage.[49] Clearly, then, we should not abandon written texts when we attempt to locate and explain acts of peasant resistance and negotiations with the state. Instead, we should open our analytical concepts to include the multiple ways in which peasants engaged policymakers on a number of strategic fronts. At times, peasants may choose to burn archives; at other times, peasants are the primary guardians of official documents, personal letters, and other written accounts of their own lives.

In addition to these sources located primarily in Mexican archives, my journey along the road to Ixtlán has been guided most directly by three Oaxacan historians. The first and for me most important guide has been Manuel Martínez Gracida (1847–1924). Martínez Gracida published thirty-one different books and essays on Oaxacan archaeological, political, ethnic, and environmental history. Incredibly, another forty-five manuscripts remain unpublished. Born in Ejutla, Oaxaca, Martínez Gracida was a lifelong liberal, partly as a result of his father's execution at the hands of a conservative general. His devotion to liberalism, however, went beyond his personal experiences. Liberalism, he believed, fostered greater tolerance for intellectual freedom and access to understanding the past without the institutional bias of Catholic dogma. He held various positions within the Oaxacan state bureaucracy, ranging from scribe to legislator, but his real passion was research and writing. He had an unquenchable curiosity about Oaxacan history and archaeology, traveling throughout the state to gather documents, artifacts, and samples of regional flora and fauna. He typically spent the bulk of his monthly income pursuing his research interests, buying books, drawings, photographs, paper, and postage for voluminous correspondence. He sent questionnaires to leading politicians and their children so that his biographies would be based on firsthand knowledge of his subjects' private lives. After typing drafts of his research, he would send copies to family members and experts so that they could cross-check his references and conclusions. He reportedly worked twelve-hour days, seven days a week. Like his research, his family responsibilities continued into old age. Following his son's execution by a Villista firing squad, Martínez Gracida assumed financial responsibility for his daughter-in-law and grandchildren. His last employer, the National Museum in Mexico City, hired him in 1919 as a staff ethnographer with the modest salary of eighty pesos per month. His friend and admirer, the Oaxacan intellectual and writer Manuel Brioso y Candiani, described Martínez Gracida as a serious and quiet researcher, the consummate investigator.[50]

More than any other Oaxacan scholar, Martínez Gracida has provided a road map for writing a history of the Porfiriato from the bottom up. He wrote detailed military histories on battles during the War of the Reform, the French Intervention, and Díaz's rebellions in 1871 and 1876. He tried to explain to Mexicans living in an era of relative stability how much of the present had been shaped by a turbulent past. I have benefited from his published and unpublished manuscripts, his research notes, and in some cases the actual letters and documents he used as primary sources. He wrote about everything from mining and agriculture to laws and the theater. I found his manuscripts in Mexico City, Oaxaca City, and even in municipal archives in the district of Ixtlán. These documents came to Ixtlán, I believe, during the 1940s and 1950s when Rosendo Pérez García wrote his own history of the Sierra Zapoteca.

Pérez García, the second Oaxacan historian whose work has provided crucial help for my own research, was a Zapotec originally from the town of Ixtlán. He returned to his boyhood home as school inspector for the district sometime in the 1940s. He traveled to the far corners of Ixtlán district and, much like Martínez Gracida before him, collected stories, documents, and knowledge about the people of the region. In 2001 I met Rosendo Pérez García's nephew, Víctor Ramírez Hernández. Víctor provided helpful insight into his uncle's life in Ixtlán and then later in Mexico City. He also helped me understand how Zapotec stories of the past continued to be relevant for people today.

Pérez García relied equally on the work of Martínez Gracida and Jorge Fernando Iturribarría (1902–1987). Iturribarría, the third historian who has guided my questions, wrote about Oaxaca's pre-Columbian past, its colonial history, its nineteenth-century civil wars, and its experiences surrounding the 1910 Revolution. Like me, he was particularly interested in Oaxaca's native sons, Juárez and Díaz, and he skillfully laid out a way for me to approach their complicated relationship. He largely focused on generals and politicians, though he had a keen understanding of the subtle and sometimes hidden conflicts between these members of the ruling class. His work deals with many of the events I write about here, particularly the civil wars before 1876. His work is marked by beautifully crafted narrative, a skill he developed as a newspaper reporter and chronicler of his native state. He has inspired the scholarly work of a large group of Oaxacan specialists, both those originally born there and those who have fallen in love with the state. In major and minor ways, these "students" of Martínez Gracida, Pérez García, and Iturribarría have all guided me on the road to Ixtlán, and their work will be discussed throughout this study, with more careful consideration in the conclusion.

Overview

I have organized this study of Porfirian Mexico around a chronology that makes sense in the Sierra Zapoteca. I begin by exploring the origins of the rural National Guard in Ixtlán district and the years of fighting in Mexico's civil wars. Chapter 1 examines the patriarchal organization of Zapotec communities and their militias during the years 1855 to 1862, detailing the crucial episodes of fighting on the liberal side. Chapter 2 explores the years of fighting for Mexico's "second independence" against the French from 1862 to 1867. Chapter 3 offers a soldier's interpretation of Díaz's revolts at La Noria (1871) and Tuxtepec (1876) and explores the further linkages formed between Díaz and the Sierra Zapoteca. I then turn to an examination of the interaction between Zapotec communities and the Porfirian state, pointing out important political and economic transformations throughout the thirty-five years of Díaz's presidency. Chapter 4 traces the origins of a pact between Díaz, his local representatives, and Zapotec peasants. Chapter 5 identifies the ways in which this pact began to come unraveled as older veterans died and a new generation of young, inexperienced, mestizo men began to dominate the regional economy and political system. Chapter 6 examines the final dissolution of the Porfirian regime, including the deep resentment the popular classes felt toward Díaz. I conclude with the internal collapse of cooperation in the district during the 1912 Ixtepeji revolt and provide an explanation of Oaxaca's transformation into Mexico's "Land of Yesterday." This new way of seeing Oaxaca provided a tempting explanation of local and regional distinctiveness, but it is a history largely based on myths and misconceptions of the twentieth century.

All too often the bright light of revolutionary studies emphasizes the final years of the Díaz regime, leaving the origins and transformations of the Porfiriato in the dark. Even Porfirio Díaz had trouble seeing into the past as the uprising against his government spread and grew more intense. In 1911, facing an inglorious defeat after thirty-five years in office, Díaz wrote in his resignation letter, "I hope . . . that when the passions which accompany every revolution have been calmed, a more conscientious and substantial study will provide a more correct judgment to arise in the national conscience which will permit me to die bearing in my heart a just recognition of the esteem which all my life I have consecrated . . . to my fellow citizens."[51] Beginning with his first military campaign in 1855 as leader of the Ixtlán National Guard, Díaz had always thought of himself as hero, savior, and protector of the nation. Now, forced into exile and betrayed by old age and advancing senility, Díaz could not grasp the hostile alienation expressed by so many Mexicans toward him and his government. Though Díaz could not see the path he had traveled to get to this point, it is my hope that this book will more clearly lay out the failures and successes of his regime. That story is best understood, from beginning to end, from the perspective of the Sons of the Sierra on the road to Ixtlán.

CHAPTER ONE

Reawakening a Zapotec
Military Tradition, 1855-1862

They resisted up to the last instance.
General José María Cobos (1860)

We know from Monte Albán, the temple fortress overlooking the valley of
Oaxaca, that warriors have occupied a central place within Zapotec society
for a thousand years.[1] Originally settled during the early Classic era (ca. 200–
900 C.E.), the inhabitants of Monte Albán drew pictographs on the walls of
temples and tombs depicting military victories, conquests, and ceremonial
sacrifices. Although these drawings reflected a powerful military tradition
that originally brought people together, underlying divisions within Zapotec society became more problematic by the beginning of the Post-Classic
era (ca. 900–1521 C.E.). By this time, families had traversed the central valley, establishing smaller priestly and military settlements that engaged in
intermittent combat with their neighbors. Some people settled in the rugged
mountain range of the Sierra Madre Oriental and with time began to diverge
in dialect and custom from the larger Zapotec population living in the valley.
Still, the Serranos, as they came to call themselves, retained a keen interest in
the achievements of warriors. In fact, their new mountain landscape became
an integral part of their military prowess, as they used the caves and peaks
to their advantage. When Mexica armies tried to conquer the Sierra in 1468,
Zapotec warriors defeated them by creating landslides along narrow passes

and firing arrows from strategic positions above their enemies. They also resisted Spanish military encroachments in the sixteenth century, using the terrain to forestall military conquest and frustrate colonial administrators. In general, the stories of military accomplishments in the Sierra Zapoteca emphasized a defensive posture that protected communities and families by repelling foreign domination.[2] This localized and relatively restrained interpretation of Zapotec militarism kept the memories of warriors alive without posing a direct threat to government officials in Oaxaca City. The Serranos adhered to a fairly simple code of conduct: treat the people of the Sierra with respect, do not encroach on their land, and they will tolerate your control over the valley.

At stake in this relationship between Zapotecs in the Sierra and Hispanic and mestizo elites in the valley was a mutually beneficial notion of "autonomy." Native communities wanted to be free of outside interference from political administrators. At the same time, valley elites wanted to make political and economic decisions without pressure from native community leaders. Elites could not risk mobilizing so many poor people.[3] The wars for independence (1810–21) and a series of administrative reforms in Oaxaca during the 1840s and 1850s fundamentally changed this dynamic. In effect, the military traditions of the Sierra Zapotec were reanimated in the struggles over nation-state formation when valley elites turned to Indian communities as allies. Porfirio Díaz had a major role in building this new relationship. He became subprefect in Ixtlán district in 1855 and immediately organized a National Guard battalion to support the liberal cause initiated by the Plan of Ayutla (1854). The Ayutla revolt against President Antonio López de Santa Anna brought together radical intellectuals, populist rural caudillos, and moderate opponents of the regime. The coalition, however, was fraught with divisions at its inception, and conflicts continued to split the group once it took control of the national government. State governments faced their own internal tensions as politicians came to terms with the new liberal regime. Like most Mexicans, Oaxacan politicians were divided into three camps: conservatives, moderate liberals or *borlados*, and radical liberals or *rojos*.[4] In the fall of 1855, Governor José María García made plans to hand over the state government to conservatives in a bloodless coup. García belonged to the moderate wing of the Liberal Party and saw no need for fundamental reform or for a civil war. The Ixtlán National Guard, led by their young commander Porfirio Díaz, forced the governor to reconsider.

Ixtlán in 1855

In August 1855 Porfirio Díaz traveled the road from Oaxaca City to the town of Ixtlán to take up the post of district subprefect.[5] Díaz, a mestizo of Spanish and Mixtec origins, entered the political stage as a twenty-four-year-old administrator of a predominantly Zapotec region; he would exit at age eighty as the president of the nation facing a growing rebellion that led to revolution. Subprefects, later renamed *jefes políticos*, represented the state and federal governments at the local level. They carried out political directives, organized electoral campaigns, collected taxes, mediated disputes, investigated criminal accusations, made arrests when necessary, and monitored the needs and sentiments of the people living in the cities and towns of their districts. Their primary objective was to maintain order; the best news a governor or president could hear from a jefe político was *"no hay novedades* [there's nothing new to report]." Often, but not always, these men came from towns outside of the districts they managed since they were supposed to remain above the partisan fray that divided villages. But usually, particularly during the Porfiriato, jefes políticos were at the center of controversy and conflict, siding with one group against another and looking for ways to earn extra money through legitimate and illegitimate means.[6]

Díaz came to Ixtlán as an instrument of political control imposed on Indian communities by a white-mestizo minority, barely 12 percent of the entire state's population in 1857.[7] Subprefects throughout the state had assumed greater importance in the early 1850s, following a series of administrative reforms designed to limit village autonomy. Political elites feared widespread unrest, especially a coordinated Indian rebellion that could threaten the administrative structure under their control. In fact, a series of violent revolts in the 1830s and 1840s demonstrated that a massive Indian uprising was indeed a real possibility. Zapotecs from the Isthmus of Tehuantepec (historically and culturally distinct from the Sierra Zapotecs of Ixtlán) rebelled in 1847 and controlled much of the isthmus until 1853. The state government finally recaptured the region, but only after a major military campaign ordered by Governor Benito Juárez.[8] From 1843 to 1848, Triqui Indians from Juxtlahuaca department, along Oaxaca's western border with the state of Guerrero, joined Mixtec Indians from Tlaxiaco and Huajuapan departments in a revolt against a military outpost in the region. The Indian rebels had the support of the liberal caudillo Juan Álvarez, who saw their struggle as a campaign against corrupt cacique and mestizo abuses. A more significant threat, however, was the rebellious example that Maya Indians offered in the Yucatán Caste War of the

A ZAPOTEC MILITARY TRADITION

late 1840s. The Maya waged a race war against white settlers at a time when the Mexican army was preoccupied in a war with the United States. The Yucatán Caste War, the Isthmus of Tehuantepec, and other regional rebellions in Oaxaca were a constant reminder to political elites of their own precarious hold on power.[9]

In 1855 a vast majority of Oaxacans, approximately 87 percent, lived in Indian communities organized internally by local customs, local leaders, and local interests. The resilience of native communities throughout the colonial period was due in part to a variegated household economy that combined subsistence agriculture with supplemental income earned in producing goods for domestic and foreign markets. Indian weavers produced cotton *mantas* (square pieces of cloth or blankets) for export to the mining centers of north central Mexico.[10] Families also cultivated the insects used to make cochineal, the red dye exported throughout the world.[11] Small gold and silver mines in the central and southern highlands of Oaxaca, along with salt mines in the Tehuantepec Isthmus, also provided Indian peasants with access to currency. By the 1860s, however, the cochineal trade had collapsed, the mines had stagnated, and most peasants found themselves without access to a viable wage economy. They had only the mountainous terrain to use for subsistence agriculture. In search of economic security and political autonomy, Indian communities were at odds with the evolving demands of a new state government bent on taxing and controlling its population from above.

The Oaxacan state government initiated a series of reforms in 1846 that began, according to historian Marcello Carmagnani, the "second conquest" of Indian communities.[12] Ironically, the major advocate of these reforms was Benito Juárez, the Zapotec Indian from Guelatao. But Juárez thought of himself as a liberal, not as an Indian. Although political eulogies would later consider Juárez the redeemer of Indian Mexico, Juárez himself did not embrace his native origins.[13] On the contrary, throughout his political career Juárez enacted policies that sought to diminish the influences of native cultures and local village customs. The net result of this apparent contradiction—the Indian politician confronting Indian communities—alienated Juárez from some peasant communities who eventually joined anti-Juárez political movements. In Ixtlán district, however, the Juárez reforms ultimately enhanced Zapotec participation in statewide and national politics. For the people of the Sierra Zapoteca, Juárez was and remains an unqualified hero.[14]

As governor, Juárez initiated two major reforms, both of which were designed to limit the autonomy of Indian villages. First, he determined that a new military establishment was needed to respond to internal unrest. In order to protect "public security" and prevent Indian communities from bypassing the law, Juárez proposed the formation of "a military force, that by its morality, its discipline, and its training can quickly respond by giving aid in any corner of the state."[15] In 1848 Juárez began organizing National Guard units to defend his regime. In the next two years, state expenditures for the new military establishment grew to more than 25 percent of the entire state budget. By 1850, 800 permanent National Guard troops were stationed around the state, and another 2,500 were available for rapid mobilization.[16]

Juárez's second reform ran parallel to his military plans. The entire state was reorganized into eight departments administered by regional governors, and then each department was subdivided into districts administered by subprefects. The regional governors were directed to monitor military activities in their regions. The subprefects had a more challenging objective. Juárez instructed that "they should not limit themselves to counting heads and dictating official letters, but rather they should do something nobler and more difficult: they should govern the people."[17] To govern the people implied a more interventionist approach to local politics than had previously existed. By controlling municipal budgets through tax collection and allocation of public funds, subprefects intended to displace the moral and political authority of communal elders.[18]

The attempt to "reconquer" indigenous Oaxaca took place over a decade through reforms designed to reconstitute the state according to a liberal vision of policymakers.[19] A new era began in Oaxaca, but it bore the familiar traits of the colonial order: a white-mestizo alliance determined to extract Indian labor and resources for the benefit of the minority population. Under the new state regime, native communities were forced to reconsider their place in the context of a republican Mexican nation. Significantly, the communities of the Sierra Zapoteca used the new institutions of state control—the National Guard and the office of subprefect—to reinscribe their own historical and political status within the nation. Under the leadership of Porfirio Díaz, they became Zapotec soldiers of the republic. Ironically, the white-mestizo alliance that had pushed through the reforms of the 1840s and 1850s had to contend with a militant and aggressive indigenous population from the central highlands after 1855. As allies of the state, the Zapotecs of Ixtlán district could enter into negotiations over political and economic issues as citizens rather than as subjects.

The Origin and Structure of the Ixtlán National Guard

Díaz initiated the formation of the Ixtlán National Guard, but its organizational structure adhered to more local, Zapotec notions of military service. Though Díaz drilled his recruits according to his own regimen of calisthenics and gymnastics, the effectiveness of the battalion came from the ways in which communal elders maintained their status within the guard. Based on the region's history of intervillage conflict, Zapotec leaders recognized the need for negotiating the gender, generational, ethnic, and class tensions of everyday life. In effect, the Ixtlán National Guard reproduced existing hierarchies within communities by reorganizing those distinctions according to military protocol. Once the battalion had been formed, individuals used military rank as markers of local leadership and authority; even during times of peace, captains, colonels, and generals retained their titles, indicating their status within the community and throughout the region.[20] At the same time, the National Guard units became a mediating element within communities, a formalization of privilege and hierarchy that reinforced status according to preexisting differences. To Díaz's credit, he did not try to organize a National Guard battalion that would undermine the influence of communal elders. Although he was the official administrator for the entire district, my guess is the young Díaz had little choice.[21]

Díaz's primary objective was to form a militia that would support the liberal cause initiated by the Ayutla revolt. Men from throughout the district assembled for training with Díaz in September 1855, but that was no way to gauge their understanding of liberal ideas or loyalty once fighting began. One month later, on October 4, Díaz called all of the men in the district to a general meeting to read, discuss, and endorse the liberal ideals outlined in a new set of organizing principles.[22] According to a report of the meeting, the leaders of nearly every town in the district endorsed the liberal plan. They called themselves "*ciudadanos* [citizens]," and they expressed their willingness to defend the liberal revolt. This document provided the first district-wide petition that asked village men to sign en masse in support of liberalism.[23] While the public pressure of signing such a document could always lead some village leaders to act against their will, there is no evidence of disagreement or coercion within this document or any other source surrounding the formation of the Ixtlán National Guard. On the contrary, town leaders who were unable to attend the meeting, like the representatives from Teococuilco, issued their own letter supporting the liberal movement. Over the next two generations, many more petitions emerged from district-wide meetings in Ixtlán, and sometimes we can identify internal conflicts within those discussions. In the absence of such evidence, however, we should not assume that the text of these petitions was beyond the comprehension of those who signed it. The 1855 endorsement of liberal ideals meant the Serranos would be putting their lives at risk; they had every reason to understand the full implications of signing this document for themselves and their families. Even when village leaders could not sign their own names, the petitions were carefully read and discussed at the meetings, and then duly signed by scribes from particular towns. Juárez's ties to Ixtlán district created an opening for liberal support, but Zapotecs also understood the consequences of entering into the partisan, ideological struggle between liberals and conservatives.

Zapotec support for the liberals continued after 1855 and after the series of reforms had begun to polarize Mexican politics even further. These reforms, including the controversial land reform legislation known as the Ley Lerdo (1856), initiated no major disputes in the Sierra Zapoteca. No haciendas encroached on communal lands in the Sierra, and most communities continued to have access to commonly held agricultural plots. There were intense border conflicts between villages, but these fights predated liberal land laws. In short, the liberal reforms posed little threat to the Zapotec villagers of Ixtlán district. On the contrary, the liberals had strengthened Indian communities by arming them.[24] Still, not all Serranos considered themselves liberal. The National Guard units effectively forced conservative supporters underground, though a few individuals made known their political views. In Ixtlán district Jacinto Juárez (not a relative of Benito Juárez), his wife Marciala, and her two sisters Anacleta and Micaela publicly criticized the anticlerical actions of the liberals. A few Serranos hid priests in their homes and collaborated with conservative armies in order to protect their religion. Unfortunately, little information remains on the roles that conservative and pro-Catholic peasants played in the district. More research into the role of the Catholic Church and, in particular, the role of local parish priests during this time period would address this important issue. The fact that we have any evidence suggests that there was probably more opposition than the liberals cared to admit.[25]

Liberal leaders stereotypically assumed that women might support priests and their conservative allies because they had been duped by Catholic lies. No doubt conservatives had supporters among the women of Ixtlán district, but many more women actively supported the liberal cause. The National Guard units, however, did not provide a formal position for women during times of war. Nor did women receive formal recognition for their service to the nation during times of peace, when memories and histories about the wars took on renewed importance. Joining the National Guard units was a privilege reserved for men only, though women fed and bandaged the soldiers and spied on enemies. Zapotec women traveled with men during war, providing essential support just behind the front lines. Although they were excluded from the formal structure of military service, women clearly experienced their own hardships during Mexico's civil wars.[26] However, as they were situated outside of the organization of the National Guard units, women did not have a place within Mexico's military history. Without that formal structure, the acts of bravery performed by women remained mostly unrecognized. Eventually, during the Pax Porfiriana, widows, mothers, and daughters would demand compensation for the sacrifices of their male relatives, but few women would claim to have served the nation in any military capacity of their own. The National Guard units reinforced male control over the conduct of war and later over the ways in which war was remembered.[27]

In similar fashion, men reserved for themselves the formal positions of local political control. Zapotec communities elected their own town councils (*ayuntamientos*) throughout the last half of the nineteenth century through civil *cargo* systems. Men were elected to one-year positions on town councils, filling ranked offices that included president, *sindico* (something like a constable), secretary, treasurer, and first and second *vocales* (or general representatives). Elder men who had served in every cargo position, known as *pasados* or *principales*, determined who should run for office. Thus, elder men held positions of higher status in their communities since they were the experienced ones and the ones who advised the town councils.[28] In this way, generational distinctions marked the formation of communities as much as gender differences. Not surprisingly, generational status became a key element of the National Guard units as well. When Díaz organized the National Guard unit in the Sierra Zapoteca, he named relatively older men to the ranks of low- to mid-level officers. Before any fighting had taken place, men in their forties and fifties became sergeants and were later promoted to lieutenant and captain over younger men from the same towns. Most men were not considered too old for military service. Rather, generational status within the communities became an essential element of directing and controlling the troops. One of the best examples of this sort of leadership came from Felipe García of Guelatao. He was promoted to captain in 1860, at the age of fifty-two, leading a regiment of one hundred men from his community. His leadership within the National Guard proved crucial on numerous occasions during war times, but he also led the community as a respected elder after 1876. In fact, he continued to use his status as a veteran until 1903, as a ninety-five-year-old leader of the community.[29]

Village-based officers were needed to negotiate the tensions within and between villages that existed prior to and apart from the formation of a National Guard battalion. Larger communities were divided into barrios, where churches and patron saints of particular neighborhoods were used as identification markers.[30] Thus, spatial differences within and between communities added to the complexities of organizing a unified military command. Conflicts between the town of Ixtlán, the district *cabecera* or administrative head town, and neighboring villages were especially intense. The subprefect's office (later the office of jefe político) was in Ixtlán, and *sujeto* or subject towns realized the unfair access that villagers from the town of Ixtlán had to formal political power. Within the National Guard battalion, village-based officers gave communities a relative sense of autonomy within the larger army. Without those bonds of community, the tensions between villages would have weakened the entire corps. Still, the formation of the Ixtlán National Guard was more complex than simply naming elder men from particular communities to the officer ranks. Ethnic and class divisions within the region complicated the overall structure at the battalion level. Young mestizo men, related through marriage and business ties to important politicians and mine owners from the region, were named senior officers of the battalion, assuming positions of lieutenants, colonels, and eventually generals.

Miguel Castro orchestrated many of these arrangements, though he did not hold a military office himself. Born into a lower-working-class mestizo family in Oaxaca City in 1813, Castro earned the favor of wealthy Oaxacans who supported his education. He became a lawyer and eventually assumed an administrative post in the Sierra Zapoteca. Through political and business contacts, Castro began to buy mine claims throughout the district, becoming by 1855 the largest and most influential gold and silver mine owner in the region. He married María Jacinta Meijueiro, a descendant of Spanish (and perhaps Portuguese) bureaucrats from the colonial era, whose family had settled in the mining town of Xiacui. The Meijueiros had retained their surname over the years, and the status of Spanish heritage, but they had lost all trappings of economic privilege. In addition to the private emotions that brought them together, Meijueiro offered Castro the honorable status of a Spanish family, and he provided her the security of financial wealth. Castro became the mentor and sponsor of his wife's nephew, Francisco Meijueiro Pérez, promoting him for minor bureaucratic posts and securing a position for him as a lieutenant in the National Guard battalion. Castro also sponsored the career of Fidencio Hernández, another mestizo born in the town of Ixtlán to working-class parents. Hernández and Meijueiro pursued military and political careers until 1876 and then dedicated themselves to using those contacts for business purposes. Like Castro, both men eventually became state governors, and both would become tremendously influential in state and national politics. In the process, they also became relatively wealthy. Hernández and Meijueiro shared one other thing in common. They married into the same family, the Delgado family of Xiacui, and had become brothers-in-law. Their sons, Fidencio and Guillermo, would be first cousins.[31] These two generations of Hernández and Meijueiro men became the caudillos of the Sierra Zapoteca, though the full meaning of caudillo status in Ixtlán requires careful reconsideration. While these men held considerable influence, Zapotec communities could limit their power and authority by recalling the contributions everyone from the Sierra had made during Mexico's civil wars. All men had an opportunity to join the National Guard, and all men could claim to have played an important role in defending the nation.

The National Guard battalion from the Sierra Zapoteca thus mediated gender, generational, spatial, class, and ethnic tensions that existed in the region. Mestizo men held ranked positions above Indian men. Elder Zapotec men commanded their younger neighbors in community-based regiments. Women were excluded from any formal position or recognition in the war effort. As we will see, while individual soldiers would receive medals and certificates of bravery for military service, regiment and battalion commanders received most of the recognition for leading their men during successful campaigns. Thus, merit and performance on the battlefield mattered little toward promotion in the National Guard since preexisting factors determined where one entered the system. Despite all of these internal divisions within the National Guard battalion and within the region more generally, the men and women of the Sierra Zapoteca would become passionate and effective defenders of the liberal cause. In each civil war the Ixtlán National Guard fought for the side that eventually triumphed.

The participation and, more important, the leadership of older men in the Ixtlán National Guard represented a much different organizational structure than that of National Guard units in other regions of Mexico. For example, in parts of the Sierra de Puebla, as Florencia Mallon argues, older men stayed at home while younger men fought for the liberals in the National Guard. When men who had fought in the wars returned to their villages, they talked about a new sense of generational rights and privileges. In particular, veterans challenged the *"pasados'* monopoly of power" whereby elder men determined who would hold communal offices and therefore negotiate internal disagreements and external conflicts with other villages and the state. Younger men who had risked their lives for the liberal cause expected a more open and responsive communal power structure that acknowledged their participation in national and communal defense. The connection between veterans and the liberal state stood at the heart of this generational conflict: "National Guardsmen held new access to state power and control over the means of violence and self-defense." And yet all discussion of "legitimate" communal authority "went through the *pasados*." In brief and contingent episodes and varying from village to village, young veterans from the Sierra de Puebla created a new "democratic patriarchy," where access to the liberal state could be used to redefine male privilege within the community.[32] Mallon emphasizes, however, that this generational challenge lasted for only a brief time. The Juárez regime attempted to disarm the Puebla National Guard battalions in 1867, and the young veterans found themselves in direct conflict with the liberal government. In addition, village elders in more indigenous communities like Cuetzalan in the eastern Sierra appear to have avoided an internal challenge to their authority. Significantly, elder men from Cuetzalan led a brief rebellion against regional and federal authorities in 1868; of the twenty men arrested as leaders of the rebellion, many were in their eighties and the oldest was 104.[33]

While the case of Cuetzalan suggests important similarities with indigenous communities in the Sierra Zapoteca of Oaxaca, the generational composition of National Guard battalions in other parts of Puebla represents an important difference. Communal hierarchy remained unchallenged in the Sierra Zapoteca, whereas the exclusive mobilization of young men in parts of Puebla created new possibilities for limited democratic participation. The generational composition of National Guard units may help explain why veterans in Oaxaca were less confrontational toward local and national elites than were the National Guard militias in Puebla. These differences would reemerge when National Guard troops were mobilized after 1867. As long as the Ixtlán National Guard bolstered established forms of communal hierarchy, military service provided no alternative models for reorganizing politics.

The War of the Reform, 1858–1861

Benito Juárez returned to Oaxaca as state governor in January 1856, and he reluctantly promoted Porfirio Díaz to a position in the regular army stationed in the Isthmus of Tehuantepec. Juárez had tried to convince Díaz to remain within the government since the pay was considerably better. As the subprefect in Ixtlán, Díaz received approximately 150 pesos per month; as a captain in the regular army Díaz earned only 70 pesos per month. After leading the Ixtlán National Guard, however, Díaz had found a career better suited to his temperament and ambitions. Other men could write laws and implement policies based on liberal ideas; Díaz relished the risks and objectives of the military. The professional contrast between Juárez as a politician and Díaz as a military leader began at this moment.[34]

Juárez served as Oaxaca governor this time for just six months. In mid-1856 he became chief justice of the federal Supreme Court, which placed him first in line to succeed the president. Significantly, Juárez's rising prominence in national politics had at least symbolic implications for the Zapotecs back in Ixtlán. Claiming that Juárez was truly one of them, local leaders officially changed the name of the district on July 30, 1857, to "Ixtlán de Juárez." From that time to the present, the region itself would be called both the Sierra Zapoteca and the Sierra Juárez, a normative association that formally linked Juárez to his birthplace.[35] While Juárez probably appreciated this gesture, the political challenges between liberals and conservatives kept him fully occupied in Mexico City. In fact, a conservative rebellion led by Félix Zuloaga challenged President Ignacio Comonfort. Conservatives and their allies were particularly unhappy about land reforms and anticlerical measures within the new liberal constitution of 1857. Rather than lead an unpopular government or a military campaign against his rivals, Comonfort simply resigned in 1858. The conservatives briefly jailed Juárez, who had become acting president, but Juárez escaped his captors, fled to Querétaro, and established a liberal government in exile.

Ideological divisions had driven Mexicans into the jaws of a bloody civil war. Ultimately, the War of the Reform (also known as the Three Years War) would cost thousands of Mexican lives and leave the country open to foreign invasion. Each side had supporters among Mexico's urban intellectual elite, and each side had peasant soldiers willing to die in defense of their respective causes. Liberals and conservatives disagreed about the role of the state in economic and social life, and they disagreed profoundly on the role of the Catholic Church in society. Even Juárez's home state did not fully endorse the liberal president. In late December 1858 a conservative army led by José María Cobos briefly held sections of the capital city, including the Government Palace on the central plaza. Less than three weeks later, liberals retook the city, forcing Cobos to retreat and reorganize before he could try another assault on Oaxaca. After ten months, in October and November Cobos once again set his sights on Juárez's home state.[36] This time Cobos and the conservative army advanced quickly through northern Oaxaca, aided by Mixtec allies who resented the reforms that Juárez had initiated in the 1840s and 1850s. As it became clear that the capital city would fall, Governor Miguel Castro ordered his government to abandon Oaxaca City. Liberal officials fled to the town of Ixtlán on November 4, 1859, just forty-eight hours before the conservative army marched into the city. Significantly, most of these men left behind their wives and families, many of whom became embroiled in the military struggle to control Oaxaca. One woman, however, fled with the liberal government. Margarita Maza de Juárez, wife of Benito, took refuge in her husband's birthplace, bringing the couple's three children with her in baskets carried on the back of a burro.[37]

Castro acted as interim governor until mid-December, when José María Díaz Ordaz returned to organize the liberal coalition against the conservatives. Díaz Ordaz's leadership energized both the liberals in exile and the local population who would be called on to retake the state. One young resident of Ixtlán, sixteen-year-old José Martínez, went to the town square, joined by others ready to go into combat against the conservatives. Miguel Castro was there, the caudillo of the Sierra, standing next to Díaz Ordaz. Near Castro stood Fidencio Hernández and the men under his command from the town of Ixtlán. Francisco Meijueiro was there, too, selecting a group of men to remain in the Sierra while other troops advanced on the enemy. Martínez recognized other regional leaders in the crowd. Felipe García came from Guelatao, heading up a contingent of one hundred men. Mariano Ibarra arrived from Lachatao with his men. And the fearless Cenobio "El Gallo" Pérez joined the battalion with the fiercest group of soldiers in the district, the men of Ixtepeji.[38] While many of the faces were familiar, Martínez did not recognize everyone there, for not all of the soldiers came from Ixtlán district. Colonel Cristobal Salinas had been named leader of the Ixtlán brigade, though he was from Puebla and not well known by most of the soldiers. Jacinto Pacheco came from Oaxaca City. Julio Ríos traveled to Ixtlán from Miahuatlán. Others came as individuals or in groups of three, five, and sometimes more. Consistent with the structure of the Ixtlán National Guard, most of the troops followed their own village leaders, who assumed mid-level officer ranks in the battalion structure. Spirits ran high among the people gathered in Ixtlán, according to Díaz Ordaz, for "each Oaxacan has come to reclaim his flag." With other men from Ixtlán district, José Martínez enlisted and soon had his chance to face the enemy.[39]

Díaz Ordaz assumed command over the liberal army—the 1,100 soldiers of the Ixtlán National Guard led by Salinas and Porfirio Díaz's regular army of

1,000 men stationed in Tehuantepec. As with most regions in Mexico, control of the state government meant control of the state capital, and Díaz Ordaz realized he would have to retake Oaxaca City. He devised a plan to assemble the entire liberal army south of Oaxaca City, near Tlacolula in the central valley, where the conservatives had stationed an outpost. The liberals intended to take Tlacolula, and then begin a coordinated assault on Oaxaca City without worrying about their rear flank. The Ixtlán National Guard set out for Tlacolula in early January 1860, expecting to join Porfirio Díaz's forces within the week. Not surprisingly, given the number of troops involved, conservatives learned of the movements and prepared their own plans to counter the liberal assault.[40] Conservative general José María Cobos assembled 2,200 soldiers at Tlacolula to face the liberals. He could rely on some volunteers, but he also used forced conscription to fill out his ranks. Wealthier conservative supporters could buy out their service obligations with loans and/or grants used to finance the war.[41] In addition to matching the troop strength of the liberals, Cobos enjoyed a distinct advantage with access to superior cannons and adequate supplies of rifles, shot, and gunpowder. In contrast, liberal generals in Oaxaca were constantly begging Benito Juárez to send arms and ammunition.[42] With better arms and plentiful ammunition, the conservatives could afford to go on the offensive. On January 22, 1860, Cobos ordered a preemptive attack on Porfirio Díaz's army, temporarily encamped at Mitla. The conservative tactic worked brilliantly and forced Díaz to abandon most of his artillery, ammunition wagons, and other supplies. The liberal army from Tehuantepec suffered considerable casualties, and those who survived scattered in disarray. Díaz would later reorganize and regain his reputation as an effective military leader, but he lost badly on this day.[43]

Following this victory, Cobos turned to the Ixtlán National Guard surrounding Santo Domingo del Valle, just northeast of Tlacolula. The liberal troops, the majority of whom were Zapotecs from the Sierra, preferred guerrilla warfare tactics rather than open field battles. They took up positions on the hillsides, digging in behind trees and rocks and popping up to take sniper shots when they could. Cobos hit them with his artillery, which, he believed, "caused profound destruction among the enemy." He then sent in his cavalry to drive the liberal forces out into the open. But the Zapotecs surprised him. They had not been injured during the artillery shelling, and they did not give up their positions. Cobos's postwar report revealed surprise and a bit of fear at this prospect when he simply stated, "They resisted up to the last instance." Cobos then ordered his foot soldiers to engage the liberals with bayonets. At this point, the lack of discipline and desire among the conscripted soldiers resulted in significant disorder. Some conservative soldiers refused to advance, while others began to retreat; Zapotec marksmen picked them off as they fled. Conservative officers tried desperately to hold the line, but many of them were killed, captured, or forced to retreat as well. In the end, Cobos not only lost the battle at Santo Domingo, but he also had to leave behind all but one of his cannons and most of his ammunition. His report, which began so glowingly, concluded that the loss of the heavy artillery "had been inevitable." Cobos retreated to Oaxaca City, followed closely by the Serranos.[44]

The liberals, however, had not won a complete victory. Díaz's army was mostly dispersed, and he needed time to reorganize and rejoin his allies in the Ixtlán National Guard. In addition, Governor José María Díaz Ordaz suffered a serious wound in the battle around the foothills of Santo Domingo. He died on the return trip to Ixtlán, leaving the liberals without a clear political or military leader.[45] The state constitution designated that the chief justice of the state Supreme Court should become governor, but that transition did not go smoothly. Citing the constitution, Supreme Court justice Marcos Pérez assumed the leadership of the liberal government in Oaxaca. Pérez, a Zapotec born in Ixtlán district, was aligned with the radical wing of the liberal party, an ally of Benito Juárez, and a former law school professor. In fact, he had been one of Porfirio Díaz's first teachers, and the two maintained a cordial relationship. In later years, Díaz described Pérez as "a man of obvious talent, vast learning, pure habits, and extraordinary integrity, honor and strength of character."[46] Other liberals in Oaxaca did not think so highly of Pérez. In particular, Colonel Cristobal Salinas argued that Pérez was an intellectual and not a military leader; the liberals needed someone who understood warfare. Salinas refused to acknowledge Pérez's authority, which complicated the chain of command for all liberal supporters in Ixtlán. For his part, Pérez notified Benito Juárez about the power struggle, probably expecting his friend to adhere to the constitutional provisions. Juárez, however, determined that an outsider and a military officer would have more success during these difficult times. In February 1860 Juárez sent General Vicente Rosas Landa to lead the Oaxaca front, but the disagreements within the liberal camp continued.[47]

Rosas Landa was accustomed to commanding well-equipped and highly disciplined troops. He knew how to fight if he had access to adequate supplies and ammunition. These things were all lacking in Oaxaca. While he desperately tried to get more arms and ammunition, Rosas Landa ordered a defensive line just outside of Oaxaca City.[48] Porfirio Díaz recognized that Rosas Landa was out of his element and tried to assert more influence on the decision-making process. With the conservatives on the run following their defeat at Santo Domingo, Díaz argued that it was time to attack Oaxaca City.[49] This suggestion only frustrated Rosas Landa, who viewed the Ixtlán National Guard and its officers like Díaz as an "undisciplined" and "unmanageable" militia. His plan to forestall an attack on the conservatives had some initial success. Zapotec sharpshooters targeted officers at the front lines, which had a serious impact on the organization and morale of conservative soldiers. Ultimately, however, Rosas Landa's plan failed because the conservatives adapted to this limited challenge by sending out their own patrols.[50] When the liberals were forced to retreat once again into the protection of the Sierra Zapoteca, Rosas Landa returned to Veracruz in order to personally tell President Juárez of the insubordination and unprofessional behavior of the troops in Oaxaca. Cristobal Salinas and Porfirio Díaz resumed command.[51]

All of these internal conflicts reveal more than simply a power struggle between men with big egos. The military and political situation was exceedingly complicated, and even now, with the benefit of hindsight and access to letters and war reports from multiple perspectives, it is difficult to explain fully what happened and why. Military leaders on both sides were working with limited knowledge about the soldiers under their command. They were uncertain how men would respond in the heat of battle. More to the point, a subtext within military reports suggests an undercurrent of racist attitudes toward the Zapotec army from Ixtlán. With the significant exception of Porfirio Díaz, most professional officers, generals in particular, for both the liberals and the conservatives had trouble believing that this group of National Guard troops had the skill or the intelligence to win on the battlefield. Rosas Landa refused to let them engage the enemy until he had reinforcements and more ammunition. Even when the Zapotecs proved capable of inflicting serious blows against the conservatives, Rosas Landa did not deem them a reliable army. Conservative general José María Cobos reacted with surprise when the Zapotecs did not run from Santo Domingo. After he returned to Oaxaca City, he allowed his troops to mock the Serranos with insults related to their place of origin, calling them "communists" and "our brothers from the Sierra." He tried to discredit all liberals by suggesting that they and their Zapotec allies were "barbarians." This attack was the particular effort of *El Boletín*, a newspaper distributed by Cobos in Oaxaca City. For example, on February 21, 1860, *El Boletín*, claimed, "The communists do not want to take up positions in the city of Oaxaca. It seems they like the sierra and the voluble temperatures of the hills; it seems they prefer to live like squirrels on the hard ground."[52] Given Juárez's Zapotec origins and ties to the Sierra, the insults aimed at the Ixtlán National Guard had political implications as well.

The fact that the liberal government took refuge in Ixtlán only heightened the animosity that conservatives had for the Sierra. The liberal exile actually created a new problem for both sides: the participation of middle-class women in the war effort. Peasant women had always been close to war, providing crucial support usually just behind the front lines. They also had to flee their homes at times, as enemy armies marched through villages in search of opponents. For middle-class Mexicans, however, women were supposed to remain safely secure in their homes while men went off to fight. When men with ties to the liberal government fled Oaxaca City in November 1859, they left behind their wives and families; naturally, these men worried about their loved ones and anxiously tried to get messages to their families. Women also sent correspondence to their husbands, fathers, and brothers in the mountains. By January 1860, a clandestine network of informants and couriers had begun exchanging letters between men in Ixtlán and women in Oaxaca City. Conservative sentries began conducting extensive searches of anyone entering or leaving the city. Discovering letters and supplies, they immediately began arresting the women involved. By May 1860, sixteen women and ten men (mostly servants) had been charged with "corresponding with the enemy" and other crimes against the conservative government. As prosecutors prepared cases against them, the women were put in jail, locked in convents, or placed under house arrest. Oaxacan historian Manuel Martínez Gracida collected the court proceedings against these women; incredibly, he also found and preserved the actual letters.[53]

Manuela Carranza and Manuela Ortigosa de Renero were the first women charged with sedition after soldiers uncovered a packet of letters discussing troop movements. Their servants, Santiago Feliciano and Agustín Aguilar, had been arrested for carrying the letters and other supplies suspected of going to the liberals in Ixtlán. Several of the letters openly discussed the military situation in Oaxaca City, sensitive information that could have aided the liberals had it arrived. An unsigned note mentioned that most of the conservative troops had left the city and that "the only ones still here are the Indians [indios] from Sachila [sic]." Manuela Carranza also sent supplies like cotton and broadcloth that could be used by the men in Ixtlán. Josefa M. de Sandoval, Clara de Fernández, and Laura Torres were arrested in March 1860 for sending supplies as well. Other women were arrested because conservative soldiers had uncovered letters written to them by their husbands. Luis Carbo sent a brief letter to his wife Dionicia León de Carbo in late March. He gave the letter, written on a strip of paper just two-and-a-half inches wide, to Agustín Bautista, a Zapotec peasant from Ixtlán. A conservative patrol found the note on Bautista, arrested him, and then arrested Dionicia León. The note told his wife how to act once the liberal army started the battle to retake Oaxaca City. He was worried that the fighting would be close to their home and that she might be in danger. He was also concerned that she and her friends might insult or even harm women supporting the conservatives. There were other notes like these, some written in faint pencil on tiny pieces of cloth. They all seemed to infuriate the conservative officers who were in charge of prosecuting these women. Pleas for leniency went unanswered, and despite having children at home most of the women remained in jails or locked behind convent walls.

By far most of the letters confiscated by the conservatives did not deal directly with the military situation in Oaxaca. Still, even getting word that someone was safe or would be unable to write for some time provided indirect military information. Husbands and wives, fathers and daughters, were mostly interested in simply making contact to reassure their loved ones that they were safe. The agony of separation during war, the pain of not knowing the fate of people caught on opposite sides of a battle line, occupied most letter-writers. Read together, these brief love letters express a poetics of suffering that reveals how deeply affected people were by the war. The letters help us understand how the memories of this war could shape their entire lives. The pet names, terms of endearment, intimate phrases, and innuendo indicate a remarkable intimacy. Few letters preserved from nineteenth-century Mexico have this quality. Salutations often expressed the most emotion: "Piece of my soul [*pedaso de mi alma*]," "My dear Lala," "My loving little mother," and "My dear little Pug-Nose [*Chatito*]." Closings were difficult, heartfelt, and often lengthy: "Good-bye dear brother and don't doubt the loyal friendship of your sister who loves you and will never forget you for even a moment"; and "The nights of insomnia lead me to beg you my *Chatito* to take care of yourself as best you can, *chico*, since you know that you are my treasure." Women in Oaxaca City and men in Ixtlán expressed similar feelings of frustration over their separation. One young woman wrote, "My Soul [*Alma mía*] my heart broke when you left since I thought I might not see you again." Another young woman wrote, "Dear Luis, tell Daniel to take care of himself . . . and tell him that I am fine and away from danger as he knows I am no longer in my home." From Ixtlán, Luis Fernández wrote his daughter, "I am good and there is nothing new to tell you since that fatal night of our separation, which has caused so much suffering." Félix Romero, who later became governor of Oaxaca, wrote his wife, begging her to stop sending letters because it was too dangerous. He wrote, "My dear love, I desire as much as you do to see each other again and

I hope to the entire world that we will! Console my family, hug my children, and stop writing me until we see each other. Good-bye!" Ironically, his letter fell into the hands of the conservatives who used it to arrest his wife.[54]

Conservatives were not hateful, evil men who enjoyed putting women in jail. On the contrary, they were frustrated by their inability to keep liberal women from risking their safety in the midst of a tense military struggle. Conservatives, like liberals, sought to keep women, at least middle-class women, out of political and military conflicts. Also like their liberal counterparts, conservative leaders maintained careful records of their fallen comrades, their widows, and surviving families in order to grant pensions once the fighting had ended. In one report, General Cobos listed the widows of officers killed in action during the first two months of 1860. This group included 45 women and 141 children.[55] Both liberals and conservatives motivated their troops by highlighting the ways in which the other side endangered women and children. In April 1860 liberal general Rosas Landa reported how "a woman had been wounded" by conservative fire just outside Oaxaca City. One month later, conservative general Cobos charged that liberals had exploded dynamite around buildings, including the convent of La Concepción, without regard for the "innocent lives" of the nuns inside.[56] By this time, mid-May, the liberal assault on Oaxaca City had failed, and the conservatives had grown frustrated with the standoff. If one side did not inflict a decisive blow against the other, more urban residents would suffer, more liberal women would contact their husbands, and more conservative women would be in harm's way. For these reasons, at least according to his reports, Cobos made a fatal decision; he decided to attack the Sierra Zapoteca.

At first glance, Cobos's decision made perfect sense. The liberal leadership had come apart, Vicente Rosas Landa had fled the state for Veracruz, and by all reports the liberals had nearly run out of ammunition. However, there was no way for Cobos to know how difficult it was for invading armies to control the mountains, no way for him to anticipate how vulnerable his army would be to sniper attacks. The stories of Zapotec resistance against the Mexica were three hundred years old; surely his army, equipped with rifles and cannons, would not be so easily defeated. But invading the Sierra Zapoteca was always the wrong decision, and as a result of this mistake Cobos lost the war in Oaxaca.

Porfirio Díaz organized the district's line of defense, working closely with village leaders from Ixtlán, Ixtepeji, and Guelatao. Desperately short of ammunition, Díaz asked the people of these towns to donate any metal they had so that he could use it to make steel shot for explosives and bullets. In the town of Ixtlán, parishioners of La Asunción chapel had recently purchased a new bell. They donated it to Díaz in exchange for a promise that the government would replace it once the war was over. It would take nearly fifty years for Díaz to honor that promise, but eventually the people of Asunción parish received a new bell sent directly by the president. That bell hangs in the steeple still today.[57] Other Zapotecs from other towns played an important role in defending the region as well. They, like Díaz, knew that the conservatives would have to pass a narrow clearing just outside of Ixtepeji, the largest town in the district. On the morning of May 15, Díaz positioned troops above the pass and ordered another contingent of Ixtepejano snipers to circle around in anticipation of the conservative retreat. The plan worked perfectly. Out of seven hundred conservative soldiers sent into the Sierra, only one hundred returned safely to Oaxaca City.[58]

Following their victory at Ixtepeji, nearly 3,500 Zapotec troops descended on Oaxaca City in late May. They established a line around the western entrance to the city and advanced slowly and methodically into the city center. After losing most of his cannons at Tlacolula and a large part of his army at Ixtepeji, Cobos could not stop this assault. His reports to conservative leaders in Mexico City grew increasingly desperate and detached as he described his impending defeat in the passive voice: "the artillery was inevitably lost," "the officers couldn't keep the troops from retreating," and "we were forced to flee the city."[59] On August 5, 1860, liberal commander Cristobal Salinas declared victory in the battle to retake Oaxaca.[60] By that time, Cobos had already abandoned his post, a decision that brought widespread condemnation by other conservative officers. Consistent with the bloody nature of this conflict, however, liberals had begun executing officers, and Cobos had little to gain by simply waiting to surrender. In other parts of the country, conservatives and liberals expressed some surprise at the turn of events in Oaxaca. Conservatives openly questioned how they could have lost this crucial state after their initial success; they still did not fully appreciate the tenacity of the Ixtlán National Guard.[61] Liberals used Oaxaca to inspire soldiers in other battles, and soon the broader war turned decisively in favor of the liberals. In fact, Porfirio Díaz left his home state after retaking the city, leading a battalion of Oaxacan troops against Generals Leonardo Márquez and Félix Zuloaga. During these last days of battle in the War of the Reform, Díaz solidified a national reputation as an effective field commander, for which he received a promotion and medal of honor for his service.[62] The war finally ended on New Year's Day, 1861, when 25,000 liberal soldiers marched in a victory parade in Mexico City.

In Oaxaca, liberal leaders arranged to grant pensions to the widows, mothers, and children of men who were killed fighting against the conservatives.[63]

Significantly, they could agree on little else since the political tensions within the liberal ranks had only increased with the conservative defeat. The disagreement between Marcos Pérez and Cristobal Salinas continued even after Salinas swore impartiality as a military officer. He clearly favored the more moderate wing of the liberal faction, which forced Pérez to resign the governorship in November 1860.[64] Locally and nationally, the divisions between the moderate and the radical liberals were not simply ideological. As local historian Rosendo Pérez observed, "A defining feature of the *borlados* party was that they would not accept Indians like Marcos Pérez and Benito Juárez as their leaders."[65] Juárez was warmly greeted on his return to Mexico City and won reelection in March 1861, but constant bickering within the legislature and the opposition press kept him on the defensive. Given the divisions within the liberal camp, the conservatives had good reason to believe they could regain control of the national government. They needed only a strong ally.

Conclusion

I have spent some effort detailing the military history of the Sierra Zapoteca during the Reform years in order to set the context for the stories that veterans told in their old age during the Porfiriato. However, a more important part of the story surrounding these events was the fact that the mobilization for war caused a rapid transformation in Mexico's rural political culture. People's lives did not materially improve, the economy did not grow rapidly, a new political philosophy did not incorporate marginal populations, but thousands of Mexicans began to think of themselves differently. Fighting in a war for political control of the nation had been a monumental period in the lives of ordinary Mexicans. For the first time, men who sought to control the central state had mobilized native populations, armed them, trained them, and led them in a struggle for national sovereignty. To coordinate and inspire soldiers from distant and diverse communities, military leaders told their followers that they were all Mexican, that they would all receive the benefits of citizenship, and that they were all fighting for the same thing: *Libertad*. We will see, however, that the meaning of *Libertad* was itself open to interpretation. While the memories of the War of the Reform animated the stories people told about themselves and their communities, the larger purpose for having gone to war itself became highly contested.

In the Sierra Zapoteca the creation of a National Guard battalion reconnected the generation of the Reform to a pre-Columbian tradition remembered as a glorious military history. Prior to Díaz's arrival in Ixtlán district in 1855, that tradition described only the distant past. In addition to creating a newfound sense of belonging to the nation, the Ixtlán National Guard revived an equally important sense of ethnic pride among Zapotec communities. Finally, the experience of fighting alongside Díaz gave these ordinary soldiers a connection to the extraordinary career of the man who would eventually rule Mexico for nearly thirty-five years. The people of this region formed an intimate bond with Díaz that would shape their actions during his presidency and their response to the 1910 Revolution that brought him down.

CHAPTER TWO

The French Intervention, 1862-1867

There are not soldiers equal to ours.
Porfirio Díaz (1862)

The War of the Reform failed to end the fundamental conflict between Mexican liberals and conservatives. Despite a bloody and devastating civil war, both sides sought a more complete victory over their rivals. Liberals moved to consolidate their reforms, particularly those measures that limited church wealth and influence. Conservatives sought to regain political power, reverse the reforms, and reestablish their own sense of Mexican nationalism, at the heart of which stood an unwavering allegiance to the Catholic Church. Although broad policy and ideological differences distinguished liberal from conservative, in many ways the heart of the conflict focused on the economic and political role of the Catholic Church. This focus created an international audience for the Mexican struggle for national power. More specifically, conservative Mexicans turned first to the Vatican and then to European governments for help in their struggle against liberals at home. By seeking international allies, however, conservatives introduced the unseemly prospect of a foreign army occupying Mexico. Not surprisingly, Mexican liberals from Sinaloa in the north to Oaxaca in the south characterized this war as the battle for Mexico's "second independence." Ultimately, the conflict that came to be known as the French Intervention settled once and for all the nineteenth-century dispute between liberals and conservatives.

Cinco de Mayo

The War of the Reform returned liberals to power in Mexico City and in Oaxaca City, but deep divisions within the liberal camp raised conservative hopes for continuing the struggle. Conservatives found a willing supporter in French emperor Napoleon Bonaparte III, who eventually committed thousands of his finest soldiers to fight in Mexico.[1] Several months after returning to Mexico City in 1861, Benito Juárez antagonized France, Great Britain, and Spain by unilaterally declaring a moratorium on the debt payments that Mexico owed each country. The three European powers blockaded the port of Veracruz with the intention of forcibly collecting customs duties until the loans had been repaid. Significantly, they did not forge an alliance against Mexico since political tensions back in Europe precluded their broad cooperation. In addition, British and Spanish officials did not endorse Napoleon's intentions to establish a new government in Mexico. By January 1862, the British and Spanish troops withdrew from Veracruz, while six thousand French soldiers prepared to move inland, along the old Camino Real that led from the port through Orizaba, Puebla, and into Mexico City.

The standard narrative of the French Intervention typically shifts from the occupation of Veracruz to the battle at Puebla on May 5, 1862. Although Mexico's victory on Cinco de Mayo only postponed the French occupation for a year, it became and remains a national holiday because it symbolized Mexico's determination for independence from foreign governments. There was, however, an event that happened prior to the battle at Puebla that had a dramatic impact on the course of the entire war against the French and deserves more careful examination.

San Andres Chalchicomula, later renamed Ciudad Serdán, was the first town travelers met on the Camino Real after crossing the steep mountains from Orizaba. Just inside the Puebla state line, Chalchicomula was an important resting point on the main road to the city of Puebla and then on to Mexico.[2] In the eighteenth century the Catholic Church built a thick, fortress-like warehouse, *La Colecturía del Diezmo*, in Chalchicomula to hold crops collected as tithes from the surrounding communities. The liberal government confiscated this warehouse during the mid-nineteenth century and used it to store guns, cannons, gunpowder, and ammunition. In early March 1862 liberal generals ordered several battalions from the Army of the East, including the First and Second Oaxaca Battalions, to Chalchicomula. The troop strength reached more than 1,500, made up primarily of mestizo, Mixtec, and Zapotec soldiers in the regular army and hundreds of women *soldaderas* who traveled with their male relatives. According to historian Jorge Fernando Iturribarría, the Oaxacans had been sent to Puebla to evacuate the people of Orizaba. They also would have used the contents of the warehouse in their defense against the French.[3]

The officers pushed the soldiers through the night to get to Chalchicomula because a tropical storm had blown across the isthmus. They arrived in the late afternoon on March 6 and immediately cleared out some, but not all, of the 46,000 pounds of gunpowder stored inside. They lined the streets and grounds around the warehouse with the barrels of gunpowder, and then prepared sleeping quarters inside. The women were busy as well, moving between dozens of vendor stands that had been set up to sell food to the army. As night fell, some of the vendors and some of the women began roasting meat and corn on wood-burning charcoal fires. More than likely, the wind blew a spark from one of these fires into the warehouse, which ignited a barrel of gunpowder. In seconds, a chain reaction of gunpowder explosions ripped through the encampment. Heavy wooden beams holding up the ceiling of the warehouse fell on those who survived the initial blasts, crushing them before they could escape. Uncontrollable fires killed more men and women who were struck unconscious by the shockwaves. In the end, the explosion killed 1,042 men, 475 women *soldaderas*, and more than 30 local vendors. Doctors and surgeons arrived within hours of the blast and continued to come for another week, but they saved only 224 of the wounded. Most of these victims had suffered terrible burns and lost limbs and eyesight as a result of the blast.[4]

The most reliable accounts of the explosion come from the medical reports collected by the Mexican Congress as part of their inquiry into the accident. As the first to arrive in Chalchicomula, Doctors Manuel Burguichani, Felipe Orellana, and José Cerrato described the scene in graphic, horrible detail, yet emphasized that the reality went beyond their descriptions. They performed amputations well into the next day, cleaned burns as best they could, and set broken bones for men who would die from other injuries in a few hours. They were shocked and unprepared for the horror of seeing so many body parts, decapitated corpses, and heads without bodies. Worse, they reported finding bones of other people lodged in the bodies of some of the survivors. Poisonous smoke filled with acid and ammonia threatened survivors, and the doctors quickly had to move a safe distance from the warehouse. They placed the wounded in a nearby hotel, and as more doctors and medics arrived, they turned to cleansing the area of the corpses and body parts that were still scattered around the ruins of the warehouse. There were too many dead to bury, and town officials feared an outbreak of diseases. The doctors formed piles of cadavers and burned them according to "the old traditions." For several days, smoke from these pyres joined with building fires and other purification fires to turn the sky black. Fearful of more explosions and of the pall of death that hung over the town, local residents locked their doors and hid inside their homes.[5]

Liberal generals and colonels from other divisions began arriving to investigate the accident, but their reports lack the detail or specificity of the doctors'. Yet even for military men accustomed to the brutalities of war, the explosion at Chalchicomula went far beyond their experiences. Their reports began like this one, found years later in Manuel Santibañez's *Reseña historica del cuerpo de Ejercito de Oriente* (1892): "I have encountered the most horrible spectacle that I have ever seen and I hope that I never see something like this again in my life." Ignacio Mejia visited the site on March 7 and reported that the scene went beyond "the spectacular horror" he had expected.[6] General Ignacio Zaragoza came several weeks later, though by this time he had been instructed to investigate the cause of the accident.[7] Within a month of the explosion the Mexican Congress began calling for a full investigation into the accident at Chalchicomula. Some people speculated that French spies had set off the explosions or, perhaps worse, that Mexican conservatives might have been responsible for the destruction. The advancing French army had actually sent their doctors to Chalchicomula when they learned about the accident. According to Mexican reports, the French assisted with the wounded for several days and provided invaluable relief for the Mexicans. Still, the Mexican army was on a heightened state of alert, and some people strongly believed the explosion had not been an accident. Mexican general Manuel Robles Pezuela quickly became a target of suspicion because of his open criticism of the liberal regime. When investigators found letters he had sent to the French about Chalchicomula and other military issues, they arrested him for treason, tried him in a hastily assembled military court, and within three weeks of the explosion, executed him.[8] No substantial evidence linked Robles to the explosion, but the Mexicans felt victimized by the accident and sought an easy target for retribution. Twenty-one senior officers had been killed in the accident; the loss of one more who appeared ready to switch sides did not seem to matter.[9]

The consequences of this explosion were both immediate and long lasting. In Oaxaca, including the Sierra Zapoteca, news of the explosion generated widespread support for the liberal cause. The first people to die in this war were Oaxacan soldiers and their female companions, and that sacrifice motivated people in the state to honor their memories. In addition, the tremendous loss of life in this accident severely diminished the number of troops available within the state. The role of the Ixtlán National Guard in defending the state grew as a direct result of the explosion at Chalchicomula. In Puebla the explosion also changed the way in which the war unfolded over the next several months. If the Army of the East had remained in Chalchicomula as an advance buffer to protect Puebla, it would have inflicted some casualties on the French that would have at least slowed down the advance. If the troops and supplies had been sent back to Puebla, the Mexicans might have completely routed the French so that Napoleon would not have pursued the intervention. From another perspective, however, the explosion appears to have altered the expectations of French commanders. After hearing firsthand reports of the devastation from their own doctors, including an easy calculation that the incident had killed nearly 10 percent of the entire regular Mexican army, French officers marched on Puebla anticipating an easy victory.[10] Did the explosion cause the French to underestimate their opponent? If not for Chalchicomula, would the French have followed a more careful attack that might have defeated the Mexicans? Napoleon and his generals had expressed their expectations for an easy victory even before the accident at Chalchicomula. After suffering such a tremendous loss of life and materiel, how could such Mexican soldiers defeat Europe's best and most experienced troops?

The French commanders led their forces to Puebla, expecting at least a warm welcome from the people of this conservative city. But the Mexicans stationed there were also seasoned soldiers. They knew how to fight against a larger and superior foe, and they imagined nothing less than a war to protect their homeland. As the crack soldiers who had won on Europe's most bloody battlefields soon learned, the Mexicans would not easily surrender. On the morning of May 5, 1862, French general Charles Lorencez plunged headlong into the battle to take Puebla, carelessly using up half of his ammunition in the first two hours of fighting. He tried desperately to penetrate the Mexican lines, but met stiff, determined resistance all along the Mexican perimeter. In the end, Mexico's peasant army delivered a stunning defeat to Lorencez; it would take the French an entire year before they could regroup and take Puebla.[11]

Many Mexicans fought courageously at Puebla, but one individual earned especially wide regard for his leadership. Porfirio Díaz, commander of the Second Brigade, led his men with daring skill. Late in the afternoon, he correctly anticipated a French assault that could have broken through the Mexican defenses. But Díaz was in his element. In his own words, he had "never had a more pleasurable day." On May 10, 1862, just five days after Mexico's victory over the invading French army, Díaz wrote to his sister Nicolasa from the battlefields of Puebla:

> On the fifth of this month the time came when we could confront those red Mamluks [*mamelucos*]; with excitement overflowing to the point of drowning the bloodshed began at 11 in the morning and it poured until 6 in the afternoon when the enemy began to run. We have suffered considerable losses, but we have killed many, many monsieur's.

> I have collected their red hats, their crosses and medals, and their arms. In short, I have never had a more pleasurable day, nor a day as great as the memorable 5th of May, a day of glory and greatness . . . .

> There are not soldiers equal to ours. Let the French brag about the battles of Magenta, Solferino, Australitz and Crimea because all of these crosses and laurels now rest at the foot of the Mexican flag. I pray to God that I do not go crazy with excitement.[12]

Many other Oaxacans, including Zapotecs from Ixtlán district, served with Díaz at Puebla. For most of them, as their testimonials and personal memories in old age would reveal, the war against the French, especially Cinco de Mayo, would become one of the most memorable events in their lives.[13]

The war, however, was far from over after this one day. Napoleon mustered another twenty thousand troops, though it took nearly a year to get them into position to attack. By October 1862, the French troops waiting for reinforcements began raiding mills and farms, picking targets near Chalchicomula since they knew there would be no significant opposition nearby.[14] A more robust and cautious French army returned to Puebla in March 1863. Rather than an all-out offensive, French commanders encircled the city, bombed it with cannons, cut off supplies and ammunition going to the defenders, and starved the Mexicans into submission. Some 12,000 Mexican soldiers surrendered to the French, including more than 1,500 officers. Porfirio Díaz was among this group, though he managed to escape before the officers could be deported to France.[15] As everyone expected, once Puebla fell to the French, only a reduced and demoralized Mexican army guarded the road to Mexico City. Facing certain defeat, Juárez abandoned the capital city at the end of May, though he swore to never surrender Mexican sovereignty to a foreign ruler. As he had during the War of the Reform, Juárez organized a roving government that managed to stay just out of reach of his enemies.

Mexico's Second Empire

With Mexico City under their control, Napoleon and his Mexican allies determined that Mexico needed the unifying symbol and authority of a monarch. Napoleon chose Austrian archduke Ferdinand Maximilian Joseph of Hapsburg, who accepted once he was convinced that the Mexican people had chosen him as well. In fact, Maximilian's insistence on a demonstration of popular support for his monarchy frustrated some of his conservative supporters. Francisco de Arrangoiz, for example, complained to one of Maximilian's advisors that Maximilian would not leave for Mexico until he had received "the certificates of adhesion . . . which clearly stated that he is being endorsed by a majority of the country."[16] Upon receiving this reassurance, Maximilian and his wife Marie Charlotte Amélie Léopoldine, known in Mexico as Carlota, left for Mexico, arriving in Veracruz in May 1864. After Agustín Iturbide's short-lived imperial government in the 1820s, Maximilian established Mexico's second empire.[17]

In Oaxaca one of the first responses to Maximilian's arrival came, appropriately, from Benito Juárez's hometown of Guelatao. On July 10, 1864, most of the men of Guelatao gathered in the community's central plaza to discuss the political events swirling around them. Many of these men had served in the Ixtlán National Guard in the 1850s during the War of the Reform, and some of them had already fought against the French in Puebla on Cinco de Mayo. All of them stated their willingness to fight against Maximilian's government and the foreign army that protected him. As their declaration made clear, they thought of themselves as Zapotec Mexicans. Their statement indicates that Felipe García, a captain in the National Guard, led the discussion, though they may have borrowed some of the language from a school textbook. For example, it was unusual for these men to speak metaphorically of patriotic fathers beyond their own direct ancestors. In this case, however, the Serranos promised to "sustain and defend the precious inheritance brought forth by our fathers from the pueblo of Dolores." They noted that the struggle against Spanish domination had endured for nearly eleven years, a surprisingly specific reference to the fact that independence had not been achieved by Miguel Hidalgo but by Agustín Iturbide. This sort of precision actually went against liberal interpretations of independence that emphasized Hidalgo exclusively. In addition, the Guelatao declaration of war against Maximilian stated that the men would fight "to maintain the form of our government, which is a popular representative republic." Whether they used a textbook or not, the Serranos had struck upon an original lesson in the war against

Maximilian and Napoleon, both mentioned by name in the statement. They could not support Maximilian because he was a foreign emperor, selected by a European ruler and kept in power by a foreign army. The fact that some conservative Mexicans, like Miguel Miramón, whom the group also singled out for criticism, supported Maximilian could not change that fundamental reality. For the Zapotecs, the war for Mexico's "Second Independence" had begun.[18]

To a great extent, the real war for control of Mexico was not fought on the battlefield. As the Zapotecs from Guelatao indicated, liberal and conservative Mexicans saw this war as a struggle over national symbols, culture, and a sense of history. Ironically, Maximilian tried to win over potential opponents by publicly endorsing the same heroes recognized by liberal supporters. In August and September 1864 Maximilian traveled to the town of Dolores to celebrate Hidalgo's revolt against Spain, and then canceled the events commemorating Iturbide's constitution on September 27. These acts infuriated his conservative allies, who had expected the new emperor to reject Hidalgo in favor of Iturbide.[19] Even Maximilian's decision to adopt a grandson of Iturbide in order to establish a royal "Mexican" lineage did not end the conservatives' complaining.

Maximilian, however, had not fully revealed his own liberal tendencies, and only slowly did conservatives suspect they had made a mistake in choosing this European emperor. They criticized a series of "liberal" decisions Maximilian carried out in 1864 and 1865. He appointed several liberals to key cabinet positions, including Juan de Dios Peza in the Ministry of War and José Fernando Ramírez in the Foreign Ministry. He alienated Pope Pius IX, the Vatican nuncio, and the Mexican Catholic hierarchy by refusing to return property expropriated from the church during the Reform. He also argued for greater religious tolerance and continued to demand that priests administer the sacraments for free. His plans went further, according to Joaquín Velázquez de León, who claimed the emperor had asked the Ministry of Justice to draft legislation that would enforce the entire set of Reform laws. Conservatives even complained that Maximilian's coat of arms did not have an obvious symbol of his faith—no crosses and no indication of his support for Catholicism.[20]

As much as liberals had targeted the Catholic Church for reforms in the 1850s, conservatives demanded unqualified support for the Catholic Church as the centerpiece for a new regime. By late December 1864, Teodosto Lares, the archbishop of Mexico City, viewed the uneasy relationship between the Catholic Church and Maximilian as "critical [and] extremely delicate."[21] Ignacio Aguilar, an advisor to Maximilian, received numerous complaints about the emperor's reluctance to return church property. Many conservative activists commented on the situation, but Aguilar's own daughter, Ana Aguilar de Solórzano, explained the issue in perhaps the clearest terms: "How sad we are with this Emperor in whom we placed so much hope for salvation; he is committing the same crimes as Juárez! In the end, if the Holy Father cannot have church property returned it makes little difference if the person committing the crime is named Maximilian or Juárez."[22] Discontent with Maximilian's refusal to return church property led to greater doubts about his government. Pablo Vergapa argued, "The council is in chaos as is the army and generally the entire public administration . . . . Maximilian is losing the confidence of all social classes." Vergapa added that the assembly of notables that had invited Maximilian was considering another meeting to select a new sovereign; "No one will be voting for Maximilian," Vergapa warned.[23]

Conservatives continued to object in 1865, even after Maximilian replaced some liberal cabinet ministers with conservatives and after the French had won several military victories against liberal armies. Conservatives openly worried that plans for an event honoring Cinco de Mayo had been allowed to proceed.[24] Maximilian, they argued, naively believed he could win over Mexicans by appealing to their sense of nationalism. These complaints, along with Maximilian's actions, signaled that the focus of the struggle between conservatives and liberals was as much about cultural and historical symbols as it was politics. In this regard, Maximilian's ambivalent attitude toward the Catholic Church antagonized his base of support. One of his fiercest critics, Francisco Arrangoiz, resigned his diplomatic post in Europe and lobbied other conservatives to abandon the monarch. In July 1865 he wrote an angry letter to Maximilian's aide Ignacio Aguilar: "*Compadre*, I did not work so hard to bring to Mexico this Juárez wearing a crown . . . . I did not work for him to insult the clergy; nor for the Empress to say in her letters that she will arrange a suitable agreement with his Holiness; nor did I work in order for him to plant his demagogic ideas in this country."[25] As late as September 1865, well after the French had achieved several important military victories, conservatives still suggested that Maximilian was "neither virtuous nor talented" in governing Mexico.[26]

Internal disagreements within Maximilian's government actually ran counter to the success his armies had on the battlefield. Soon after capturing Mexico City, French commanders turned their attention to other regions of the country, including Monterrey, Sinaloa, and Oaxaca. As many occupying armies have learned, however, an initial sweep through cities and towns is much easier than actually holding territory and pacifying local populations. This experience characterized fighting particularly in Oaxaca. The French siege of Oaxaca City began in late December 1864.[27] Porfirio Díaz led the defending Mexican army, finding himself once again in a position to repel a French assault on an important city. But this time Díaz faced insurmountable odds. Eight thousand French soldiers had been assigned to capture the state, joining forces with another one thousand Mexicans supporters; Díaz's troops numbered only about 3,500. In an attempt to save the city from the French, Díaz nearly destroyed it. He leveled buildings and shot holes through walls in order to have a clear aim on the enemy. He demanded war taxes from wealthy citizens, removed elected officials, confiscated and occupied church property, and essentially took the supplies his troops needed for defending the city. People argued that he was doing more damage to the city by trying to protect it than the French would do in trying to capture it. The French attack began in the southern part of the city, where they quickly secured artillery positions to attack the republicans. Díaz desperately tried to reposition his cannon but soon realized he could not repel this attack. When he surrendered on February 9, 1865, many people in Oaxaca City were simply glad to have the ordeal finished.[28]

National Guard troops from the Sierra Zapoteca fought with Díaz in Oaxaca City and hurriedly returned to their homes once it was clear Díaz would surrender. French commanders understood the need to keep these soldiers inactive, and they dispatched a regiment to convince regional leaders in the Sierra Zapoteca to end the fighting. French colonel Agustín E. Brincourt met with Miguel Castro to discuss the terms of a possible modus vivendi; significantly, they did not describe their negotiations as surrender. Castro had little choice. He could either commit the remaining soldiers to certain defeat or find a way to live with the French. In exchange for an end to hostilities, the French commander agreed to allow Castro to name the region's jefe político. Castro opted to end the fighting and chose his nephew, Francisco Meijueiro, to be the jefe político.[29] On the face of it, then, Castro and Meijueiro had entered into a collaborative agreement with the invaders. Significantly, however, no one from the Sierra had been forced to sign a pledge of loyalty to Maximilian. Former general Cristobal Salinas was not as fortunate. On April 28, 1865, he swore allegiance to Maximilian in exchange for his life, promising to refrain from taking up arms against the government and to keep military leaders informed of his whereabouts.[30] The terms of a truce with the Serranos were more temporary, a "gentleman's agreement." To a certain extent, they simply chose to fight another day, and most Oaxacans agreed with that decision.

Maximilian's liberal policies and the hostility of conservative Catholics toward the emperor had actually created an opening for some liberals to cooperate with the monarch, if only for a short time. This narrow middle ground between liberals and conservatives existed in Oaxaca as well, where the empire's administrator tried to reach out to both factions. Juan Pablo Franco, a lawyer from Chiapas, administered Oaxacan affairs with a gentle touch. He refused to punish liberal supporters, and he echoed the liberal voice of Maximilian. In fact, the most significant group of people who were unhappy with Franco's tenure was the state's Catholic bishops, who believed he had moved too slowly to undo liberal restrictions against the church. Thus, the ambiguous policies of the imperial government in both Mexico City and Oaxaca City demonstrated the contingent nature of politics surrounding the entire French Intervention. Even staunch liberals like Castro and Meijueiro, personal friends of President Juárez and allies of Porfirio Díaz, could get along with the new regime in the short term. In the long term, however, few citizens were willing to yield Mexican sovereignty to a foreign ruler.[31]

After surrendering to the French, Díaz was sent to prison in Puebla, fortunate that his captors decided not to execute him on the spot. In fact, the French treated him with considerable respect, allowing him to live in an apartment instead of a jail cell and providing him with a servant. They had tried to convince him to switch sides, but he refused. His only concession was a promise to not escape. He broke that promise in September 1865, though years later he claimed that this decision still bothered his sense of honor. Accomplices helped him stage a dramatic escape in which he used a rope to climb down from a second-story window. He quickly mobilized a small guerrilla band and waged hit-and-run attacks on the French.[32]

Díaz's efforts coincided with a growing popular insurgency in Oaxaca's central valley, led by Luis Pérez Figueroa, and in the Sierra Zapoteca, led by Cenobio "El Gallo" Pérez from Ixtepeji. Although Castro had signed an agreement not to lead an assault against the French, Zapotec officers had not agreed to those terms. Through the summer of 1865 and into the fall, Zapotec units of the National Guard staged their own attacks on French outposts in the Sierra. Cenobio Pérez and his band of soldiers defeated the French in several skirmishes throughout the district, including battles at Yolox and the Rio Grande. Although he could not threaten Oaxaca City, Pérez demonstrated once again that an occupying army could not control the central highlands. Even if liberal leaders like Castro and Meijueiro had agreed not to resist the imperial government, Zapotec soldiers determined their own course of action.[33]

Two weeks after Díaz's escape, Maximilian signed an executive decree ordering the immediate execution of anyone caught resisting his government.[34] For conservatives, Maximilian's decree represented the shift in policy they had expected from the beginning. From their perspective, he needed to eliminate those stubborn opponents who refused to recognize his government. Díaz's escape proved that too many liberals were willing to continue the fight indefinitely. For liberals, however, the decree energized their determination to defeat this regime. It confirmed their understanding of the war as a fight to the death, and liberal officers used notices of the decree to rally troops, telling them of the certain death that would follow if they lost on the battlefield. News of the decree reached deep into the liberal ranks. In fact, Zapotec National Guardsmen were executed as a result of the decree. In August 1866 a small unit of the imperial cavalry swept into Ixtepeji in the middle of the night and captured Cenobio Pérez in his home. Telling his family that he would be imprisoned in Oaxaca City, they executed him just outside of town, according to Maximilian's executive decree.[35]

By 1866, however, the French army was mostly on the defensive. Díaz had reorganized the resistance in southern Mexico, and liberals had regained lost cities and states in the north as well. Simultaneously, Maximilian was beginning to lose support in Europe, and despite his policy changes, he never completely won over his conservative critics in Mexico City. Napoleon III ordered most of his troops back to Europe in order to carry out wars in the Continent, and the French armies began a slow withdrawal. As the international and national alliances that had kept Maximilian in power since 1864 began to fray, the fortunes of war shifted to the liberal side. Porfirio Díaz personally led the charge to retake Oaxaca City in April 1866, joining his troops in hand-to-hand combat against the enemy. It was during these battles, in the retaking of Oaxaca and later in the retaking of Puebla, that Díaz regained his reputation as a brilliant and courageous military general. When he drove the French from Oaxaca City, Díaz suffered a serious leg injury. Passing by his family's residence in order to make sure his sister Nicolasa and niece Delfina (who became Díaz's wife the following year) were safe, Díaz stopped to empty the blood that had filled his boot. But he refused to get off his horse, rejecting his family's plea to tend to his wound. With the French on the run, Díaz wanted only to retake the city.[36] He spent the summer and early fall of 1866 securing his position in Oaxaca. He removed local officials who had collaborated with the French, replacing them with men loyal to him. In Ixtlán, however,

Díaz could not or would not dislodge Castro and Meijueiro. He needed their support, and he needed the Zapotec soldiers they could mobilize. Within the year, the jefes políticos and other officials named by Díaz would be called on to support Díaz's candidacy for president. Significantly, Castro and Meijueiro would remain loyal to Juárez.

In October 1866 Díaz learned that an advancing column of 1,500 Austrian and Hungarian troops intended to retake Oaxaca for the empire. Anticipating the enemy's movement, Díaz determined that he would rather fight in the mountains than in the city. Díaz's army marched north from the capital to the town of Etla, arriving eventually at a hilltop area known as La Carbonera. Díaz placed the Ixtlán National Guard under the command of his younger brother Félix and granted these troops the "honor" of fighting in the vanguard position.[37] The battle began at dawn on October 18, and by late that afternoon Díaz's army had routed the enemy. Once again, the Mexicans had been badly outnumbered and had faced a superior enemy with greater arms and ammunition. But Díaz and his soldiers had the advantage of fighting in the hills they knew best, and the added incentive of fighting for their homeland. By the end of the day, the Mexicans had captured dozens of foreign officers, hundreds of enemy soldiers, and all the arms and ammunition they could carry. It was a decisive victory, a turning point in the southern front, and Díaz received full credit for defeating Maximilian's best troops. Several weeks after his victory, Díaz petitioned President Juárez for a medal to commemorate these Oaxacan victories. The medal, "for my comrades in arms," showed that even as a young commander, Díaz understood the importance of inspiring his men with public expressions of patriotic gratitude.[38]

The battle at La Carbonera would later be considered one of Díaz's most glorious victories. Indeed, it was crucial since it sealed the fate of the empire in Oaxaca and opened the door to retaking Puebla and Mexico City. Altogether 65 Mexicans lost their lives at La Carbonera, and another 113 were wounded. From the Sierra Zapoteca, thirteen men of the Batallón de Tiradores de la Sierra were killed; forty others were wounded. In general, however, the fighting had gone well, and the casualties were minor given the tremendous odds faced by the Oaxacans.[39] Félix Díaz honored his troops from the Sierra Zapoteca by issuing them a congratulatory letter. He thanked the Serranos for responding to the nation's call for protection, knowing that they had left behind their families. With tremendous pride and gratitude he dismissed them, but he cautioned that their work was not fully complete and that the nation would most likely need their services again: "return to your homes bearing arms, which should be guarded as a sacred gift that the Patria has granted to you."[40]

Some Oaxacans continued to fight alongside the Díaz brothers as members of the Army of the East. They recaptured Puebla and then reclaimed Mexico City. For most of the Serranos, however, the fight against foreign invaders had ended. The Zapotecs could return home with their weapons, with the means of defending themselves and their nation when threatened. A medal or a certificate of bravery was not worth as much as the right to carry weapons, a right the Serranos would defend for the next two generations. If Díaz had cast the right to bear arms in terms of the sacred, then the Serranos would guard that privilege religiously.

Exacting Revenge

The depth of hostility that liberals felt toward the empire became clear as former administrators and then Maximilian himself fell into their hands. In Oaxaca, Juan Pablo Franco, the imperial administrator, had tried to negotiate terms of surrender, but Díaz refused to concede on any issue. Franco was particularly concerned about the safety of Archbishop José María Covarrubias, who had been an ardent supporter of the conservative cause and personally responsible for excommunicating local liberal leaders. In an exchange of letters Franco asked Díaz how he would protect Covarrubias after liberals took control of the city. Díaz responded that he would treat him no differently than any other conservative; he would be happy to execute him in "his fine bishop's uniform."[41] Franco and Covarrubias immediately fled for Puebla. Soon after, Franco traveled from Puebla to Tehuacán to meet his family in flight from Oaxaca. Díaz's scouts learned of Franco's whereabouts, captured him, and brought him back to Díaz for sentencing. To the surprise of many Oaxacans, even those who supported the liberals, Díaz decided to execute Franco for treason. Rejecting an emotional appeal for clemency on the part of Franco's family, Díaz carried out the execution in late January 1867.

For many Oaxacans Díaz's decision appeared bloodthirsty and heartless. Newspapers reported the trial and plans for execution, and emphasized Franco's tolerance when he had been administrator. According to one newspaper account, more than five hundred women wrote asking Díaz to pardon Franco.[42] The gravity and emotion of the unfolding events were painful to watch, and painful perhaps to recall many years later. In the middle of a sleepless night before his execution, Franco wrote his wife a final letter:

Today at noon I was informed that they have sentenced me to death, and tomorrow morning at six I will be executed. An injustice has been committed against me, but with all my heart I forgive those who have done it. . . .

I am content and at peace, and let me tell you: I would be without sorrow if it were only a matter of my life, which I offer to God, but I am leaving you, who have been the gentle and faithful companion of my life, and our dear children, and my poor mother and other family, and this breaks my heart. . . .

May God make my homeland happy. May God take care of you and of my poor children. Goodbye, goodbye forever. . . . Goodbye, my dearest wife. Goodbye, my beloved children.[43]

The official reason Díaz gave for Franco's execution focused on the decree that Maximilian had signed that sentenced to death anyone captured fighting the government. Díaz simply argued that he was administering the same sort of justice handed out by the imperial government. The decision to follow through with the execution, however, appears somewhat arbitrary. According to historian Erika Pani, Franco was the only civilian administrator in Maximilian's government to meet this fate.[44] We can speculate about several other factors that may have played a role in Díaz's decision. First, the execution demonstrated exactly how political opponents would, or more important, could be treated by the victorious liberals. Many people had collaborated with the imperial government, and Díaz quickly removed some local officials from office. By killing Franco, Díaz sent a signal to anyone who might challenge his authority. Second, Franco had enjoyed some popularity in Oaxaca City and had proven he could work with both conservatives and liberals. By eliminating Franco as a potential rival, Díaz strengthened his control over his home state. A third possible reason relates as well to Oaxacan and national politics. By executing Franco, Díaz proved his staunch allegiance to the liberal cause and sent a signal to Benito Juárez. In that regard, Díaz created the conditions whereby Juárez would have to match his example. How could Juárez pardon other senior imperial administrators when Díaz had already set execution as the "proper" course of liberal action?

Whereas Franco's execution had drawn local and regional condemnation of Díaz, the execution of Maximilian generated widespread national and international criticism aimed at Juárez. Emperor Maximilian fled Mexico City at the last possible opportunity, as Porfirio Díaz marched from the south and other liberal generals advanced from the north. The emperor made it only as far as Querétaro, where he was forced to surrender on May 15, 1867. One month later, on the Cerro de las Campanas on the outskirts of Querétaro, Maximilian was executed by firing squad along with two of his Mexican generals, Tomás Mejía and Miguel Miramón. Ignoring the broad international appeal to spare Maximilian's life, Benito Juárez determined that too many Mexicans had died and suffered because of the French Intervention. In order for the nation to heal its wounds, in order for the world to understand the price of violating Mexican sovereignty, Maximilian had to die.[45] But the dawn of the Restored Republic opened a difficult period for Mexico when things might have been different. Juárez had intended Maximilian's death to signal an end to the conflicts and divisions that had plagued Mexico for more than a decade. After years of civil war, after suffering the effects of a massive foreign invasion, including the deaths of some fifty thousand Mexicans, the national government had been restored. Still, the opportunity for advancing toward a more stable political order did not deter members of the Liberal Party from challenging Juárez for the presidency. Oaxaca's other native son, Porfirio Díaz, became Juárez's chief opponent.

Conclusion

For the people of Ixtlán district, fighting in the War of the Reform and then during the French Intervention marked a turning point in their lives. While they looked to Juárez's success as a sign of their own potential, they knew firsthand how important military service had been to the liberal cause. After fighting in Mexico's civil wars, some of them gained local and regional prominence and became leading members of Oaxaca's political establishment. Some earned medals and certificates of bravery for defending Mexico on the battlefields, rewards they later used to barter for political protection and economic aid. And some died in combat, leaving behind families and communities who would recall their lost relatives as heroic patriots. But for all of them, the experience of fighting changed the way they thought of themselves and of their place in the nation. In short, the Zapotec peasants of Ixtlán became Mexicans. These feelings caused no material changes in the region; it did not create a new road or new connections to Mexico City. But the Serranos imagined new ties, new relationships, and new alliances between themselves and the men in power. Oaxacans had died at Chalchicomula, and then at Puebla, and then in the series of battles to regain Mexican sovereignty.

Although Díaz had initially armed and then led Zapotec troops through two wars, there were limits to his influence in the Sierra. The Ixtlán National Guard provided another way to reproduce communal hegemony, allowing elder men in each village to maintain the decision-making process within their communities. The potential for a more radical, more open approach to organizing politics did not exist, even if everyone believed they had played a part in defending the nation. When Díaz began to challenge the old order under Benito Juárez, few Zapotec soldiers would support him. The structure of the National Guard battalions represented a stable and familiar context within which peasant communities could understand and negotiate the political changes taking place in their district and their nation. And though the foreign invaders had been defeated and liberalism reigned triumphant, more instability loomed on the horizon.

CHAPTER THREE

Rebellions and Promises in the Restored Republic, 1867-1876

And this will be the last revolution.
Porfirio Díaz (1871)

Following their victory over the French, Mexican liberals christened a new beginning for the nation, a time they called the "Restored Republic." They had won a decisive military struggle against their conservative opponents, and more important, they had won the opportunity to redefine Mexico's political culture according to their own ideology and view of history. Herein lay the origins of a secular political culture built around Mexico's military history. A coherent articulation of these ideas would take years to assemble, however, in part because the Liberal Party remained as divided as before the war. Liberals could not overcome their own legacy of internal divisions, which featured intense ideological debates and armed uprisings against rival liberals. Prewar debates between radical liberals and moderate liberals reignited over legislative initiatives dealing with social and judicial reforms. Much of this conflict centered on an ideological tension within Mexican liberal thought more broadly: the precarious balance between the institutional power of the state and individual liberties.[1] While Benito Juárez and his supporters argued for broader executive authority, opponents countered that a powerful president would likely infringe on the rights of individuals. Significantly, many Mexicans, including those who had fought against the French in both the regular army and the National Guard units, argued that the war had been fought for

Libertad or liberty. Thus, any hint that liberty might be diminished by executive fiat invited quick reactions among veterans. In fact, references to military service became a new feature of the debates within liberal ranks, creating a discursive link between men from different generations, classes, and ethnic groups. Their wives and children would eventually take up this language in letters they wrote to state officials, but initially the conversation involved primarily men. This emphasis on military service, however, generated a new source of conflict between men who had chosen careers in politics and those who had pursued careers in the military. The two native sons of Oaxaca, Benito Juárez and Porfirio Díaz, stood at the center of this dispute. And the other sons of the Sierra, the Zapotecs of Ixtlán district, played a decisive role in that dispute.

In 1867, 1871, and 1876 Díaz pursued a "Oaxaca strategy" for gaining national power.[2] In his electoral bids and in his armed rebellions, Díaz always began in his home state. He tried to establish a political and/or military stronghold in Oaxaca, and then advance from the south into Puebla and, finally, into Mexico City. Díaz knew from experience how effective this path to power could be since he had helped defeat the conservatives during the War of the Reform using this route, and he had done the same against the French. Despite his earlier military successes, however, Díaz failed in 1867 and 1871. In fact, Díaz did not gain power until 1876, the only year the Ixtlán National Guard joined his cause. Eventually, Díaz and his supporters would look to their victory in 1876, rather than their previous defeats, for reassurance that they had been destined to establish a new political order. Veterans merged their memories of these battles with stories about victories over conservatives and the French, forming a more linear war narrative that celebrated Díaz's rise to power and their role in helping him get there. In the process of writing that narrative, they had to forget or intentionally omit the complexities of this history.

The 1867 Elections

Díaz had decided not to pursue Maximilian to Querétaro, turning back at Mexico City to allow other armies to carry out the final defeat and eventual execution of the emperor in June 1867. Díaz had already ordered enough executions and did not need another on his hands, though by staying away from Querétaro Díaz also avoided the national and international controversy surrounding Maximilian's execution. Díaz had decided instead to tour the regions of the center-south, Puebla and Oaxaca in particular, to lay the foundations for a postwar run at the presidency. This task involved appointing men loyal to him to positions of local office. He had already appointed many of the jefes políticos in Oaxaca. In Puebla Díaz named new local administrators and replaced provisional governor Rafael J. García with Juan N. Méndez, the popular National Guard general from the Puebla highlands. Within a few short months, Méndez would prove more loyal to Díaz than to Juárez.[3]

Díaz did not publicly declare his intention to run for president since he was still a commissioned officer serving at the discretion of President Juárez. Instead, he allowed others to speak for him through newspapers he controlled. He began publishing *El Boletín de Oriente* in November 1866 and others, including *La Victoria*, several months later. *El Boletín* chronicled the achievements of the Army of the East; *La Victoria* was more openly partisan, announcing the formation of political clubs for Díaz in February 1867 and backing him for the presidency in June, a month before Juárez actually returned to Mexico City.[4] Thus we see the two unwritten rules of electoral politics taking shape rather soon after liberals had won the war. The first informal rule prevented individuals from openly campaigning for political office since leaders were expected to remain above the partisan fray; they were to be seen as reluctant servants rather than as ambitious ideologues. The second rule involved naming local administrators, particularly jefes políticos, in order to sway the actual voting. If the first rule implied a nonpartisan political system, the second demonstrated the real cutthroat nature of the electoral process.[5]

Although it is easy to see how Díaz prepared for the 1867 campaign, it is not as easy to explain why. He had become a major war hero and a symbol of the nation's determined fight for sovereignty since he had been at Puebla in 1862 and again in 1867, and he had helped lead the Mexican forces to victories both times. He had the backing of the regular army and of many of the National Guard battalions throughout the country. Many of these supporters encouraged him to run in order to protect the interests of those who had fought against the French. Some historians have argued that Díaz was mostly interested in enhancing his own political power to satisfy an oversized ego. That argument may look correct from hindsight, knowing as we do that once he gained the presidency he stayed in power until he was forced out by a nationwide revolution. I would argue, however, that in 1867 Díaz ran for office because he could. He had fought to protect Mexico's democratic process, as flawed as that process may have been. And so he challenged Juárez because he had a constitutional right to do so. He was not planning an armed revolt against Juárez in 1867, and, as often happens in electoral campaigns today, if he did not win the first time he could always run again. Díaz expressed these ideas in an 1867 letter to Miguel Castro, the acting governor in Oaxaca. About the possibility of rebellion, Díaz wrote, "Once the Nation goes down that path (which frightens me to imagine), we would find ourselves lost, without a compass and without a rudder." The country was protected by its constitution, Díaz argued, not by the good intentions of individuals: "An intelligent and democratic people should not base its future on the qualities of a single person, but rather on its institutions. Individuals are worth very little in any government and worth nothing in a Republic. Mexico is democratic, sensible, and enlightened and knows its path."[6]

Like Díaz, Juárez used surrogates to help with his campaign and appointed local officials to sway the vote in other parts of the country. Still, his return to Mexico City had taken longer than he had hoped, and Díaz's upstart campaign showed signs of gaining traction. One month after returning to the capital, in August 1867, Juárez tried to regain the initiative with a set of executive decrees. The *Convocatoria* contained several significant directives. It set the date for the next presidential elections for October 6. It proposed several amendments to the 1857 Constitution that were designed to strengthen the executive branch. And it offered a general amnesty to Mexicans who had collaborated with the imperial government. Many parts of the country reacted quickly and angrily to the *Convocatoria* since Juárez had proposed amending the constitution without legislative approval, a clear violation of the constitutional process. Ultimately, he was forced to withdraw the reforms until after the presidential elections. Mexicans were also angry at Juárez's willingness to so easily forgive collaborators. Thousands of loyal citizens had sacrificed their lives and their homes in putting down Maximilian's regime; to simply ignore those sacrifices, to refuse to punish acts of treason against the nation, violated a widely shared sense of fair play. But Juárez was on the defensive in his bid for reelection. Díaz's political threat was real, and Juárez needed to gain ground in order to retain his office. More than anything else, the *Convocatoria* represented an authoritarian response to Díaz's growing popularity.[7]

Oaxacans in the Sierra Zapoteca and in Oaxaca City reacted rather mildly to the *Convocatoria*. They had shared an ambivalent experience with the imperial regime, and many leading liberals had actually found a way to coexist with the empire's administrative system. Miguel Castro, for example, had seemingly been a collaborator, though no one would publicly challenge his liberal credentials. Few Oaxacans, in the countryside or the cities, wanted to continue the civil strife by refusing to forgive their fellow Mexicans. Díaz learned this lesson most clearly when he executed Juan Pablo Franco.[8] Instead of protesting the *Convocatoria*, Juárez's supporters in Oaxaca reacted angrily to Díaz's bold attempt to challenge the president. General Luis Pérez Figueroa advised Juárez to appoint new governors in Oaxaca, Veracruz, and Puebla, the three states where Díaz was strongest. These states needed "men with pure intentions," Pérez Figueroa argued, which meant simply men who were more loyal to Juárez. The new governors would then appoint new jefes políticos to carry out the election.[9] Miguel Castro stated the issue more clearly: "frankly, Don Porfirio has changed much and he no longer serves you as a loyal and good soldier."[10] But just as clearly, the debate within Juárez's own camp was not about democratic practice. Juárez's supporters wanted the president to act unilaterally, to remove popular but pro-Díaz officials, and to limit Díaz's ability to actively campaign for the presidency. No one in Oaxaca, neither Castro nor Pérez Figueroa, called for an entirely new and open system where voters would be able to make their own unencumbered decisions about the candidates for office.

Though his supporters pushed the president to limit Díaz's campaign, going into the elections Juárez acted with restraint. Even after it became clear that Díaz would likely win Oaxaca, Juárez did not suppress the Díaz campaign. Castro anticipated the results of the elections and predicted Díaz would get a majority of the votes in the state: "since both of them [Porfirio and Félix Díaz] get along so well with most of the jefes políticos, which as you know, are the ones who oversee the elections; and all of the other people do what they [the jefes políticos] tell them to do."[11] Juárez calmly told Castro not to worry: "It is necessary to work for and maintain assurances of order and proper administration in your state."[12] He would not prevent Díaz from organizing a campaign. However, Juárez's loss in Oaxaca would expose how little Castro could influence the electoral process, demonstrating his inability to manipulate the system as he and presumably Mexico City wanted. For that reason, Castro's political role in Oaxaca was greatly diminished for Juárez. In other parts of the country, pro-Juárez forces had done exactly the same thing that the Díaz brothers had done in Oaxaca. But there was an interesting counterpoint to events in Oaxaca. By allowing the Díaz brothers to move forward with their plans, Juárez could effectively monitor and gauge their ultimate objectives. Juárez may have been "smoking out" Díaz, allowing him to organize in order to create a public record of disloyalty and blind ambition.

Still, Juárez supporters were angry about the prospect of losing the president's home state. José Silva, an ardent supporter of the president, declared, "Will we, those of us who want you to continue to guide the destiny of our country, allow this nightmare to take place? A thousand times no. Let other states do so, in good time, but here, which is your homeland, which you have done so much to help and save from misery, this would be a true scandal."[13] Díaz's "Oaxaca strategy" was having its desired effect. Castro grew increasingly convinced that Díaz would win a majority of the votes for president in Oaxaca and that then Félix Díaz would win the vote for governor one month later:

> Chato [Félix Díaz] expects to win a majority among the jefes políticos because [Porfirio] Díaz appointed them; they are essentially soldiers and they obey him completely. For this reason if you do not take extraordinary precautions right away, the elections will be completely lost. I am completely isolated in the government. . . . I cannot count on the soldiers because all of the officers support Chato since he trained them and fought with them; I cannot count on the political process working since it is arbitrary.[14]

Another Juárez ally, José López Viascán, advised the president to mobilize the Zapotec armies of Ixtlán district in order to force the Díaz brothers into submission. Too many military leaders in Oaxaca "no longer obey the government," López Viascán warned; "The jefes políticos put into office by Porfirio Díaz are in the opposition and the good and loyal liberals that we have . . . fear getting stabbed in the back by the opposition if Díaz wins. . . . With this in mind, Señor Castro should call on several jefes políticos who could organize a militia from the Sierra in order to enforce the law. But as a highly principled person he probably would not want to do so because he has no accusation to act upon and does not want to spill more blood since so much has already poured."[15] Neither Castro nor Juárez endorsed the prospect of using the Ixtlán National Guard to contain Díaz; the risks of starting a civil war were too great.[16]

As Castro and others had predicted, Porfirio Díaz won a majority of the votes for president in Oaxaca. With the important exception of the Sierra Zapoteca, Díaz's control over the state was nearly complete.[17] Still, Juárez easily won a majority of the electoral votes throughout the country: Juárez received 7,422 electoral votes (72 percent), Díaz received 2,709 votes (26 percent), and 240 were cast for other candidates (2 percent).[18] In effect, Juárez had told his Oaxacan supporters not to worry about the local election because he had installed enough local officials in other parts of the country who could sway the national vote. He did not need Oaxaca to win the election. In typical fashion, however, knowing that Juárez was probably going to win at the national level would have placed even greater pressure on the Oaxacans to bring the state over to the president. Loyal states might expect compensation for their support, while "disloyal" states could expect nothing. It was crucial to be on the winning side.

Elections for governor in Oaxaca were set for November 1867, providing juaristas and porfiristas with another opportunity to square off. Governor Castro warned Juárez that mail service was in the hands of pro-Díaz administrators and that his correspondence was not confidential. Castro suggested naming someone else to direct the post office, but Juárez refused, probably because the Díaz brothers had clearly eclipsed Castro's influence within the state and Juárez would need to find another ally. By this time, late October 1867, Castro knew that Félix Díaz would become the new state governor since Félix was personally directing hundreds of "*malditos soldados* [damned soldiers]" to do as he wanted. With this flash of anger, Castro also reminded the president that Díaz had another four thousand soldiers under his command in Tehuacán, Puebla, who were prepared to enforce the outcome of the gubernatorial elections in Oaxaca if needed. As expected, Félix Díaz won the election for governor.[19]

Miguel Castro understood that fundamental political disputes of this nature could only go so far before they turned violent, especially in a place and time like Mexico during the Restored Republic. In early November 1867 Castro advised Juárez to remove Porfirio Díaz as chief of the army's Second Division, "in order to avoid another revolution."[20] Other Oaxacans sought a settlement. The state legislature gave Díaz a small hacienda on the outskirts of Oaxaca City in recognition of his years of service. The hacienda of La Noria pleased the general, who appeared to enjoy the quiet life of a landowner over the rough-and-tumble pursuits of a field commander. Some Oaxacans believed Díaz was now in the mood to negotiate. Juárez's relative, Joaquín Mauleón, informed the president that they had tried to talk Díaz into ending the dispute: "Your friends met with General Díaz and encouraged him to work on consolidating the peace, hoping he would forget his past electoral defeat. He seems to be content with his small property, which was given to him, and he has dedicated himself to improving it."[21]

In contrast to his restraint before the elections, once reelected to the presidency Juárez moved more forcefully against Díaz's supporters and potential allies. But in his zeal to limit Díaz's strength, Juárez cut away at his own support. For example, he determined that all Oaxacan National Guard units should be disbanded and disarmed, a major miscalculation since the most important battalion of the National Guard, the soldiers of the Sierra Zapoteca, had voted for the president and continued to support him. When he had originally created the National Guard in the early 1850s, Juárez did not foresee a time when he could not control them. An armed citizenry in a state governed indirectly by his major rival was by itself a threat to his regime.[22] But the Zapotecs of the Ixtlán National Guard had fought for Juárez almost continuously since 1855, and they had voted for him in the 1867 elections. They believed that they had earned the right to carry arms, and they were angry that Juárez would so quickly turn his back on them. They decided that they would not give up their arms without a struggle.

General Luis Pérez Figueroa, who had fought alongside Díaz at the battle of La Carbonera, advised the president to reconsider his order to disarm the Sierra. Pérez Figueroa had grown leery of Díaz's political maneuvering and saw the soldiers of the Ixtlán National Guard as crucial allies should violence breakout. Pérez Figueroa also realized that disarming the Zapotec National Guardsmen would be a delicate and potentially dangerous undertaking. In late November 1867 Pérez Figueroa forwarded a letter to Juárez from a representative of the Ixtlán National Guard. It was clear from the letter that disarming the Sierra would have to be done forcibly. Ramón Sarmiento, from the town of Ixtlán, dictated a clear and direct message to a professional scribe and then sent it to various officials. Sarmiento declared, "We will not experience the humiliation of being disarmed." The Zapotec armies knew their participation had been instrumental in the recent struggles and demanded more respect. As Sarmiento explained, "You would have us believe that all of our sacrifices have been in vain, even though we fought without stopping and defeated the invaders." If Juárez insisted on disarming them, there could be only one conclusion: "In a word Mexico has triumphed but we are still slaves."[23] Juárez backed down. Unlike his aggressive pursuit of arms and military leaders in other parts of Mexico, Juárez simply turned a blind eye to the fact that peasants from the Sierra Zapoteca still kept their weapons.[24] Local and regional leaders would not enforce the directive, and Juárez was unwilling to send troops into a state that was controlled by the Díaz brothers.

Díaz wrote Juárez in early 1868 to congratulate him on his new term as president. Choosing his words carefully, Díaz wrote, "I cordially congratulate you for your victory and I desire that, during the legal period, the country will experience the good fortune, which it so desperately needs."[25] The key phrase in this note was "during the legal period," which for Díaz meant that Juárez would be constitutionally ineligible to run for reelection. In effect, Díaz warned the president to step down once his term expired. Within two months of the "congratulatory" letter, Juárez learned that Díaz was planning a trip to the United States to buy arms and ammunition. Several months later, in November 1868, Díaz's arms shipment arrived in Puerto Angel in Oaxaca, and rumors about Díaz's intentions began flying widely. One report had him using the arms to fortify Chiapas and Oaxaca and then staging an invasion of Guatemala, where he would become *"Presidente vitalicio* [president for life] *de Guatemala.*" Other rumors reaching Juárez were that officers from the First Brigade stationed in Puebla intended to rebel in support of Díaz. Most of the officers came from Oaxaca and openly favored Díaz over Juárez. Finally, another rumor suggested that Díaz intended to establish a República de Oriente, made up of the states of Veracruz, Guerrero, Oaxaca, Chiapas, Tabasco, and Yucatán, and then make himself president.[26] While these rumors proved false, they suggest that Díaz and his supporters were maneuvering behind the scenes in anticipation of another opportunity to challenge Juárez.

These plans were complicated in Oaxaca by a public disagreement between Díaz and his brother Félix. Díaz had tried to select his younger brother's cabinet appointments, but Félix ignored his advice. Their dispute became public when the governor named Francisco Rincón as his secretary. Rincón had worked with Juan Pablo Franco during the French Intervention, and his presence in the government angered both the juaristas and the porfiristas. The Díaz brothers eventually reconciled, but their discord made organizing a united opposition more difficult. Félix Díaz also removed Fidencio Hernández as jefe político in Ixtlán district, a decision that frustrated both Castro and Porfirio Díaz.[27] But Félix had his own plans for making inroads into the Sierra Zapoteca, and he sought his own representative. He tried to shift the balance of power within the district away from Ixtlán and the mestizo caudillos like Castro, Hernández, and Meijueiro and toward the Zapotec leadership in the largest town in the district, Ixtepeji. Félix Díaz had personally led the Ixtepeji unit within the National Guard, particularly during the final battles of the French Intervention. Using these military ties to communal leaders, the governor provided Ixtepeji with several tangible benefits. He gave them funds for a new school; he released the people of Ixtepeji from their obligation to provide labor for road maintenance in the district; and he curtailed speculation in the local corn market by setting a fixed price. All of these measures undermined the influence of people in the town of Ixtlán, the district *cabecera*. To show their appreciation, Ixtepeji community leaders renamed their town in honor of the governor. In doing so, they indicated that they were likely to support both Díaz brothers in the next round of elections.[28]

Tensions increased within Ixtlán district for another reason. Although they supported the liberal cause and Juárez's 1857 constitution, Zapotecs rarely expressed support for the anticlerical measures at the heart of the liberal/conservative conflict. In fact, Serranos more often described themselves as "republicans" and not as members of the Liberal Party. Still, we should properly consider their religious practices something like "liberal Catholicism." They tolerated the presence of both priests and liberal ideologues as long as neither group tried to impede the patriarchal lines of communal authority. Moreover, tensions between liberals and clergy did not necessarily impede the religious views of Zapotec parishioners. In fact, this church/state conflict created a more autonomous space for Zapotecs to integrate pre-Christian notions, like the supernatural powers that animated the peaks and caves throughout the region, with orthodox Catholic ideas like devotion to the saints. When priests went too far, as one apparently did in 1870 by speaking against the Juárez government, Zapotecs reported him to officials and then allowed his arrest and removal from the district. And when liberal officials went too far, as the jefe político did in 1871 by trying to suppress religious processions and meetings of local cofraternities, the people rebelled. In this case, the state government conceded and removed the overzealous jefe político.[29]

In general, the four years between 1867 and 1871 were marked by political intrigue and lingering tensions between supporters of Juárez and Díaz. These tensions mounted as Juárez proved unable to resolve the country's economic and political malaise. Mexico City newspapers roundly criticized the president, accusing his regime of corruption and arbitrary repression. By 1871, with the next round of presidential elections fast approaching, Juárez was in a more vulnerable position than in 1867.[30]

The Rebellion of La Noria, 1871

Juárez faced two opponents in the June 1871 elections: Sebastián Lerdo de Tejada, the chief justice of the Supreme Court, and Porfirio Díaz, who had "retired" to his hacienda in Oaxaca. In the general election Juárez won a plurality of the electoral votes (46.7 percent), though accusations of corruption and fraud undermined the legitimacy of his victory. By law, if no candidate received more than 50 percent of the electoral votes, Congress would have to choose the next president. Juárez stacked the legislature with his supporters and easily won a majority of the votes for president. Though Díaz complained bitterly, he could do little to change the outcome. The Díaz brothers concluded that Juárez could only be removed from office by force of arms. Once again Díaz planned his Oaxaca strategy as he prepared openly for a revolt against Juárez. He and Félix would secure their home state, advance into Puebla, and from there take Mexico City.

But Díaz had one major problem: with the exception of Ixtepeji, most Zapotec soldiers in the Ixtlán National Guard had become unhappy with the Díaz brothers and Mauro Vazques, the jefe político imposed on them. In January 1871 Vazques had tried to enforce a new head tax throughout the district. When Zapotec village leaders gathered to protest the tax, he threatened to have the state government order the Ixtlán National Guard out of the district. "They are a mobile unit," Vazques advised the governor, "and they can be sent to other districts."[31] Ironically, the Serranos refused to pay the new tax precisely because of their military service. Then in April Vazques prevented public processions for religious celebrations and accused the Serranos of forming secret religious societies that kept out state authorities. Four months later, the Serranos rebelled against Vazques and by implication the state government. They occupied the jefe político's office and took up defensive positions in anticipation of a counterassault by the regular army stationed in Oaxaca City. Porfirio Díaz rushed to Ixtlán to calm the Serranos. He planned to negotiate with them, but he was also prepared to use force if necessary. And for the first time, and I believe the only time, Díaz expressed disrespect for the Zapotecs of Ixtlán. In a private letter sent to his wife Delfina, Díaz wrote, "Everything is over now and if those foolish Indians [indios tontos] had known that I was coming we would not have had to fire a single shot."[32] But the Serranos were not so "foolish" after all. They achieved their goal when Félix Díaz removed Vazques as jefe político and replaced him with Fidencio Hernández. Díaz had expected Hernández to support his impending rebellion against Juárez, which Hernández had indicated he would do in several letters. But Ixtepeji was the only community that supported Díaz; the others remained loyal to Juárez and prevented Hernández from pulling them into the rebellion.[33]

The structure of the Ixtlán National Guard, however, prevented unilateral military action on the part of individuals like Hernández or single communities like Ixtepeji. The stockpile of arms and, more important, ammunition was controlled by village leaders in Ixtlán, who continued to support Juárez. Other village leaders also supported Juárez, viewing Ixtepeji's independence as a threat to the entire region. Ultimately, the hierarchical structure of the rural National Guard units guaranteed that Ixtepeji would follow the command of battalion leaders. Still, a small number of individuals within the community joined the effort, but even they were subjected to retaliation after the war or, as Celestino Pérez described it, "una guerra sorda [a stubborn and silent war]" of aggression and hostility.[34] When Félix Díaz quickly lost the battle to control Oaxaca, most Ixtepejanos were probably glad that they had not enlisted in a losing cause.

As with most political issues in his native state, Juárez knew of Díaz's plans and did little to alter the course of events. A network of informants kept the president abreast of Díaz's moves. The best way to eliminate Díaz as a threat was to allow him to rebel, defeat him militarily, undermine his legitimacy as a war hero, and expose his disloyalty to the nation. If Díaz rebelled, Juárez would be able to rid himself of this opponent once and for all.[35] In fact, the United States Consular agent, L. L. Laurence, blamed the ensuing violence on Juárez: "it must have been known to the Federal Government that he [Díaz] was preparing this Revolution and with the facts so notorious should the Federal Government not be held responsible for all of this ruin and destruction caused by him."[36] Juárez finally acted when he learned that the American ship *Ada May* had docked at Puerto Angel in Oaxaca, carrying a shipment of arms and ammunition purchased in San Francisco. Secretary of the Interior (*Gobernación*) Matías Romero wrote to Félix Díaz ordering the state government to report the cargo to federal authorities. But Governor Díaz stalled the request, reassuring Romero that an agreement could still be reached.[37] Five days later, on November 8, Porfirio Díaz and his brother announced their rebellion at the hacienda of La Noria.

Published by the Oaxacan state press, the Plan of La Noria has been closely analyzed by historians. Some historians, like Daniel Cosío Villegas, have criticized the plan for lacking a clear ideology or purpose, interpreting it as a chaotic complaint of a young man obsessed with gaining presidential power. More recently, Florencia Mallon has called our attention to the plan in a new way. She argues that it was "an important, experimental articulation" of popular demands against an increasingly authoritarian state. Written and signed only by Porfirio Díaz, the plan recognized "the people's contribution to the Liberal Revolution and to its defense against Conservatives and Interventionists." In this way, Díaz appealed to veterans who felt abandoned and abused by the Juárez regime. In an attempt to bring this coalition together, Díaz spoke to their multiple interests, crafting a plan that he hoped would attract as many Mexicans as possible. Mallon argues that the strength of the Plan of La Noria lay in its undetermined character, in its openness to multiple viewpoints and experiences. The "incoherent" nature of the document, so roundly criticized by Cosío Villegas, was actually its greatest asset.[38] The plan offered a new approach to liberal politics in Mexico, a perspective that emphasized the role of popular classes in national history. As such, the Díaz-led grassroots movement against Juárez had the potential of bringing to power a regime that recognized its debt to ordinary Mexicans, a regime that owed its very existence to the courage and loyalty of the peasantry. Hoping and expecting the popular classes to join him against the antidemocratic Juárez regime, Díaz concluded his call to arms with one simple statement: "Let no citizen dominate and perpetuate the exercise of power, and this will be the last revolution."[39]

Mallon analyzes the internal text of the plan, in particular, the document's open invitation to organize politics in a new, more populist fashion. If we compare the Plan of La Noria to other rebel programs before and after 1871, its radical nature and direction become even clearer. In almost all of the plans prior to La Noria, a rebel caudillo or coalition identified the corrupt practices of a particular ruler by name. Significantly, Antonio López de Santa Anna garnered the greatest amount of criticism and inspired the most rebellions. The Plan of Ayutla (1854), for example, identified Santa Anna and declared openly that he would be removed from office. After 1871, in Díaz's Plan of Tuxtepec (1876), in Francisco Madero's Plan of San Luis Potosí (1910), and in Emiliano Zapata's Plan of Ayala (1911), sitting presidents were all targeted by name. The choices were clear: support the ideals of the plan by opposing the man in office.[40] The Plan of La Noria, however, did not mention Juárez by name. Díaz made vague references to "the Government and its agents," and he criticized "an oligarchy as incompetent as it is unproductive and unpatriotic," but he did not identify Juárez as the object of his rebellion.[41] La Noria emphasized instead the principles of no reelection, of democratic process, and of popular participation in the political system. The goals of La Noria, as stated in the original plan of 1871, were more about putting into practice certain ideals and less about bringing down a certain individual. This distinction made it unusual among Mexico's political plans. In addition, by not naming Juárez as the object of the rebellion, Díaz could hope to win over people who might otherwise be reluctant to join. The Zapotec soldiers of the Ixtlán National Guard might support the principles of the Plan of La Noria, but they would not want to criticize Juárez so directly.

The potential of La Noria's ideological challenge to Juárez, however, did not translate into a sustained military threat. The reasons for Díaz's failure were not fully discussed at the time or even after he succeeded in his 1876 rebellion. For most of the rebels, including Díaz, La Noria was a bad memory. During the Porfiriato, when veterans recalled their years of service to the nation as the most important time in their lives, La Noria was largely ignored. It was rarely mentioned at all, and never mentioned by itself. At times, veterans, usually friends of Díaz, would say something like, "the challenge we set at La Noria was achieved at Tuxtepec." But for most veterans, and most likely for Díaz himself since his younger brother Félix lost his life in the revolt, the memories of La Noria were universally bad. As early as 1877, Concepción Prieto, the widow of Captain José Reyes, asked Díaz for aid "in name of the victims of the Plan of la Noria." [42] Many years later, in 1903, another Oaxacan veteran, Trinidad Gamboa, wondered if Díaz remembered their failed revolt at La Noria: "Do you recall, Señor General Díaz, that time of unspeakable hardship? Do you remember my General all of the twists and turns on that journey through uncharted paths? I believe you must, because the footprints of past suffering can never be erased from the hearts of men!" [43] Rather than emphasize the reasons for his 1871 loss, Díaz and his supporters accentuated the reasons for their eventual victory in 1876. La Noria became tied to Tuxtepec, but the two rebellions were dramatically different in terms of their military execution. Díaz lost in 1871 for three reasons. First, Juárez enjoyed significant support among the federal army and enough support among the popular classes to limit Díaz's military threat. Second, Díaz failed to offer decisive leadership on the battlefield, and he did not personally engage the enemy throughout the entire rebellion. And third, internal divisions within the rebel forces undermined their effectiveness and demoralized the troops. Other historians have stressed the impact of Juárez's death in July 1872 as the determining factor in ending the rebellion. But, as we will see, the rebellion was almost completely defeated by that time, and Juárez's death had little influence on the outcome of the war. [44]

In preparing for war, the Díaz brothers used their previous experience to plot a strategy. They would begin in Oaxaca, exactly as their triumph against the French had begun, and then move into Puebla, where Juan N. Méndez and the National Guard battalion of the Sierra de Puebla would join in marching to Mexico City. Porfirio Díaz intended to use his brother's status as governor to establish a legitimate alternative to the Juárez regime. But he made one major miscalculation in his Oaxacan plans: most of the Zapotec peasants of Ixtlán district remained firm supporters of Juárez. Without their backing, Félix Díaz could not hold on to the state. The federal army delivered a stunning defeat to Félix Díaz's troops in a ferocious nighttime battle on December 22, at San Mateo Xindihui in the Oaxacan district of Nochixtlán. Félix Díaz fled Oaxaca City, traveling eventually to the coastal town of Puerto Angel near the Isthmus of Tehuantepec. The people of Juchitán learned of his whereabouts and pursued the fleeing governor; they sought revenge for an incident several years earlier in which the governor had ordered the mutilation of Juchitán's patron saint. When they found him, the Juchitecos peeled the skin off the governor's feet, forced him to walk several miles, and finally cut off his feet before they killed him. They sent his disfigured body back to Oaxaca City in a box. [45]

When Félix Díaz broke with the federal government, Félix Romero, the president of the state Supreme Court, assumed the governorship in accordance with the state constitution. Just as Governor José María Díaz Ordaz had done in 1858, Romero left Oaxaca City to take refuge in the Sierra Zapoteca. On January 8, 1872, Romero resigned, allowing Miguel Castro to become interim governor, backed once again by a Zapotec army. After the Díaz rebellion failed in Oaxaca, within the first two months of its inception, other states were left without the coordinated leadership they so crucially needed. Juárez could deal with the uprisings one at a time. The rebel forces suffered military defeat in Veracruz next. Ramón A. Alor from Cosoleacaque, Veracruz, recalled how his house had been the headquarters for assembling arms and ammunition for the 1871 rebellion. Led by General Eulalio Vela, the rebels' effort failed completely, and General Vela was gravely wounded, barely escaping capture.[46]

The west-central state of Jalisco proved to be a more important theater of operations for the rebellion. Rebels had tried to bolster their forces with a shipload of arms and ammunition, but government agents intercepted it in December 1871.[47] Still, the rebels survived longer in Jalisco than they did in most other states. Díaz personally toured the Jalisco campaign in March 1872, and after meeting with rebel leaders, he determined that he should revise his original Plan of La Noria. The rebels were losing in most parts of the country, and Díaz hoped to win supporters with a new pronouncement. They plotted to capture the town of Ameca, announce that the tide had turned against the government, and then release a revised plan for establishing a new government. More than likely, Díaz had predated his revisions since the battle to capture Ameca ended in utter defeat; moreover, Díaz was not present when the revised plan was released on April 3, 1872.[48] The major revision of the plan allowed for the head of the Supreme Court, in this case Sebastián Lerdo de Tejada, to become president upon overthrowing Juárez. With this move, Díaz hoped to draw Lerdo and his supporters to the rebellion by offering him the presidency. But more than anything else, Díaz's revision showed how desperate he was; the modifications in his plan represented a step away from the bottom-up populist tone of the original Plan of La Noria. The head of the Supreme Court had always been first in line to succeed the president according to the constitution. The revision at Ameca signaled that the old political structure would not give way to a more open system of selecting national leaders. In any event, Lerdo did not take the bait. Díaz's rebellion had lost most of its energy, and the rebels failed to capture Ameca.[49]

In fact, the battle for Ameca came to represent the frustration of the entire rebel movement. In a series of three long letters written between January 1899 and September 1900, a veteran of the Jalisco campaign, José Rosas Landa, emphasized the disorganization of the troops fighting for Díaz. As soon as Rosas arrived at the camp, "everything was filled with danger and anxiety, hardship and deprivation, though you already know that since we were in such an unequal fight against Juárez's forces who had more provisions and greater discipline." The rebels faced government troops in several towns, but in most encounters, "our luck was almost always bad." Rosas and his comrades could not come down from the hills since the people in the nearby villages still supported Juárez. On several occasions villagers fired on the rebels: "Our situation was very sad," Rosas recalled.[50]

The battle for Ameca proved equally disastrous. The federal army had taken up a position around the church, and fighting began as the rebels crawled into the town square. The rebels could not dislodge the federal troops, and the order was given to retreat. Rosas recalled, "Upon seeing our retreat, the enemy began playing 'Diana' with their clarinets. Then some of our boys began to show their dissatisfaction [with the order to retreat], and several officers ordered our troops to play '*Media vuelta*.'" Mocked by the federal army, rebel troops were frustrated by their leaders' call for retreat, and shouts of "let's kill them [the officers] and rob the town" rose up among the ranks. The officers tried desperately to silence those cries, Rosas explained, but he feared that "some malcontents had already committed crimes and that [their actions] had stained the cause for which we were defending." After calming the unhappy troops, "the retreat continued in an orderly fashion and we spent the night in a hacienda near Ameca, continuing the next day on the road to the Mesa de los Ramos."[51]

Insubordination soon split the officers' ranks as well. Marching from Ameca to Etzatlán, Commander Manuel Fernández of the Third Cavalry revolted against Coronel Casiano Morales. As he fired shots from his sidearm, Fernández cried, "*arriba el tercero* [rise up men of the Third]." But soldiers loyal to Morales disarmed Fernández, and the rebel commander was executed on the spot, at the Hacienda San Sebastían near Etzatlán. Captain Clemente Parra had been ordered to carry out the execution. But Parra and Fernández were both from Guadalajara, and Parra's role in his friend's death drove him to distrust the rebel leaders. Soon after the execution, Parra slipped away from camp in the middle of the night. Rosas was promoted to captain after Parra deserted, though Rosas had also sympathized with Fernández. The whole episode was agonizing for Rosas to recall; "who would have thought that after twenty-five years I would have to refer to all this."[52]

The rebel army of General Pedro A. Galván was disbanded at the hacienda of San Diego, just outside of Techaluta in June 1872. Rosas described their desperate situation: "We were reduced to a small group of men with few weapons, fewer horses, almost naked and forced to experience every kind of deprivation and suffering; because of our ineffectiveness, we had to walk from one place to the next always on the defensive." The group functioned as a guerrilla army, moving by night and surprising the enemy with hit and run assaults: "in this way we managed to play with the enemy and avoid complete elimination." They had several small victories, but the group was finally captured at Amacueca by Captain Antonio Zamora, transported back to Guadalajara, and jailed. They remained imprisoned "until the amnesty law issued on account of Señor Juárez's death, which saved us from such a sad situation." Some historians have suggested that Juárez's death brought an end to Díaz's rebellion since an outpouring of grief and a sense of uncertainty swept the nation. The desperate and dismal situation of the rebel movement, as described by José Rosas Landa, suggests the rebellion had failed long before Juárez died.[53]

Juárez Dies

News of Juárez's death on July 18, 1872, spread quickly. The official announcement went out to all state governors early the next day, and the ritualistic mourning and patriotic deification of Juárez began in earnest. Like sons who had not fully realized the strengths and accomplishments of their father until it was too late, Mexican officials rushed to express their grief and sorrow over the loss of a president who had continually been challenged by foreign invaders, internal strife, and insubordination. By proclamation, interim president Sebastián Lerdo de Tejada declared, "the Mexican people will never forget the important services that Benito Juárez gave to our country during the most challenging days of the civil war and foreign intervention." For the first time in more than two decades, Mexicans would have to settle their political differences without the reassuring and sometimes repressive presence of Benito Juárez.[54]

Juárez's death came at a precarious time for the federal government. Though Juárez's troops had largely defeated the porfirista rebels by the spring of 1872, no one quite knew what would happen now that the president had died. Would the federal army remain loyal to Lerdo? Or would its members join their former comrade Porfirio Díaz to secure the influence of military men within the government? In the year before his death, Juárez had been roundly criticized in the Mexico City press for ruling the country ineffectively and with an authoritarian hand. He had failed to bring prosperity to the nation, and he had failed to abide by the constitutional ban on reelection. Juárez did not die as a popular hero.[55] Even in Oaxaca, Juárez's home state, Félix Díaz had won reelection to the governorship, and Porfirio Díaz had won a majority of the votes for the presidency in 1867 and 1871. The Zapotec peasants of Ixtlán district remained Juárez's only dependable source of allies. When the Díaz brothers rebelled, Juárez quickly handed over the state government to his friends from the Sierra Zapoteca. And when Juárez died, these friends expressed their undying loyalty to his memory. Interim governor Miguel Castro, Juárez's longtime political ally, wrote to the secretary of the interior on July 20, 1872, "The unfortunate news of the death of Benito Juárez, Constitutional President of the Republic, has filled this state with pain. . . . For such an irreparable loss, I offer you the most sincere condolences . . . and I assure you that these sentiments are shared by all of the inhabitants of the state where the memory of the great man who has departed from the public stage will be everlasting."[56] Castro's letter, echoed in less personal ways by governors from throughout the nation, spoke of the public stage, the political arena that Juárez had occupied for most of his adult life. And like the theater, where playwrights create archetypal characters for public consumption, stories of Juárez became collective dramas where individuals rewrote their own versions of national history.

Miguel Castro signed another letter that day, but not in his official capacity as governor of Oaxaca. Castro, along with village leaders, businessmen, and other officials from the Sierra Zapoteca, expressed the special significance Juárez had for the people of this particular region. Calling themselves "*los hijos de la Sierra* [the sons of the Sierra]," the writers asked that Juárez's remains be returned to his birthplace in Guelatao, which thereafter became known as "the glorious cradle of the Caudillo of the Reform." The deep personal loss expressed by these men established the tone and sentiment of later eulogies to Juárez, immediately elevating the practice of remembering Juárez to an art form, albeit art of dubious taste:

Sirs:
Our voices are silenced by sorrow and our hearts pound with pain upon asking that the remains of the hero who has just died be returned to us for interment in Villa Juárez, glorious cradle of the Caudillo of the Reform. . . . Providence has subjected Oaxaca to a most terrible challenge, bringing down its dear son, symbol of nobility and bravery; our souls are deeply wounded and our imaginations can barely conceive of a disaster so insolent and so colossal. . . . His remains will inspire us by his

unequaled heroism, his abnegation, and his immutable consonance; he will be the holy aura whereby we swear to be free, strong, and happy. We will place in his tomb a glorious crown and we will write, as the only epitaph, the name of the Caudillo, locket of love, treasure of virtues, source of life itself, a name eternally blessed so that no one can utter it without trembling nor hear it without feeling proud.[57]

Upon Juárez's death, the Serranos began a national campaign to emphasize the leader's Zapotec origins. They intended to enhance their national stature by arguing that they had nurtured, and then shared, Juárez with the nation. For the Sons of the Sierra, memories of the dead president were more about the Sierra Zapoteca than about Juárez. His story was their story. Their effort directly challenged the view in Mexico City, which diminished a specific regional identification of Juárez in order to broaden his appeal to the entire nation. In fact, Juárez eventually become known as *"Benemérito de las Americas* [Distinguished One of the Americas]," freed even from the territorial boundaries of Mexico, an example of patriotism and good government for all of the Americas. In later eulogies Juárez was remembered as "a bird without a nest" and as a "disinherited Indian."[58] But for the people of the Sierra Zapoteca, the origins of Mexico's greatest political hero were an essential ingredient of their own importance and identity. In short, their sense of belonging to the Mexican nation went through Juárez.

Several days after Juárez died, the Oaxacan poet Bernardino Carvajal, a former priest and steadfast supporter of Juárez during the 1860s, wrote a twenty-five-verse lament, which anticipated the romanticization of Juárez's life.[59] Carvajal wrote:

Juárez has died!
The Defender of the Mexican People,
The Defender of Mexican Honor,
The Genius of the American Continent.
Juárez has died!
The Sublime Democrat,
The Man of the Future, of Progress,
The Man who saved Mexico from its Past.
Juárez has died!
The immortal patriarch
Who sacrificed his entire life
For the Good of the Country.

Juárez has died!
The Model of Citizenship
And the Symbol of Good Government
For Mexican Fathers and Mothers.
Juárez has died!
The People cannot hide the pain
that rips through them.
We Cry ceaselessly,
Juárez no longer exists.[60]

Memories of Juárez were expressed through poems like Carvajal's, speeches, letters, songs, statues, paintings, and eventually the monument in downtown Mexico City known as the Hemíciclo.[61] It would be easy to dismiss this glorification of Juárez as the disingenuous expressions of people who wanted to use Juárez for their own gain. Clearly, there is something disturbing about the maudlin sentimentality surrounding the Juárez imagery, which leads us to dismiss its significance. But just as clearly, the sentiment echoed by so many people seems most often sincere, whether they benefited from such an expression or not. Countless people reproduced Juárez in their own ways. A single poem or song by itself offers nothing new to historians of Mexico. We have all seen examples of homage to Juárez in the archives, in the official speeches, in the statues that stand in cities and villages throughout the country. But it is exactly this universality that should call us to attention; it is the formulaic way in which similar stories are told, embellished, and modified that requires closer scrutiny. My point here is that the mythogenesis of a Juárez cult began in 1872, immediately after Juárez died. Díaz encountered the depth of praise surrounding Juárez when he witnessed the public grieving for Juárez, when he returned to Oaxaca in 1876 for his Tuxtepec rebellion, and when he returned as state governor in 1881. Díaz eventually championed Juárez as a central hero of the nation, but the major push for establishing Juárez as the father of Mexico's "second independence" came from Oaxaca itself, from Oaxacans living in Mexico City, from officials in state government, and from the Zapotec villagers in the Sierra Juárez.[62]

On July 18, 1872, the day Juárez died, porfirista general Donato Guerra defeated Luis Terrazas at Tabalopa, but for all practical purposes the military threat of the La Noria rebellion had passed away long before.[63] In fact, rather than save the federal government, Juárez's death posed a challenge to constitutional order that went beyond Díaz's rebellion. Upon assuming the presidency, Lerdo needed to consolidate his position within the government.

There was the possibility that Juárez's supporters would not allow Lerdo, a former electoral opponent, to become president, since troops loyal to Juárez were not necessarily loyal to Lerdo. Juárez had experienced his own problems with the military, relying on Ignacio Mejía, his minister of war, to negotiate a working order with army officers. Lerdo needed to demobilize these troops as quickly as possible. For that reason he sought an immediate truce with the lingering bands of porfirista rebels. He also retained Mejía as minister of war until 1874.[64]

Juárez's death did not end the revolt. A lack of leadership, a lack of broad-based popular support, and a superior enemy defeated Díaz's first attempt to bring down the government.[65] After La Noria, Díaz and his officers had their property confiscated in the state of Oaxaca.[66] But few Oaxacans, including the Serranos, harbored ill will toward Díaz for an extended time. Because the federal army had defeated Félix Díaz so early in the rebellion, the Ixtlán National Guard did not fight directly against the Díaz brothers. The Serranos had successfully, perhaps luckily, found a way to support Juárez without confronting their former jefe político. Over time, this subtle distinction would prove important to Díaz and the Zapotecs of Ixtlán district. In fact, after Juárez's death, many Serranos began to see Díaz as the state's new favorite son. Díaz had initially justified his rebellion by claiming to stand up to the authoritarian impulses of the central government. For the Serranos, the potential for achieving more radical local autonomy justified their renewed support for Díaz. Eventually, the Serranos reimagined their historical relationship with Díaz, emphasizing the years of fighting with, not against, the general. Díaz never punished the Serranos for opposing him in 1871; he did not punish Castro, Meijueiro, or Hernández; he did not even seek revenge against the Zapotecs of Juchitán for mutilating and killing his brother. La Noria had been a "nightmare" that no one cared to recall.

Miguel Castro governed Oaxaca from 1872 to 1874, but he faced tremendous opposition from the "*borlado*" or moderate liberal supporters of President Lerdo. The leader of this group, José Esperón, sought alliances among former anti-Juárez Oaxacans, including Díaz. In August 1874 Esperón complained to Díaz that Castro "believes he is above the law, [and] more infallible than the vote of the people."[67] But Díaz largely kept his distance from Oaxaca, residing instead on his estate in Veracruz. In November 1874 Esperón won the election for governor and, typical of every new administration, began replacing local jefes políticos with men loyal to the new regime. When he turned to the district of Ixtlán, the Serranos jailed the new administrator, declaring themselves in open rebellion against the state and federal governments.[68]

The Tuxtepec Rebellion, 1876

On January 21, 1876, a Zapotec army advanced from the district of Ixtlán to Oaxaca City. Reminiscent of the march in 1855, the group intended to remove a moderate governor and replace him with a liberal who would respect the important role of the Serranos in statewide politics.[69] As in 1855, Zapotec soldiers carried their rifles, their machetes, and their courage as they began their dusty walk to the outskirts of the capital city. But this time, the Zapotecs were highly experienced troops, men who had been fighting almost continuously since 1855. They did not hesitate before they entered the city. They did not pause to consider the significance and risks involved in their actions. They moved with determination and purpose, confident that they would be successful. They alone had been on the winning side in every major war of the last twenty years. Porfirio Díaz could not make that claim, nor could other National Guard battalions in neighboring states. The Serranos understood war by 1876, and they understood their own important role in Mexican politics.[70]

From the perspective of the Zapotec National Guardsmen, history began to repeat itself in other ways as well. Once again, they embraced their old jefe político, Porfirio Díaz, pledging their loyalty to him by supporting his Plan of Tuxtepec. Díaz showed in his 1876 rebellion how much he had learned from his previous revolt in 1871. He did not allow elections to take place at all, which might have given the government the opportunity to defraud him. He galvanized the optimism and excitement for change going into the elections and turned that movement into an armed insurrection. The Serranos justified their rebellion by claiming their actions were in defense of the 1857 Constitution. President Lerdo had trampled their rights by plotting to defraud Díaz of the presidency. Ironically, they claimed to be acting in the spirit of Benito Juárez, who had defended the constitution against rebel conservatives, foreign invaders, and rival liberals. Clearly, they had already begun to rewrite Mexican history, asserting a continuous link between Juárez and Díaz when, of course, the two men had been at war with each other just five years earlier. But the Serranos were inspired by the notion that President Lerdo and Governor Esperón threatened the principles for which they and their comrades had sacrificed so much blood.

Many of the same men who had fought in earlier battles joined Díaz in his Tuxtepec rebellion. Former lieutenants Francisco Meijueiro and Fidencio Hernández became generals for the Ixtlán National Guard. Ordinary soldiers like José María Martínez, now thirty-three years old, marched from Ixtlán to

Oaxaca City. And Mariano Ibarra came again from Lachatao. But there were also men who were fighting for the first time; they had been too young to fight against the French but now had a chance to join the National Guard themselves. Men like José Zorrila from the town of Ixtlán, Dionisio Santiago from Xiacui, Rosalino Santiago from Yatuni, and Miguel López of Santiago Comaltepec fought on Díaz's side for the first time.[71] The promotion of Meijueiro and Hernández to the rank of general represented, however, a new and significant change for the Sierra. By assuming Miguel Castro's influence, these two brothers-in-law became the leaders of a region that had proven instrumental in every major political and military event of the last quarter century. Castro had grown frustrated with Lerdo's maneuverings in Oaxacan politics and had decided to retire to his property in the Sierra Zapoteca. Mexican politics had become an occupation for younger men, and the rise to power of a new generation strengthened the hierarchical and ethnic-based patriarchal structure of communal life in the Sierra. The National Guard battalions continued to reinforce that system.[72]

On January 15, 1876, Díaz declared in his Plan of Tuxtepec that the government of President Lerdo had lost its legitimacy and had trampled on the constitutional rights of all Mexican citizens. Six days later, the people from Ixtlán district announced their support for Tuxtepec with their own rebel pronouncement. The Plan of the Sierra Juárez proclaimed support for Díaz since he alone would protect the 1857 Constitution, principles that "had cost the people much blood and sacrifice to sustain." Fidencio Hernández called on all Oaxacans to join the rebel movement, once again invoking the importance of protecting the 1857 Constitution: "I invite you all to help me defend the Constitution. Long live the Code of 1857! Long live the invincible General Porfirio Díaz!" In rallying the people of Oaxaca to the Tuxtepec cause, Hernández told them, "We already belong to the most patriotic and most liberal state in the Republic. From this day forward, our state will return to the rule of law and constitutional order."[73] Hernández worried that the rebel movement would be seen as merely a way of gaining power for a new group of political elites. He tried to reassure the people of Oaxaca that this time things would be different: "We are taking up arms, then, not to attack, but to defend ourselves; not to violate the rights of citizenship, but rather to reestablish them." The Plan of Tuxtepec and its Ixtlán endorsement, he told them, "mark the end of the degenerate ambitions [*ambiciones bastardas*] of a perpetual presidency, establishing [instead] a single principle: No Reelection."[74] Eventually, this indignation over a "perpetual presidency" would ring hollow, given Díaz's long

grip on power. But in 1876, in the infancy of the Porfirian state, Díaz successfully convinced his followers of his honest and limited intentions. In fact, Díaz
remained committed to the principle of no reelection until at least 1884.

To prove his own lack of interest in formal political power, Fidencio Hernández appointed Francisco Meijueiro governor of Oaxaca in February 1876.
For himself, Hernández assumed the task of leading the Oaxacan National
Guard against the federal government. The Zapotec soldiers under Hernández's command had grown to trust this mestizo leader, calling him in their
own language, "*viejo chuc-quia*," the one with the strong gaze. Notions of
strength and masculinity infused the Oaxacan National Guard at this point.
The Zapotec soldiers had come to believe that they had inherited an ancient
tradition of fighting against all enemies. It was their duty to uphold that tradition, to affirm the honor of their ancestors, and to serve their nation when
called on.[75] In a handbill distributed by Díaz in early autumn 1876, the troops
were told that Lerdo and Esperón no longer respected the Oaxacans: "They
believe we are divided, that you have lost the manly spirit [*varonil energía*] to
fight. But because of your rapid cooperation and engagement in this struggle,
they will be mistaken at their own peril."[76] The country needs you once again,
Díaz wrote:

> Do not forget that the mercenaries of reelection imprison the innocent,
> insult the defenseless and assassinate those they capture. Remember
> that they will loot the people, lay waste to the fields, and stain the honor
> of our families. Possessed by a justifiable indignation caused by these
> outrages, rise together as one man and begin to fulfill your obligations,
> confident that you will also be fulfilling mine. The danger grows closer
> and I am ready: if you decide to share this danger with me, I await you on
> the battlefield as your old comrade in arms.[77]

Encouraged by Díaz, and led by Hernández and Meijueiro, the soldiers from
the Sierra Zapoteca assumed a prominent place in the military effort to topple
Lerdo's government. In a separate handbill Díaz singled out the Sierra Juárez
for its role in the coming war: "Lerdo and Esperón still expect to find us weakened because they do not see many battalions under arms. But they forget
that among us, and above all in the Heroic Sierra Juárez, there is a true National Guard, as ready to take up arms against enemies as to return to their
homes and labor, satisfied and proud of their glorious efforts."[78] Díaz tried to
guide the overall military strategy even before he could get back to Oaxaca.
In March 1876 he pleaded with Hernández to advance on Puebla with caution, with a sense of respect for local leaders from the Sierra de Puebla: "If,

as I suspect, you enter the state of Puebla before I arrive or before I get near the capital, be very careful to always follow the instructions of Señor Juan N. Méndez for the provisional organization, [both] political and military of said state."[79] Hernández followed Díaz's advice in the short term but ultimately ignored working with Méndez as part of the larger campaign.[80] In spite of their boastful proclamations of invincibility, Fidencio Hernández and the soldiers under his command were captured on July 14, 1876, near Jalapa, Veracruz. Hernández was sentenced to the prison at Santiago Tlaltelolco in Mexico City. Learning of Hernández's capture, Díaz assembled his troops once again in order to rally the men around Hernández's "heroic" example. Let our imprisoned comrades and our martyred brothers inspire you by their example, Díaz told his soldiers; "Liberty demands it; honor requires it."[81] In Ixtlán Lieutenant Colonel Rafael Jiménez Rojas convened a meeting of all community leaders in the district to discuss Hernández's imprisonment. Like a wounded lion prepared to defend itself to the death, Rojas claimed, the people of Ixtlán should uphold their honor and seek revenge for Hernández, "the lost son of this community, the good citizen, the good friend, who is now paying with his precious life the cost of loyalty, civic duty, bravery, and love of his people."[82] Hernández's capture had little consequence on the outcome of the war. On November 16, 1876, porfirista troops defeated the federal army at the battle of Las Lomas de Tecoac, and Lerdo's government was overthrown.

Conclusion

Díaz had begun his long military career in the remote mountain district of Ixtlán, Oaxaca, in 1855. More than twenty-five years later, he would begin a new political career in Mexico City, the center of national power. For the people of Ixtlán, Díaz would become fixed in their stories and memories as the young brave soldier who had trained them, armed them, and honored them with the privilege of defending the nation. The history of the previous civil wars began to take on a new meaning. Clearly, their sacrifices had not been in vain. Their willingness to risk life and home against all enemies had not been a misguided adventure for the benefit of only a few. Díaz's rise to power had become their cause, their purpose, and their glory. Now they would use their memories of those years to write a new history of their important role in building the nation.

Díaz was constantly reminded that he had not been alone on the battlefields of Oaxaca. Zapotec peasants and their families wrote Díaz of their own place in Mexican history, recalling the sacrifices they had made during two decades of civil war. Veterans paraded through their towns on national holidays, assumed prominent positions within their communities, and told stories of the triumph and terror of fighting for liberty. During the Porfiriato, these veterans were celebrated as local heroes of Mexican sovereignty. But these veterans were not unique. Their identification with Juárez and Díaz may have been grounded in a deeper and broader sense of collective memory because of the personal histories of both Juárez and Díaz. Zapotec peasants may have reflected on and redefined that relationship more openly than other people. However, their experiences in defending the nation and their memories of that time were shared by thousands of rural inhabitants throughout Mexico.

CHAPTER FOUR

Recognition and Reward in the Early Porfiriato, 1876-1890

For the benefit of those patriotic pueblos.
Porfirio Díaz (1889)

In the first days of victory following the triumph of the Tuxtepec rebellion in 1876, Porfirio Díaz hosted a banquet in the mountains of the Sierra Zapoteca. Dozens of soldiers walked from their separate villages, escorted in small groups by their parents, wives, and children. Some families had been at the designated place all morning, preparing the site for such a gathering and cooking the beef, black beans, corn tortillas, and coffee that everyone would share. As they came closer, General Díaz greeted his guests, warmly embracing his fellow soldiers and inviting those with obvious war wounds to sit close to the head table. The wounded deserved special recognition for their sacrifices, and Díaz would make sure to honor them during his speech. As he rose to speak, Díaz looked out over the people sitting and standing in the fields of their ancestors. From his vantage point he could see the horizon and the distant peaks and valleys that cut through the Sierra. He must have momentarily reflected on his own journey to this point. His military and political career had started here, and it was to these people that Díaz owed the most. He chose his words carefully that afternoon, and for the assembled crowd those words would not be forgotten. He thanked them, of course, and told them that it had been an honor to fight alongside such brave soldiers. They had believed in him personally and had risked their lives for the good of the nation. And then the emotion and magnitude of their combined efforts overwhelmed Díaz. His eyes filled with tears as he pledged to remain loyal to his soldiers. He would never abandon them, he promised, and they could always call on him for protection. Finally, as he looked off in the distance, as if thinking of the journey to Mexico City to assume the presidency, Díaz rallied his men once more by declaring that together they would continue to fight for justice.[1]

This single moment effectively captures Díaz's appeal as a military hero and the origins of his popularity as a political figure. In 1876 Díaz spoke as easily and freely with poor Mexicans as he did with the rich. He understood the contributions that ordinary citizens had made to defend the country against foreign enemies, as well as to establish a regime under his personal direction. Moreover, he framed the challenges of the future in a context that acknowledged the accomplishments of the past. After years of leading soldiers on the battlefield, after years of organizing political clubs and associations around his candidacy for the presidency, Díaz had learned how to inspire Mexicans to think of themselves as historical actors. From the perspective of these Zapotec peasants in rural Oaxaca, Díaz would always remain their young commander, the first person to arm them and trust them with the duty of protecting their homes and nation against all enemies. But Díaz was moving to Mexico City in 1876, and the men and women who ate with him at the banquet would now have to deal more directly with local and statewide officials. Ultimately, the history of the Porfiriato in rural Oaxaca, as throughout the entire country, was shaped more by these immediate local relationships than by anything Díaz did in Mexico City. My focus, therefore, will remain on the men and women Díaz left behind rather than travel the more familiar historical path that led to the urban metropolis. How did local officials meet the expectations of the rural people whom Díaz could so gracefully inspire? And how did these Zapotec citizens continue to be actors in their own history?

On the morning after Díaz hosted his celebratory banquet, life returned to normal in the district of Ixtlán. Fernando Pérez of Ixtepeji had suffered a serious wound at the battle of La Carbonera, but he could still work a plot of land owned by the village. Dionisio Santiago returned to his village of Xiacui, where he eventually found work in the mine at Natividad. Mariano Ibarra of Lachatao remained in the military for another five years and used his connections to secure a job for his daughter at the new textile factory in Xía. At age sixty-three, Felipe García of Guelatao took up subsistence farming again, basking in the honor fellow villagers bestowed on him as a celebrated war hero. Francisco Meijueiro, the mestizo general from Ixtlán district, continued to serve as governor in Oaxaca City. And, of course, Porfirio Díaz moved to Mexico City to become the nation's president.[2]

Other veterans from Ixtlán district were not as fortunate. Mariano Paz's leg had been shattered by a bullet, leaving him unable to walk or earn a living. He relied primarily on his wife, Luz López, and on the contributions of his neighbors. Julián Medina had been forced to have his leg amputated. He tried to use a prosthesis, but medical care in rural Mexico in the 1870s left him with few opportunities and little hope. Clemente Martínez fought alongside his son Ramón against the French, but when the war ended, he had to return to Ixtepeji to tell his wife, Rosalia García, that Ramón had been killed in battle. Many years later Rosalia wrote that she continued to mourn the loss of her son. José Pacheco still bore the scars of the beating he had suffered at age thirteen when he had been forcibly conscripted into the conservative army. And José's father, Jacinto, fell ill during one of the long campaigns and died without ever returning to his family in Oaxaca. The generation of men and women from the Sierra Zapoteca who lived and died during Mexico's civil wars had paid a tremendous price for the honor of seeing Benito Juárez and then Porfirio Díaz occupy the presidency.[3]

Along with every name of every soldier who ever fought in the Ixtlán National Guard was a story about war and its consequences on everyday life in rural Mexico. Although these stories would begin to repeat themselves—loved ones lost, held prisoner, wounded, and killed—the impact of those experiences should not be easily dismissed. Indeed, these veterans and their families would not allow political leaders to forget the sacrifices they had made for the sake of saving the nation from foreign invaders and rival politicians. Porfirio Díaz may have been walking into the president's office in Mexico City, but there were thousands of people in the countryside who believed they had opened the door for him. The Zapotec soldiers of Ixtlán district, along with their families, expected both recognition and reward for their years of service. Significantly, veterans asked for very little during this time: job security in the region's mines, a new bridge, the right to keep their arms and ammunition, fair adjudication of land disputes, and the freedom to choose their own representatives to local town councils. Even when specific Zapotec demands became more varied and ambitious, after 1890, the larger objectives remained much the same: political autonomy, economic security, and cultural recognition.

Zapotecs were constantly engaged in a balancing act with mestizo elites, at times cooperating, at other times resisting, and at all times negotiating and discussing delicate political and economic decisions. During the early years of the Porfiriato, this slow process was tolerated because Díaz, his local allies, and rural peasants and workers generally sought a consensus rather than a confrontation on key issues. While the terms of that pact were always shifting, the need to negotiate with individuals and communities who had actively supported the military goals of the regime remained constant. Clearly, the Porfirian state was not born arrogant and strong; it developed those characteristics over time, as it aged and lost touch with the people who had risked their lives during the nation's civil wars.[4]

When Porfirio Díaz moved to Mexico City, he left the Oaxacan state government in the hands of his trusted ally from the Sierra Zapoteca, Francisco Meijueiro. Díaz remained, however, an active interlocutor with rural Oaxacans, writing and receiving hundreds of letters from people throughout the state. Meijueiro served as governor for less than two years, but he continued to manage the affairs of Ixtlán and by extension all of central Oaxaca as the major figure behind most economic and political decisions affecting the region. Like Miguel Castro before him, Meijueiro relied on his ties to the Ixtlán National Guard to bolster his status in valley politics and business.[5] However, Meijueiro's connections to the people of Ixtlán district were deeper than Castro's. Meijueiro had rather humble origins, similar in some ways to the people who worked in the region's fields and mines. Although his grandparents had been minor Spanish bureaucrats, Meijueiro himself had worked as a day laborer at the gold mine at Natividad. His Zapotec friends had called him "*Tío Chico Cacle*," a teasing name that referred to the sound his sandals made when he had been a young child, and a name he kept as he grew older.[6] He knew many of the people of the Sierra Zapoteca personally, and he assumed the status of local patriarch fully intending to live up to the reciprocal obligations inherent in that role. Although he amassed substantial wealth and personal prestige, Meijueiro also dedicated himself to meeting the demands of the rural population in Ixtlán. In effect, Meijueiro treated the Zapotec peasants as limited partners in developing the Sierra. He would seldom place their needs before his own, but he rarely acted unilaterally and without first consulting communal leaders.

The relationship between Meijueiro and Zapotec peasants, however, was far from idyllic and harmonious. The class and ethnic divisions that separated them could only be transcended at times by the efforts of both sides and by the direct intervention of Porfirio Díaz. Zapotec peasants enjoyed two powerful bargaining advantages. First, they had legitimate and well-documented histories of having fought in the civil wars over the last twenty years. They claimed to be heroes, equal in their own ways to the assertions Meijueiro and

Díaz made about themselves. Second, and more important, Zapotec peasants were unwilling to surrender their arms. They had won the right to carry weapons by defending the nation, and they would not relinquish that right without a fight. During these early years of the Porfiriato, they only needed to remind officials that they had the arms; they would not take up armed struggle again until the final days of the regime. The Serranos trusted Meijueiro, and the years before his death in 1890 were relatively calm. Meijueiro kept well informed about events throughout the district. He knew of complaints against the jefe político, of land disputes, of problems in the mining sector, of efforts to create new factories, of the obstacles involved in building new roads and bridges. He knew when villagers faced serious divisions within their own communities over issues like access to land, water, and municipal offices. He knew when international businessmen were coming to Oaxaca, seeking investment opportunities. He knew when Mexico City engineers were seriously considering the development of a railroad line to Oaxaca. And he knew Porfirio Díaz, a man of his own generation. Díaz and Meijueiro considered themselves good friends; indeed, they were *compadres*, forming a fictive kin relationship through their children. Meijueiro's importance to Oaxaca in general and Ixtlán in particular cannot be overstated. He consistently argued for more jobs and better treatment for the Zapotec people of Ixtlán district, fulfilling the promise of rewarding people who had risked their lives for Díaz and the nation. When Meijueiro died in 1890, an era ended in Oaxaca. An important link to the past, to the communities of the Sierra, and to Mexico City had been lost.[7]

The Origins of Discontent in Ixtepeji

Located twenty-five miles up a winding dirt road from Oaxaca City, Ixtepeji was the first town travelers met as they entered the Sierra Zapoteca. Because of its location, the people of Ixtepeji regularly monitored the road that passed by their community, effectively controlling access to the Sierra and assuming the responsibility of protecting their neighbors. As early as 1468, Ixtepejanos had been instrumental in forcing the invading Mexica armies to forgo their occupation of the Sierra. Although the town was nominally under Mexica control, Ixtepeji resistance effectively limited the Mexica to the valley of Oaxaca. In recognition of its population size and history of military accomplishment, Ixtepeji became the district *cabecera* during the early colonial period. At about the same time, 451 tributaries from Ixtepeji were assigned to the *encomienda* of the Spaniard Juan de Aragón. They provided Aragón with chickens, corn, beans, cacao, salt, honey, and of course, labor. In addition, they were required to pay him more than 220 pesos per year. In the seventeenth century Ixtepejanos used their town's size and juridical status to effectively practice their own style of expansionism, forcibly taking over lands from smaller villages like Huayapan, Tlalixtac, Tomaltepec, Chicomezuchil, Jaltianguis, Zooquiapan, and Nexicho. In 1702 colonial officials tried to shift the balance of power in the district away from Ixtepeji. They removed its *cabecera* designation and renamed the smaller town of Ixtlán *cabecera* in its place.[8]

Many historians have identified this demotion and lingering resentment against district officials as the cause of the hostility that grew between Ixtepeji and Ixtlán.[9] Eventually, the underlying animosity in the region erupted into open warfare in 1912, when people from Ixtepeji attacked neighboring settlements and threatened to take over the district militarily. Other towns ultimately united to defeat the Ixtepeji rebels, making sure the villagers would never again cause problems. The entire town was sacked, and hundreds of men, women, and children were forced into exile. Ixtepeji never recovered its population or its regional prominence.[10] We do not need to go back as far as 1702, however, to find reasons for discontent in Ixtepeji. In fact, the 1912 rebellion had its origins in the early years of the Porfiriato, in 1877, when Francisco Meijueiro orchestrated a new landholding syndicate just outside the Ixtepeji town limits. Due to its expanding population in the mid-nineteenth century, farmers from Ixtepeji had begun cultivating cornfields and fruit orchards on lands near the town but outside of the legally defined area reserved for village residents. Acting in his official capacity as governor, Meijueiro convinced the people of Ixtepeji that they needed to make legal arrangements in order to prevent other towns or individuals from designating these lands as *terrenos baldíos* or unclaimed lands. The two parcels, known popularly as Estudiante and Yovaneli, supported a wide variety of crops: corn, avocados, peaches, pears, apples, and almonds. In 1877 there were no indications of any disputes involving these two parcels, but it was easy to imagine potential conflicts, given the richness of the land. Besides, Ixtepeji was continually involved in other land disputes with neighboring villages on several fronts; one more would not have been surprising.[11]

Meijueiro wanted to keep the Ixtepejanos satisfied by protecting their access to the two parcels. Most of the men of the village had enthusiastically enlisted in the National Guard, and they maintained a keen sense of their own importance within that military unit. In addition, many people in Ixtepeji were already unhappy about losing access to a large tract of land that had been sold to English industrialists who planned to build a textile factory.

Given their willingness to take up arms, Meijueiro could not risk destabilizing the entire district as well as the state government. It was in Meijueiro's interests to keep the Ixtepejanos busy with farming. But Meijueiro also had a plan to enrich himself and his family.

He drafted and published the *Reglamento aprobado por el Pueblo de Ixtepeji en 22 de Noviembre de 1877* as a pamphlet.[12] He wanted to publicize the land deal to ward off any potential challengers and to guarantee to the people of Ixtepeji that their claim was now legal. The *Reglamento* granted thirty-two original signers of the agreement with equal partitions of Estudiante and Yovaneli (Article 1).[13] These men became known as "los rancheros" and governed themselves in a highly organized structure consisting of a *junta directiva* (board of directors) made up of three representatives and a treasurer (Article 2). Annual reports were required every November; elections for the *junta directiva* were held on the first Sunday in December; officers began their terms every February. Article 20 of the *Reglamento* protected the rancheros by declaring that they could change the terms of their agreement if they so desired. Significantly, for the generation of original rancheros there were few problems with the agreement as they signed it, though the potential for conflict existed within the document itself. Article 19 ordered the rancheros to pay one-fifth of their produce as a tax on their property. A small portion, twenty-two pesos, was to go directly to the Ixtepeji town council. The other proceeds were set aside, "to be invested in projects or improvements as determined by the people." Meijueiro convinced the villagers that his representation was the best investment they could make with the remaining proceeds from the ranchero lands. With the exception of twenty-two pesos per year, Meijueiro had one-fifth of the produce from the ranchero lands delivered to him personally on his estate. In effect, Meijueiro had reproduced a system of state-sponsored graft, one that looked remarkably similar to the tribute collected by both Indian caciques and Spanish *encomenderos*.

It seems unlikely, however, that Meijueiro had fooled the Ixtepeji rancheros to enter into an exploitative relationship. Article 20 reassured the rancheros that they could have altered the agreement in some way if they had so wanted. And, as we will see, Meijueiro worked diligently on development projects for the region up until his death in 1890. He fully intended to use at least some of the money from Ixtepeji rancheros to offset the costs of building roads and bridges in the district. But there was no way of knowing in 1877 just how far Meijueiro's family would abuse the ranchero agreement over the next generation. By 1906, the ranchero population had doubled, and Francisco's son, Guillermo, had begun hiring his own accountants to enter the orchards and fields before harvest in order to charge a more onerous tax that was, at least from the perspective of ranchero families, exceedingly unfair. Guillermo Meixueiro ignored the complaints of the villagers who argued that he was taking too much. It was at this point, beginning in about 1906, that the rancheros claimed that Francisco Meijueiro had originally misled them. He had acted like their friend and representative, they told Díaz, only to betray them for his personal gain.[14]

In many ways, whether his intentions had been for good or bad, Francisco Meijueiro was responsible for the discontent that led Ixtepeji to rebel in 1912. By setting the ranchero land apart from the rest of Ixtepeji, Meijueiro effectively divided the pueblo into two interest groups—the rancheros and everyone else. Ixtepejanos who did not have to pay 20 percent of their production to the Meijueiro family did not share the same resentment over the tax. In one generation this division would split the *ayuntamiento* (the town council) and the town more broadly. Contrary to other accounts, the 1912 rebellion was not supported by the entire community. The rancheros had decided to take matters into their own hands. Significantly, they first attacked the textile factory in the nearby settlement of Xía.

Indians and Industry: The Textile Factory at Xía

During the Porfiriato, dozens of men and women from Ixtepeji worked in the cotton textile factory located at Xía. They would generally rise before dawn, prepare their midday meal, and begin a two-hour walk over narrow mountain trails to arrive at the factory. As they drew near, the early morning mist would be slowly lifting from the valley, weaving and mixing with thin lines of white smoke that rose from scattered cooking fires of resident workers. The company had allowed some families to build small shacks in the valley, and these people had permanently resettled in the area.[15] In fact, the entire valley seemed to have been taken over by construction. The owners of the factory built houses for their managers, a company store, a chapel, and a school. They were constantly adding new rooms to the factory, extending the boundaries of the plant well beyond the original structure. Even with this constant expansion, most workers walked to the factory, arriving just in time for the company whistle to call them to their labor.[16] Mornings were always a busy time at Xía, as workers gathered at the gate of the massive building, clustered in small groups around the main patio. Horse-drawn wagons lumbered over rain-washed roads, bringing food and supplies up to the settlement and taking away the finished cloth that would be sold in the city. With people constantly moving in and out of Xía, the tranquility of a pastoral life appeared to be gone forever. As the workday began, the once quiet valley would be transformed into a noisy cacophony of banging spindles, crashing looms, and hissing steam-powered engines. But some things remained the same. The workers of Ixtepeji would join their Zapotec neighbors at this new factory, just as they had come together in the Ixtlán National Guard. And, just as before, old animosities and rivalries would not completely disappear.[17]

In 1877 Francisco Meijueiro was concerned about calming the people of Ixtepeji because they had lost access to the land on which the new factory was built. During Félix Díaz's tenure as governor (1867–71), English investors obtained the concession rights to establish a textile factory in the Oaxacan town of Santa Cruz, in Zimatlán district. After the failed rebellion at La Noria, when men with more direct ties to the Sierra Zapoteca controlled state politics, the concession was modified so that the new factory would be built in Ixtlán district.[18] Fidencio Hernández and Francisco Meijueiro had lobbied hard and skillfully to have the factory built in their home district. New jobs were needed for the Zapotec veterans who expected greater opportunities following their years of military service. In addition, Hernández and Meijueiro saw the new factory as a sign of Ixtlán's advance toward "progress," as an example of the modernization efforts taking place throughout the nation. There was only one other cotton textile factory in Oaxaca at the time, San José located in Etla near the capital city. Securing the new factory in the Sierra Zapoteca was a major coup for Hernández and Meijueiro, although the lingering dispute over the particular parcel of land threatened to undermine their efforts.[19]

The site chosen by Hernández and Meijueiro was situated in a river valley between the towns of Chicomezuchil and Ixtepeji. A mountain river cut across the land and gave the area its Zapoteco name "*Schoo-riia,*" which translated as Río Jícara, or Small Gourd River. Both Chicomezuchil and Ixtepeji claimed portions of the Xía valley since its fertile soil could support large expanses of corn, beans, and fruit orchards. But because neither village held legal title to the land, each could only farm it as long as custom and appeals to "time immemorial" kept other users away. Not surprisingly, during the mid-nineteenth century, a major portion of the disputed land passed into the hands of a private owner. Antonia Martel Rojas, a widow originally from the Oaxacan town of Tlacolula, obtained legal title to Xía, though she did not intend to farm the land for her own benefit. As part of the deal brokered by Hernández and Meijueiro, the Martel Rojas family agreed to sell the land title to Mowatts and Grandison, Inc., an investment company established by English nationals living in Oaxaca City. Although Chicomezuchil and Ixtepeji would each continue to claim the land, there was little they could do to prevent its transfer to foreign investors. They did, however, secure promises from Hernández and Meijueiro that people from their villages would be guaranteed jobs in the new factory.[20]

Mowatts and Grandison had great expectations for their factory. A reliable and accessible source of waterpower would provide inexpensive energy for the hydraulic equipment they planned to install. An equally accessible source of labor power would provide an inexpensive workforce to operate the machinery. Workers came from throughout the district but primarily from the towns of Ixtepeji, Nexicho, Chicomezuchil, Lachatao, and Yahuiche. In 1878 the factory produced 25,000 pounds of cotton yarn, worth an estimated 55,000 pesos, and 15,000 finished cloth pieces, worth some 44,312 pesos. By 1902, the value of goods produced at Xía had climbed to 271,000 pesos, for 721,000 pounds of finished cloth. Products were sold primarily in Oaxaca City, Ixtlán, and Villa Alta. At its peak, some 148 men and 115 women worked in the mill at Xía. They operated 9,000 spindles and 280 looms. In the late 1870s men were paid sixty centavos per day, and women earned forty centavos. These were relatively good wages, especially for the women, who had little or no other options for finding wage labor. The men may have been able to find work in the region's mining industry, but that work was more difficult and dangerous than operating a machine at the textile factory. In many ways, working at the Xía textile factory was a preferred occupation. But wages were slow to rise for the workers at Xía. By 1902, wages had increased just ten centavos for a day's labor. By this time, textile factory workers in other parts of the state could expect to earn 1¼ pesos, nearly 60 percent more than the Zapotec laborers at Xía.[21]

Industrial development was slow and uneven across Oaxaca during the Porfiriato. Investors' and promoters' enthusiasm about the state's industrial potential always outpaced actual development; compared with other regions, Oaxaca drew only minimal capitalist investment. Still, comparisons with other regions of Mexico tell only part of the story of industrialization during the Porfiriato. Macroeconomic analyses of railroad expansion and manufacturing development identify national trends and long-term economic growth. Based on these studies, we can gauge the obstacles, potential, and trajectory of the Porfirian economy.[22] The fundamental impact of economic change during the Porfiriato, however, was a much more local event. As the textile factory at Xía demonstrated, the Porfirian industrial revolution reached far into rural Mexico, transforming the daily lives and occupations of local populations. From the perspective of Zapotec communities, a new factory that employed over 250 wage laborers represented a crucial change in their economy. It was precisely this kind of local industrialization that mattered most to rural inhabitants during the Porfiriato.[23]

The textile factory at Xía benefited Zapotec communities in a number of ways. First, it provided scarce wage jobs during a time of political stability and declining emphasis on military careers. Second, it rewarded former veterans and their families with the security of a steady income. Third, some peasant communities could rent water rights to the new factory. Ixtepeji, for example, charged annual user fees for drawing water from the Grillo River, which the factory used for its hydraulic equipment. These lease agreements received much attention by village leaders and eventually became a major source of funding for the town. They also became highly contested issues when Ixtepeji demanded an increase for water rights.[24]

Other problems limited Xía's potential for stimulating further industrial expansion in Ixtlán. The Sierra Zapoteca lacked a reliable road system that could withstand the seasonal rains and floods that plagued the mountains. Wooden bridges were especially vulnerable during the rainy season and had to be rebuilt every decade. An unreliable transportation system also increased the time and cost of delivering raw cotton to the factory. Cotton supplies came primarily from Tututepec in Juquila district, arriving by mule train after a twenty-day journey.[25] Even buying the cotton could be a problem. Merchants would often monopolize the cotton supply in order to set the price for the factories in Oaxaca.[26] Finally, competition with more efficient and more capitalized factories in Puebla posed a challenge for factory owners at Xía. In many ways, the Xía factory represented a limited start toward industrialization in the Sierra Zapoteca; however, it was a start, a first step toward rewarding those patriotic communities with reliable wage jobs. To go beyond this initial phase would require more direct intervention on the part of the state and federal governments. Of course, the people of Ixtlán and Oaxaca had an advantage over other parts of Mexico: Porfirio Díaz oversaw much of the state's economic policy. His involvement in the Oaxacan economy began in earnest when he returned to the state as governor in 1881.

Local Patriarchy and the Right to Bear Arms, 1880–1884

In the Plan of Tuxtepec (1876), Porfirio Díaz had proclaimed that he and his supporters were fighting for the principle of "No Reelection," that is, for an end to self-perpetuating, autocratic presidential power. As Díaz's first term came to an end, however, the challenge of living up to that pledge caused

Díaz's supporters great consternation.[27] Francisco Meijueiro, for example, encouraged the president to remain in office in order to protect the fragile stability won during the previous years. Clearly, Meijueiro stood ready to set aside the promises of Tuxtepec. But Díaz was not, at least not yet. In an October 1879 letter, Díaz gently scolded his friend:

> I understand that you are leaning toward an extension of my term, which would avoid the serious challenges that exist in arranging a peaceful transition of power, but would require a new constitutional decree allowing reelection for another four-year term. I am greatly honored that you would think so highly of me; but the method [*is absolutely unconstitutional*] *does not follow the prescript of the constitution* [the bracketed portion was crossed out in the draft letter and the second written in pencil to replace it], even if you could come up with some kind of plausible excuse to support your position.[28]

Although Díaz felt strongly about the issue of no reelection, he did not want to insult his friend, and so changed the tone of his letter but not his insistence on stepping down in 1880. I want to emphasize, however, that Díaz was not calling for greater democratic participation. He assumed for himself the right to name an official candidate, and he reserved the right to run again in another four years. He may have been willing to step down, but not to step aside.

Meijueiro had no choice but to accept Díaz's decision to allow someone else to become president. But Meijueiro was determined to influence exactly who that person might be. By November 1879, Díaz had not publicly announced which candidate he would choose, though he was leaning toward his minister of war, General Manuel González. González had been a supporter of the Tuxtepec revolt, but he also carried the rather antiliberal baggage of having fought for the conservatives during the War of the Reform. Other members of Díaz's cabinet were also lobbying for the nomination, especially Justo Benítez, minister of hacienda. Benítez had been a more consistent liberal, one of the *Tuxtepecos netos*, as the Mexico City press called him.[29] But Benítez did not have the backing of key regional leaders around the country. Meijueiro endorsed González and rallied the local commanders of the Ixtlán National Guard to do the same. In fact, if someone other than González received the nomination, Meijueiro and the veterans from the Sierra Zapoteca threatened rebellion.

In November 1879 González wrote a surprisingly candid letter to General José Guillermo Carbó in which he complained of the conflicts within the cabinet and the challenges that lay ahead in organizing a political movement.[30] He spoke of the real "antagonism" between himself and other cabinet members, especially Protasio P. Tagle, secretary of the interior (*gobernación*) and an open supporter of Benítez. González told Carbó, "Every day that passes convinces me even more of the need to resign from the cabinet so that my supporters and I can have more freedom to act." Because of the "promises made to the people in the Plan of Tuxtepec," González argued that Díaz should not be hampered by accusations of undue influence. For that reason, Díaz and González devised a strategy whereby González would announce his resignation at a cabinet meeting, which would then pressure Tagle to do the same. As it happened, however, the entire cabinet offered to resign so that the president could choose a new group of ministers. Díaz and González had not expected this move, which produced a rather dramatic moment at a critical transitional juncture. But Díaz was getting pressure to nominate González, and he needed to make a decision. As González explained to Carbó, "If the supporters of Señor Benítez believe that General Díaz supports him, they are hugely mistaken. Oaxaca and many other states have announced that they would prefer civil war to the candidacy of Señor Benítez. The President knows this, and for that reason I assure you that General Díaz is no supporter of Señor Benítez." [31] Why would Meijueiro and the Ixtlán National Guard support González? As minister of war, González would have maintained better relations with veterans and with commanders like Meijueiro, who retained his military rank and a military salary. Beyond that reason it would be difficult to say. Unfortunately, known documentary evidence surrounding these years is silent on key questions. Events immediately following the 1880 election reveal, however, that rebellion in Oaxaca was indeed a real possibility. [32]

The threat of rebellion in Oaxaca surrounding the issue of presidential succession indicated to Díaz that he needed to gain a firmer grip on his native state. He thus returned to Oaxaca after he resigned the presidency, assuming the governorship until 1882. And, just as Meijueiro had been willing to ignore the promises of Tuxtepec regarding presidential succession, Díaz made plans to renege on assurances he had made to allow the Ixtlán National Guard to remain armed. During his first week as governor, Díaz decided to disband the National Guard battalions throughout the state, which meant Indian communities would have to surrender their weapons. In particular, Díaz demanded that the arms and ammunition of the Ixtlán National Guard should be confiscated by the state government. As the Serrano historian Rosendo Pérez García observed, thirty years after training them to fight, their old general now saw the soldiers of 1855 as a threat. [33]

Díaz's attempt to disarm the Zapotec peasants violated the implied provisions of their historical pact. Unilaterally, Díaz was trampling on the very right that the Serranos guarded most carefully. They had risked life and limb for the nation and for this particular president, but now Díaz wanted to treat them as ordinary peasants, as second-class citizens unworthy of the trust they had earned on the battlefield. It had been easier for the Serranos to get along with Díaz while he was in Mexico City. These weapons represented more than a sign of trust between the president and the people. Local leaders used their status as real and potential military commanders to protect their own patriarchal status within communities. This issue demonstrated, however, that despite Díaz's national stature, his authority in the Sierra Zapoteca proved more limited. As in previous attempts to disarm local militias, the Serranos refused to comply with the order. Community representatives, municipal presidents, and National Guard officers gathered in Ixtlán to discuss their options. After much debate, they determined that they would deliver to the state capital only those weapons and ammunitions that had become useless because of time and disrepair. They would maintain a majority of their weapons, and they would not surrender these voluntarily. In effect, they had found a way to meet Díaz partway, and they were unwilling to go any further. Díaz understood that he could not push them to do more and went along with their ruse. Although everyone realized that the Zapotec soldiers of Ixtlán district still had arms, Díaz officially accepted their compromise; he announced that the Sierra had been disarmed and would no longer be a threat.[34]

But who exactly felt threatened by the Sierra, and why? Obviously, even Díaz could not completely control the communities of Ixtlán as long as they had their own autonomous means of defending their interests and/or of occupying Oaxaca City with their own army. It seems improbable, however, to argue that Díaz himself felt threatened. More than likely, Díaz's intent was to disarm the Sierra so that other people in state government, especially the future governors whom he would appoint, would not have a problem enforcing their decrees. For the most part, Díaz understood how to negotiate with Zapotec community leaders. He knew how to speak to them, how to appeal to their sense of history, and how to convince them that he was on their side, though he came dangerously close to violating their trust when he asked them to turn in their arms. But other political leaders in the state did not have that skill or the personal experience of living and fighting alongside these people. Díaz sought to limit their autonomy, but he knew that he could not simply order federal troops into the district to force the Serranos into compliance. History and his own experience had taught him the futility of invading Ixtlán district.

The relationship that Zapotec peasants had with Díaz was always being tested, always being negotiated in minor and major ways. Díaz had tried and failed to change that relationship in his attempt to disarm the people of Ixtlán district. Instead, Zapotecs communities maintained their arms from 1855 to 1920. For more than two generations, their access to weapons, their experiences on the battlefield, and their willingness to confront officials bolstered the relative sense of autonomy for the Serranos. Failing in his attempt to completely disarm the Sierra, Díaz turned his attention to developing the Oaxacan economy. At the top of his list was the mining industry, especially the gold and silver mines throughout the district of Ixtlán. Perhaps this economic plan had been Díaz's motivation for disarming the Sierra all along. Investors, both foreign and domestic, felt uneasy about the distribution of weapons throughout the district.

Mining in the Sierra Zapoteca

Mine owners, their managers, and engineers may have been concerned about the potential for unrest throughout the Sierra, but from 1876 to 1890 there were actually few instances of organized resistance to the mines. In one case, in July 1885, Governor Luis Mier y Terán reported to Díaz that Natividad, the state's largest and most productive gold and silver mine, located in the district of Ixtlán, had been the target of recent robberies. Mier y Terán put Juan Meijueiro, Francisco Meijueiro's brother, in charge of a small contingent of soldiers sent to guard the mine. However, the English engineer at the mine did not think the group was sufficient to end the "hostility." The engineer complained to Díaz, "If it's simply this group of eight men which Meijueiro has then that's O.K., but I was talking about an entire battalion." [35] Obviously, political leaders determined that the engineer was overreacting to the situation. A string of robberies was a serious issue, but it hardly warranted a complete militarization of the region. In many ways, the relative absence of conflicts involving the mines was surprising because the mines did not produce a significant profit for investors until the 1895 worldwide boom in the price of precious metals. During the first decade of the Porfiriato, mining profits were limited by a lack of a railroad to the state, a reliable source of credit and investment, and a failure of the mines to find any new veins. There was great hope for Oaxacan mining, but little or no expansion. The peasant workers of the region, however, initiated fewer conflicts during this time than they did in later years. As long as the mines continued to provide jobs, the Serranos did not pressure for higher wages or more favorable working conditions. In fact, during the early years of the Porfiriato, managerial and financial problems posed a greater obstacle to the mining industry than did popular resistance.

Natividad was an important source of jobs for several hundred day laborers living in the neighboring towns of Xiacui and Calpulalpam. But the mine itself, founded in 1785, produced little profit for investors. Internal problems on the corporation's board of directors plagued the management of Natividad and nearly forced the mine to shut down completely. Porfirio Díaz and Francisco Meijueiro were at the center of these internal disputes. Both men had invested heavily in Natividad, and they both waited anxiously for the mine to return a profit. Unlike other investors, however, Díaz and Meijueiro realized that the mine could not shut down entirely, even if it were a money loser. Too many people depended on Natividad for their livelihood; if it closed, the Zapotec residents in the area would go hungry.[36]

In April 1882, while he was still governor of Oaxaca, Díaz maneuvered to take control over the board of directors at Natividad. Other investors, most notably Jacobo Grandison, owner of the textile factory at Xía, and Oaxacan businessman Juan Rey, had a majority of votes on the board and wanted to begin slowly cutting jobs at the mine unless workers discovered a new vein. Encouraged by Manuel Dublán, Benito Juárez's brother-in-law and a Natividad investor, Díaz decided to personally sit on the board for a brief time and then name someone he trusted to assume his position.[37] In fact, Díaz was on the board for just two months, until he resigned as Oaxacan governor in July 1882. Although he was leaving the state, Díaz emphasized that his greater purpose was to aid in the economic development of Oaxaca. In his resignation letter Diaz reminded his fellow Oaxacans that his "constant yearning and single aspiration has always been to aid in the enrichment of the state." He promised that he would continue to use all of his connections, all of his influence, and all of his energy to search for businesses that would invest in Oaxaca. He would also call on the federal government to assist his home state in utilizing the riches of Oaxaca and the "genius of its inhabitants."[38] His direct intervention in managing the affairs of Natividad had a profound impact on the Zapotec peasants living and working in the region. Clearly, Díaz had a fondness for Oaxaca, a fundamental and core attachment to the place of his boyhood. He may have lived amid European architecture, European furniture, and men with European ideas, but Díaz never forgot his roots or his taste for things from his native state. When he was president and living in Mexico City, Díaz ate black beans from Ocotlán, drank coffee from Villa Alta, and requested a particular wheat from Ixtlán district to make his bread. Díaz did not drink alcohol, but he kept mescal on hand so he could offer his friends a taste of Oaxaca's pure-grain alcohol.[39]

Three years after Díaz left Oaxaca, after becoming president for a second term, Natividad and the other mines in Ixtlán district were still not profitable. Francisco Meijueiro wrote Díaz frequently with bad news, referring to the situation in August 1885 as "the financial crisis in the mines." Because he was losing money in his mining investments, Meijueiro asked Díaz to continue to send him a military salary as general of the Ixtlán National Guard, a request Díaz fulfilled.[40] In fact, Díaz himself appeared to be somewhat short of money that year. In November Meijueiro invited Díaz to buy into another mine in the district, a relatively small investment and a potential bargain since the current owner wanted to sell quickly. Díaz responded that he did not have enough money to do so.[41]

Managerial and financial problems continued at Natividad through most of 1886, when Francisco Meijueiro was named to the board of directors. The other board members represented some of the state's most important businessmen: Constantino Rickards, Manuel Allende, Demetrio Sodi, and Manuel Peralta.[42] If this group could not rescue Natividad, then the mine was doomed. Contrary to the downward trend in the mining industry, Meijueiro directed an aggressive investment plan designed to expand Natividad's operations. He could not, however, turn to bankers since the mine had already mortgaged all that it could afford. Meijueiro looked instead to the group of men who stood to profit if the mine prospered. Díaz, along with all other stockholders, was asked to invest thirty pesos per share per month in Meijueiro's plan. Meijueiro was confident that a new and profitable vein would soon be discovered, at which time the additional investments would no longer be needed.[43] Not surprisingly, Díaz and other shareholders were unhappy about making more investments while the mine was not producing. But Meijueiro assured Diaz of the importance of keeping the mine operating. "The principal objectives are these," Meijueiro told Díaz, "to make sure the company has the money it needs to operate, and to make sure that the mine is not abandoned so that the people will have work."[44]

Meijueiro's plan essentially represented a last-ditch effort to keep the mine in the hands of local businessmen who had both a financial and moral stake in the region's economic prosperity and political stability. Foreign owners would lack the kind of commitment and understanding of the Zapotec labor force that would be necessary to keep the peace. Outsiders could buy smaller mines, but Meijueiro wanted to keep Natividad under local control. In August 1886 Meijueiro visited Natividad to see how his plan was working. Although shareholders had recently invested 20,000 pesos, Meijueiro reported, "they had not taken out a single centavo."[45] Few shareholders were as optimistic about the plan as Meijueiro. Díaz, for example, regularly complained that Natividad was costing him too much. In response, Meijueiro could only promise that "there will either be dividends or the mine will be sold."[46] Meijueiro's ultimate goal was to simply keep the mine open.

Díaz, on the other hand, was clearly looking to get out of the mining business in Oaxaca. In late 1885 he began to steer foreign investors to his native state, advising them on particular mining operations and encouraging them to take advantage of the state's low labor costs. Díaz's help was particularly crucial for one investor, N. S. Reneau, a Frenchman with business ties to the United States.[47] Every time Reneau visited Mexico he would call on Díaz in Mexico City. Díaz would then write Meijueiro, directing the Oaxacan to help in whatever way he could. Meijueiro served as Díaz's personal representative in Oaxaca, hosting Reneau in his home and escorting him to potential investment sites. Within a month of his first visit to Oaxaca, Reneau found gold mines that interested him in Ixtlán district, though Natividad was still not for sale. He bought several smaller mines and promised to return for more. Díaz's enthusiasm was high: "I believe he will be returning with even better propositions and with the means to establish his mining operations which will greatly benefit the state."[48]

Reneau returned to Oaxaca in early 1888 and agreed to buy the plant and mining operation at Cinco Señores y Socorro from the aging Miguel Castro for 50,000 pesos. Upon closing the deal, Reneau personally thanked Díaz for his "powerful influence" in getting the two sides together.[49] But Reneau was interested in even larger transactions. The Frenchman bragged about associates in the United States who had 150 million dollars ready to invest in railroads and mines in Mexico.[50] Several months later, in August 1888, Reneau returned to Mexico with two engineers from the company he had formed in Chicago. Reneau proposed a straightforward investment scheme to buy mines in Oaxaca, Guanajuato, and Chihuahua. Reneau and his backers would own 80 percent of the stock in all their investments, and the Mexican government would own the remaining 20 percent. This plan proved too large for Díaz, despite his initial enthusiasm, though the president was willing to talk further. He reassured Reneau, "You know that for my part I am prepared to help you in whatever way possible."[51]

Meanwhile, the other stockholders at Natividad grew tired of losing money and approached Meijueiro with a request to buy them out. Meijueiro asked Díaz to join him on this deal, stating, "I would never think of undertaking a business venture without inviting your participation." Meijueiro, the eternal optimist about Ixtlán's potential in gold mining, appeared somewhat surprised by the prospect. "Despite our efforts to raise the spirit of the mine owners in these parts," Meijueiro wrote Díaz, "the majority of the associates of Natividad are actually discouraged and I believe they would sell us their shares at an extremely low price." If they could get the other shares for a bargain, Meijueiro believed the miners would either discover a new vein or the entire operation might be sold to an individual or company that would pay a better price for the whole thing. Díaz feigned interest, doubting if Natividad were really that promising of an investment.[52]

Ultimately, there was little Meijueiro could do by himself to alter Natividad's profitability. He remained a committed and enthusiastic supporter of the mine for the remainder of his life, giving gold and silver nuggets from Natividad to his friends on special occasions.[53] He tried to limit regional competition by advising Díaz not to develop mines in the neighboring state of Chiapas: the veins were poor, the distance from Mexico City was too great, and the Jesuits there were all "rebels."[54] In the end, the structural forces of the international market for precious metals were beyond Meijueiro's control. In addition, the limitations of an inferior transportation infrastructure within the region posed an insurmountable obstacle that no individual could solve. The major problem, as Reneau, Castro, and Meijueiro all recognized, was that Oaxaca did not have a railroad in the 1880s.[55] Díaz could promote Oaxacan mining and even get some foreign investors to risk their money in his native state, but without a railroad those investments would never prove lucrative. Díaz reassured Reneau and Meijueiro that a railroad was his top priority. In terms of the local economy in Ixtlán, other improvements were just as important as a railroad. In particular, a steel girder bridge across the district's Río Grande was the most important project for the Serrano communities. In fact, Meijueiro and the Zapotecs expected these improvements because Díaz had promised them he would build a bridge in exchange for their support in the Tuxtepec rebellion.

A Lasting Symbol of Recognition and Reward

For various reasons, it was difficult to build the infrastructure of rural Oaxaca. People regularly stole telegraph posts and wire in remote areas, forcing the government to duplicate its efforts and guard the improvements as they went along. Robberies were especially frequent in the districts of Ixtlán, Etla, Cuicatlán and Teotitlán, where peasants would use the posts for reinforcing their own buildings, or for fencing, or even for firewood.[56] But projects like a telegraph system offered peasants only limited improvements in their personal lives. It was hard to see how these lines of wire and wood could make their lives any better. Other development projects—a railroad, schools, and especially a bridge—represented more tangible signs of the government's dedication to the regional economy of Oaxaca.

Plans for connecting Oaxaca to Mexico's growing railroad network had been developed as early as 1875, but the line between Oaxaca City and Puebla was not completed until 1892.[57] The state government, in concert with Porfirio Díaz in Mexico City, sought investors in Europe and the United States. In 1886 Governor Mier y Terán believed he had finally secured a contractor to build the line after he offered broad concessions to José Sibenater, who represented a European company. The concessions included generous lines of credit, tax rebates, and a lease on the railroad for ninety-nine years.[58] Sibenater's company agreed to build the first fifty kilometers of track within one year of breaking ground. After that initial phase, the state government of Oaxaca would hire the company to finish the line at a cost not to exceed 20,000 pesos per kilometer. Despite the promises made by the governor, the state government could not come up with enough capital to get the construction underway, and the deal collapsed.[59]

Finally, with more direct help from Porfirio Díaz, a deal to get a railroad built appeared to be on track. In 1889 Díaz had the federal government finance a lucrative contract with Read and Campbell, Ltd., of London. In addition to the terms outlined in the previous contract, the federal government rather than the state government agreed to subsidize the company nearly 2,400 pesos per kilometer for the railroad from Puebla to Oaxaca City, a grant that would eventually cost more than 11 million pesos.[60] Díaz's participation in this deal was crucial. In fact, Díaz played a critical role in deciding exactly where the line would run. The planning engineer for Read and Campbell, a Mr. Earley, was sent to Oaxaca to plot the direction of the track. Earley had to make a decision regarding which side of a riverbed he should lay track, which would have implications for continuing the line into Oaxaca City. Earley's escort, Francisco González y Cosío, wrote to Díaz for advice. From his desk in Mexico City, Díaz could imagine the valleys and hills of the region. He had lived there, encamped with his soldiers during the many military campaigns of his earlier career, and he knew exactly which route the railroad should follow. Díaz wrote confidently that the railroad should run along the Río Blanco and climb gradually toward Sayocatlán. The line should follow the south bank, continuing until it reaches "the gold mines of Chilua Clero, which used to belong to the Martínez, a Spanish family." From that point, Díaz advised, "the most accessible slope will be on the left going toward Oaxaca City because this side would need fewer and smaller bridges than the right side, which would be the south side."[61] While many people acknowledged Díaz's support in getting the railroad built, few people knew that the president had actually determined the course of the railroad in Oaxaca.

From Díaz's perspective, the people of Oaxaca deserved and badly needed the railroad. As he explained to Oaxacan governor Albino Zertuche in 1889, the railroad "will be for the benefit of those patriotic pueblos in particular and the country in general."[62] The railroad offered one other important benefit for Oaxacans. Hundreds of workers would be needed to prepare the route and then to actually lay the track. Díaz advised Read and Campbell executives on the availability of labor in rural Oaxaca and made a specific request that the company hire workers from Ixtlán district. For Díaz, as well as for the Serranos, the railroad represented both an immediate and a long-term reward for having fought in the nation's civil wars. But simply making jobs available would not satisfy the Serrano communities or the hundreds of other peasant laborers who sought work with the railroad company throughout the state. Francisco Meijueiro, fulfilling his role as regional patriarch, expressed gratitude to Díaz for having recommended workers from the Sierra to Read and Campbell engineers, though he doubted the workers would be treated fairly by the company. Although Sir Rudston Read himself had invited Meijueiro to a meeting to discuss the terms of a labor contract, Meijueiro did not expect to reach a settlement: "I'm going [to the meeting] with little hope or no faith that we can come to an agreement because, in general, throughout the Republic foreigners treat Mexicans poorly [tratan mal a los mexicanos]."[63] Díaz tried to reassure Meijueiro that Read and Campbell was different, but he acknowledged that Meijueiro's first responsibility was to protect the people of the Sierra. After an exchange of letters with Díaz on this issue, Meijueiro appeared satisfied that he had the latitude to demand a more favorable contract for the Serranos.[64]

Railroad construction workers in other parts of Oaxaca experienced the mistreatment that Meijueiro anticipated. They were abused, Benjamin Cartas explained to Díaz; "the way the people are treated, from what I'm told is not appropriate to keep them working. The people are abused and harassed, which is the reason many of them come for a week and never return." As for those workers who migrated from central Oaxaca to work on the railroads, Cartas noted, "they have simply gone home." Even when they stayed, workers would be fined for lost or damaged equipment, and often times the company would withhold their paychecks altogether. Governor Zertuche reported troubles in Tehuantepec, where workers had begun raiding the railroad supply centers in order to sabotage the project in southern Oaxaca. Indian peasants in Oaxaca, especially in Tehuantepec, would not be so easily exploited.[65]

Despite these problems, the railroad line from Puebla to Oaxaca City was finally completed in 1892. In recognition of his tireless effort to link Oaxaca with the rest of the country, state leaders invited President Díaz to officially open the Mexican Southern Railroad. At the inauguration of the Puebla-Oaxaca route, Díaz announced that the railroad would do two things: it would bring into the state more banks, credit, and investments, and it would export Oaxaca's agricultural goods, manufactured products, and mineral resources.[66] The major project that everyone considered essential for developing the Oaxacan economy had been completed. The Serranos had helped build the railroad and dreamed of adding their own spur line into the important mining region of Natividad. That project was never begun.

For the Zapotec communities of Ixtlán district, other state-sponsored development projects were even more important than a railroad. The Serranos wanted the government to build more schools in their district so that their children could learn to read and write and, more important, learn about Mexican history, especially about the role of Benito Juárez in that history. To a limited extent, the state government made an effort to support education for Oaxaca's popular classes. In 1884 three hundred educational grants were budgeted "for the children of those who were killed in the wars of the Reform and Intervention."[67] These "orphaned" children had a special place in Oaxacan society. In addition to receiving money for education, they were also granted eight pesos per month for food aid. But there were limits to what the state could afford. Governor Mier y Terán tried to balance the needs of these children with the costs of supporting the jefes políticos, the expense of wiring Oaxaca City with electricity, and the general maintenance of running the state government. As for Díaz, his obligation to the children of his comrades was genuine but also limited. He advised Mier y Terán to worry less about expanding educational programs in the state and to concentrate instead on providing basic primary instruction. "We are obliged to make men not scholars," Díaz told the governor.[68] Nevertheless, the state's investment in education, especially its aid program for the families of soldiers killed in action, demonstrated a commitment to rewarding those men who had served in the National Guard. Education in rural Mexico was a profoundly optimistic approach to dealing with social problems since it entailed a commitment of precious time and resources to people with little formal educational experience. The return on that investment was distant and difficult to calculate. But rural populations demanded schools, and the government had to respond, if only in a limited fashion.

There was always the need for more and better schools in Oaxaca. In 1888 Francisco Meijueiro virtually begged Díaz to spend more money on education. Public instruction, Meijueiro wrote, justifiably concerned all state governments. But in Oaxaca, the problem deserved particular attention since a majority of the population lived in remote Indian communities. Simply increasing the number of schools in Oaxaca City would not solve the state's education ills. New schools, according to Meijueiro, had to be built in rural communities: "We need capable instructors and the schools need to be located near the students."[69] As the patriarch of Ixtlán district, Meijueiro had an obligation to meet the needs of his constituents. To a certain extent, he lived up to that obligation.

Meijueiro's commitment to developing the Sierra Zapoteca and meeting the expectations of his peasant neighbors was particularly obvious in his efforts to have a steel girder bridge built across the district's Río Grande. The only road through the district relied exclusively on a bridge over this particular river, and a new bridge had been a pet project of Meijueiro's throughout the early years of the Porfiriato. He believed a new bridge would aid the expansion of the mining industry in the district. As "the financial crisis" in the mines deepened, Meijueiro argued in 1885 that a new bridge would raise the hopes and spirits of everyone living and working in the district.[70] Meijueiro expected to be involved in the project, but only because he saw it as a local issue, as something that mattered most to the people who would use it everyday.

In the last year of his life, Meijueiro became virtually obsessed with the bridge. He mentioned it frequently in his letters to Díaz, and it became his final effort to improve the lives of the people of the Sierra. In 1889 he began talking about the bridge as a passageway to a new era. He saw the project as a lasting monument both to Díaz and to those veterans who had served the nation so bravely. He told Díaz, "I want all of the inhabitants of the Sierra to be convinced that they enjoy your gracious consideration as one of their good friends." He even offered to finance the construction project himself: "If you would have the kindness to grant me this small project, I would put up the necessary financing." And he pushed Díaz to act quickly, telling him, "this year has been very dry; there has never been a better opportunity than this to do the job." The patriarch of the Sierra longed to see the bridge completed and awaited Díaz's reply: "I will be in my home, surrounded by my family, attending to my businesses and mines, calculating how many people will be needed for the important task of the bridge. I will remain here with my entire family, living happily right here until the job is finished."[71]

Meijueiro was not acting alone. Zapotec communal leaders from around the district gathered in Ixtlán town to draft a more personal petition to Díaz. They met on February 5, 1890, and dispatched their letter to Díaz on the same day: "Those of us survivors [veterans], municipal authorities, former subordinates of yours, and the others of us sons of this District, recall that in September of 1876, you told us that you would order the renovation of the bridge over the Río Grande. We now humbly bring our petition before you since said bridge is completely ruined and surely will not be able to withstand the swift currents of the next rainy season." More than likely, these Zapotec peasants were recalling a promise Díaz had made to them at the banquet celebrating his victory in the Tuxtepec revolt.[72] They drew on their common history with Díaz, explaining "the respect and sympathy that you have demonstrated has inspired us ever since the time you were our jefe político." Yet they were also thinking of the future. If he would grant them this small request, they wrote, "the name Porfirio Díaz will be forever in the hearts of every true Serrano. You will leave us with an offering that our children will learn to respect." Díaz wrote back that he would assign an engineer to the project.[73] Unfortunately, financial and bureaucratic obstacles delayed construction until 1898, and the new bridge did not open until 1900. Francisco Meijueiro had died a decade earlier, never knowing of this lasting symbol of recognition and reward for the Serranos.

The Politics of a New Generation

Francisco Meijueiro's dedication to developing the economy in Ixtlán district had made him a fairly wealthy man. He had gone from being a day laborer at Natividad to directing the mine's board of directors. He invested in land and businesses in Oaxaca City and Ixtlán district, and he was able to raise his family in comforts that he himself had not known as a young child. One of his more lucrative practices proved to be the legal advice and representation he sold to peasant communities and individuals throughout central Oaxaca. In addition to representing the rancheros of Ixtepeji, for which he was handsomely rewarded, Meijueiro sold his advice to other peasant communities engaged in land disputes, water conflicts, and other business negotiations with a political nature. Although he had not been trained as a lawyer, his political influence with state and federal officials could often guarantee a favorable settlement for the side he represented.

His other special talent was securing jobs for people. For Zapotec men and women his efforts brought new manufacturing jobs to the district at the textile factory, protected miners at Natividad, and obtained positions for laborers on the railroad. For his friends and family Meijueiro proved even more effective at dispensing good-paying jobs in the government. The status of regional patriarch brought with it expectations that Meijueiro could provide jobs for the people who respected his unofficial authority. No doubt Meijueiro received considerable compensation for his efforts. In 1882 Meijueiro helped his cousin Miguel Meijueiro become the jefe político for Ixtlán district. In return, Miguel appeared to understand that he owed his position exclusively to his cousin. As a result, other regional elites held little sway over the new jefe político. For example, Manuel Toro, an influential mestizo landowner and former military commander, had settled in Ixtlán district and had established a system of providing peasant communities with "protection" in exchange for substantial payments in cash and agricultural products. Miguel Meijueiro challenged Toro and defended the Zapotec communities who resisted Toro's extortion. As the jefe político explained in a report to Díaz, "I have become his [Toro's] enemy simply because I no longer let him rob the communities and the citizens, as has been his custom."[74]

Other friends and family members of Francisco Meijueiro also received special consideration for political appointments. Fidencio Hernández, Félix Romero, and Dr. Manuel Ortega received government positions based on Meijueiro's recommendation.[75] In 1886 Meijueiro asked Díaz to return "our good friend" Pascual A. Fenochio to the national congress since Fenochio's only income was the salary he received as a representative. Fenochio's other investments were doing poorly, according to Meijueiro, and he wanted to help his friend. In the same request, Meijueiro also asked Díaz to appoint his brother Pablo Meijueiro as representative from either Oaxaca or any other open seat in the national congress. He did not elaborate on his reasons for supporting Pablo's appointment. Díaz endorsed both of Meijueiro's recommendations.[76] Díaz, however, did not always accept Meijueiro's nominations. Indeed, Meijueiro wrote so frequently to Díaz asking him to appoint friends and relatives to positions that there was no way Díaz could accept all of them.[77] Still, Meijueiro's requests were usually met with approval by Díaz, which enhanced Meijueiro's reputation and status as the leading figure in Oaxacan politics.

Toward the end of his life, Francisco Meijueiro secured government jobs for two of his children. In 1885 Meijueiro asked Díaz to appoint his son Carlos tax collector for the principal highway through the entire state of Oaxaca, from Tehuacán, Puebla, to Puerto Angel on the Pacific coast, a huge stretch of road that must have provided considerable opportunities for graft. Carlos received the appointment.[78] In 1889 Meijueiro requested the position of *jefatura de hacienda* in Oaxaca for his other son, Guillermo. Guillermo was only twenty-six years old, and this position began his long career in public life.[79] By 1889, Francisco Meijueiro had allowed Guillermo to assume many of the responsibilities of running other parts of the family business. Francisco's health had been declining, and Guillermo needed to become more familiar with his father's vast dealings. More than anything else, Francisco sold influence. To market that intangible commodity required a more delicate touch than Guillermo seemed to realize, however. Unlike his father, Guillermo had known only relative wealth and prestige. In addition, Guillermo had not served in the Ixtlán National Guard side by side with the Zapotec soldiers of that district. Guillermo would eventually get his chance to organize a militia from the Sierra, but that opportunity would come late in his life during the upheaval of the 1910 Revolution. There was a certain wisdom and understanding about working and living with the people of Ixtlán district that the elder Meijueiro could not teach his son. In particular, Guillermo had little understanding of the unwritten consensus and cooperation shared between veterans of the nation's civil wars.

On October 8, 1889, President Díaz received a distressing letter from the widow of a prominent veteran from Ixtlán district. Monica Cruz de Pérez, widow of Cenobio "El Gallo" Pérez from Ixtepeji, hired a professional scribe to explain to Díaz that she had not received her husband's pension for nearly an entire year. Her son Fernando Pérez, along with other veterans' widows Luisa Ramos and Cármen Sánchez, testified that they, too, had not received the pensions that they deserved. The group charged that Francisco Meijueiro and his son Guillermo had stolen the money that rightly belonged to the heirs of Zapotec veterans. The Meijueiros acted as brokers for dozens of peasant families in the Sierra who received money from the government because they or their relatives had served in the National Guard. Every two or three months, as Monica Cruz explained, they would travel to Oaxaca City to collect their pensions from the Meijueiros, who had obtained the money from the state government. Since December 1888, Monica Cruz told Díaz, they had received nothing, "not a single centavo." The Ixtepejanos were upset with Díaz because Guillermo had told them "that you [Díaz] no longer feel anything for the people of the Sierra de Juárez." Guillermo claimed that the government had ended their pensions. But they believed he was lying to them, that he had simply taken the money himself, and so they put the issue squarely before the president: "On behalf of the widows and children of those Patriots who died for the Fatherland, those who loved you dearly, grant us your unflinching protective hand and in this way liberate us from the insatiable avarice of those traitors and assassins of our dearly departed martyr, Señor General Félix Díaz." Monica Cruz and the others played their trump card, reminding Díaz that throughout the Sierra only the people of Ixtepeji had supported his Plan of La Noria in 1871. Francisco Meijueiro, "Don Pancho" as Monica Cruz called him, had fought against the Díaz brothers. Surely Díaz would recognize the loyalty of the Ixtepejanos.[80]

After receiving Monica Cruz's letter in Mexico City, Díaz quickly dispatched a letter of inquiry to the Meijueiros in Oaxaca. Díaz's ire seemed to have been raised over this issue, and he intended to correct the problem. Although Guillermo had handled (or mishandled) the matter, Díaz wrote only to Francisco. In replying to Díaz, Francisco first claimed that Monica Cruz had not traveled to Oaxaca to pick up her pension. Then he said she had not presented her papers to the *jefatura de hacienda*, Guillermo's office, and so the pensions had been suspended. Finally, Francisco admitted that he was not fully informed on the entire affair and would have to look at it more carefully.[81] Two months later, in December 1889, Fernando Pérez learned through his own inquiries that his father's pension had been sold to a third party, a Juan Morales. Pérez pleaded with Díaz: "By these acts you should now be completely convinced Señor General, of the way Meijueiro has abused us and continues to abuse us because of our ignorance; and he is doing the same thing to other people through false representation; only he is capable of such a crime."[82]

More than likely, Guillermo had acted in the name of his father and had sold the pensions to a third party in an attempt to steal the money. He was young, impatient, and overconfident; he probably thought he could put off these peasants, and the theft would go unnoticed. But "El Gallo" had been an important leader of the Ixtepeji militia, and his family would not simply accept Meijueiro's explanation. For his part, Francisco Meijueiro consistently seemed uninformed about the case, though he denied any wrongdoing on his or his son's part. In the end, Díaz ordered the pensions restored to their proper recipients.[83]

The system of rewarding veterans and their families with government pensions was prone to corruption as long as middlemen handled the money for peasant recipients. But prior to 1888, for more than twenty years, the Pérez family had received the pension earned by Cenobio's years of military service. Clearly, Guillermo Meixueiro, as a representative of a new generation, did not fully comprehend the pact his father and Díaz had made with these citizen soldiers and their families. The incident over Monica Cruz's pension may have appeared minor to Guillermo, but it signaled the end of one era and the beginning of another. Although Guillermo no doubt had heard the stories of war and revolution from his father, the fundamental lessons that had been learned on the battlefield had not passed from one generation to the next. The importance of mutual cooperation, loyalty, and dedication to people born with fewer privileges than him seemed to elude the young Meixueiro.

Conclusion

Across south-central Mexico, but especially in the small mountain district of Ixtlán, Oaxaca, thousands of men and women had fought alongside Porfirio Díaz during the nation's civil wars and had supported his drive to become the nation's president. Although these people usually remain anonymous in the annals of Mexican history, Díaz knew who they were. In 1876 he traveled to Mexico City on their hopes and expectations that he could and would change their lives. They wrote to him in the president's office, sharing their personal stories of suffering and sacrifice, and humbly requesting both recognition and reward for their years of service. During the early years of the Porfiriato, Díaz and his political allies understood the terms on which they had gained power.

In Oaxaca, Francisco Meijueiro represented the face of both the state and federal governments to local populations. He settled land disputes, encouraged new industrial manufacturing, expanded mining operations, demanded fair contracts for railroad workers, and advocated for better schools and roads. He left Ixtlán and Oaxaca a better place than he had found it. But he also left behind the potential for major conflicts that could drive a wedge between the people of Ixtlán district and the government. The rancheros of Ixtepeji did not anticipate how much of their production they could lose to taxes and corruption. The owners of the textile factory, along with mine owners, wanted to make money and not necessarily make the people of Ixtlán district happy or keep them employed. Finally, there would be more disputes with veterans and their families regarding military pensions. Unfortunately for the Serranos, Francisco Meijueiro did not leave behind a more open democratic system of dealing with these conflicts. Díaz was not interested in such reforms; neither was the new generation of local political leaders. Instead, after Francisco Meijueiro's death in 1890, Zapotec peasants were forced to rely more and more on Porfirio Díaz's direct intervention to settle disputes with their neighbors and with local elites. As long as Diaz lived up to the promises of an earlier era, the people of Ixtlán district could challenge the effort to dismantle the consensus that had been forged on the fields of war. To survive, those stories would have to be passed to a new generation so that they could remind local, state, and national elites of the important role played by the people of the Sierra Zapoteca.

CHAPTER FIVE

Porfirians against the Regime, 1890-1906

Grant us the same considerations that we have always enjoyed.
People of Ixtepeji to Porfirio Díaz (1898)

After Francisco Meijueiro's death in 1890, men who had been too young to fight in the civil wars of the mid-nineteenth century began to dominate Oaxacan politics and business. As before, these men had close ties to Ixtlán district and the Zapotec people of that region. Guillermo Meixueiro stood at the center of this group. He was only twenty-seven years old when his father died, but he was responsible for a vast network of political and business transactions involving his extended family. Guillermo's first cousin Fidencio Hernández was another important member of this generation. Like their fathers before them, Guillermo and Fidencio attempted to use their ties to the militias and industries of Ixtlán district to bolster their influence in Oaxaca City. Other young men from prominent families also began to enter the small circle of Oaxacan public life. Jacobo Grandison inherited the Xía textile factory from his father, Thomas, and then expanded his family's real estate holdings into gold mines and coffee plantations throughout central Oaxaca. Emilio Pimentel, a young intellectual originally born and educated in Oaxaca, became an active member of the group surrounding President Díaz known as the *científicos*. Pimentel returned to Oaxaca in 1902 as Díaz's handpicked governor, eager to put into practice the social ideals he had helped formulate in Mexico City. Félix Díaz, the president's nephew, was an opponent of Pimentel's. He had encouraged a grassroots campaign to become Oaxacan governor but was reprimanded and punished by his uncle for acting unilaterally. Finally, Benito Juárez Maza, the son of the hero of the Reform, assumed a position in the national legislature and began laying the groundwork for his own run at the Oaxacan governorship. Not surprisingly, the young Juárez Maza was most popular in the Sierra Zapoteca, the birthplace of his father.[1]

Although their names were familiar to almost every Oaxacan, this group of young elite businessmen and politicians failed to reproduce the system of benevolent patriarchy that had characterized the relationship between their fathers and rural populations. These men, and many more of their generation, had come of age during the Porfirian era of political stability and relative economic prosperity. They had been raised during the triumphant years of liberal ascendancy, missing out on the monumental struggles faced by their fathers. As they learned in school and heard repeated at state-sponsored commemorative events, the liberal victory had been preordained because of its merits. They did not fully realize that the actual outcome had been uncertain and precarious, nor did they understand how important ordinary peasants had been to the liberal cause. As privileged individuals, they assumed it was their birthright to direct local, regional, and state politics. As a group, they were uninterested in placating the interests of the majority underclass of Indian peasants in Oaxaca.

Generational changes had also begun to shape political and social life in rural Oaxaca. In Ixtlán district, for example, most Zapotec veterans who had fought alongside Porfirio Díaz and Francisco Meijueiro did not live to see the new century.[2] The impact of losing these men was profound. In just one case in the town of Ixtlán, Manuel Jiménez, Estanislao Jiménez, Luciano Ruiz, and Julio Hernández had served on the town council throughout much of the early Porfiriato. They all passed away in the 1890s, and, as some disgruntled observers noted, a new group of "*jovenes*," or young men, assumed the responsibilities of town leadership. Critics claimed that the younger generation of Zapotec peasants did not share the same sense of loyalty and comradeship with neighboring communities as those who had fought in the civil wars.[3] The district-wide cooperation and sense of unity that had grown from fighting in the Ixtlán National Guard were slowly giving way to politics based primarily on community interests.

Still, enough "*antiguos soldados* [old soldiers]" survived to keep alive the memory of a political culture that emphasized cooperation and consensus within and between Zapotec communities and local elites. When confronted by foreign businessmen, expanding corporations, or urban politicians, Zapotec communities could quickly reassemble and make collective demands. Besides, these people had never interpreted the recognition and privileges granted to veterans as exclusive rights for them only. Just as Guillermo Meixueiro and Fidencio Hernández expected to assume the status of their fathers, Zapotec men and women believed that their elders had won broad citizenship rights for everyone in the district. Years of honoring both living and dead veterans on Independence Day and especially on Cinco de Mayo had taught them that they had all acted heroically to save the nation. The government's debt to its soldiers and their heirs could not be a onetime payment; it had to be an ongoing social relationship built around trust and reciprocity. And the Zapotec peasants of Ixtlán district believed they had one powerful ally in their struggle against the new attitude and arrogance of the young mestizo elite— their former jefe político, Porfirio Díaz.

This chapter highlights the complicated transitional years of the Porfiriato when the consensus of heroic patriarchy was challenged by a new generation of men who did not understand or appreciate the role Zapotecs had played in establishing the regime and in maintaining its legitimacy. As a new generation of men assumed positions of authority within and over the district of Ixtlán, the underlying tensions between rich and poor and the struggle for survival that pitted one community against another rose to the surface. The irony of these post-1890 conflicts was that Mexico was experiencing an unprecedented era of presidential continuity amid an even more spectacular period of economic growth. Clearly, the fundamental problem after 1890 was not the threat of civil war or the frustration with a stagnant economy. Rather, conflicts increased because a new generation of men initiated a unilateral and heavy-handed approach to controlling regional politics in Oaxaca. At the same time, peasant veterans and their families still expected a more open and cooperative approach to managing the affairs of their communities, and therefore they initiated more direct forms of resistance as they tried to reconnect to the political practices of an earlier generation. The slow erosion of a Porfirian consensus began in 1890 and had completely collapsed by 1906.

Significantly, Porfirio Díaz himself, along with other appointed bureaucrats, tried to defuse the social conflicts between rural populations and local elites. In Ixtlán district, even the jefe político was directed at times to protect the interests of the Zapotec peasants against the avarice of wealthy landowners and businessmen.[4] But local elites pursued their own interests, even if they had to go against the wishes of Porfirio Díaz to do so. In effect, the Porfirian ruling faction in Oaxaca split much earlier than the rebellion initiated by Francisco I. Madero in 1910, though the Oaxacan break remained nonviolent and far more subtle. For the most part, however, peasant communities were forced to struggle on their own for the protection of their political and economic rights. They simultaneously fought against the authoritarian impulses of Guillermo Meixueiro and for a return to the implicit consensus they had shared with his father. In that sense, their struggle was both for and against patriarchal order.[5] If we pull apart this apparent contradiction, we can see more clearly the actual issues at stake in Ixtlán district during the late nineteenth century. As a system of male control over social life in terms of culture, the economy, politics, and the family, "patriarchy" during the Porfiriato underwent profound transformations over time.[6] Gender and, more important, generational conflicts led rural and urban populations to use new explanations to connect Mexican history to contemporary politics. As the veterans of Mexico's civil wars began to die, archetypal symbols of nationalism, bravery, patriotism, and the family became even more important to Mexican citizens. Major disagreements between generations emerged when appeals to those symbols evoked divergent responses. The primary generational conflict during the Porfiriato did not come from the fact that Díaz and many of his advisors grew old in office and uninterested in the lives of ordinary Mexicans. The fundamental generational conflict in rural Mexico came from the interference of relatively young local elites in the daily lives of peasants who largely supported the regime.

In Oaxaca Guillermo Meixueiro tried to impose his will from the top down, pursuing his interests against all others. He had assumed the prerogatives of a caudillo without learning the reciprocal responsibilities inherent in that role. To counter Meixueiro's interference, Zapotec village leaders sought to maintain and/or strengthen their own patriarchal order within their communities. Marginal populations within the region—women, disfranchised mestizo peasants—would never be the primary beneficiaries of Zapotec communal politics. During the years 1890 to 1906, we find times when the former order of Francisco Meijueiro, Porfirio Díaz, and the peasant communities held sway, and other times when the interventionist tendencies of Guillermo Meixueiro, Fidencio Hernández, Jacobo Grandison, and Emilio Pimentel predominated. The back-and-forth struggle between these two trends played out through these years around a series of economic and political disputes.

Rather than follow a linear chronological explanation, I have organized this chapter according to the two patriarchal tendencies at work during this period. I begin by discussing the ways in which consensual politics continued after 1890. In disputes involving tax increases, water rights, and the role of the local jefe político, three elements of consensus-based politics emerged most clearly: (1) collective action; (2) limited protection and reward for peasant communities; and (3) recognition of the historic role played by Zapotec National Guardsmen. The second part of the chapter focuses on the breakdown of a consensus between ruling elites and rural popular classes. The slow assertion of an authoritarian impulse also came in three ways: (1) a breakdown in the cooperation between peasant communities, which led to more autonomous village action and greater intervillage conflict; (2) a breakdown of the cooperative working relationship between rural populations and local industries, which led to more frequent conflicts at the textile factory and mines; and (3) a breakdown of a political consensus around electoral politics at the state level and municipal politics within the district.

Collective Action and Taxes

Although many of the men who had formed personal friendships and political alliances based on a common military history had died by 1890, the Porfirian consensus shared between ruling-class elites and rural popular classes continued to influence significant political and economic transactions. Peasant communities could still coalesce around mutually agreed upon forms of collective action; state officials could still provide peasants with limited bureaucratic protection; and Zapotec peasants could still expect elites to recognize the historic military contribution of the Sons of the Sierra. The legitimacy of the Díaz regime, from the perspective of the Serranos, depended on the maintenance of this consensus. No issue threatened the potential for cooperation between peasants and the government as much as taxes. More than any other issue, the imposition of higher taxes, or even the rumor of a tax increase, would cause village leaders to convene district-wide meetings, write strongly worded protest letters, and threaten broad resistance. In simple terms, the Serranos expected exemption from higher taxes since they and their elders had fought in the civil wars of the mid-nineteenth century. Their presumed right to special consideration was a fundamental part of their identity as loyal Mexican citizens. If the government no longer respected them enough to grant them special status, then they would no longer respect the government. They found strength and courage in their collective action against higher taxes, and they found a way to continue to cooperate with each other.

Porfirio Díaz had originally used the issue of taxes to try to galvanize popular support for his rebellion in 1871. He had called for the abolition of the despised interstate taxes, the *impuestos de alcabala*, in his Plan of La Noria, but once he assumed the presidency Díaz moved slowly to make any significant tax changes. In 1886 he chastised his friend, Oaxacan governor Luis Mier y Terán, for attending a meeting of fellow state governors who wanted to unilaterally end the tax on goods traded between their states. Mier y Terán assumed Díaz had supported the abolition but pointed out that "in all frankness . . . the government of Oaxaca could not stay behind the others in regard to a question that seems on first glance to be progressive and useful."[7]

Individual head taxes posed a greater threat to rural populations than did taxes on trade. In 1896 the state government imposed a new head tax of five centavos on all citizens. As historian Francie Chassen-López explains, rural populations throughout the state reacted to the 1896 Ley de Hacienda with fierce opposition, generating in Oaxaca "the major indigenous protest movement of the Porfiriato."[8] People complained to their town councils, district jefes políticos, state legislatures, and governor. Peasants feared that the new tax would be collected but then spent paying off corrupt officials rather than improving the roads and transportation systems of the state as designated. Tax protests were especially intense in Zimatlán, Juquila, and Ixtlán districts.[9] For the people of Ixtlán district, the new tax was especially troublesome. They argued that they should be exempt from the head tax because they and their parents had successfully defended the nation against foreign invasions; they had fought for this government and for this president, and they expected special recognition for their efforts. With Porfirio Díaz's support, the state government granted the Serranos their request. On Wednesday afternoon, April 15, 1896, Zapotec officials from every town council in the district gathered in Ixtlán to receive official notification that they had been excused from paying the new head tax. Ramón González, the district jefe político, called the meeting to order and read a letter from the state governor. On hearing of their exemption, the room full of Zapotec men erupted into shouting, cheering, and whistling. They shouted "*Vivas*" to the state government, "*Vivas*" to President Díaz, even "*Vivas*" to the Ley de Hacienda from which they were now free.[10] Their exemption was a huge victory, a true sign that they could expect ongoing special rights and privileges as a result of their military service to the nation.

After the room quieted down, Ramón González again addressed the audience. Several newspapers in Mexico City had reported that widespread unrest regarding the new tax had taken place in several parts of Oaxaca, including Ixtlán district. The newspapers were correct, but González complained that they had misrepresented their actions and opposition. "They have accused us of acting contrary to civilized society and the principles of humanity," González told the assembled crowd. The good reputation of the Sierra had been damaged by these reports of "barbarism" and unrest. In response, González encouraged the Zapotec leaders to draft a collective letter to their fellow citizens throughout the district and to share that letter with the newspapers. The letter began, "To the Brave People of the Sierra. You have demonstrated on numerous occasions, as History will bear witness, that you are patriots and good liberals. During times of Mexico's greatest afflictions, our dear patria has counted on your support, which you extended spontaneously and without selfish interests." The letter explained that the people of Ixtlán district had received exemption from the tax because of their historic contribution to the nation, and not because they had organized an opposition movement that had threatened the social order. Their collective action in 1896 echoed the collective spirit with which they had fought in the civil wars of an earlier era, and they continued to act together as they publicly expressed their support for their president. In a highly ritualized endorsement, all of the municipal presidents signed a petition supporting Díaz's candidacy for another term as president. Clearly, the Zapotec leaders believed their familiar relationship with Díaz had protected them once again and they were eager to see that he continue to serve as president.[11]

The unusual recognition and protection afforded to the people of Ixtlán district bothered state officials. Governor Martín González resented the special treatment these people received, but he could do little to undermine their privileges since the primary order coming from Mexico City was to keep them satisfied and calm. In 1902 a new jefe político in the district explained to President Díaz that the people were still not willing to pay higher taxes. There was no way to force them to pay more taxes, Salvador Bolaños Cacho told Díaz. Rather, we should "calm the sons of this place, and with affection rally them in an era of peace and respect."[12] The jefe político insisted on negotiating with the Serranos, seeking a way to make the case for higher taxes without offending their sense of history and privilege. He did not suggest a heavy hand, the stick and boot so often described as political practice during the Porfiriato. But the Serranos were unwilling to compromise on taxes. They found no legitimate reason to pay higher taxes and consistently refused to do so. They also were aware that other individuals, especially wealthy landowners, received tax advantages. The Sons of the Sierra expected no less.[13]

Although their reputation for challenging new taxes was widely known, each new Oaxacan governor found it necessary to try to test the resolve and ability of the Zapotec communal leaders to organize an opposition movement against higher taxes. In 1904 Governor Emilio Pimentel proposed an increase in personal head taxes. He originally wanted to double the tax to ten centavos per person but was concerned about causing unrest among the *"clase prole-taria"* as he called them, especially among the Zapotecs of Ixtlán. Pimentel proposed a "compromise" with the Serranos. In order to avoid "the alarm so frequent among us, especially on the issue of new taxes," Pimentel asked Díaz if an increase of three centavos would be satisfactory. Almost everyone in the state was willing to go along with this increase, Pimentel told Díaz, everyone except the people of Ixtlán district: "It seems they are preparing to create difficulties for me, even though I took great pains to explain the mat-ter to them and despite the special treatment that the government constantly grants them so as to keep them happy."[14]

Díaz wrote back a month later in a somewhat cynical tone, advising Pimen-tel to go forward with the smaller increase. Díaz said that if he received any complaints, he would simply explain that the tax was unequivocal, except for those who had served the nation during times of war and who could prove it with documents from governmental archives. Díaz reassured Pimentel that only a very few veterans were still living.[15] But Díaz seriously underestimated the broad interpretation of rights that veterans from the Sierra Juárez as-sumed. They believed that individual veterans should be granted special privi-leges, and so should their families who had made sacrifices of their own. Everyone in the district should therefore be excluded from the new taxes. When the policy went into effect, the Serranos blamed Pimentel for ignoring their historical contribution to the nation. They initiated a broad opposition movement directed at forcing Pimentel from office. They also began to sus-pect that Díaz had forgotten about the promises he had made to them.

Negotiating Contracts

In addition to favorable treatment regarding tax increases, state officials granted Zapotec communities limited protection in preparing long-term con-tracts between native town councils and capitalist investors. To that extent, Zapotec village leaders and state officials pursued an unwritten but widely shared notion of the importance of working together on protecting the inter-ests of native people in the district. While consensus politics remained viable, cooperation rather than confrontation predominated.

Issues surrounding water rights have received far less attention in the his-torical literature on rural Mexico than have land disputes, though in many cases conflicts over water mattered as much or more than those over land.[16] In fact, after the turn of the century, when foreign investors sought even greater opportunities in rural areas, water rights became the most important source of cash revenue for Indian municipalities. But because water was also so important for maintaining subsistence agricultural plots, leasing water rights to a mineral processing plant or a hydraulic-powered factory could undermine food supplies. The standard interpretation of Porfirian disregard for the interests of rural populations, especially on issues involving foreign economic exploitation, fails to explain the ways in which Oaxacan state bureaucrats intervened on issues of water resource management. Instead, consistent with the earlier era of consensus-based politics, Porfirian officials aggressively protected the interests of Zapotec communities in the face of unfair or potentially harmful water contracts.

In 1901 American George S. Clark signed an agreement with the Zapotec villages of Lachatao, Amatlán, and Yavesía for use of the water in the river "Las Vigas." Clark owned several mines in the district and planned to build a processing plant powered by hydraulic generators. With promises of employment opportunities, village leaders agreed to give Clark access to the water free for twenty-five years and then charge him seventy-five pesos per year for another twenty-five years.[17] Fidel Sandoval, a secretary for the governor, reviewed the contract before the state government would approve it. Although he was under tremendous pressure by the district jefe político to endorse the agreement, Sandoval carefully read the document, looking for any prejudicial clauses that might eventually harm the villagers. He sought more information about where the river began, its exact course, its depth, the volume of water it normally carried, and whether other villages or businesses used the river. The jefe político provided Sandoval with the information he requested and impatiently urged final approval of the contract in order to settle the matter.[18]

Sandoval still had serious reservations about the contract, however. "The concessions appear too broad," he explained to the governor. In particular, Sandoval was concerned that Clark did not have to pay rent for the first twenty-five years, nor did he have to pay any indemnification for building an aqueduct over private or communal property. Sandoval proposed significant changes to the agreement. The concession could still be for fifty years, but Clark would be exempt from paying rent for only the first ten years. After that, Clark would pay 150 pesos per year instead of just 75, a 300 percent increase in the total cost of renting the water. Clark was also required to pay for any damage to property along the aqueduct route. Moreover, he was prohibited from subletting his rights without prior approval of the village town councils, and he had to pay any filing and legal fees. Finally, rather than simply promising to provide jobs for village residents, Clark had to agree in writing that he was obliged to hire "capable and honorable residents of the contracting villages."

After reviewing the new contract as amended by Sandoval, the villagers met with Clark in Ixtlán, and all parties signed the agreement.[19] Sandoval clearly had the best interests of the villagers in mind.

This case was not an isolated example of Sandoval's protection of peasant interests, nor did Sandoval act alone. The demand for greater access to water increased during the mining boom of 1895 to 1907, and many villages were being pressured to lease their rights to nearby rivers and streams. If Zapotec villagers signed unfair contracts, unrest and dissatisfaction would surely build. Clearly, it was in the best interest of the state government to protect villagers as much as possible. Sandoval similarly reviewed and revised water-leasing agreements between Jacobo Grandison and the town council of Tlazoyaltepec in Etla district. And in some cases Sandoval simply refused to allow water contracts to go into effect. Even Fidencio Hernández, one of the mestizo strongmen of the Sierra, could not get a water contract he sought. Sandoval advised the governor that renting the water that Hernández requested would cause too much disruption for the people in the area.[20]

In addition to relying on state bureaucrats like Sandoval, Zapotec town councils often hired their own representatives to negotiate favorable contracts with foreign and Mexican businessmen. Several towns, including Ixtepeji, Guelatao, Chicomezuchil, and Lachatao, hired José Ruíz Jiménez to represent their interests in political and economic transactions. Ruíz Jiménez's father, Rafael, was originally from Ixtlán district and rose through the military to become a colonel during the French Intervention. José benefited enough from his father's military career to obtain a modest education, which enabled him to gain a position as a scribe in the Secretaría de Gobierno of the state of Oaxaca. During his tenure as a professional writer, Ruíz Jiménez learned the convoluted and formulaic language of official correspondence. He also developed a distinct calligraphy, which gave his letters a polished and sophisticated look. In 1886, at age twenty-nine, Ruíz Jiménez abandoned his government position and began a long, frustrating career as a representative for town councils and individuals from the Sierra Juárez who had business with Oaxacan and federal officials. He fancied himself as a self-taught legal and technical advisor, as someone who could aid the uneducated peasants of Ixtlán district and make a handsome profit doing so. During the last two decades of the Porfiriato, Ruíz Jiménez wrote dozens of letters to President Díaz and to Oaxacan governor Emilio Pimentel, letters that most often complained of the unfair treatment his ideas of reform had received. When he began advising Zapotec communities in Ixtlán on various land, water, and political disputes, he earned the animosity of regional elites who resented his interference. But Ruíz Jiménez was an eloquent and assertive representative, who easily convinced villagers of his usefulness. He presented himself as a fellow Serrano—indeed, he could speak Zapoteco—and he openly challenged state and district officials (in whom many people had only limited confidence anyway). In short, he was a *Guadiaa*, a chronicler possessed with the knowledge of reading and writing texts.[21] In many situations, Zapotec town councils turned to Ruíz Jiménez because they felt overwhelmed by the opportunities for profit or loss as Mexican landowners and foreign capitalists tried to expand their investments in Ixtlán district.

The Role of Jefes Políticos

As the regional economy heated up after 1890, even the district jefe político found it necessary to defend the rights and interests of peasant communities against intense pressure by mestizo landowners. There are few detailed studies of the role of the jefes políticos in rural Mexico during the Porfiriato, but most historians generally regard these rural strongmen as oppressive and brutal representatives of the dictatorial regime.[22] In Ixtlán district, however, the jefe político often tried to protect the rights of peasant communities against an onslaught of elite intervention. The men who occupied the office of jefe político in Ixtlán were probably not so different than their colleagues around the country; they simply had to deal with a more assertive population, who had personal and historic relationships with the president. Zapotec peasants were more willing to complain about abuses and hardship directly to President Díaz; and Díaz occasionally responded to their pleas for help, often enough, at least, to keep the abuses of the jefe político in check. The jefe político's most important task was to maintain peace and stability in his district, but he could only do his job if the peasants did not accuse him of corruption and turn Díaz's eye on his actions. The peasants of Ixtlán guaranteed that the jefe político would consider the majority population in carrying out his responsibilities.

If the role of the Ixtlán jefe político provides an alternative to the standard interpretation of abuse and intimidation at the hands of local officials, then it was because mestizo elites held unofficial positions of authority and power within the region. In many ways, the Ixtlán jefe político had to protect peasants against the aggression and interference of nominal allies of President Díaz. Men like Guillermo Meixueiro and Fidencio Hernández did not hold formal office, but they contributed directly to the growing conflicts within the region. The situation was further complicated by the fact that the actual jefe político changed frequently in Ixtlán district, perhaps because Meixueiro and Hernández could never find someone to be their lackey. Men would often serve short terms of just one or two years. After working in Ixtlán, many men advanced to higher statewide positions within the government. If things went well, the office of jefe político in Ixtlán district could be a stepping-stone to higher political appointments and opportunities.[23]

In contrast, the man often accused of causing problems for Zapotec communities was the secretary to the jefe político, Federico H. Toro. Toro's father, Manuel, had been a well-known officer in Díaz's regular army and had settled in Ixtlán district on a ranch near Ixtepeji. Through his father's connections and his own hard work, Federico Toro served as the secretary to the jefe político for more than twenty years. Over the same period, Toro simultaneously held the offices of district postmaster and stamp agent. It was the frequent transitions within the jefe político's offices that allowed Toro to consolidate for himself many of the administrative, judicial, and police powers of the office. Oftentimes, Zapotec peasants would simply ignore the current jefe político and complain directly of the abuses at the hands of his secretary. But Toro had a softer side as well. He enjoyed classical music, poetry, and rural folk stories. He mastered several musical instruments and passionately conducted regional orchestras on special occasions. In many ways, Toro embodied the quintessential man of the Porfiriato; he balanced a love of the "progressive" arts with a demand for local autocratic power.[24]

Despite, or perhaps because of, Toro's interference, the particular appointment of a jefe político in Ixtlán district was always a delicate issue. For example, in 1899 Governor Martín González wanted to make a new appointment, but he feared antagonizing the people of the district. He agonized over his decision, consulting directly with Díaz and openly expressing his desire that the new jefe político would be acceptable to the people of the district. After some deliberation, González appointed Sebastián Trejo Zerril, someone he believed "could get along well in Ixtlán." Nevertheless, González feared that Trejo Zerril might have difficulties since "some malcontents from the *Cabecera* have started to cause trouble."[25] Significantly, Díaz expressed equal interest in the appointment. He wanted to know how much the jefe político position paid—130 pesos per month—and he wanted to be kept informed on Trejo Zerril's progress.[26] A similar situation presented itself in 1902 when the Ixtlán jefe político, Salvador Bolaños Cacho, was reassigned to the jefe político position in Tlaxiatac. When word spread to the communities that Bolaños Cacho was leaving, hundreds of Zapotec men gathered to protest his departure. Bolaños Cacho had effectively limited Toro's abuses, they claimed; Salvador was the only man who could maintain peace throughout the district.[27] However, the decision had already been made to transfer Bolaños Cacho, and the plea from villagers was ignored. Just as the letter-writers had warned, the new jefe político, Lázaro Ruiz, could not peacefully negotiate the disputes that were growing between native communities, elite landowners, and industries. In 1904 Ruiz formally asked for military aid to help him calm disturbances in Calpulalpam, Natividad, Ixtepeji, and other points throughout the district.[28]

As in Ixtlán, other rural districts in central Oaxaca required the jefe político to negotiate conflicts rather than impose a resolution by force of arms. In fact, archival data suggest that many jefes políticos had severe limitations on the amount of coercion that could be used to settle disputes. In the district of Villa Alta, for example, the jefe político had to carefully negotiate land disputes and could not unilaterally impose his decisions. But even in these cases, peasants understood that negotiations did not necessarily mean that their interests would be protected. For example, José Luciano Zuñiga from the village of San Francisco Cajones in Villa Alta district complained that the jefe político was a lawyer; therefore, "it is in his interest to have the villages in continuous upheaval so that he can more easily exploit us, even as he claims to defend our interests." Significantly, the jefe político in Villa Alta was Miguel Meixueiro, one of Guillermo Meixueiro's cousins.[29]

Through their constant dialogue with Porfirio Díaz, Zapotecs effectively imposed significant limits on the unilateral authority of district jefes políticos. As long as Díaz listened to their complaints and responded enough to give them satisfaction, peasants could hold their relationship with Díaz over the heads of district officials. As for Díaz himself, rural Oaxacans, like most Mexicans, rarely if ever blamed the president for their problems. In fact, they had an unwavering perspective on good fortune. When political and economic events favored a particular village, they credited President Díaz for his paternal intervention, even referring to him at times as "Papá Grande."[30] When political problems went against the interests of a particular village, Zapotec peasants blamed local administrators and the state governor. Peasants did not publicly consider the possibility that Díaz had abandoned their particular cause; to do so would have dismissed the only possible chance they had at preventing or reversing the situation. For the same reasons, they almost always credited him for positive change. And because Díaz occasionally assumed the role of a deus ex machina in local politics in the Sierra Zapoteca, intervening in the affairs of the region from above, peasants granted him godlike qualities: he was all-powerful, all-knowing, and all-good. Once again, the contours of Catholic culture shaped the possibilities of Mexico's secular political culture. When bad things happened in Ixtlán, the contradictions of an omnipotent, omniscient, and benevolent ruler did not dissuade peasants from their steadfast allegiance to Díaz, at least not until 1906.[31]

The hegemonic order of the Porfiriato was based in large part on the negotiation and resolution of a political culture that celebrated a common military history, though the implications of that history meant different things for different people. Díaz and his middle-class supporters viewed the experiences of war much differently than did Indian peasants. For Díaz, individual citizens had been called to serve the nation, to preserve its institutions, and to protect its sovereignty. For the rural popular classes, entire communities had gone to war to protect their homes and their nation in times of political crisis. Over time, the contrast between these two historical views led to divergent notions of citizenship rights and privileges. In effect, ruling elites and rural popular classes answered these questions differently: who served, who sacrificed, and who deserved state aid?

In their correspondence with government officials, many letter-writers referred to themselves or their relatives as *antiguos soldados*, literally "old soldiers." In this context, however, the direct English translation of "old" for *antiguo* misses important connotations. An *antiguo soldado* was an old man, but the term implied more than chronological age. *Antiguo* also meant "former" and "past," while retaining a sense of ongoing relationships and commitments. Veterans and their families used the term *antiguo soldado* to express their continued loyalty to the nation and to remind political leaders that they still expected special recognition and privileges because of their years of service.[32] Díaz personally knew hundreds of them. Some veterans had known Díaz or his extended family before the civil wars of the 1850s, and many of them later served with Díaz during his numerous military and political campaigns in the state. If Juárez had become the distant ancestor, the founding father who had died to protect the nation, then Díaz became the living father, the patriarchal figure who could intervene to protect the lives of his metaphorical children. In effect, the Serranos embraced Díaz as an extended member of their communities. Once again, the people of the Sierra Zapoteca were not acting alone. Other Oaxacans and other rural Mexicans looked to Díaz in exactly this way. Some of them shared personal memories of having met the president. Others reminded Díaz of his ties to Oaxaca. Many rural Mexicans hoped Díaz would aid and support them like a father.

By reminding the president of a personal encounter at some time in the past, letter-writers hoped to establish a bond that could be used in the present. Enrique Romero claimed to have played on Díaz's Hacienda La Noria as a young child. Vicente Garcés, a veteran from the Oaxacan town of Jamilte-pec, recalled that his family had cared for Díaz in 1857, following the battle at Ixcapa. Díaz had been badly wounded, and Garcés's mother, aunt, and sister tended to his injuries. Jacinta R. de Perzabal reminded the president that she had brought him a drink of water in 1866 when he had stopped to make sure his sister and niece were safe during the retaking of Oaxaca City. He had been badly wounded in the leg, Perzabal noted, but he had bravely refused to rest. Manuel Reyes claimed to have been the person who carried the Plan of La Noria from the printer's table to Díaz for his signature in 1871. Later, Reyes had been captured and imprisoned for his role in the La Noria rebellion.[33] It is difficult to determine if any of these encounters actually happened, though they all seem plausible. The subtext within these and other stories of chance encounters with the president pointed to a time in the past when Díaz had needed help. Letter-writers hoped that Díaz would reciprocate the aid that they had once extended to him.

Within and beyond Oaxaca, the most popular reference to Díaz projected him as father of the nation and, in many ways, as a surrogate father in the lives of ordinary citizens. One of the earliest examples of casting Díaz as a father figure came from his good friend Francisco Meijueiro. In 1889, after encour-aging Díaz to support the construction of a new bridge in Ixtlán district, Mei-jueiro described the importance of a paternal bond between the president and his people: "In any case I am determined to show the people of Oaxaca and the Serranos that only from you can we expect considerations as a fa-ther and that we should remain obligated to you as if we were your children."[34] This relationship required loyalty on the part of the Oaxacans and special considerations for development projects on the part of the president. Pater-nal relationships, as Meijueiro understood, encumbered both the father and his children. In 1903 Tomás Ramos echoed Meijueiro's sentiments exactly: "You know, my General, that all of the Republic considers you as a true father, particularly the state of Oaxaca and even more the soldiers of the Sierra de Juárez."[35] Similarly, from the village of Guelatao dozens wrote to Díaz express-ing their hope and satisfaction for his paternal intervention: "We know and understand that our affairs are in the hands of Papa Grande and we seek no other recourse."[36]

Women also wrote to Díaz. María Manzano, a woman from the Zapotec vil-lage of Analco, complained to President Díaz that a dispute with a neighbor-ing village had begun to threaten the civility and security of her community. Dictating her letter to a professional scribe, Manzano told Díaz that women deserved to be protected by the government because they too had served the nation: "During difficult times in the past, our fathers, husbands and sons were accompanied by their women and we too cooperated in the defense of our rights."[37] Significantly, Manzano assumed an adult status in her correspondence with the president. She referred to herself and the other women of the region as "*la mujer serrana* [the women of the Sierra]." There were, however, few people as bold and assertive as three Zapotec women from Ixtepeji. Josefa Jiménez, Mauricia Jiménez, and Juana Sabina Santiago wrote Díaz fourteen times in three months. Their six telegrams and eight letters complained about the abuses committed against their community by Guillermo Meixueiro. These women argued that they and their husbands deserved better because they all had served the nation when called upon. Their husbands had been veterans and had become rancheros on the land set aside in 1876. Their greatest concern was that Guillermo Meixueiro and his cronies had told them that Díaz no longer felt obligated to the Serranos: "They tell us that you no longer care for the Serranos, which is a clear attempt to upset us and disrupt the public order."[38] They were confident that Díaz would continue to grant them special privileges. Too many of them had risked their lives for him to so easily forget his obligations.[39]

The Slow Erosion of the Porfirian Consensus

From 1890 to 1906, the Porfirian consensus came under increasing pressure. The cooperation and goodwill that had carried Díaz to power in 1876 and had lasted during the early years of the regime began to ebb once a new generation of men assumed positions of authority and influence within the district and the state. Conflicts increased after 1890 on three fronts: (1) intervillage disputes over land divided the rural population and led to more autonomous rather than collective peasant action; (2) disagreements about managing and protecting the region's natural resources led to more frequent and volatile conflicts between peasants and industries; and (3) elite interference in municipal politics, coupled with Porfirio Díaz's imposition of handpicked governors, led to greater political disagreements. From the perspective of the men and women who believed they had been responsible for Díaz's military victories, the legitimacy of the regime was at stake. Díaz could either support the people who had always stood ready to defend him, or he could allow a new generation of men to destroy the spirit of consensus and cooperation that had once characterized his administration.

Land disputes between neighboring villages in the rugged mountains of the Sierra Zapoteca dated back at least as far as the early colonial period. Communal survival depended on maintaining adequate agricultural lands in order to feed local populations and to pay the onerous tribute taxes charged by Indian caciques for Spanish overlords. Land disputes continued after independence, but during the civil wars of the 1850s and 1860s, issues of national defense and political sovereignty forced most communities to set aside their disagreements over land. Even during the early years of the Porfiriato, from 1876 to 1890, most communities in Ixtlán district found ways to settle their disputes without state intervention. Beginning in 1890, however, the cooperation that had predominated for roughly an entire generation gave way to intense confrontation and hostility over landowning arrangements.

The ongoing conflicts between villages were exacerbated by middle-class demands for more land for commercial agriculture. In the summer of 1890, the Oaxacan state legislature ordered peasant communities to provide written title to the lands they farmed. As a first step in determining which lands remained unclaimed (*terrenos baldíos*), the state government intended to finally put into practice the December 1883 Colonization Law passed by the national Chamber of Deputies. The 1883 legislation was designed to put unused land into production and to "whiten" the racial mix of rural populations through European immigration. State legislators hired private surveyors to map unclaimed lands and planned on granting those lands to new European immigrants. In exchange for their work, the survey companies received title to one-third of the land they mapped. Although the underlying racialist premise of the 1883 legislation probably doomed the program from the outset, the practical application of the law as social policy failed since few European immigrants were interested in settling in rural Mexico. The potential economic gains of creating a small landowning class also failed since the survey companies ultimately received or purchased more than half of the land they surveyed. These companies were the only real beneficiaries of the 1883 legislation.[40]

In rural Oaxaca many communities resisted the 1890 land title requirement and only reluctantly agreed to mark off their properties. From their perspective, the new law could only diminish their farmlands since the state would learn that some communities farmed on parcels that did not legally belong to them. Other communities had more complicated landholding arrangements that would have been threatened by the new regulation. In Ixtlán district, for example, some communities farmed collectively and would have had difficulty determining exactly which lands belonged to which community. José Vásques, Felipe López, and Manuel Fernando Cruz, the municipal presidents of Yavesía, Amatlán and Lachatao, explained the problem this way: "Since time immemorial we have joined the communal property that belongs to our populations, without a fixed and determined line as to which particular lands belong to which village, having always enjoyed mutual use of these lands without the slightest problem." Typical of grassroots resistance to state intervention, these three municipal presidents dragged their feet in complying with the directive, requesting a two-month extension to complete the survey. If they were going to acquiesce to state regulations, they would do so on their own time.[41]

Zapotec communities in the central highlands had good reason to limit the state's intervention. Foreign investors were using the new laws to claim lands in all districts surrounding Ixtlán, and businessmen with direct ties to the Sierra Zapoteca were behind some of the largest transactions in the state. Jacobo Grandison, the English industrialist and owner of the textile factory at Xía, led this group. Taking advantage of the colonization law that favored foreign immigration, Grandison began a major land grab in the early 1890s. He already controlled a significant amount of land in Ixtlán district: the massive textile factory and all of the buildings on the property, as well as a dozen mines scattered throughout the district. But because Zapotec communities had successfully guarded the titles to most of their communal properties, Grandison and other land speculators could not buy large agricultural expanses in the district.[42] He turned his attention, therefore, to the districts surrounding Ixtlán. In 1891 Grandison requested a grant in Choapam district for more than four thousand hectares, nearly twice the legal limit allowed for a single individual. Grandison could avoid the size limitations by assigning portions of his land claim to his extended family—his sisters Isabel, Inés, and Regina and his Scottish brother-in-law Henry "Guillermo" Trinker, who managed the Xía textile factory. Three years after his request, Grandison received a colonization grant from the *secretaría de fomento*.[43]

Grandison intended to add this new property to his existing coffee plantation in Choapam district. The peasant populations living near Grandison's plantation, however, opposed his expansion and refused to acknowledge his ownership. Claiming that he had planted coffee trees beyond his property line, the peasants regularly entered the coffee orchards, harvested the beans of their own accord, and took other natural resources for their own consumption. Grandison could only complain to state officials: "They cut pine trees and take firewood; they tap rubber trees. . . . The Indians believe that they will always have a right to the things that grow wild in the forest even when those lands have been sold."[44] Indian peasants had other reasons for mistrusting coffee planters. Laborers were regularly mistreated on the coffee plantations; they were driven to work long hours, were sometimes cheated out of the pay they deserved, and were always vulnerable to exploitation at the stores managed by the plantations. Peasants would retaliate by stealing from the plantations or simply refusing to work for the most oppressive owners.[45] Clearly, tensions were high in the coffee zone, and Grandison and the other coffee planters who sought to expand their holdings were not interested in reaching a consensus with local peasants.

Grandison's thirst for more land continued unabated throughout the Porfiriato. In 1901 he purchased another 47,000 hectares in Choapam district, an incredibly large amount that made him one of the state's largest landowners. He also sought a potentially lucrative contract for the extension of a railroad line from Ejutla district to Huatalco on the Pacific coast.[46] During the years of rapid economic growth in Porfirian Mexico, the demand for land increased throughout Oaxaca, and Grandison and others like him sought a lion's share. The scale of this massive land transfer to foreign businessmen was felt throughout the state, including in Ixtlán district. As the pressure for land increased during these relatively prosperous years, intervillage conflict throughout the Sierra Zapoteca grew.

Intervillage Conflicts

There were numerous intervillage conflicts after 1890—between Ixtlán and Guelatao, Atepec and Analco, Teococuilco and Guelache, Ixtepeji and Tlalixtac, Las Llagas and Quiotepec—but the most protracted land dispute pitted the village of Abejones against Maninaltepec.[47] The duration and bitterness of this conflict, more than any other land dispute, demonstrated that the brief era of collective action between villages was coming to an end. The people of each village acted in their own interest, and state officials could do little to get them to cooperate. Ultimately, this conflict also revealed the weakness of the jefe politico, who could not force a settlement on either side. The conflict between Abejones and Maninaltepec began at an undetermined time but had its most divisive manifestations in 1896 and 1912. Maninaltepec held legal title to a small section of farmland located near the town of Abejones. People from Abejones had farmed the land prior to 1889, but Maninaltepec had never completely surrendered it. In 1889 leaders from the two villages signed an agreement giving Abejones the right to farm on the land until 1896, after which Maninaltepec would assume control over the property. In 1896, however, Abejones refused to surrender the parcel. Both sides prepared for armed conflict, while state officials scrambled to find a peaceful solution.[48]

On July 23, 1896, Ramón González, the district jefe político, ordered leaders from both towns to meet him at a neutral site in order to reach a final settlement. González wanted to end the conflict before it became even more complicated and perhaps violent. He was already too late. After Abejones had refused to surrender the land, Maninaltepec began renting it at a low price to villagers from Comaltepec, yet another neighboring village.[49] Maninaltepec leaders hoped to get the Abejones farmers off the land without risking any of their own labor or resources. Nevertheless, the July 1896 meeting appeared to produce results. In exchange for half of the year's harvest, Abejones agreed to surrender the land to the renters.[50]

By the end of the year, however, the municipal president of Abejones, Nestor Bautista, claimed that the settlement was unfair. "No one knows who owns it," Bautista complained to the jefe político.[51] Bautista also pled his case directly to Governor Martín González. "The situation is difficult and dangerous," Bautista wrote; "it seems, Señor Governor, that the authorities of Ixtlán pay no attention to our complaints." Bautista, who did not know how to read or write and so dictated his letters to a secretary, argued that the concessions were "absurd." "This agreement cannot be enforced," Bautista explained, "or take effect when it has not been legally ratified; and we further request that you grant us aid and protection so that neither our properties nor our lives will be attacked or offended." [52] The irony, of course, was that Abejones still had possession of the land and yet claimed to be the victim of abuse at the hands of the jefe político.

On the advice of the jefe político and the Secretaría de Gobierno, the state government of Oaxaca issued Resolution Number 6393 on December 16, 1896, to end the dispute between Abejones and Maninaltepec. The resolution simply ordered the two sides to abide by the original agreement of 1889. In protest, the town council of Abejones refused to attend any more meetings with the jefe político. Its members understood that possession continued to matter more than the written regulations or agreements. As his frustration grew, the jefe político ordered the arrest of Bautista and his cabinet, along with the arrest of village leaders from Maninaltepec and the renters from Comaltepec. González wanted to knock some heads together, intimidate the disputants with his authority, and force them to end their fighting.[53]

While Nestor Bautista sat in jail, his relative José Domingo Bautista acted as Abejones's municipal president. The new president dispatched a letter to the governor, notifying him of alleged abuses committed by the jefe político.

Villagers from Abejones had been jailed; two other people had disappeared and were feared dead. The people of Abejones felt isolated because, according to the municipal president, villagers from Yolox and Comaltepec had joined Maninaltepec. And still, Bautista told the governor, "the authorities in Ixtlán have done nothing about this and the *vecinos* [residents] of my town along with their leaders are suffering every kind of abuse and violence."[54] The governor grew concerned by the latest report from Abejones; perhaps the jefe político had gone too far. Governor González ordered an inquiry into the allegations made by the Abejones village leaders since more than anything else he wanted to maintain order.[55] In response to the governor's questioning, the jefe político reported that the people of Abejones were only trying to delay a transfer of the land: "Far from complying with the provisions, the municipal president of Abejones wants to bring these issues to a head; he admits that the entire village has invaded the land belonging to Maninaltepec." The jefe político also refuted charges that Yolox and Comaltepec had entered into the dispute, as those two villages were located some distance from the land in question. Nor was it true that the two "missing" men—Anastasio Bautista and Sixto López—had been killed since they had been seen recently in their village. The people of Abejones, according to the jefe político, "invent slanderous accusations of all kinds in order to secure some relief."[56] On this point, archival evidence supports the jefe político rather than the leaders of Abejones. By complaining directly to the governor, Abejones officials hoped to delay the land transfer for at least another year. The interesting point is that the governor felt compelled to investigate the allegations further. Abejones did not encounter an unsympathetic bureaucracy—a wall of silence—from which complaints from poor peasants received no reply. On the contrary, the people of Abejones followed a consistent and largely successful strategy of resistance in order to maintain their control over the land. Even with the threat of arrest, the jefe político was ultimately incapable of forcing a settlement that would be honored by both villages.

In November 1898 Abejones leaders reported to the governor that they had agreed to abide by the ruling granting the land to Maninaltepec. In actual fact, Abejones had held a town meeting at which residents had agreed to let the issue be settled by "impartial judges," a further delaying tactic since they knew it would take some time to organize the adjudication process. Village leaders anticipated the outcome, claiming that they were "tired of protecting the people from so many injustices that have resulted from this affair."[57] The dispute nevertheless resurfaced in 1900 and again in 1912 when Abejones leaders complained that "the question of land has never been fully settled."[58]

By 1912, however, an entirely new set of political circumstances would shape the tentative resolution of this dispute.

This case, more than any other land dispute, best demonstrates the relative weakness of the jefe político's office vis-à-vis direct action on the part of individual communities. Abejones leaders consistently claimed to be the victims of intimidation and harassment, but they had possession of the land. They publicly stated their desire for a final resolution, but in their minds the only acceptable resolution was their continued access to land that neighboring communities, legal documents, and district officials agreed belonged to Maninaltepec. No doubt intimidation took place, though there was actually very little violence. The jefe político's reaction to this conflict was one of frustration since he could not get the issue settled. And contrary to every assumption we have about the power of district jefes políticos, Ramón González could not end the dispute by simple decree. Even Governor Martín González expressed his frustration over the numerous land disputes involving Zapotec communities. As he lamented to President Díaz, "these questions about land and the abuses that have been committed, exploiting the Indians, demanding reports, obscuring the truth, they are a true challenge that only God will be able to sort out."[59]

Martín González had been a soldier, not a politician, a man of action unaccustomed to listening to the cacophony of complaints and accusations that erupted over intervillage land disputes. In desperation, González pledged to study the issues and to enact policies that would "avoid any conflict."[60] Clearly, Abejones had successfully multiplied the number of patriarchal authorities involved in this issue, diffusing the power of the jefe político by appealing directly to the governor and the president.[61] As a lasting consequence of this and other land disputes, Zapotec villagers began to question the motives of their neighbors. Greater pressure for land had pushed most of the communities to protect the limited resources under their control.[62] Although their parents had fought side by side to defend their homes and nation against foreign invaders, the men and women living in Zapotec communities after 1890 often found themselves at odds over basic issues of cooperation.

Conflicts with Capital

As with conflicts between villages, confrontations with capitalist industries grew after 1890. The irony, of course, is that Oaxaca's rural economy was expanding rather than contracting. Increased competition, and not limited deprivation, led to greater unrest in Ixtlán district. The dozens of gold and silver mines scattered throughout the district and the cotton textile factory at Xía became the immediate targets of peasant discontent.

In 1895 a sudden increase in the international demand for precious metals ignited greater interest in the Oaxacan mining industry. Foreign and Mexican investors looked to the potential of mines in the state, and most observers believed that Oaxaca was Mexico's "Land of Tomorrow."[63] In particular, the richest and most promising mining region in the state, the Sierra Zapoteca, became the focus of intense foreign investment. The state's largest gold and silver mine, Natividad, finally began earning a profit for shareholders after the 1895 boom. Porfirio Díaz, for example, received more than five hundred pesos in dividends in the fall of 1898 alone. His old friend Francisco Meijueiro would have been pleased to know that Natividad had finally paid off.[64] Still, familiar obstacles to growth continued to hold back more sustained economic expansion for Natividad. The need for new and improved roads throughout the district increased as traffic to and from the mine grew during the boom years, and the call for a railroad spur reaching Natividad became even louder.[65]

Other complaints surfaced for the first time. In 1900 Manuel Muñoz Gómez complained to President Díaz that certain factors prevented Oaxaca from reaching its potential in the mining industry. As a newcomer to Oaxaca, Muñoz Gómez wanted to invest in the region, especially in Ixtlán district, but the "provincialism" and "ignorance" of the working people concerned him. Muñoz Gómez thought it would be better to bring in more experienced laborers from northern Mexico.[66] But this suggestion would not have impressed Díaz. Jobs, rather than economic growth and profits, were responsible for maintaining peace and stability in the district. The mining boom may not have produced tremendous wealth for investors, but it guaranteed jobs for the people.

Oaxacan mines ultimately produced only a fraction of the anticipated profits, but the mining industry in Ixtlán district still changed dramatically during the boom years. New owners tried to impose new restrictions on Zapotec laborers, and the workers began for the first time to directly challenge the exploitative labor contracts under which they suffered. From 1879 to 1900, the number of mine claims in Ixtlán district remained relatively constant, ranging from forty-six to forty-one. Most of the mines remained idle, but they belonged to wealthy Oaxacans either living in the district or in Oaxaca City. In 1879 just twelve different families owned all of the mines. Miguel Castro owned twenty-two mines, by far more than any other individual. José Ferrat owned eight mines; Constantino Rickards owned six; and Pedro Meixueiro

TABLE 1. Mine Claims in Ixtlán District, 1879, 1900, and 1903

Year	Total Mine Claims	Foreign and Corporate-Owned Claims	Foreign and Corporate Claims as Percentage of Total
1879	46	7	14
1900	41	9	22
1903	82	42	51

Source: Archivo General del Estado de Oaxaca, Fomento 16-02, "Boleta para recoger datos sobre la industría mineria," April 13, 1900; Archivo General del Estado de Oaxaca, Fomento 16-05, "Boleta para recoger datos sobre producción de la minas," 1903.

owned three mines. Together with other wealthy investors, most of the Ixtlán mine owners also held shares in Natividad. By 1900, only modest changes had taken place among the mining elite in the district. Jacobo Grandison owned twelve mines, mostly purchased from Miguel Castro or his estate. The Meixueiro clan (Pedro, Gonzalo, Ramón, and Manuel) owned nine mines, and Constantino Rickards still held four. As before, many of these men also owned shares in Natividad.[67]

By 1903, however, significant changes had taken place within the mine-owning class itself (see table 1). First, the number of mine claims doubled in just three years, growing from forty-one to eighty-two. Second, foreign investors and corporations had taken over a major share of the mines, especially the new mine claims. Corporations owned twenty mines and claims in 1903, compared with just three in 1900; foreigners owned claims to twenty-two mines in 1903, compared with just six in 1900.[68] Although most of these new properties were simply claims and not fully operating enterprises, the increased competition caused by the new investors led to conflicts that had never before existed. The experience of workers at Natividad demonstrates these problems best.

During the boom years, the labor force at Natividad expanded to nearly five hundred men and women, who worked continuous shifts to get the ore out of the ground, processed, and on its way to the city.[69] Significantly, mine workers at Natividad were paid wages well below the national average and relied heavily on the informal trade of ore to supplement their meager earnings. Serranos earned only one peso per day for working in Natividad, compared with the three pesos per day mine workers could earn in other parts of the country. In general, Mexican miners were paid according to nationality and ethnic background, rated by the number of expected tons loaded per day: "Americans loaded ten tons per day, Blacks eight tons, Italians six tons, Japanese five tons, Chinese four tons, and Mexicans only two tons."[70] Zapotec miners in Ixtlán, along with other Indian miners in the state, ranked even below "Mexicans."[71]

The Zapotec miners justifiably argued that they had a right to a *"pepena,"* a small chunk of ore acknowledged as a part of their wages. Illicit ore collection sparked a steady market in mercury, gunpowder, candles, picks, sacks, and other tools used to produce the tiniest grams of gold. Of course the gold itself was also traded. Zapotec men and women defended the practice of taking whatever they needed from the mine as part of their inherited ancestral rights and, most revealing, because they had defended the country against foreign invaders. Villagers argued that they had a right to take from the mines enough to satisfy their basic needs. This was no different, they claimed, than the people who went into the forest to gather wood for their fires, animals for their food, or lumber for their houses; it was just like the people who took salt from salt mines and water from rivers: "By the rights we have inherited from our ancestors and defended with our lives against foreign invasions, we are the owners of these lands, of all that is on the surface and beneath the ground. . . . Those who call themselves the owners of the mines have abused us in complicity with the government, taking advantage of our ignorance and poverty."[72]

During and after the boom years, administrators at Natividad tried desperately to limit access to abandoned mine shafts, waste piles, and runoff water used by their processing plant. They wanted to terminate the *"pepena,"* and to do so they would need to end the entire informal economy surrounding that practice. In 1904 Manuel Arreortúa and his brothers Andres and Pedro were charged with stealing from Natividad and imprisoned by the jefe político in Ixtlán. They had been panning the runoff waters from Natividad's processing plant, and officials had decided to make an example of them. However, they felt they had been unfairly accused and punished, they explained to Díaz, since people from throughout the district had done the same thing for generations. They asked Díaz for help, reminding him that they were the sons of José Eligio Arreortúa, a former comrade of Díaz's on the battlefield. Díaz ordered their release, though district officials were slow to acquiesce. It was becoming clear that the president had a different understanding of the rights of the Serranos than did this new generation of district officials and mine owners.[73] After the collapse of the mining industry in 1907, relations between workers and administrators at Natividad would become even more hostile.

By that time, however, Zapotec peasants realized that they were essentially on their own in their struggle against mine owners.

Tensions between Zapotecs and the owners of the cotton textile factory at Xía also grew after 1890. The people of Ixtepeji had always been ambivalent about the textile factory because they believed the land had actually belonged to them. But for more than a generation, the villagers had found a way to live with the factory so close to their community. Many Ixtepejanos worked there, and the town had signed a water lease agreement with factory owners. On January 13, 1893, Margarito Hernández, the municipal president of Ixtepeji, agreed to lease to Jacobo Grandison the water from the Grillo River. Grandison agreed to pay 60 pesos per year for nine years plus a signing bonus of 240 pesos.[74] For the people of Ixtepeji the river formed an essential part of their ancestral patrimony. Beginning at a point known by its Zapoteco name as "Xoo retze landa," the river was formed by the confluence of two streams, the "Xoo lo diss" and "Xoo manzanilla," and cut across land belonging to Ixtepeji. As with most geographic markers in the Sierra, all legal references to land and water used their Zapoteco names rather than their Spanish translations. These culturally specific titles imparted a sense of pre-Columbian ancestry, custom, and ownership rights.

The 1893 contract expired in 1902, and many Ixtepejanos expressed their desire to use the water for themselves rather than continue to rent it to the factory. Guillermo Meixueiro and Federico Toro tried to influence the internal debate going on within Ixtepeji by arranging for the election of their own candidate to the office of municipal president. But other Ixtepejanos complained to President Díaz, noting that in addition to problems surrounding their own municipal elections, "the jefe político is acting as if he were a direct representative of the factory at Xía."[75] Meixueiro and Toro were ordered to back off. Still, the net effect of their interfering in local politics guaranteed that many Ixtepejanos would oppose renting water to the factory. After the original contract expired, Pedro Illescas, the municipal president of Ixtepeji, presided over a town meeting to discuss the delicate issue of renting water to the factory. Illescas put the question to the assembly: should we continue to rent water to the factory, or should we use the water for our own fields? Illescas was against signing a new contract with the factory, and he wanted government officials and the owners of the factory to know that he was prepared to abandon the rental agreement. He spoke for the faction that believed the town would have to irrigate more agricultural lands to feed their growing population.[76] Felipe Santiago, president of the ranchero syndicate, spoke next. He argued that the community should negotiate a new contract with Grandison, but one based on new assumptions with higher fees. The people needed to convey the importance of the water, Santiago noted. This water represented a life force running through the community; the people of Ixtepeji shared a spiritual bond with this water that must be taken into consideration. Then Santiago invited the other men to speak on the subject as well.[77]

After a long discussion, the men decided they would rent the water to the factory, but that the price would rise to 500 pesos per year. They still wanted a nine-year contract, and they promised that they would guard the river while the factory leased the water. As the meeting ended, the entire assembly agreed that the village had made a significant sacrifice by surrendering their rights to the water. They could have used the river to irrigate more crops, but they were willing to make this concession in the best interest of the regional economy.[78] Two months after this meeting, the company still had not responded to Ixtepeji's terms for a new contract, and the villagers were beginning to get angry. They complained to the governor, noting that the old contract had expired at the start of the year; surely the need for a new agreement was obvious to everyone.[79] Ultimately, the factory owners would delay the signing of a new agreement for nearly two full years—until late December 1903. They continued to pay for the water, but they paid only sixty pesos per year as in the previous agreement. Nor did the Ixtepejanos get the five hundred pesos per year that they had originally sought. Grandison and his brother-in-law Guillermo Trinker agreed to pay only 150 pesos per year.[80] A lasting bitterness toward Grandison settled over many of the Ixtepejanos who had attended the 1902 meeting to draft a new contract. Some Ixtepejanos blamed Guillermo Meixueiro for not supporting their demand for a fair contract. Others simply ignored the contract and used the water for their own irrigation needs.[81] But the lingering hostility between the factory owners and the people of Ixtepeji was far from over. In 1912 an armed rebellion against district officials would begin at the factory, and many of the Ixtepeji soldiers would seek their revenge.

Political Disputes

In many ways, the 1912 revolt was directed as much toward Guillermo Meixueiro as it was against the factory. After his father died, Meixueiro abandoned all restraint in trying to control Ixtepeji politics from the inside. Rather than pursue the slower and more unpredictable path of cooperation and negotiation, Meixueiro simply tried to have his own candidate become municipal president. He succeeded in 1898, when he rigged the election of Pablo

Cruz. But, as Meixueiro should have expected, many other Ixtepejano peasants complained to President Díaz about Meixueiro's meddlesome interference in their communal affairs. Margarito Hernández, for example, challenged the fraudulent elections that placed Cruz in office. In retaliation, Cruz arrested Hernández and several other men and had them thrown in jail. Pánfilo Méndez also complained that no one from Ixtepeji had voted for Cruz. Accusing Cruz and Meixueiro of trying to arrange a sweetheart deal with Jacobo Grandison of the Xía textile factory, Méndez told President Díaz that "these traitors want to continue selling the blood of the Sierra."[82]

Cruz eventually went too far in abusing his opponents in Ixtepeji, and Guillermo Meixueiro could no longer protect him. Along with his allies Tereso Hernández and Pablo Castellanos, Pablo Cruz violated the sanctity of Ixtepeji's church by removing important relics, including objects buried with former priests in the high altar. Meixueiro was then forced to remove his crony from the municipal office, temporarily holding him in jail in the town of Ixtlán. It was clear, however, that a majority of Ixtepejanos wanted even greater punishment for Cruz. An influential group of village elders asked President Díaz to exile Cruz to some distant part of the country. As they had repeated in so many other letters to the president, this group of men asked that their rights be respected because of "the important and loyal services that our dear fathers and some of those present with us have given in defense of the Republic."[83]

Predictably, as Guillermo Meixueiro increased his interference in communal politics, Ixtepejano peasants had to look for legal aid beyond their community.[84] They turned most often to José Ruíz Jiménez. But Ruíz Jiménez's involvement only made Meixueiro even more determined to control a "dissident" town like Ixtepeji. A rising spiral of hostility, fueled by charges and counteraccusations, developed between Meixueiro and the people of Ixtepeji. When Meixueiro could no longer have his own candidate run the town, he tried to remove his most vocal opponents by having them forcibly conscripted into the military. In one case in 1898, Meixueiro used the pretense that a group of men had stolen a bull and should therefore be forced into the army. However, an organized group of Meixueiro's opponents quickly dispatched a letter to Díaz: "Continue to grant us the same considerations that we have always enjoyed so that our brothers will not be consigned to the army, but that the crimes or errors that they have committed may be judged and punished in our tribunals in compliance with existing laws." This same group of Ixtepejanos pointed out to Díaz the irony of unfairly compelling them to serve in the military. They had always volunteered to serve the nation during times of crisis, and it was because of that service that now their rights as citizens should be respected: "You know good and well that when the Nation was threatened all of us bravely and willingly volunteered, leaving our families and our homes to spill our blood in defense of the Government and our institutions; we have always been prepared to offer our humble personal service if it were necessary." Díaz ordered Meixueiro to allow the accused to go free.[85]

Still, Meixueiro resorted to forced conscription at other times after the 1898 incident. In 1906 Meixueiro arrested Eusebio Hernández from Ixtepeji and prepared to have him conscripted into the military. Eusebio's father, Antonio Hernández, turned to José Ruíz Jiménez for help. The elder Hernández spoke only Zapoteco and needed the aid of a translator to make the case that Meixueiro had unfairly harassed his son. Once again, Díaz ordered Meixueiro to release the young man.[86] Antonio Hernández may not have spoken Spanish, but he understood the underlying reasons behind Guillermo Meixueiro's bold interference in communal politics throughout the district, especially his intervention in Ixtepeji. Meixueiro wanted to become governor. In order to become governor, Meixueiro needed to consolidate his "electoral base" within communities by controlling votes through the local town councils. He also wanted to secure greater revenues in the form of taxes and tribute that village councils would dedicate to him for legal representation and "protection." Finally, Meixueiro's plan to become governor included a scheme to convince President Díaz that peace and stability in the region, and by extension the entire state, depended on Meixueiro's ability to settle disputes. Unrest played into Meixueiro's hand since he would either be called on to settle the conflict through expensive negotiations or paramilitary force. Many peasants, however, already had their favorite candidate for governor, the president's nephew Félix Díaz. As Antonio Hernández related to the president, "Don Félix Díaz will be our shield and our flag in every situation."[87]

Meixueiro's actions during the 1890–1906 period and the responses they generated by peasants suggest that the major issue at stake for everyone involved was control over the electoral process and the state governor's office. In 1894 President Díaz began to intervene even more directly in Oaxacan state politics, installing his friend and ally General Martín González as Oaxacan governor. González proved to be an unpopular governor, both alienated from the Oaxacan ruling classes, who saw him as an outsider, and disconnected from the popular classes, who viewed him as an unsympathetic autocrat. González practiced an unusual strategy when faced with sustained opposition on key decisions. When the local press openly criticized him, or when opponents rallied against his government, González would simply leave the state, temporarily forcing a constitutional transfer of power to an interim governor. When the criticism quieted down, he would return. During his tenure as Oaxacan governor (1894–1902), González spent nearly a third of his time outside of the state.[88]

President Díaz personally arranged González's first reelection in 1898 since few Oaxacans actively supported the governor.[89] In exchange, González granted Díaz veto power over key appointments to state and federal offices. In practice, however, the list of names promoted by González would have been pruned even before reaching the president's desk. Not surprisingly, Díaz's usual response, as it was in June 1899, was that "all of the friends whose names you mention are fine with me."[90] As González's second reelection approached in 1902, opposition to the state regime grew bolder and more widespread. Anti-González newspapers, the Oaxacan middle class, and Oaxaca's rural population favored a candidate they assumed would meet with Díaz's favor, his nephew Félix Díaz.[91]

Félix Díaz, like Guillermo Meixueiro, enjoyed a political pedigree more in line with Oaxaca's emphasis on military accomplishments and local ties—their fathers had both been generals and then governors of the state. Like most Oaxacans, the peasants of the Sierra Zapoteca enthusiastically supported the young Díaz as they sought a return to more familiar forms of patriarchy, though they had no real guarantee that Félix would meet their expectations. Unfortunately, from their perspective, President Díaz refused to endorse his nephew. Instead, the president ordered both González and his nephew to renounce their candidacies. González went into early retirement, and Félix Díaz was exiled to the Foreign Service for his unabashed self-promotion. As historian Peter Henderson has observed, President Díaz would not be pressured into action; he "treated Oaxacan politics as an exclusive, personal sphere in which he brooked opposition from nobody, not even members of his own family."[92] But the younger Díaz remained a popular symbol for many people, especially for the peasants of the Sierra Zapoteca. From 1902 to 1910 they continually wrote personal and community-wide letters to the president, asking that Félix Díaz become their governor.[93]

Porfirio Díaz, however, had plans of his own, and the first indications of a breach between the president and the Zapotecs who had always supported him began to emerge. Díaz selected Emilio Pimentel as the official candidate for governor, and he appointed Miguel Bolaños Cacho interim governor to handle the electoral process. Pimentel's political career was due entirely to the stability of the Pax Porfiriana. Born into a middle-class family in the Oaxacan city of Tlaxiaco, he was an intellectual, not a soldier, who was more impressed by nineteenth-century romantic poetry and classical music than by the heroic stories of military glory told by veterans. In an era of peace and stability, intellectuals like Pimentel could succeed in politics, which would have otherwise kept them on the margins. After graduating from the Instituto de Ciencias y Artes in Oaxaca in 1876, Pimentel enjoyed a long career serving both the state and federal governments. Most of his positions were administrative appointments granted by men of an earlier generation who had defended Mexico on the battlefield, men who had proven how to lead and how to speak the language of heroic patriarchy that permeated urban and rural Mexico. But Pimentel spoke a new language; he talked of reforms and ideas, of moral, intellectual, and economic progress. He had little concern for placating the sense of honor that moved so many ordinary peasants. Pimentel represented the generation that fell between Mexico's two great wars—the war against the French and the 1910 Revolution. His lack of military experience, along with his disregard for the military experiences of others, alienated Pimentel from significant sectors within Oaxaca.[94]

Pimentel began his political career as personal secretary to Oaxacan governor Luis Mier y Terán (1884–87), and later became a foreign consul in Rio de Janeiro, a federal deputy, and then municipal president of Mexico City. During his time in Mexico City, Pimentel cofounded the group of young intellectuals who became known as the *científicos*. He was an active member of the group, challenging especially Justo Sierra on issues of educational reform.[95] Although Oaxaca's political elite organized clubs and newspapers in support of Pimentel's election in 1902, they never fully sympathized with a governor who was imposed on their state. Guillermo Meixueiro, the prominent lawyer and landowner from the Sierra Zapoteca, had hoped to become Díaz's candidate in 1902. Along with other opponents of Pimentel, Meixueiro appeared in a newspaper article critical of Díaz's decision. The Porfirian ruling class in Oaxaca was beginning to come apart.[96]

Once Pimentel's election was a certainty, however, Meixueiro tried desperately to reassure President Díaz that he remained a loyal supporter. In a long, four-page letter to Díaz, Meixueiro spoke as a wayward son, as a younger man caught going behind his elder's back. "Allow me to offer a simple and loyal explanation," he began. "Because of sincere convictions, I was not a friend of General González; my sympathies were wholeheartedly in favor of the candidacy of Major and Engineer Félix Díaz." Nevertheless, Meixueiro understood the political realities of his day, and he granted Díaz unflinching support: "I recognize that you have the authority to advise us and intervene with a decisive vote in our affairs."[97] Díaz appeared convinced of Meixueiro's loyalty, at least for the moment, but he still turned to someone other than Meixueiro to organize Pimentel's 1902 election in the district of Ixtlán.[98]

Significantly, the Zapotecs of Ixtlán district did not so easily surrender their loyalty to Félix Díaz or their hostility toward a candidate imposed on them. Interim governor Miguel Bolaños Cacho had one objective during his few short months in office; he had to organize the election of Díaz's candidate Emilio Pimentel. The people of Ixtlán, however, publicly criticized both the official candidate and the autocratic process whereby Pimentel would become governor. Angered by their insolence, Bolaños Cacho wrote Díaz that these *vecinos* were "disrespectful" and "disobedient." They refused to vote for Pimentel, even though Pimentel was clearly going to win. After Pimentel's victory, Bolaños Cacho explained to Díaz, "the people of Ixtlán will see that they are not absolutely indispensable to the functioning of the Government and the State."[99]

Despite the obvious tension between the popular classes and the governor, political officials from the Sierra Zapoteca tried several times during Pimentel's first administration to demonstrate the region's support for the governor. In May 1904 Federico Toro organized a celebration in honor of the governor's *onomástico*, his feast day. The entire program was organized from the top down, and little spontaneous enthusiasm emerged for the governor. Toro paid pueblo bands to perform during the entire day of Sunday, May 22, and he ordered municipal officials to send a collective telegram congratulating the governor on his special day. In addition, he had the schoolchildren sing national hymns, and he sponsored a writing contest for students. At four o'clock in the afternoon he released balloons as an ostentatious sign of the district's support for the governor. Then, at seven in the evening, he illuminated all public buildings and convened a nighttime serenade in Ixtlán's main plaza. But these official celebrations could do little to convince the Serranos that they should support Pimentel, a governor who regularly intervened on issues that threatened their status quo and who continued to disregard the historical contribution of the Sierra in national history.[100] For the Sons of the Sierra, Pimentel's candidacy was unpopular in 1902, and his reelection bid in 1906 nearly led them to rebel against his regime.

Conclusion

Francisco Meijueiro's death in 1890 marked a turning point in Oaxaca. As veterans, soldiers, and officers like Meijueiro passed away, a new generation of men assumed positions of economic and political importance throughout the state. This younger generation did not fully understand or appreciate the degree to which their fathers had relied on popular classes for support during times of war or for the cooperation and goodwill that allowed the Porfirian regime to establish a stable federal government. By 1890, the consensus shared between ruling elites and rural popular classes was under attack. In Ixtlán district, peasants found it more difficult to engage in collective action since intervillage conflict forced communities to protect their resources against neighboring villages. Zapotec village leaders did not turn against industrial enterprises in the district, but they did challenge unfettered capitalist development, which would relinquish control over natural resources to outsiders, especially to foreign investors. Veterans and their families still expected recognition and reward for their years of service, but local elites like Guillermo Meixueiro opted to intervene more directly in the internal affairs of Zapotec villages. By 1906, the Serranos could no longer rely on the protection and cooperation of middle-class elites. In short, the demise of reciprocity in rural Oaxaca signaled the end of Porfirio Díaz's popular legitimacy among Zapotec peasants.

In many ways, the struggle over the legitimacy of the Porfirian regime represented a conflict between the past and the future, a fundamental disagreement over recognizing the historical contributions of popular classes or allowing for the new accumulation of capital and political power by a generation of men who had not fought in the nation's civil wars. But the conflict, as I see it, does not represent François-Xavier Guerra's notion of "tradition vs. modernity."[101] There was little that was "modern" about the patriarchal order that Guillermo Meixueiro and his young cohorts sought to impose on the communities of the Sierra Zapoteca. If anything, this generation of elites pursued a more "traditional" hierarchical structure, where power emanated from the top down. In a sense, Zapotec peasants desired a more "modern" democratic approach to governing their villages and region—a consensus with middle-class elites that was firmly grounded in constitutional provisions that protected their rights as loyal citizens of the nation. In short, Guerra's framework rests on a distinction between "tradition" and "modernity" that proves to be a false dichotomy in explaining the case of rural political culture in Porfirian Oaxaca.

Nevertheless, a more pronounced struggle over history and historical memory began to take shape after 1890. As veterans who had fought in the civil wars of the mid-nineteenth century began to pass away, the Porfirian regime put forward a new symbolic order centered on Benito Juárez and mediated through the personal military history of Porfirio Díaz. The irony, of course, is that at precisely the moment when supporters of the regime began talking about the importance of "progress" and the future course of Mexican society, history itself became more politicized as a contested reference. With the death of each veteran, the need for official ceremonies increased in order to underscore the loyalties and accomplishments of previous generations. In effect, public rituals grew as personal memories faded. But the families of departed veterans expected more than official platitudes. The Porfirian consensus between ruling elites and rural popular classes began to unravel as history itself became more politicized and as official interpretations of historical events ignored the accomplishments and contributions of ordinary Mexicans.

CHAPTER SIX

The Failure of Order and Progress, 1906-1911

Did we risk our lives for this when we were fighting at your side?
"Los Serranos" (1906)

In 1908 the American journalist James Creelman shocked the Mexican political establishment by publishing an interview with Porfirio Díaz in which the president announced that he would not seek reelection. But there was much more in that interview than contemporary readers or later historians recognized. In particular, Díaz's interview showed a man who had become nostalgic for the past, and a man who was cognizant of and moved by the popular support he had once enjoyed. Creelman captured the moment like this: "Over the city drifted the smoke of many factories. 'It is better than cannon smoke,' I said. 'Yes,' he replied, 'and yet there are times when cannon smoke is not such a bad thing. The toiling poor of my country have risen up to support me, but I cannot forget what my comrades in arms and their children have been to me in my severest ordeals.' There were actually tears in the veteran's eyes."[1] Reminiscent of the emotion he displayed at the banquet for his Zapotec soldiers in 1876, Díaz recalled how thousands of Mexicans had risked their lives for the nation and for him personally. Díaz's nostalgia in 1908, however, ignored the fundamental reality for too many Mexicans, including the Sons of the Sierra in Ixtlán district. By this time, Díaz had allowed local elites to trample on the pact he had originally formed with veterans and their families, the very people Díaz imagined in his conversation with Creelman.

As I have argued, three distinct periods of economic and political transformation characterized the Porfirian history of the Sierra Zapoteca. First, from 1876 to 1890, peasant communities in the Sierra expected and received compensation for their years of service in the form of basic infrastructural improvements and new industrial jobs for the region. The men and women who had fought alongside Díaz—the generation of the Reform—knew Díaz and his mestizo allies personally, and they used those relationships to their advantage. A second period began in 1890 when Díaz's longtime ally Francisco Meijueiro died, leaving his son Guillermo Meixueiro in charge of the family's vast business and political dealings. From 1890 to 1906, a generation of men who had not fought in Mexico's civil wars directed the region's economic and political fortunes. Although this was a time of relative economic prosperity led by an expansion in the mining industry, intense conflicts over tax increases, industrial development, land disputes, and gubernatorial elections threatened the stability of the region. Zapotec communities began to feel betrayed and abandoned by the regime and its local representatives during this transitional period. Significantly, 1890 was also the point at which Díaz began to systematically organize public celebrations of Mexican heroes, most importantly, celebrations of Benito Juárez.

During the final period of the Porfiriato, 1906 to 1911, the local political establishment, along with the Porfirian regime in Mexico City, came under increasing criticism. An economic downturn combined with antidemocratic and repressive measures ended the period of consensual politics that Díaz had formed with his Zapotec supporters. This earlier consensus gave way by 1906 to a shared sense of betrayal. Zapotecs were indignant and angry not because they had been abused for so many years, but because they sensed that the rights won by previous generations were under attack by the regime. The end of cooperation between the Porfirian regime and the Serranos started with Mexico's first major centennial celebration in 1906, the one-hundredth anniversary of Benito Juárez's birth. Other conflicts surrounding the 1906 and 1910 elections for governor in Oaxaca, the collapse of the state's mining industry, the intensification of regional conflicts over land and water, and the rebellion of Francisco I. Madero marked the closing of one era and the beginning of another.

The 1906 Juárez Centennial and Local Conflicts

As the end of the nineteenth century approached, Mexico City officials began to highlight Benito Juárez's birth (March 21, 1806) as the original moment when Mexico began to fulfill its liberal destiny. They described his birth as a preordained event, which led eventually to the great Reform era and, in turn, led to the Porfirian era of peace and prosperity. Stories of Juárez never drifted far from the metaphors of Catholic narratives. Mexicans understood the story of a savior born into poverty and the reductionist interpretation of historical events as the fulfillment of a divine plan. But the discursive shift to Juárez's birth made sense for other reasons as well. The primary objective for officials in Mexico City always had been to draw on Juárez's popular appeal as a means to bolster support for the Porfirian regime itself. By emphasizing Juárez's birth, these officials could more easily ignore the fact that his death came in the midst of Díaz's rebellion at La Noria, an issue that seriously undermined any symbolic continuity between the two regimes. In addition, the new emphasis on Juárez's birth offered Porfirian Mexico its first major centennial event.

Preparations for the one-hundredth anniversary of Juárez's birth began on March 21, 1903, exactly three years in advance of the actual celebration. Díaz actively participated in the early planning by naming committees, proposing legislation, and encouraging state governors to promote the Juárez centennial. He named Félix Romero, a fellow Oaxacan, an original signer of the 1857 Constitution, and an experienced organizer of Juárez celebrations, as national commissioner in charge of overseeing the nationwide event.[2] Romero wanted his Comité Patriótico Liberal, the national planning committee, to serve as a clearinghouse for advice and assistance for celebrations throughout the country. He anticipated the spontaneous formation of local committees in all parts of the nation, which would generate their own ideas about how to celebrate Juárez. Local committees, Romero believed, would know best how to make Juárez relevant to the daily lives of most citizens and demonstrate the broad respect Mexicans felt for the hero of the Reform. In 1903, however, Romero's committee stood alone since few communities were ready to begin planning and paying for an event that would take place three years hence. As a result, Romero realized that he would have to take a more active role in organizing local celebrations since no spontaneous movement had emerged on its own.[3]

Romero determined that his committee should immediately turn its attention to Juárez's birthplace, Guelatao, in the district of Ixtlán. The national planning committee proposed an ambitious project to erect a new monument to Juárez, which would stand next to a new school for the region's Zapotec children. Just as Juárez had risen from poverty through education, so too a new generation of children would walk out of the Sierra Juárez as educated citizens. With plans to dedicate the building on the centennial of Juárez's birth, Romero notified Governor Emilio Pimentel of the committee's recommendation, and word soon reached the people of Guelatao that they had been chosen for this special honor. The new century had already ushered in a period of significant political change for Guelatao, a small town of just three hundred inhabitants. On December 12, 1900, the Oaxaca state legislature promoted Guelatao to the status of *villa*, an administrative distinction that formally separated Guelatao's municipal affairs from the town of Ixtlán, the district *cabecera*. To show the town's gratitude for the promotion, ninety-three-year-old Felipe García, Guelatao's most prominent living veteran, organized a new association, La Sociedad Progresista Porfirio Díaz. García had served with Díaz in numerous battles, as far back as 1860, and had achieved the rank of captain. The new society named in honor of the president would continue García's relationship with Díaz, even if that relationship were primarily symbolic. Through this ongoing dialogue between local and national patriarchs, the villagers of Guelatao envisioned a continuous effort to advance the "material and moral progress" of their community.[4]

The villagers saw the plans for the Juárez celebration as the first tangible sign of their national prominence. When Guelatao's town council learned of the new school and monument, it organized its own committee, the Mesa Directiva de la Junta, "Juárez y Progreso," which officially endorsed the idea. Echoing the notion of progress, the name chosen by the local committee demonstrated how well its members understood the real import of the event. In fact, the people of Guelatao interpreted the connection between past and present even more directly than did the national leaders. Community leaders in Guelatao determined that the new school should not only educate children but should also be a place where adults could learn to read and write. The adults who had been deprived of an education in the past should not be dismissed as a lost generation in the present. To be good citizens, to participate more fully in the political and cultural affairs of the community and the nation, all Serranos should have access to education. This access was a "right" conferred on all Mexicans by Juárez, the "unconquered Indian Redeemer, who proclaimed the rights of man and secured the second Independence of the Mexican people."[5] From the outset, the villagers of Guelatao had begun to reshape the centennial project into something better suited to their own immediate needs.

The formation of Guelatao's committee revealed another significant step toward the assertion of local control over the Juárez centennial. In order to succeed, the community needed to unite around a common plan; they needed to speak with one voice about the purpose and goals of the new school. Any controversy would have doomed the project since the town was going to rely on government grants and individual pledges to complete the monument and the school. There appears to have been little disagreement within Guelatao, but that was due in part to the way in which the Mesa Directiva was organized. When the group gathered to discuss the project and to select a local committee, Felipe García, now ninety-five years old, chaired the meeting. García had recently asked for and received a generous pension of twenty-five pesos per month, evidence that he continued to be respected by officials in Mexico City.[6] In 1903 García was the oldest and highest-ranking veteran from Guelatao. More than any other person, he represented the living heroism that was to be celebrated in honor of Juárez. And because he had commanded the fathers (and grandfathers) of most of those present at the Juárez centennial meeting, García could expect the respect and obedience of the entire community. His endorsement of the school project enhanced the prospect that the families of Guelatao would unite around a single plan. Together, as a unified community, they hoped to determine where the school would be built and how the school would ultimately serve the district. Felipe García was too old, however, to manage the volume of correspondence that was required of the planning committee. Anastasio Juárez was elected president of the Mesa Directiva, and Felipe García's son, also named Felipe, was appointed first secretary. For help in Oaxaca City, the committee appointed José Ruíz Jiménez honorary president of the committee.[7]

The school was to be built with funds collected from around the country. The Mesa Directiva sent letters to all state governors and to the newspapers *Diario del Hogar* and *El Imparcial*, informing them of Guelatao's plans and asking for whatever support could be afforded. Wealthy individuals and state governors began pledging funds soon after the announcement. General Manuel Sánchez Rivera offered one hundred pesos within two weeks of the proclamation. The state governor of Tlaxcala pledged two hundred pesos. The state legislature from Hidalgo granted forty-five pesos. Finally, the governor of Veracruz promised to help in whatever way he could with both moral and financial support. Encouraged by the rapid nationwide response, the Mesa Directiva commissioned the project as the Escuela Nacional Juárez.[8]

Although the idea for a school originated in Mexico City, it quickly became a local project. Moreover, in the context of local and statewide politics in Oaxaca, the plan to build a school easily became a contested issue. Governor Emilio Pimentel doubted the feasibility of the plan from the very beginning. Having formed his views on Indian education well before he became governor, Pimentel believed the new school was a waste of time and money. In fact, Pimentel had always opposed universal education, especially when it came to Mexico's indigenous citizens. In 1887 he had challenged portions of Justo Sierra's educational reforms on the grounds that Indians could not overcome their "ignorance" and "backwardness." Significantly, Sierra won this particular debate with Pimentel after invoking the memory of Juárez.[9] As governor of Oaxaca, the state with the largest Indian population in the republic at the time, Pimentel reluctantly went along with the plan for a new school in Guelatao. Several times he reminded Díaz that Guelatao already had a school; a new one would be redundant and a violation of the rational allocation of state money and energy. But the push from Mexico City was too strong, and Pimentel designated an engineer to survey where the new school and monument should be built.[10]

When the engineer's report came back in July 1903, Pimentel informed Díaz that only one or two sites were adequate for the new building. He recommended that land owned by Benito Juárez Maza, Benito Juárez's son, would be the best, and should be the only land used to build the school.[11] Juárez Maza, of course, did not farm himself; he was a congressman in Mexico City. The current tenants, therefore, would have to find alternative land. Ruperto Juárez, most likely a distant Juárez family relative, leased one of the plots, and Santiago Ruíz rented the other. However, the issue was more complicated than it first appeared since Ruíz was from the neighboring town of Ixtlán. Arable land remained a precious commodity in this mountainous region, and Ruíz's search for a new plot posed a hardship on Ixtlán, a town of nearly one thousand inhabitants.[12] The ensuing debate over where to build the new school and where the current tenants would go for new land ignited a dispute between Ixtlán and Guelatao that lasted well beyond the centennial of Juárez's birth. By limiting the possible sites where a new school could be built, the governor effectively continued his obstructionist tactics toward the entire project. Unknowingly, however, Pimentel had set into motion a series of debates and conflicts that he had not anticipated. People from both villages began to criticize Pimentel more openly, joining other communities from the Sierra who had their own reasons for distrusting the *científico* governor.

Village officials from Ixtlán resented the attention and funds aimed at Guelatao for the new project. To remind the residents of Guelatao that Ixtlán should be regarded as the more important town in the district, especially in light of Guelatao's upstart attitude as a new *villa*, Ixtlán's *ayuntamiento*, assisted by the jefe político, began to reassert the town's authority as the district's *cabecera*. In September 1904 it determined that more money was needed for maintaining the district jail, operating the municipal school, and organizing celebrations on national feast days in Ixtlán.[13] To raise more money and in response to the decision to relocate Santiago Ruíz, Ixtlán also initiated changes in more significant land agreements between the two villages. In particular, Ixtlán's town council decided to double the rent on a tract of land that peasants from Guelatao had been renting for nearly two decades. The land was of minor importance for farming, but Guelatao's primary source of water, a small tributary river known by its Zapoteco name *Xoo vetó*, flowed through this tract. If Guelatao lost access to this water, all households in the community would be threatened. In effect, no piece of land was as vital to Guelatao as the one now disputed by the two villages.[14]

Guelatao's town council was caught off guard by Ixtlán's decision to double the rent. Since 1888, it had paid twenty-five pesos per year, delivered every September 15 (on the eve of Independence Day), for the use of the land in question. Even before 1888, the villagers of Guelatao had used the land to pasture their livestock, gather firewood, and collect water in cisterns connected to a modest irrigation system. Ixtlán's demand to double the rent violated the terms of the signed agreement and challenged the practices established by previous generations. But the dispute centered on a mere twenty-five pesos per year, a relatively small amount equal to the monthly pension Felipe García received from the secretary of war. More than money, the struggle between Ixtlán and Guelatao became tied to issues of male honor, municipal autonomy, and the rights of due process.[15]

At first, village leaders in Guelatao argued that regional strongmen Guillermo Meixueiro and Federico H. Toro had created the dispute. Meixueiro still aspired to become Díaz's candidate for governor in the 1906 elections. If the district were on the brink of bloodshed, and if the only person who could end the dispute were Meixueiro, then his importance to the region and the state would be unchallenged. But the villagers from Guelatao saw through Meixueiro's strategy. As they reported to President Díaz, Meixueiro intended to sacrifice their welfare for his own personal gain: "he's trying to antagonize both pueblos so that later he can call us together and appear as our savior or defender."[16] They complained that Meixueiro was dividing the two towns and threatening the fraternal goodwill that had characterized years of cooperation.[17] They could not ignore, however, that Toro and Meixueiro had convinced many people from Ixtlán to support the changes in the land agreement. The *ayuntamiento* of Ixtlán had changed in recent years, and a new generation was in control of the municipal government. Villagers from Guelatao reminded Díaz that the "*principales* [elders]" of Ixtlán had died and that a new group of "*jovenes* [young men]" was now in charge. The older generation, men like Manuel and Estanislao Jiménez, Luciano Ruíz, Julio Hernández, and others, would not have supported the conflict with Guelatao.[18] From the perspective of people in Guelatao, Toro and Meixueiro had manipulated the younger generation of leaders in Ixtlán to go along with a plan that threatened regional harmony.

The young village officials from Ixtlán made their own accusations. They argued that José Ruíz Jiménez was behind the conflict since he caused trouble wherever he went. The decision to place Ruíz Jiménez on the Juárez centennial committee had come back to haunt Guelatao. His presence irritated Toro and Meixueiro, and Guelatao would have to pay the price. Governor Pimentel also blamed Ruíz Jiménez for much of the difficulty, calling him "the black bird in this business" and arguing that Ruíz Jiménez fired the intransigence of Guelatao and destroyed "all spirit of conciliation."[19] Pimentel's accusation lost some credibility, however, since the governor eventually blamed everyone but himself for the ongoing dispute in Ixtlán. Three months after criticizing Ruíz Jiménez, Pimentel complained to Díaz that the fundamental problem was "the ignorance and malicious character of the people of Ixtlán."[20] Pimentel grew increasingly frustrated by his inability to settle the dispute; both villages ignored his recommendations and openly challenged his authority to intervene on the issue.

Through most of 1904, Ixtlán refused to pay its portion of taxes due to the state until a decision had been made on its request for the increased rent payments. In August, just one month before Guelatao would have paid for the next year's rent, Governor Pimentel ratified Ixtlán's plan to increase its budget. Guelatao, however, refused to pay Ixtlán the higher rent fee since the request had been made unilaterally. As the village had done since 1888, Guelatao paid Ixtlán only twenty-five pesos. Pimentel's search for a settlement quickened. In February 1905 he ordered officials from both towns to attend a general meeting in Ixtlán where a resolution might be found to the satisfaction of both parties. But that effort failed miserably, and negotiations broke off soon after the meeting began. As the delegates from Guelatao began their walk home, Ixtlán officials reconvened their own meeting to nullify the 1888 agreement. Rather than settle the dispute, Pimentel's decision to bring the parties together actually escalated the conflict. One day later, on February 26, 1905, Federico Toro took matters into his own hands. Acting on Toro's orders, a small contingent from Ixtlán led by Melitón Pacheco, Lázaro Ruíz, Manuel Pérez, and Antonio Hernández set dynamite charges around the cisterns Guelatao villagers used to collect water from the river. The explosion destroyed the irrigation system, as well as the confidence people from Guelatao had in their governor. They placed their last bit of hope in the hands of President Díaz.[21]

Tomás Soto, Guelatao's municipal president, claimed that "before the discovery of America," Guelatao and Ixtlán had established a common bond and working relationship based on equality rather than violence and aggression. In fact, Guelatao was originally founded by "sons of Ixtlán." Nowhere will one find a document, Soto advised Díaz, that says Guelatao must pay rent to Ixtlán.[22] Soto had thus shifted to a discourse of historical memory, looking back to the original founding of town limits, that emphasized temporally vague but strongly held notions of the rights established by earlier generations.

Ixtlán was prepared to make the same argument and had at their disposal seventeenth-century documents supporting the request for larger rent payments. Ixtlán's municipal president, Manuel Pacheco, forwarded to Díaz a copy of the original land settlement, which established the boundaries between Ixtlán and Guelatao and, more important, demonstrated Guelatao's obligation to help pay for feast days held in Ixtlán. Written in 1636, this document represented the people of Ixtlán's most prized village artifact, a remnant handed down from their ancestors and a tangible sign of their historical importance in the district. In 1636 Ixtlán and Guelatao formed a major portion of the *encomienda* held by Diego Sánchez Ramírez. The two towns lived uncomfortably close to each other, and royal officials frequently had to settle land disputes. On August 8, 1636, the viceroy's office, along with *alcaldes, corregidores, regidores*, regional caciques, and *principales*, ordered the Zapotec residents of each town to attend a general meeting in Ixtlán. With the help of an interpreter, both sides settled their differences through a land/rent agreement. In exchange for land on which to build a church to San Pablo, and for farmland that would be used for growing corn, Guelatao agreed to pay Ixtlán six pesos in gold every year. In addition, Guelatao agreed to help Ixtlán celebrate the feast day of Santo Tomás with donations of flowers, decorations, and music. The document stressed that Ixtlán maintained ownership of the land and that Guelatao "has been and will be considered tenants and renters of these lands without the right to acquire any other title or legal right to the property since these rights currently and absolutely belong to Ixtlán." In forwarding this document to President Díaz in 1905, Ixtlán's young leaders argued that Guelatao effectively remained its possession and was therefore bound by the decisions of Ixtlán officials. Governor Pimentel also received a copy of this document and immediately rejected its argument. It may have been acceptable in the seventeenth century, he wrote to Díaz, "but a legally constituted town cannot be the property of another town in our time." Díaz agreed. The people of Ixtlán were complicating the issue since the problem did not actually focus on ownership but rather on the signed rental agreement of 1888.[23]

In May 1905 Guelatao began rebuilding the cisterns that its residents had used "since time immemorial." But Federico Toro once again ordered his men to destroy them. Pimentel finally focused his energy on getting Toro to accept a compromise, evidence that the people of Guelatao were correct in their assertion that Toro was making the decisions in Ixtlán. Pimentel pressured Toro to accept thirty-five pesos per year instead of fifty, an increase of just ten pesos over the original agreement.[24] But still, the people of Guelatao refused to budge, in part because they distrusted Toro and Pimentel so completely by this point. Instead, Guelatao chose to make its strongest appeal directly to President Díaz. The "honor and dignity" of our town is at stake, Guelatao's *ayuntamiento* wrote to Díaz. We are "a people who believe that we are acting in our full rights authorized by the Constitution of 1857, which we defended and restored when we came together on the fields of honor."[25] The men of Guelatao argued that their honor could not be trampled so easily. They and/or their fathers had fought for the right to protection under the constitution's guiding principle: *Libertad*. We see in this context how the people of Guelatao interpreted *Libertad* to apply to their collective rights as a town that had sacrificed for the nation. The young men on Ixtlán's town council, along with Federico Toro and Guillermo Meixueiro, threatened this fundamental principle.

Díaz did not disappoint the people of Guelatao. Assuming his role as supreme arbitrator, Díaz ordered Governor Pimentel to establish a *fundo legal* for Guelatao, a land grant paid for by the state and federal governments. Guelatao would get the land, some two hundred hectares, and access to the water that was so vital for their crops. In return, Ixtlán would receive the money they wanted and needed for maintaining and operating municipal and district offices. In October 1905 Pimentel acknowledged Díaz's resolution, sending engineer Juan E. Martínez to inspect the village boundaries and to plot the land grant for Guelatao.[26] But true to the contentious nature of this conflict, the villagers of Ixtlán reacted angrily to Díaz's proposal, claiming that the *ayuntamiento* of Guelatao would now hold Ixtlán's crops hostage. Ixtlán reminded Díaz that they, too, had fought for the nation, that they were also "former subordinates who joined with you in taking up arms and defending the institutions which guide us."[27] And though they pledged their loyalty to Díaz, the villagers of Ixtlán were prepared to resist the president's decision in more subtle ways, mostly by influencing Governor Pimentel's final determination of the land grant. Ultimately, with the help of Federico Toro, Ixtlán's town council successfully lobbied for changes in the survey that limited Guelatao's access to the river. Guelatao could only complain to Díaz that Pimentel was not following presidential orders; Pimentel, they claimed, was acting as Toro's lawyer.[28]

The struggle over land and water between Ixtlán and Guelatao erupted quickly and then drifted quietly into the background of daily life in the Sierra once the 1906 centennial passed.[29] As with most land disputes in the region, violence entered into the equation, but only limited violence that did not plunge the two villages into outright war. The real battle was waged by the scribes and secretaries who dispatched dozens of letters on each side, who provided notarized copies of original land agreements, and who wrote the arguments for and against each respective village. In the conflict between Guelatao and Ixtlán, the pen was indeed mightier than the sword.[30] After 1907 both villages faced a more serious economic crisis with the collapse of the regional mining industry. Still, there were several unintended consequences that had a lasting effect in the district. First, the tension between Ixtlán and Guelatao destroyed the plans for a new school and monument in honor of Juárez. The major losers were the generations of Zapotec adults and children who did not have access to an adequate school.[31]

Second, the conflict between Guelatao and Ixtlán disrupted planning for the centennial of Juárez's birth in the Sierra Zapoteca and throughout the state. The villagers of Guelatao lowered their expectations when it became clear that they would not get their new school or even a new monument. Instead, they made a humble request to Díaz for new musical instruments with which they would honor the hero of the Reform.[32] But even this request signaled deeper divisions within the region. Prior to the town's 1906 conflict with Ixtlán, musicians from Guelatao participated in a district-wide philharmonic corps made up of fifty-six men, mostly veterans.[33] Philharmonic corps, as historian Guy Thomson has argued, recreated the spirit of cooperation and competition between communities as veterans performed the music from their years of service in the National Guard.[34] Guelatao's request for new instruments indicated an attempt to gain greater autonomy from their Ixtlán neighbors. Díaz sent them instruments, though not until several months after the Juárez celebration. In Guelatao the centennial of Juárez's birth was celebrated in a much quieter and more subdued manner than had originally been hoped. Only a small group from Oaxaca City, led by the Asociación Juárez, the most vocal anti-Pimentel organization in the state, made a pilgrimage to the birthplace of the nation's hero.[35]

Planning for the Juárez centennial throughout the state also fell behind. In September 1905 Díaz scolded Pimentel for his failure to prepare adequately for the important event. Pimentel promised to do more, pledging to "double my efforts."[36] One month later, Pimentel wrote that he had decided on sponsoring a series of writing contests to celebrate Juárez, a completely unoriginal and uninspiring idea that did not require much effort on the part of the governor. Borrowing from previous Juárez celebrations, Pimentel settled on three writing themes: poetry honoring Juárez, histories of Juárez as state governor, and legends based on an episode of Juárez's life. Of course, this kind of celebration excluded the full participation of people who could not write, which effectively marginalized the vast majority of the population. In that sense, the home state of Juárez would celebrate the centennial of his birth in a predictably elitist fashion.[37]

Not surprisingly, on March 21, 1906, Oaxaca City rather than Guelatao took center stage in honoring Juárez. Governor Pimentel unveiled the giant statue of Juárez on the Cerro de Fortín, overlooking the entire city.[38] The state government purchased the house that Juárez had lived in during the years he was Oaxacan governor. Teachers organized the normal series of parades with schoolchildren cleaned up to wave at adoring family members, followed by a series of predictable speeches to remind Oaxacans of their special bond with the hero of the Reform. But even Oaxaca City had been the site of some controversy because of the Juárez celebration. A week before the 1906 celebration, Pimentel charged Ismael Puga y Colmenares and Heliodoro Díaz Quintas, the editors of the local newspaper *El Bien Público*, with collaborating with the Flores Magón brothers and their opposition newspaper, *Regeneración. El Bien Público* had been a constant critic of Pimentel, and its opposition voice interfered with the governor's plans to celebrate national unity, despite the obvious contradictions of any such unity. The contestation behind the planning of the Juárez centennial, in urban and rural Oaxaca, belied the patina of harmony and cooperation reported by newspapers that were loyal to the governor.[39]

Finally, the third consequence of the conflict between Guelatao and Ixtlán was the emergence of an intense rural opposition movement to the reelection of Governor Pimentel in the 1906 elections. Villagers from both towns joined a growing chorus of voices calling for a new candidate. Pimentel had proven unable to settle the dispute and unwilling to recognize the important historical role the entire district of Ixtlán had played in Mexico's past. As Zapotecs turned to Pimentel for help in commemorating Juárez's birth, they encountered a governor who thought it was a waste of time to educate Indian children and who refused to acknowledge the honor and heroism felt by all in the district of Ixtlán. The Sons of the Sierra demanded that respect and, they were determined to get it.

The 1906 Gubernatorial Election

The campaign for governor in June 1906 marked a major turning point in Porfirio Díaz's relationship with the people of the Sierra Zapoteca. These events exposed a breach between the president, his handpicked governor, and the people who had offered their loyalty to the regime for thirty years. From the perspective of the Serranos, Governor Pimentel threatened their liberty and the terms of their continued support for the regime. Díaz had a choice: he could support his veterans and their families who had proven their devotion in battle, or he could stand by his governor. On this issue the Zapotecs joined a growing anti-Pimentel movement that tried to block the governor's reelection. However, the Zapotecs went further than any other group. They not only challenged Pimentel, but they also confronted the president.

In Oaxaca City Pimentel's most vocal opponents were a group of liberals who looked to Benito Juárez for inspiration: the Asociación Juárez (AJ).[40] According to Francie Chassen-López, the AJ began in 1901 with the objective of honoring Juárez's death every July 18. Like liberal clubs throughout the nation, this group brought together sectors of Oaxaca's landed elite with an emerging professional class. As long as the club focused on consensus issues like the importance of Juárez in Mexican history, Oaxaca's ruling classes could stand together. Guillermo Meixueiro, for example, became the organization's president in 1902. By the end of 1904, however, the AJ had split into radical and moderate factions over disputed municipal elections in Oaxaca City and Francisco Bulnes's polemic *El verdadero Juárez*.[41] In the wake of these controversial episodes, landowners abandoned the AJ, leaving it in the hands of more radical middle-class members. Lawyers Heliodoro Díaz Quintas and Ismael Puga y Colmenares restructured the AJ and, by 1905, began publishing an anti-Pimentel newspaper, *El Bien Público*. They openly attacked Pimentel's regime on issues of corruption, abuse, and intimidation. In response, Pimentel harassed the AJ leaders and forced them to give up teaching positions in the university.

Pimentel's actions initiated a new offensive against any potential rival who might become a public critic. As a result, Pimentel unnecessarily antagonized many respected and admired Oaxacans who had supported him in 1902, and who may have done so again in 1906. Pimentel determined that his main rival was Miguel Bolaños Cacho, the former interim governor who had worked hard for Pimentel's first election. Pimentel accused Bolaños Cacho of stealing funds from the state treasury, an accusation that forced Bolaños Cacho to resign his position as a federal Supreme Court justice in order to defend himself. The AJ energetically supported Bolaños Cacho and reprinted his denial in its newspaper. The association countered that the real criminals were Pimentel and his *científico* cohorts who had abandoned the liberal cause established by Benito Juárez and who could not be trusted in the cause of liberty. The AJ and *El Bien Público* were consistently anti-Pimentel and anti-*científico*, but they were careful not to cross the line and become anti-*Porfirista*. Supporters of the AJ came primarily from Oaxaca's urban professional classes—lawyers, doctors, shop owners, schoolteachers, and university students. They made little effort to incorporate the complaints of Oaxaca's urban and rural poor. But these sectors, representing a vast majority of the state's population, had their own perspective on statewide politics, and they expressed those views in personal letters and petitions to President Díaz.[42]

In April 1906 several dozen men from Oaxaca City signed a letter accusing Pimentel of abuses and unfair treatment. Calling themselves "*los pobres hijos de Oaxaca* [the poor sons of Oaxaca]," they blamed Pimentel for widening the differences between rich and poor: "he does not hear the complaints of the poor, nor does he grant us any aid from his administration. He only favors and listens to the desires of the rich." Firmly believing that President Díaz had more sympathy for their plight, they recalled the promises Díaz had made during the Tuxtepec rebellion in 1876. They reminded Díaz that he had promised to protect them, a pledge Díaz reiterated during each visit to his native Oaxaca. They asked simply for Díaz to nominate someone else from his inner circle, but someone who had more concern for all Oaxacans: "please nominate a person among those around you, someone with more affection for this your birthplace [*su país natal*] who might come to govern us for the well-being and happiness of everyone, not only the rich."[43] Like Pimentel's middle-class critics, these urban poor petitioners did not openly turn their frustration with Pimentel into contempt for the president. Some of Pimentel's rural opponents, however, recognized that they could not be anti-Pimentel without also challenging Díaz. In this regard, the Sons of the Sierra went further than any other sector in Oaxaca by calling into question the entire political order.

The Zapotecs of Ixtlán district gave three reasons for opposing Pimentel's reelection in 1906: (1) they resented his election in 1902; (2) they resented his imposition of new taxes; and (3) they resented his interference in local disputes over land and water. The Serranos never forgot that Pimentel had been a compromise candidate in 1902, and they never completely abandoned their hope that Félix Díaz would become their governor. The state needed the guidance of someone whose antecedents were better known, someone who could be trusted to respect the years of dedication and service offered by the Sons of the Sierra. Félix Díaz's father had led many of them in battles against the French. They assumed that the son of this illustrious general would maintain the bonds of patriarchal reciprocity that they had formed with his father. Of course, they had no tangible evidence that the young Félix Díaz would treat them as his father had, but they imagined a historical bond that tied them together and that made it possible to establish a pact to their mutual benefit.

Pimentel had proved immune to this sort of appeal. Instead, Pimentel had established a record of enacting policies that went against their interests. He had, after all, proposed a tax increase in 1904. They did not realize, as we saw in the previous chapter, how much Pimentel had fretted about this increase. Nor did they realize how he had originally favored a doubling of the tax but had settled for a smaller increase so as not to antagonize the Serranos. But the Serranos also opposed Pimentel's reelection in 1906 because he had interfered in intervillage disputes over land and water and had only made these conflicts worse. The clash between Ixtlán and Guelatao was just one example, but it was potent evidence of Pimentel's meddlesome misadministration. Pimentel had stirred the fires of discontent between Ixtlán and Guelatao, and he could no longer contain the widespread dissatisfaction that villagers from both towns felt toward his entire regime. Divided over issues of land and water rights, the Zapotec communities of Ixtlán district were united in their support for Colonel Félix Díaz, Porfirio Díaz's nephew.

Villagers from Ixtlán, Guelatao, Ixtepeji, Chicomezuchil, and other towns scattered around the district wrote letters to President Díaz complaining of Pimentel's haughty disposition and disregard for their historic role in defending the nation. These Zapotec men argued that they were the true defenders of liberalism; Pimentel had betrayed the cause for which they and their fathers had fought. In December 1905 the villagers of Guelatao led other communities in the call for a new gubernatorial candidate. They challenged Pimentel's liberal credentials and openly compared him with their favored candidate, Félix Díaz: "The people of the renowned District of Juárez, always firm in its republican convictions, desire to be governed by the honorable liberal Colonel of the Army Corps of Engineers, CITIZEN FÉLIX DIAZ. He is a real democrat, free of conceits, and falsehoods; he has no absolutist aristocratic leanings, nor does he proclaim democratic principles in order abandon them later, like others do."[44]

Their condemnation of Pimentel echoed the complaints of Oaxaca's urban poor—Pimentel's class bias—and of Oaxaca's urban elite—Pimentel's disregard for liberal principles. Yet the Serranos went even further. They called Pimentel "a useless person, unprepared, lacking physical and moral fortitude, a despot who comes disguised with the cape of liberalism and later steps on those who have fought for liberty and for the rights of citizenship enjoyed by the people of Oaxaca." The Sons of the Sierra spoke with authority and confidence. They had little regard for the pretense of civility that characterized urban criticism of Pimentel. Nor were they concerned that they might be punished for speaking so boldly. They and their fathers had fought alongside Porfirio Díaz and his brother in battles against the French. Now they wanted a governor born and raised in that tradition; they did not want someone they could not trust: "we do not want someone of doubtful antecedents." Their concern with origins and history formed an essential part of their complaint against Pimentel and their justification for their support of the president's nephew. They called on all Oaxacans to join with them: "People like us who have had leaders with glorious records, not mercenaries; we will not accept any other candidate other than the one that we have already designated."[45]

A similar letter and petition were circulated throughout Ixtlán district in December 1905. Villagers from Miguel Abejones, Santa Ana Yareni, Alocapam, Yolox, Totonatla, Temextitlán, Tenchitlán, Las Nieves, Las Yagas, and Analco told the president that Félix Díaz should replace Pimentel. "We are free to select our own state governor," they reminded Díaz. Altogether, more than five hundred men signed a petition asserting their right to have a governor to their liking.[46] Their actions went against the wishes of local elites like Guillermo Meixueiro and Federico Toro; these villagers were not coerced into signing such a direct and challenging letter to the president since there was little to gain from those who had the greatest influence on their lives.

By the spring of 1906, it was clear that President Díaz was not going to nominate a different candidate. One month after the Juárez centennial, the Zapotecs could no longer ignore the fact that Díaz favored Pimentel over his old soldiers. Growing increasingly unsure of Díaz's loyalty, they began to challenge their president more directly. On April 30, 1906, letter-writers from the Sierra expressed contempt for Pimentel in the strongest possible language. They spoke of popular rights guaranteed by the 1857 Constitution. They defended the honor and legitimacy that ordinary Mexicans had gained by guarding the principles of the Constitution on the battlefield. Finally, they articulated the most openly anti-Díaz sentiment expressed by any single group in Oaxaca, including the radical liberals of the Asociación Juárez in Oaxaca

City. Díaz's relationship with the Sons of the Sierra was under tremendous strain as a result of Pimentel's governorship. The Serranos threatened rebellion against Pimentel, fully aware that they were courting hostilities with the Díaz regime as well. But they felt abandoned and abused by the political system, and so they protested loudly rather than remain silent. Significantly, the letter-writers refused to sign their individual names, calling themselves simply, "Los Felixistas y los Serranos," a wise decision since political repression had become widespread in the final months before the June elections. The writers no doubt came from among the group of five hundred individuals who had signed the December 1905 letter asking Díaz to name a new gubernatorial candidate. Most likely, supporters of the 1906 anti-Pimentel/anti-Díaz letter came from the towns of Guelatao, Ixtepeji, Chicomezuchil, and the town of Ixtlán itself. Individuals from these towns had complained bitterly to Díaz of the abuses caused by Pimentel's regime, especially of the corruption he tolerated at the hands of local strongmen Guillermo Meixueiro and Federico Toro. The full impact of the letter is expressed best in its entirety:

Dear Sir:
The time has come in which we must make use of the most sacred rights that the Constitution grants us: TO GIVE US A GOVERNMENT THAT WE FIND SATISFACTORY, since it is for this that we have shed our blood on the battlefield when you, the valiant sons of Oaxaca, gave us to believe that in truth you were fighting for the People.

Our rights and our security are in danger in the hands of this WORTHLESS GOVERNOR whom you imposed on us in a dark hour. This Don Emilio person and his holy band [*santa comparsa*] are a revulsion for the sons of the people, which we cannot tolerate, and we are on the verge of overthrowing him, even if it should happen, unfortunately, that you should wish to sustain him. Señor Don Porfirio, now is the time for you to give us complete liberty [*entera libertad*] to name our governors and not impose your favorites on us, as you are accustomed to do all over the country.

This letter does not have as its goal to ask you for a candidate; its sole and absolute purpose is to tell you that if you retain that man Pimentel in power, we will set in motion the great struggle to remove him by the means that are within our reach, because we are very disgusted with him and with his circle of hypocritical men and worthless scoundrels. Did we risk our lives for this when we were fighting at your side, or was this the goal for which you sought, to sacrifice us in order to later turn your back on us?

We are resolved that if you do not relieve us from this man, we will respond by whatever means are necessary to achieve this for ourselves.

We want Don Félix Díaz, and if we do not sign, it is because we reserve for ourselves the right to do so when we present a copy of the present letter to you in person.

The Felixistas and the Serranos [47]

From the very beginning of the letter, in its salutation to Díaz, the Serranos asserted their right to speak to the president as citizens with equal rights under the constitution. They avoided the usual form of addressing Díaz as "Illustrious President," speaking to him more directly as "Dear Sir." They called him by his first name, Don Porfirio, and not by his title as president or, as they usually referred to him, as general. Throughout the letter the writers emphasized the collective history of a people who had earned the rights of citizenship. They used a form of the pronoun "*nosotros*" sixteen times, and always referred to themselves in the verb tense as "we." More than anything else, they wanted the right to select for themselves who should be their governor. They had spilled their blood on the battlefield, fighting only for the rights of "the People." And now, because Díaz was imposing Pimentel on the people once again, these rights and guarantees were in danger. They asked Díaz to restore the liberty for which they and their ancestors had fought. Finally, they reserved their right to challenge Pimentel and Díaz without signing their names. They were the Sons of the Sierra; that should have been enough to have their rights respected.

Clearly, they saved their greatest condemnation for Pimentel, this "WORTHLESS GOVERNOR." Pimentel and his illegitimate cronies could no longer be tolerated. If Díaz did not remove him, they would do so through armed insurrection, the only honorable avenue still available to them. But just as clearly, the Serranos could no longer ignore Díaz's hand behind this unpopular governor. They realized that they were calling into question the entire political order. They could not trust Díaz since he obviously preferred an autocratic politician to his loyal soldiers. And so they openly challenged the president as much as Pimentel. They reminded the president that he had placed Pimentel in office. Moreover, they had no illusions about Díaz's role in local politics, telling him, "now is the time for you to give us complete liberty to name our governors and not impose your favorites on us, as you are accustomed to do all over the country." Díaz had taken for granted the importance of these men and their fathers in national history. How dare he forget that they had been fighting for the rights of the people? How dare he turn his back on them now: "Did we risk our lives for this when we were fighting at your side, or was this the goal for which you sought, to sacrifice us in order to later turn your back on us?" Pimentel was the problem, but for the first time in thirty years, the Serranos held Díaz responsible.

More indications of their hostility toward Díaz can be surmised by what was not said in the 1906 letter. The Serranos did not pledge loyalty to Díaz, the formulaic and expected closure to any correspondence sent to the president. And they did not mention Benito Juárez by name. Their complaints were more specific and more personal. Symbols of the past did not speak as eloquently as had their own actions. They had been on the battlefield with Díaz, and they deserved better. Clearly, Díaz's relationship with the Sons of the Sierra, the veterans and their families, had reached a turning point. Significantly, Pimentel was reelected, and the Serranos did not declare open rebellion. They did, however, resist the status quo in other ways. They confronted local elites like Guillermo Meixueiro; they challenged the owners of capital in the mines and the textile factory; and they sought political support from Benito Juárez Maza, Benito Juárez's son.

After 1906 Díaz could never again count on the unwavering support of the most militant sector in his native state. Without that support, Díaz had no chance of putting down the widespread rebellion that broke out in 1910. As we will see, when Francisco I. Madero declared his revolt, the Zapotecs of Ixtlán district offered only tepid support for Díaz, hesitating to form their militias. For the Sons of the Sierra, the fight that lay ahead was not for the reestablishment of the Díaz regime but for the restoration of the principles of the 1857 Constitution, the very ideals their fathers had fought for a generation earlier.[48] In 1906, however, Díaz had problems beyond the Sierra Juárez. His regime faced its first major political crisis led by opponents who had organized a new political party with Juárez in mind—the Partido Liberal Mexicano (PLM). But the PLM's role in turning people away from Díaz was limited. Díaz ruled for thirty years before the PLM revolt in 1906, and he ruled for five years after. He maintained autonomous and historical relationships with peasant communities that could not so easily be changed by an anarcho-syndicalist call to arms. The PLM spoke little to peasants, concentrating their energy and organization around the interests of Mexico's growing industrial working class. In short, Porfirian hegemony did not fail until Mexico's peasants turned away from Porfirio Díaz for their own reasons. There were experiences before and after the so-called precursor movement that determined Díaz's fate more directly. But these were local experiences, grounded in the daily lives of Mexico's rural population. And these were more subtle experiences, void of the international drama that characterized the movement led by the Flores Magón brothers.

The Recession of 1907–1911

One such event was the collapse of the mining industry throughout Mexico. Although the ensuing economic recession that began in 1907 touched the entire country, the impact of that recession can best be understood by analyzing the social problems generated by economic hardship at the local level.[49] The recession of 1907–11 led to greater conflicts in the industrial and agricultural sectors of the economy in the Sierra Juárez and led to calls for greater political reform. Riots and disturbances at the district's largest mine, Natividad, and at the district's only textile factory at Xía threatened the social order and came dangerously close to igniting a district-wide rebellion. Increased pressures for agricultural plots from men returning to the fields from the mines set off a series of intense intervillage conflicts that provoked alarm throughout Ixtlán. At the same time, corrupt district officials sought more coercive ways to graft profits off of their impoverished neighbors. Everyone was pushed to the edge during the recession, and everyone fought to control as much of the limited resources as possible.

Following the completion of the Mexican Southern Railroad in 1892, Oaxacan mines flourished. For nearly fifteen years, Oaxacan mine owners expressed the optimistic enthusiasm associated with economic booms. But the boom went bust in 1907, and most mine owners saw their entire investments wiped out in a few short years. Foreign investors and foreign managers of Oaxaca's mining operations began leaving the state in search of better opportunities. Mexican investors tried desperately to negotiate better credit terms in futile efforts to remain solvent during these bad times. However, more than any other group associated with mining, workers faced the brunt of this recession. Many families had come to depend on the wages, and many other families relied on the extensive network of petty capitalism that provided food, supplies, clothing, and entertainment for the mining industry. The impact of the economic crisis in mining was far-reaching and long lasting.[50]

The recession began with a worldwide collapse in the markets for precious metals. In less than a decade, from 1900 to 1909, the price of silver fell

17 percent, and the price of copper fell 23 percent.[51] Falling prices led to a nationwide credit crisis, and mine owners quickly learned that they could not ride out the recession through loans and promissory notes on the future. In Oaxaca all mining regions were affected, and mines began closing in Taviche, Tlacolula, and in the Sierra Juárez. Even Natividad faced the uncertainty of shutting down its operation rather than run the risk of sinking money into an unprofitable enterprise. Natividad had employed more than five hundred workers during the boom years of 1892–1907. Porfirio Díaz had once been a shareholder in the mine's stock, and regional leaders looked to Natividad as an essential ingredient in their economy. If Natividad closed, then even more hardship would befall the entire district.

The owners of Natividad had always felt threatened by competing mine owners and by local residents who regularly panned Natividad's discarded water and waste for small bits of precious metals. Administrators at Natividad tried desperately to limit all requests to use the nearby river for hydraulic power and tried repeatedly to limit access to abandoned mineshafts and waste piles.[52] But mine workers at Natividad were paid wages well below the national average and relied heavily on the informal trade of ore to supplement their meager wages. During the 1907–11 recession, wages were reduced at Natividad by 25 percent to seventy-five centavos per day.[53] Now more than ever, the informal network of household smelting operations became a key means of survival for the Serranos. Some of the illicit ore came from workers who could conceal small chunks and either sell it or process it themselves at home. But most of the supply of gold and silver for the informal markets came from men, women, and children who panned the river into which runoff water was poured from the processing plant, and from men and women who entered parts of the mine undetected and went about digging their own sacks of ore. Although one could get more ore by digging it oneself, this was also the most dangerous way of obtaining it. Informal mine workers were sometimes killed by floods or avalanches, and families were left to recover the dead bodies without official assistance.[54] Working conditions in Oaxacan mines were generally more dangerous than in other parts of Mexico. In 1907 forty-three mineworkers lost their lives in Oaxaca. In the same year, 101 deaths were reported in Durango, and 89 in Coahuila, two important mining regions in northern Mexico. As a percentage of all mineworkers in each state, however, 2.6 percent were killed in accidents in Oaxaca, compared with just 1.7 percent in Durango and 1.2 percent in Coahuila.[55] Workers at Natividad faced great physical danger and low wages; they assumed it was their right to take a little bit from the mine.

The recession of 1907–1911 only increased Natividad's siege mentality. In 1909 Natividad's administrators surrounded the entire compound with an electrical fence, which extended over two public roads that ran near the mine's operations. Villagers from the nearby towns of Xiacui and Calpulalpam protested vigorously about the injustice of mine owners limiting roads that had been used "since time immemorial by the people of these villages," and they challenged regional and state officials to dismantle the fence. A dog was killed and several people were injured by electrical shocks from the fence. From the perspective of the villagers of Xiacui, the fence threatened their fundamental right to circulate freely. On September 16, 1909, residents of Xiacui used their annual Independence Day parade as an excuse to march wherever and whenever they wanted. They intentionally followed a route that led them along one of the fenced-off roads. After an intense standoff, mine officials finally conceded and allowed the parade to continue. Tensions were on the rise around the mine, and the district jefe político and Governor Pimentel determined that the fence across the two roads should be removed and that the electricity should be shut off on the fence that remained. "All of these issues have raised the animosity of the people in that area," Pimentel told Díaz, "who, without a doubt, have made threats against the company."[56] But mining officials ignored the governor's order and refused to pay a fine of fifty pesos charged by the jefe político.

Administrators of the mine, who were unwilling to concede on any issue, caused further problems for their Zapotec neighbors. In December 1909 wagons carrying new machinery for the processing plant destroyed a private fence belonging to Trinidad Pérez, and mine officials refused to offer indemnification.[57] Word spread throughout the district that the mine owners were abusing the rights of the Serranos. One week later, Rafael Aguirre Cinta, a leading member of Natividad's board of directors and the president of the Banco Nacional office in Oaxaca City, was traveling through the district to consult with Natividad officials on financial matters. He stopped for an overnight stay at the textile factory at Xía on a Sunday night, and was repeatedly harassed and insulted by factory workers who had had the day off. They were drunk, Pimentel reported to Díaz, but their hostility should not be ignored. Pimentel blamed the administrators at Natividad. They had closed two roads, electrified their fences, and had begun threatening to import workers from Pachuca, "which would leave the Serranos without work."[58] Pimentel appeared to have learned how important it was to keep the Serranos satisfied; he knew they did not support him personally, but he also knew that they could cause serious problems for his administration.

Aguirre Cinta was more concerned than Pimentel about the situation in the Sierra, describing an impending race war should the "Indians" go unchallenged. The authorities feared the Serranos, Aguirre Cinta reported; "most of the Indians set up road blocks, steal, and threaten, and expect everyone to do as they ask; and since the authorities tolerate this behavior, simply out of fear, the result is that no one is safe." The government needs to send a new jefe político to Ixtlán, Aguirre Cinta concluded, someone "who has the honor, bravery, and energy to protect capital and [white] people, and who will put an end to the demands of the Indians, who have become arrogant simply because they know everyone is afraid of them."[59] In a separate incident, a driver for Natividad was imprisoned for traveling on public roads through the town of Guelatao. Furthermore, reports were leaked to the public that Natividad had polluted the river water with cyanide used for processing.[60] Tensions increased further. The Serranos were getting restless, Pimentel warned Díaz, and the mine owners had to find a way to calm them down.

Administrators conceded on one issue: they shut off the electricity to the fence. But this decision gave peasants the opportunity to exact revenge against the mine. Several people entered the mine's compound at three o'clock in the morning on February 11, 1910. Careful not to draw the attention of the armed security guards, they intended to teach mine owners a lesson: if mine owners harassed the pueblo, then the pueblo would harass them. Under the cover of darkness, they intentionally set fire to the company's warehouse, causing more than one thousand pesos in damage. Huntington Adams, director of Natividad, requested an immediate increase in security for the mine: "In light of such a hostile act, I believe it is urgent to make preparations for the security of the refinery as soon as possible since no one knows when the next attempt of this nature will happen, which would be disastrous for the company."[61] Adams asked for permission to run electricity through his fence again: "I am asking you to allow me to run electricity at night since it's certain that if the fence had been electrified they could not have penetrated inside the compound as they did to set fire to the warehouse." The night after the fire, individuals bombarded the finishing patio with rocks, breaking a light and causing workers to flee the area, which resulted in "considerable losses." Adams once again threatened to bring in replacement workers: "if this disorder continues, I will fire every single person from Natividad [*todo hijo del pueblo de Natividad*], and this is my last arm of defense; I'm afraid that it won't be enough to contain these people."[62]

Governor Pimentel ordered a full inquiry into the fire and ultimately determined that the villagers should not be blamed. He emphasized instead the rapid response of neighbors and mine workers who eventually extinguished the fire, saving Natividad from greater losses. The real problem, according to Pimentel, was the ongoing dispute between the mine operators and the neighboring pueblos; "after coexisting with the mine for so long, difficulties and disagreements have emerged between the Administrator, the officials of the mine, and the people of Natividad and Xiacui." Pimentel argued that the operators of the mine did not know how to work with their employees: "the cause of all these problems is the absence of any tact on the part of the principal employers, who are foreigners, and who tend to treat the Indian workers with disrespect and force." It seems strange that this man, who had opposed spending money on universal education for Indian children, would complain that the foreign owners at Natividad did not treat the Zapotec workers with respect. Still, Pimentel had always treated the Serranos with a certain amount of deference, even if they thought it had not been enough. Also, Pimentel suggested that the mine operators were actually trying to find a way to blame someone else for the mine's failure during the recession: "It's also possible that the employers are exaggerating their problems in order to make it look like these events have contributed to the failure of the business, which is certainly very bad as they owe a great deal of money and cannot improve their operations since the mine has run dry and because its technical directors are broke."[63] No one was arrested for setting the fire at Natividad, mostly because regional and state officials realized that an arrest would only inflame the hostility villagers already felt toward the mine. Mine owners paid for their own security, increasing the number of armed guards who patrolled its compound.

Nonetheless, the mine was still in trouble as a result of the recession, and, like everyone else in the district of Ixtlán, its administrators turned to President Díaz for aid. In November 1910 Antonio Allende, president of the Compañía Minera de Natividad, begged Díaz for help in securing a loan to keep the mine solvent. Allende claimed that the company had discovered a new vein, which promised great returns, but the mine needed a loan of 80,000 pesos to update their electrical plant and to pay off another loan that was coming due in December. "The Company's existence is seriously threatened at this time," Allende warned Díaz.[64] If the mine closed more than five hundred workers would lose their jobs. These men, "the working sons of the Sierra Juárez," had no other means of survival since there was no other mine in the region still operating by late 1910. For everyone's sake, for the stockholders, for his own, and especially for the "affection you express for your fellow Oaxacans who dearly love you," Allende asked Díaz to "use your good offices among your friends, the Directors of the National Bank, so that they will cooperate in our effort to raise capital."[65] November 1910, however, was too late in the political scheme of things for Díaz to offer meaningful help. His government was under attack by supporters of Francisco I. Madero, and in a few short months, Díaz himself would be in exile. During the 1910–20 Revolution, Natividad was taken over by Zapotec armies who fought against the Constitutionalists. In 1920, when peace was reestablished in Oaxaca, the lingering effects of the 1907–11 recession, followed by a decade of neglect and civil war, forced mine owners to declare bankruptcy. But that is getting ahead of the story.

Corruption and Abuse

Intervillage conflicts in the Sierra Juárez had been a problem well before 1907, but during the recession these conflicts increased significantly. The recession forced more people to survive solely on agricultural production rather than on a combination of agricultural and wage labor. Natividad was the only mine in the district still operating during the recession, and peasants could not find seasonal work to supplement their household incomes. In addition, Guillermo Meixueiro and Federico Toro fomented disputes that had to be settled by legal representation. Meixueiro was a lawyer and constantly sought clients in the district. In any land dispute Meixueiro could become the "hired gun" for one side or the other. He had little conviction about the veracity of any particular claim, preferring to side with whatever community paid his fees. Federico Toro, as the secretary to the district jefe político, was used to enforce agreements. To carry out governmental and court orders, Toro expected to be paid. He harassed individuals who did not abide by court rulings or acquiesce in the face of official pressure. To stand up to Meixueiro and Toro, opposing communities often hired José Ruíz Jiménez to represent their interests to officials in Oaxaca City. Ruíz Jiménez was not a trained lawyer, but he too was a "hired gun," a legal strategist who understood the regional power structure and who was not afraid to challenge that structure. Like Meixueiro, Ruíz Jiménez cared little for which side he represented, though his appeals usually challenged the hegemonic establishment in Oaxaca. These men, Meixueiro, Toro, and Ruíz Jiménez, did not take advantage of helpless communities who wanted only to be left alone. Intervillage conflict in Ixtlán district had a history that predated any interference on the part of these three men. But the 1907–11 recession added to the desperation of some communities, and Meixueiro, Toro, and Ruíz Jiménez had little problem finding conflicts that could be exploited for their own profit.

It was common knowledge that Guillermo Meixueiro had an interest in the ongoing litigation between villages. Antonio Hernández, a Zapotec peasant from Ixtlán, complained that Meixueiro's intervention had exacerbated the problems between Ixtlán and Guelatao, Atepec and Analco, Teococuilco and Guelache, Ixtepeji and Tlalixtac, Abejones and Maninaltepec, and Las Llagas and Quiotepec.[66] The details of all of these intervillage conflicts were remarkably similar. One village had invaded the land of another, an invasion that either violated the terms of a signed agreement or made it necessary for an agreement to be put in place. One reason intervillage conflict in the district remained problematic for so long was that few issues were ever completely settled. Land and water disputes may have temporarily given way to discussions about presidential politics and the possibility of civil war, but intervillage conflict had become almost a way of life. Another reason was that district officials and legal representatives benefited from these conflicts. There were limits to how far they could push Zapotec community leaders, and limits as well on the power of so-called mestizo caudillos. It was in the interest of some villagers to keep conflicts in the district undetermined. Even disagreements that seemingly had been set aside could be reopened years later if one village did not approve of the outcome.

In the case of Chicomezuchil's conflict with neighboring villages, for example, disputes of the past resurfaced during the 1907–11 recession. In 1894 the village of Lachatao claimed a section of the Río de Salinas that Chicomezuchil had been using for irrigation. Men from Lachatao destroyed Chicomezuchil's water tank and hired Guillermo Meixueiro to defend their actions. Two other villages, Amatlán and Yahuiche, joined Lachatao in barring Chicomezuchil from using the river. Meixueiro devised a plan whereby Chicomezuchil would rent water rights from Alejandro Juárez, who owned a private plot along the Salinas River. Without Chicomezuchil's knowledge, and acting as representative for the other towns, Meixueiro went to Governor González and told him that his plan had been agreed to by all sides and that the governor needed only to sanction the accord. He then returned to the people of Chicomezuchil, telling them that the governor had ordered the town to pay Juárez eight pesos per year for using the Río de Salinas. The people of Chicomezuchil claimed they had been tricked: "this whole thing shows how we have been deceived; we are uneducated Serranos who have been abused by the pernicious actions of those who have plagued and dishonored the Sierra, whose sons are all known and respected for their loyalty and honesty."[67]

In 1906 Alejandro Juárez died, and Meixueiro returned to Chicomezuchil, demanding that now they had to buy the land for "the enormous sum of 800 pesos." The villagers could collect just four hundred pesos but paid Meixueiro anyway, hoping he would be satisfied. He returned again in 1908, telling them this time that he needed another four hundred pesos. Enrique Martínez, Chicomezuchil's municipal president, refused to sign Meixueiro's latest contract. Martínez had briefly attended primary school in Oaxaca City; he knew how to read and write, and he knew when his people were being exploited: "I have not signed nor will I sign in defense of my humble people and my personal honor." Rather than go along with Meixueiro's extortion, Martínez said he would rather resign: "If I cannot be useful to my people, then I do not want to aid in their ongoing exploitation and vile treatment as is happening now and happened in the past for the Indian Serrano during the disgraceful colonial period." He would not betray his people, he insisted; he would be neither "a traitor nor an apparent accomplice in the theft of those 400 pesos." He understood the risks he was taking in standing up to Meixueiro, but he claimed his village was protected by the guarantees of the 1857 Constitution: "I have advised my people that even though we are humble and uneducated we are under the sacred protection of our Constitution, which was acquired by the blood of our fathers who cooperated in defending and guaranteeing our rights as Citizens." [68] Meixueiro had already instructed Martínez to refrain from discussing "local" issues with the president, who had to deal with more important "national" concerns. But the villagers of Chicomezuchil wrote Díaz anyway, asking for protection should Meixueiro punish them as he did other people. Meixueiro backed down for the moment, but he refused to return the four hundred pesos Chicomezuchil had already paid him, and he ignored their request for legal title to the land that gave them access to the Salinas River.

During the 1907–11 recession, Toro and Meixueiro also used more coercive means to extort money throughout the district. Toro began arresting individuals who could not pay a head tax, releasing them only when their families had paid equivalent amounts in coffee and cloth, plus a surcharge for failing to pay the tax on time. Peasants like Juan Ramírez complained to Díaz, "We live by our own work in the fields; we do not appreciate the offices of the Government that are here, as if they were stores for Federico H. Toro who sells justice as he sees fit." The Serranos wanted to live in peace, Ramírez told Díaz, but Toro made that impossible: "all of these complaints about land are provoked by the same Toro, who defends the person who pays him the most even though he does not have the right; he mistreats the poor who do not pay or who do not want to sustain these questions of pueblo against pueblo." [69] Toro and Meixueiro also devised a scheme to control corn prices in the region.

They made it illegal to sell corn except in the district *cabecera* and then purchased most of the corn available during the harvest. In 1909 and 1910 they raised prices in Ixtlán, forcing families to pay extra for this basic food.[70] Regional caudillos thus pressed the Serranos to the breaking point during the recession. Zapotecs complained bitterly; they attacked the legitimacy of those men who took advantage of their hardship; and they called for political reform. Díaz needed to decide which side he supported.

The 1910 Centennial and Elections

The 1910 Centennial offered a possible way out of these escalating conflicts by emphasizing the common history and cooperation of all Mexicans in the struggle for independence.[71] But good feelings alone could not mollify years of rancorous disagreements. One of the ways in which the regime mitigated the effects of the recession was to pour tens of thousands of pesos into rural Mexico through building projects designated for the centennial of national independence. With President Díaz's encouragement, towns in even the most remote parts of rural Mexico received money to build new schools, new bridges and roads, and new municipal offices. Díaz invested in rural Mexico at a time when the effects of the recession were greatest. The building projects provided jobs for unemployed mine workers and extraneous field hands. Moreover, the projects gave entire communities a sense of importance and a sense of their own future just as they were looking back on Mexico's past. There are no aggregate statistics for the amount of money Díaz spent on such projects around the centennial, but the investment in rural Mexico was plain to see in the new buildings photographed upon completion, in the volumes of correspondence between local representatives and officials in Mexico City, and in the infrastructural improvements throughout the country. Centennial planners expected world leaders to see that Mexico was a part of the modern era. For these reasons, Díaz could not allow rampant poverty to force rural workers into Mexico City, which he purged of homeless and poor residents in the months before the centennial anyway.[72]

By 1907, the people of the Sierra Zapoteca had been making political and economic demands on state officials for more than a generation. But the organization of local centennial committees empowered Zapotec peasants to criticize more directly and to question unpopular representatives more thoroughly. Ever mindful of the sacrifices they and their ancestors had made for national sovereignty, these rural citizens saw the 1910 Centennial as a way to regain their influence over local and statewide political affairs. In addition to criticizing the corruption of local elites, Zapotec peasants used their local centennial commissions to challenge the 1910 reelection bid of Governor Emilio Pimentel. The Serranos still maintained that Díaz had "imposed" Pimentel on the state, and they were prepared to challenge the president's decision to support this unpopular governor. This time they backed a candidate worthy of winning office in this year of national remembering: Benito Juárez Maza, the son of the "hero of the Reform." The formation of local centennial committees facilitated the creation of more overtly partisan electoral clubs as well. New clubs backing Juárez Maza were formed in the most important towns of the district: the Club Cuahutémoc de Ixtlán de Juárez, the Club Cuna de Juárez de Guelatao, the Club Benemérito de las Americas Lic. Benito Juárez de la Villa de Ixtepeji, the Club Melchor Ocampo de Chicomezuchil, and the Club 18 de Octubre de 1866 de Jaltianguis.[73] In many cases, the same individuals served on both the centennial commission and the electoral clubs supporting Juárez Maza. As in 1906, their challenge to Pimentel turned into a confrontation with Porfirio Díaz.

Prior to the elections, a small delegation from Ixtlán traveled to Mexico City to discuss their opposition to Pimentel with the president. Onofre Jiménez, the municipal president of Ixtlán, spoke for the group, but the moral leader of the delegation was Mariano Ibarra of Lachatao, an old veteran who fought under Díaz during the French Intervention. Díaz warmly received the group, which indicated they still enjoyed enough clout to actually meet with the president. And he even listened to their complaints against Pimentel and their desire to support Juárez Maza. But when they finished, he expressed his strong disagreement with their position. He told them that Juárez Maza could not be trusted and that it was their obligation to support the official candidate. Jiménez and his comrades boldly informed the president that Juárez Maza enjoyed widespread support in the state and that they were prepared to work for his campaign. At an impasse, Díaz threatened these former allies. As Jiménez recalled, "He then told us that he did not want any opposition in the country, and that any rebel outbreaks would be immediately repressed since he could count on a powerful and well-equipped army with modern weapons and that the best thing for us to do was to leave things in the state the way they were."[74]

Jiménez and the other delegates left Mexico City unconvinced by the president's argument and undeterred by the president's threats. Díaz turned for help from his longtime allies, the sons of his former military comrades, Guillermo Meixueiro and Fidencio Hernández. On June 1, 1910, Meixueiro and Hernández wrote an open letter to the people of the district, instructing them to reject Juárez Maza and support Pimentel. "We understand," they wrote, "that some people intend to cause difficulties in the district. . . . These people are not sincere friends of the Sierra because without a doubt they want us to appear before the Republic and before History as an ungrateful and disloyal people."[75] Meixueiro and Hernández reminded the people of their long history of supporting Díaz, emphasizing the participation of the Serranos in the 1876 Tuxtepec rebellion. They asserted that President Díaz had rewarded them with ample evidence of his loyalty: "He has granted pensions to the families of our brothers who fell in war or who were incapacitated by war; he has generously attended to every complaint or request that has come from the Sierra; he has ordered the construction of expensive projects that have had a particular benefit for our District, like the beautiful bridge over the Río Grande; he has reduced to a minimum our property taxes." Finally, Meixueiro and Hernández argued that to go against Díaz's command would represent a violation of their long-standing devotion to their former jefe político: "As long as General Díaz is alive we Serranos should remain faithful and loyal to him, because we honor the fidelity demonstrated by our fathers." For these reasons, they concluded, "we should vote for Licenciado Pimentel."[76] If anything, Meixueiro and Hernández revealed how far out of touch they were with popular sentiment in Ixtlán district. It was precisely because of their years of support for Díaz that Zapotec peasants expected to have a more direct voice in deciding who should govern the state. Although Juárez Maza appeared a reluctant candidate, the Zapotec peasants of Ixtlán district easily rejected the order to support Pimentel.[77] Not surprisingly, they were angry when obvious acts of fraud allowed Pimentel to hang on to the governorship.

Official results gave Pimentel 93 percent of the popular vote, though the Serranos and other Juárez supporters around the state argued that the results were fraudulent.[78] Two days after the elections, on June 28, 1910, more than five hundred men from Ixtlán district wrote President Díaz, explaining their opposition. They had specific complaints against Pimentel—he had neglected agricultural and industrial development throughout the district and he had imposed higher taxes—but more than anything else they asserted that it was their right to choose their own leaders.[79] They and their ancestors had fought for liberty and independence, and during this year of national celebration these rights should have been respected. Pimentel's reelection threatened to "choke the will of the people and suffocate popular liberty." As they reflected on their own role in national history, they realized that Díaz no longer respected their rights or their freedom. Onofre Jiménez and the hundreds of other men who had challenged the president over the reelection of Governor Pimentel argued that they had earned the right to choose their own leaders because of the contributions of "the old soldiers who survive and those that have passed away."[80] History, an interpretation about the meaning of the past in the context of the present, formed the basis of rural political culture during the Porfiriato, from its beginning to its impending collapse.

Conclusion

This chapter began by analyzing the 1906 Juárez centennial and ended with the collapse of the Porfirian regime in the wake of the 1910 Centennial. During both events, celebrations of national history gave way to discord. As they marched through a town plaza or stood around the pedestal of a statue, people reflected on their role in shaping national history. Through the performance of patriotic rituals at commemorative events, Zapotec men and women were reminded of their expectations for a more egalitarian Mexico.[81] They reimagined national history through these rituals, and they generated dozens of documents detailing their grievances and their demands for change. These documents provide a new perspective on intervillage conflict in Mexico in several ways. First, as with the conflict between Guelatao and Ixtlán and the numerous disputes that emerged from the economic recession that began in 1907, intervillage conflict should be understood beyond the narrow parameters of local conflict; it was tied to issues of national politics as well. Local politics were bound together with national politics—the two are not so easily separated.

Second, the volume of correspondence between officials and peasant communities provides us with a key perspective on peasant consciousness. To a certain extent, the villagers of Guelatao had been correct when they argued that Pimentel, Meixueiro, and Toro were responsible for their conflict with Ixtlán. The governor and his local representatives took advantage of the precarious balance between adjacent villages by proposing new land arrangements that threatened the existing modus vivendi. It should not be surprising that peasants from Ixtlán and Guelatao would so quickly set aside years of cooperation and turn to competition given the increased demand for agricultural land and the potential for substantial state aid for funding a Juárez memorial. More surprising, however, is that the 1906 Juárez centennial, and the land disputes tied to that event, revealed the multiple ways in which peasants challenged the wishes of local caudillos and the state governor. These documents call into question the notion that "onstage" peasant discourse is somehow false or unreliable—the idea that peasants said one thing, did something else, and believed an altogether different set of assumptions.[82]

Of course, these and other documents about land and political conflicts in Oaxaca should not be read as transparent windows into peasant conscious- ness. But neither are they trap doors that drop the historian blindly into the path of subterfuge. Read together, from the multiple perspectives of indi- vidual community members and state officials, these documents point to the attitudes and objectives that guided peasant actions.[83]

And third, the correspondence between villagers and government officials reveals a surprising element within the ruling regime itself: the ability of peasant communities to challenge regional and state officials through Díaz's populist intervention. After Díaz had decided to settle the dispute between Guelatao and Ixtlán through a land grant, the villagers of Guelatao were repri- manded by regional officials and by Governor Pimentel for writing directly to Díaz.[84] The president should not have been distracted by this local problem, scolded Pimentel and Federico Toro. But peasants from Guelatao vigorously defended their right to petition Díaz for the redress of grievances. Guelatao effectively held local officials at bay because Díaz read his mail and occasion- ally responded to the requests of local populations. By elevating local affairs to presidential scrutiny, villagers multiplied the number of patriarchal do- mains in play on any particular issue.[85]

Díaz himself understood how effectively his intervention kept regional offi- cials in line. By responding to ordinary Mexicans, Díaz encouraged letters from peasants, using their eyes, ears, and voices as a way to monitor his own officials. Because of the autonomous and historical relationship Díaz had with peasants from the Sierra Zapoteca, regional officials could not contain local disputes. By the time Mexicans gathered to celebrate the one-hundredth anniversary of independence from Spain, the Porfirian state had become a regime of surveillance, a complicated and complex network of information moving in both directions. Surveillance, Michel Foucault reminds us, "rests on individuals, its functioning is that of a network of relations from top to bottom, but also to a certain extent from bottom to top and laterally. . . . [It] constantly supervises the very individuals who are entrusted with the task of supervising."[86] Ultimately, the month-long proclamation of national unity and solidarity set for September 1910 did not erase the lingering resentment that Serranos felt toward Pimentel or the growing realization that Díaz no longer respected their notion of citizenship rights.[87]

Oaxaca, Land of Yesterday

Peace is made by the people who fight.
Isaac Ibarra (1919)

It is an understatement to say that the decade between 1910 and 1920 witnessed profound transformations throughout Mexico. Oaxaca was no exception. The revolutionary experience in Oaxaca and the particular history of resistance to the Constitutionalists has been thoroughly studied by historians; it is not my intention to revise that narrative.[1] Rather, as a final glimpse on the dynamics of Porfirian social and political life, I want to briefly consider the ways in which the legacy of the Old Regime continued to shape the ideas and actions of the Sons of the Sierra in a Revolutionary context. For in many ways the decade of fighting and upheaval represented a final statement on the Porfiriato itself. As the people of Ixtlán district quickly realized, the political and social relationship between center and province fundamentally changed during this time. In fact, the Mexican Revolution became *the* defining moment in Oaxaca, much more than it did in Morelos, Chihuahua, or Sonora. As day to night, Oaxaca's claim as Mexico's "Land of Tomorrow" gave way to an emphasis on ancient ruins and "backward" native populations. Oaxaca became Mexico's "Land of Yesterday," while new state-sponsored economic and political initiatives flourished in other parts of the country.[2] If the Revolution represented a new chapter in other parts of the country, it became a conclusion for the Sierra Zapoteca.

For the most part, the men and women who fought in the Revolution were all too young to remember the civil wars of the mid-nineteenth century. In fact, we could say the children and grandchildren of veterans who had fought alongside Díaz went to war because of him. Popular militias and their leaders justified their actions in light of the real and imagined brutalities of the Porfirian regime, in support of Francisco I. Madero's rebellion against the dictator, and in pursuit of their own demands for land and fair wages. With the exception of Venustiano Carranza, "the old man of the revolution," all of the major leaders of revolutionary movements were men in their thirties in 1910: Madero (thirty-seven, born October 30, 1873), Ricardo Flores Magón (thirty-seven, born September 16, 1873), Francisco "Pancho" Villa (thirty-two, born June 5, 1878), Emiliano Zapata (thirty-one, born August 8, 1879), and Alvaro Obregón (thirty, born February 19, 1880).[3] The majority of men and women who followed these leaders were of the same generation. This generational dynamic, according to historian Frank Tannenbaum, represented one of the key features of Revolutionary upheaval: "The Revolution was conceived by young men; it was fought by young men; it has been controlled and guided by young men. It was, in a sense, a new generation displacing an older one."[4]

Still, Mexicans of this new generation essentially believed they were fighting to protect the same principles as had their parents: for "*Libertad*," the central ideal of the 1857 Constitution; for "Effective Suffrage, No Reelection," the mantle of Porfirio Díaz's revolt at Tuxtepec in 1876; and for local autonomy, the right to farm their own communal lands and select their own village leaders. Eventually, new military heroes emerged from the battlefields of revolution, replacing Díaz as the symbolic figure of patriarchal order, though memories of Díaz remained a key element of Mexican political culture. No longer considered Mexico's heroic general, Díaz became the evil dictator who had suppressed civil society and sold the nation's wealth to foreign investors. The antithesis of Juárez, Díaz represented the archetypal enemy, the reason and justification for a bloody civil war. To a certain extent, the dark image of Porfirio Díaz and the Old Regime was as crucial to the construction and maintenance of a new Revolutionary political culture as were its own heroes. The Díaz of 1910 obscures the Díaz of 1855.[5]

In 1855 a young Porfirio Díaz organized the first rural National Guard battalion in Ixtlán district and revived a dormant Zapotec military tradition. Although myths of regional unity and military superiority animated Zapotec cultural identity, local conflicts and internal divisions actually formed an everyday part of life in the district. However, these conflicts were effectively mediated during the civil war years because of the structure of the Ixtlán

National Guard. Elder Zapotec men commanded their younger neighbors in community-based regiments, and landowning mestizo men served as officers over the entire corps. Gender, generational, class, and ethnic tensions were negotiated within the National Guard by recognizing these preexisting distinctions within the battalions. The military success of the Ixtlán National Guard invested veterans and their relatives with a sense of belonging to the nation, a core belief that they had served the nation in its time of need. Years later, as veterans grew older and died, their children would recall the wartime memories of their fathers and mothers. In exchange for fighting in wars and rebellions from 1855 to 1876, the Zapotec people of Ixtlán district argued that they had earned the right to elect their own political leaders, work in their communally owned fields, earn fair wages as miners and textile workers, and recount their own place in national history. This set of rights, broadly viewed in the Sierra Zapoteca as the rights of citizenship for all loyal Mexicans, motivated their actions again during the years of Revolutionary upheaval.

The Xía Factory as a Metaphor of Ruin

When Francisco I. Madero proclaimed his revolt against Díaz in October 1910, he found support throughout parts of Oaxaca, including some support in the Sierra Zapoteca. But these early maderistas had little room to maneuver since the state government immediately began watching them and eventually had them arrested.[6] Still, as news of Madero's revolt circulated throughout Oaxaca, Díaz grew concerned that the Serranos might use this opportunity to rebel against Pimentel. Once again, for the second time in four months, Díaz dispatched Guillermo Meixueiro and Fidencio Hernández to calm these erstwhile allies. Rumors of an impending assault on Oaxaca City had become so serious that Hernández, Meixueiro, and Emilio Pimentel tried to pacify the urban residents with a public announcement: "The people of Oaxaca [City] can rest assured regarding the position of the Sierra de Juárez, since the sons of the District have no intention whatsoever of attacking the Capital, as some misinformed persons have suggested. . . . There will be no revolutionary movement in the Sierra Juárez."[7]

In many ways the Sons of the Sierra could not escape their past—their fathers had supported Díaz, and they could stray only so far.[8] Still, they realized that there were several ways to get what they wanted from the president. They could join a rebel movement led by men from northern Mexico, or they could negotiate with Díaz and try to recreate the pact he had once formed with their relatives. The Serranos chose the latter path. In exchange for their loyalty the Serranos expected two things: first, they sought to regain a voice in selecting the officials who served over them, and second, they wanted to form a new militia—the First Battalion of the Sierra Juárez. Hernández and Meixueiro endorsed these demands since both proposals enhanced their authority in the district and therefore in Oaxaca City and Mexico City.[9] Turbulent times created new opportunities for social promotion among the Porfirian elite as well. Almost immediately, the Zapotecs achieved their first goal. Vicente Garcés, the Ixtlán district jefe político responsible for conducting fraudulent elections the previous June, was the first official to be removed from office. Garcés was fired in early December 1910, as "it was clear that the people no longer respect him as they should." At about the same time, Díaz agreed to the terms for reorganizing a popular militia throughout the district.[10]

The remobilization of a militia in the Sierra Zapoteca, however, had lasting and tragic consequences for the people of Ixtlán district. In contrast to the National Guard battalions of the mid-nineteenth century, the First Battalion of the Sierra Juárez, formed in 1910, could not overcome the intense hostilities between neighboring communities. As before, mestizo landowners assumed officer ranks above the Zapotec soldiers; Hernández and Meixueiro appointed themselves generals and commissioned their brothers as captains.[11] But in a significant departure from the National Guard units of the 1850s and 1860s, Hernández and Meixueiro recruited only relatively young men between the ages of eighteen and thirty-five for the new militia. With the important exception of Onofre Jiménez (age thirty-nine), Hernández and Meixueiro tried to supplant the authority of village elders by limiting their participation in the new battalion.[12] Once again, this generation of caudillos failed to recognize the crucial participation of village elders within the structure of the militia. Village autonomy under the guidance of communal leaders had always protected the integrity of the entire corps. Without that autonomy, fewer communities were willing to join the new battalion, and Hernández and Meixueiro had to coerce some communities to send delegations for military training.[13]

In the early months of 1911, as maderista rebels increased their attacks against the regime, tensions within Ixtlán district grew as well. Doubts about the cohesion and loyalty of the First Battalion prevented Hernández and Meixueiro from sending them into combat.[14] Ultimately, the collapse of the Porfirian regime in Oaxaca came quickly and rather quietly. Governor Pimentel resigned on May 4; President Díaz resigned on May 25, 1911. The Serranos had finally achieved their long-sought objective—the removal of Pimentel—but it had come at the cost of Díaz's own resignation. Surprisingly, because most of them had only lived in Mexico under Díaz, few Serranos voiced any concern about the transition.[15] But the Serranos were distracted by tensions within and between their own communities. Before they could participate in the rapidly moving effort to reform the nation, they first had to try to relocate their own sense of purpose as Sons of the Sierra. This last task proved impossible.

In the power vacuum created by the collapse of the Porfirian state, neighboring communities turned against each other to exact revenge for long-held grievances. Reports of land invasions, looting, and killings spread as new governments in Mexico City and Oaxaca City tried to prevent growing unrest. Many of the violent confrontations during the decade of Revolutionary fighting took place at the Xía textile factory. The first episode happened just days before Díaz resigned. Late at night on May 21, 1911, an angry group of twenty-six workers ransacked the company's *tienda de raya*, the company store, stealing merchandise worth more than three thousand pesos. They had been drinking most of the day, a Sunday, which was their usual habit. But this time some of the workers put into action the complaints and grievances that found expression when they turned to alcohol for courage. Shouts of rioting and chaos rang out, and most of the workers who did not participate in the uprising fled the area around the factory. The leaders of the riot, Eliseo Moreno and Julio López, moved through the Xía valley and headed for Natividad. They cut telegraph wires along the way and announced that they were seeking supporters among the mine workers who had been engaged in their own struggle against capital.[16]

On the morning after the riot, Fidencio Hernández, acting now as the jefe político, established a base of operations at Xía. He called for volunteers to capture those responsible and to restore order to the district. To his surprise, several hundred Zapotec men, organized into village units from Ixtepeji, Ixtlán, Lachatao, and Amatlán, reported to him for service.[17] The call to arms provided the Sons of the Sierra with an opportunity to flex their military muscle and to demonstrate their willingness to fight, if needed. It is unclear, however, whether so many Zapotec militiamen came to Xía to put down the revolt or join it. Hernández stressed to them that the rioters had been outsiders, men from Etla, and so this was not a rebellion by people from Ixtlán. But he also quickly tried to demobilize these volunteers. He paid them twenty-five centavos, less than they would have earned in the mines, and thanked them for their "patriotic service." Clearly, Hernández had determined that it was too dangerous to have armed groups roaming the district, even if they claimed to be helping officials keep the peace. There were too many villages that had ongoing conflicts with their neighbors, and given the earlier disturbances at Natividad, the litany of complaints against Meixueiro and Toro, and the animosity publicly expressed toward Pimentel, Hernández's hold on the district was tenuous at best. In fact, the rioting spread, and community elders, no longer a part of the militia, issued urgent pleas for help in restoring order.[18]

Things should have calmed down in September 1911, when Benito Juárez Maza became governor of Oaxaca. After more than fifty years, the Sons of the Sierra had helped to elect another Juárez to the Oaxacan statehouse. But Juárez's administration, like his father's before him, was plagued by ethnic unrest in other parts of the state. In particular, the Juchitán leader José F. "Che" Gómez rebelled in the Isthmus of Tehuantepec and threatened the stability of the state government. Exercising his strong ties to the Sierra Zapoteca, Juárez called on Onofre Jiménez and the Battalion of the Sierra Juárez to protect Oaxaca City.[19] After a brief occupation of the capital city, however, soldiers within the battalion rebelled. In particular, most of the First Company, composed primarily of men from the towns Ixtepeji and Nexicho, initiated a bloody civil war against Guillermo Meixueiro, Fidencio Hernández, and the villagers of Ixtlán town. Known as the Ixtepeji revolt of 1912, this bloody intra-district war signaled the complete collapse of regional unity. The heirs of a valiant Zapotec military tradition started killing each other.[20]

While most historians of Oaxaca have argued that the Ixtepejanos revolted because of their lingering resentment of Ixtlán's *cabecera* status, an administrative change that had happened several centuries earlier, I suggest the actual causes of the rebellion were more immediate and tangible. They were also more complex. When Francisco Meijueiro encouraged a group of Ixtepejanos to form a separate landowning syndicate in 1877, he introduced a new division within the larger Ixtepeji community. In exchange for control over their land, the new rancheros had to pay one-fifth of their agricultural production as tribute to the Ixtepeji town council and the Meixueiro family. By 1907, the ranchero population had doubled while the land base remained constant.[21] Not surprisingly, the children of the original rancheros deeply resented the fact that they had to pay so much tribute to the Meixueiro family. Guillermo Meixueiro had actually begun abusing the original agreement his father had established with these people and refused to listen to their complaints. In fact, he had escalated the real cost of the tribute by sending his own accountants into their orchards and fields before the crops had actually been harvested.[22] When a ranchero would refuse to pay Meixueiro, as Francisco Santiago did in 1909, Meixueiro would order his arrest, charge a fine, and collect interest on the unpaid tribute.[23] After years of complaining to Díaz and Pimentel, the rancheros used the opportunity created by the collapse of the state and federal governments and the remobilization of the military to exact revenge against Meixueiro and his allies in Ixtlán. Exposing deep tensions both within the community of Ixtepeji and the district more broadly, the rancheros led a major assault against the town of Ixtlán and the mestizo caudillos of the district. Ixtepeji itself was roughly divided down the middle—half of the residents supported the rebellion, and the other half fled the region.[24] But a vast majority of other villages sided with the rebel cause against the *cabecera*. Onofre Jiménez, the former municipal president of Ixtlán, recalled, "The major part of the Sierra was on the side of the rebels."[25]

The revolt began boldly in May 1912 when a group of rebels killed the Ixtlán jefe político and two other men at the gates of the Xía textile factory.[26] The rebels then marched to Ixtlán town, ransacked the offices of the municipal president, and selected their own jefe político. The people of Ixtlán fled their homes, taking refuge in the surrounding mountains. Fully in control of the Sierra Zapoteca and aware that Meixueiro's political power lay in Oaxaca City, the Ixtepeji rebels turned their attention to the state capital. They planned to install their own governor and begin negotiations with President Madero. In September some four hundred rebel troops, most of them poorly armed, attacked federal soldiers protecting the city. In response, President Madero ordered eight hundred federal troops into the Sierra Zapoteca.[27] Eventually, a small militia of Ixtlán villagers joined with Madero's forces to defeat the rebels. The government troops proved decisive, according to Jiménez; "without the support of the *federales* we would have been at the mercy of the rebels and inevitably we would have lost."[28] But the rancheros and rebels who had resisted Meixueiro's abuses lost instead. The town of Ixtepeji was burned to the ground; dozens of people were arrested and eventually exiled to northern Mexico. The Ixtepejanos who had not participated in the revolt were forced to live in temporary shelters in Oaxaca City and at the Xía textile factory. The town never recovered its population, and in many ways, it has yet to overcome the trauma of 1912.[29]

Although unsuccessful, the Ixtepeji revolt ultimately weakened the mestizo grip on power in the Sierra. Meixueiro and Hernández remained nominal leaders and influential politicians in Oaxaca City, but they were forced to more fully acknowledge the role of indigenous community leaders like Onofre Jiménez of Ixtlán and Isaac Ibarra of Lachatao. The strategy of separating elders from the militia had failed miserably. In addition, the battalion lost the largest and most aggressive unit within their army when the Ixtepejanos rebelled. For generations, units from Ixtepeji had been the most effective and successful fighters within the entire corps. Without their participation, the

Zapotec militia was severely weakened, and mestizo politicians with ties to the Sierra posed less of a threat to rivals in other parts of the state.

Hernández, Meixueiro, and village leaders from Ixtlán spent the next three years trying to rebuild a coalition of Zapotec communities that could be mobilized to take control of the district and the state capital if the opportunity arose. The untimely death of Benito Juárez Maza, the assassination of Francisco Madero, and the counterrevolution orchestrated by Victoriano Huerta in Mexico City provided the Oaxacan leaders with time to reorganize. In the Sierra Zapoteca, village leaders from Ixtlán town carefully negotiated the terms of cooperation with leaders from neighboring towns. Elders from Lachatao, Amatlán, and Yavesia formally pledged their allegiance to Ixtlán and offered to mediate for others. People who had fled the region during the Ixtepeji revolt wanted to return to their homes and their fields, but Ixtlán wanted assurances of respect and loyalty. These negotiations were particularly difficult for the people from Guelatao, who had challenged Ixtlán town leaders in the years leading up to the revolt. In May 1914 the Ixtlán town council held a general meeting to consider a petition from Guelatao residents to return to their homes. The Ixtlán leaders reviewed each individual name and specifically denied permission for seven families "because of the hostile attitude they assumed against the *cabecera* and its destruction." One year later, in 1915, the Ixtlán town council held another meeting to formally draft an agreement for organizing a new militia. The implied terms of cooperation that had been at the heart of the National Guard in 1855 no longer sufficed. In the wake of the Ixtepeji revolt, Ixtlán leaders sought greater control over the military apparatus. No military decision could be made without first "consulting the *Cabecera* of the District, which is where the General Quarters will be located." Ixtlán town leaders sought complete administrative and military domination over the entire district.[30]

In Oaxaca City political elites settled on a declaration of state sovereignty, a formal rupture from the rest of the nation. In June 1915 political leaders in Oaxaca City, bolstered by the new militia of Zapotec soldiers from Ixtlán, announced that in accordance with the principles of federalism, they were officially claiming their sovereignty until constitutional order could be reestablished. By this time, Venustiano Carranza and the Constitutionalist armies had gained greater control over Mexico City. Like the Villistas in the north and the Zapatistas in Morelos, the Oaxacan anti-Constitutionalists saw Carranza as a tool of the United States. From their perspective Carranza was "an automaton of the White House," and Carranza's supporters were "traitors to the fatherland who will never rise to the public offices to which they aspire because they will always carry in their impressionable souls the diabolical evil of their fathers, the 'Yankees.'"[31] Leaders of the sovereignty movement in Oaxaca attempted to form ties with other rebel groups—the Zapatistas and Villistas in particular—but ideological and logistical limitations prevented any widespread military front from threatening the Constitutionalists.[32] The Zapotecs faced the Constitutionalists alone.

A major battle between the two armies took place at the Xía textile factory. Zapotec soldiers took up defensive positions inside the factory that had once provided crucial jobs for people in the Sierra. The battle completely destroyed the factory, which was never rebuilt. Eventually, the owners received compensation as part of the settlement paid to English landowners who had lost property during the decade of revolution. The land itself went back to farmland, even though the ruins of the factory still stand as a reminder of the Porfiriato. Still, like the Mexica army in the sixteenth century, the Spanish army in the seventeenth century, and the conservative and French armies in the nineteenth century, the Constitutionalist army could not dislodge the Serranos from the mountains. But neither could the Zapotec army drive the Constitutionalists from Oaxaca City.

After nearly four years of a stalemate, in early 1919 Guillermo Meixueiro began looking for a way to exit the conflict. The Constitutionalist generals were eager to see him retire because they feared Meixueiro might form a new southern front with Manuel Pelaez in Veracruz, exposing a serious weakness in their defense of Mexico City. But before a treaty could be signed, Meixueiro still had to negotiate with individual community leaders from Ixtlán district.[33] Clearly, Meixueiro had not consolidated his power in the district; indeed, many community leaders seriously distrusted this mestizo politician as much now as they had when he began his career in 1890. Writing for the people and militia from Lachatao, Isaac Ibarra rejected any peace negotiations that did not include actual representatives from Zapotec communities. Ibarra criticized "political men who dress in revolutionary uniforms" but who ultimately betrayed the people risking their lives, a direct attack on Meixueiro's lack of dedication to the Serranos. The people of the Sierra wanted "a commission composed of military men and not lawyers."[34]

> In short, the people of the Sierra do not fight for riches or jobs or public offices . . . the people of the Sierra do not sell the blood of their brothers; they know how to sacrifice their lives, but all for the general good and not for the particular benefit of a single man. . . . The Sierra is not repre-

sented and will not recognize any agreement or compromise. Peace is not purchased with money; peace is made by the people who fight. That does not mean that the Sierra opposes peace in the state, that is, an honorable peace sanctioned by the good name of the region, a peace that will be honored in the pages of history books. All of the blood spilled by our brothers will honor the future descendants of this heroic Sierra. What a shame that you do not know how to interpret our ideals, and what a shame that there are malevolent people willing to mislead us; do not be confused into thinking that there are no people in the Sierra who can speak Spanish.[35]

After several months of negotiations, the Serranos finally agreed to lay down their arms if they could participate in new statewide elections and pledge allegiance to the 1857 Constitution.[36] On May 4, 1920, after more than five years of defending the Sierra Zapoteca from an invading Constitutionalist army, the Zapotec soldiers of Ixtlán district celebrated a peace agreement by parading through the cobblestone streets of Oaxaca City. As the sounds of horse hooves and marching feet echoed down urban corridors, "the defenders of Oaxacan sovereignty" basked in the enthusiastic praise of onlookers—"*Viva la Sierra Juárez*," "*Viva Oaxaca*," and "*Viva la Constitución de 1857*." Although the rest of the nation had either willingly or reluctantly adopted the laws of the new 1917 Constitution, the people of Oaxaca had uniquely won the right to maintain allegiance to the 1857 Constitution. For the Zapotec peasants of Ixtlán district, history and memory had always been their source of inspiration. Like their parents and grandparents before them, defending the 1857 Constitution had become a duty and an opportunity passed from one generation to the next. But the parade and "victory" celebration of 1920 quickly proved hollow. Within three weeks Oaxacan political leaders recognized the new constitution and began a sustained effort to rejoin the rest of the nation in rebuilding institutions and lives after a decade of fighting. In many ways, Mexicans in other parts of the country had stopped looking to the past and had begun imagining a new future. History could no longer protect the Sons of the Sierra.[37]

The Juárez Legacy as Interlude

Just as they had done during the initial years after Juárez's death in 1872, the Serranos kept alive the memory of the "hero of the Reform" during the initial years of Revolutionary state building. According to Charles Weeks, Juárez's popularity receded somewhat on the national stage as Revolutionary leaders looked to their own heroes for symbolic legitimacy. In general, President Alvaro Obregón and the other Constitutionalists of the 1920s remained ambivalent about recreating the Porfirian cult around Juárez.[38] In December 1920, less than six months after the war had ended in Oaxaca, villagers from Guelatao proposed the construction of a major Juárez monument as a way of creating a national "tourist attraction." They envisioned a grand statue, a school, and an interpretive center that would convey the profound importance of Juárez's ideas and accomplishments. The people of Guelatao noted that their village and other towns in the district required aid for rebuilding after "the civil dispute," a clear recharacterization of the war against the Constitutionalists. Juárez, they hoped, would bring them much needed federal aid. Obregón had other ideas. He shuffled the request between various ministries, reluctantly going through the motions of supporting the plan, or at least not rejecting it outright. Manuel Vargas, Obregón's secretary, eventually wrote back that there were no funds available for rebuilding villages, though he was keenly aware that Guelatao was Juárez's birthplace. As for the Juárez monument itself, an engineer was assigned to the project in 1923, more than two years after the initial request, though the project eventually floundered.[39] In addition, Obregón, throughout his years as the major political figure in Mexico (1920–28), refused all requests to attend Juárez memorials in Guelatao.[40]

The people of Ixtlán town also had a plan for gaining state aid. In early 1921 they organized the "Junta Protectora de Enseñanza" with the specific purpose of securing educational funds for Indian children. The organization's letterhead proclaimed, "*Por la Raza y la Patria* [For Race and Nation]," a motto advanced by proponents of indigenous nationalism in other parts of the country as well.[41] Calling for Obregón's "enthusiastic protection of the Indian Race," members of the group pointed out that their children, "*la raza de Juárez* [the people of Juárez's race]," should have the opportunity to learn about Juárez's contributions to national history.[42] Obregón had a more hostile reaction to this request. Arguing that separate schools for Indian children created a special class within Mexican society, Obregón stated, "I believe it would be a grave error to turn the Indian into a separate caste with separate laws and advantages; it was an error carried out for many years and one that I intend to eliminate. The Indian should already be considered only as a Mexican citizen; but if we consider [the Indian] as such, then [the Indian] should have all of the advantages and all of the obligations that every other Mexican citizen enjoys under the laws of the country."[43] Obregón's stance on Benito Juárez and

Indian education sought to diminish ethnic differences tied to particular regions. Ironically, his views probably reflected more accurately Juárez's own attitudes. Still, for the people of the Sierra Zapoteca, memories of Juárez represented the most important and, after the nationwide repudiation of Porfirio Díaz, the only remaining symbol of their connection to the nation. The Sons of the Sierra had gone to war against the Constitutionalists invoking Juárez's name and defending the principles of the 1857 Constitution. They would not so easily set aside their devotion to the hero of the Reform.

Throughout the 1920s and 1930s, villagers from Guelatao made repeated requests for financial assistance to help raise the level of commemorative events around Juárez to national prominence. Mexico City officials almost always denied these requests.[44] Celebrations and memorials recalling fallen heroes of the Revolution received more direct support from the government.[45] Finally, in 1937 President Lázaro Cárdenas traveled to Guelatao to celebrate Juárez's birth and to inaugurate a new government boarding school dedicated to educating Zapotec children.[46] As Cárdenas's government began pulling away from more radical social policies, the Revolution itself would be reinterpreted as the fulfillment of the Liberal Reform of the nineteenth century.[47] Steadfast in their assertion that Juárez deserved nationwide praise, the Sons of the Sierra could finally imagine themselves as a part of the Revolutionary community that formed the Mexican nation.

The Díaz Legacy as Conclusion

The 1910 Mexican Revolution set into motion a decade of violence and upheaval, as thousands of men and women took up arms against a corrupt regime. By weaving together the origins of Díaz's political and military career with the lives of people who fought alongside him in Oaxaca, I have explored the nature of grassroots expectations toward, support for, and alienation from the Porfirian regime itself. Rather than the Revolutionary image of Díaz as an unwavering brutal dictator, I have identified important discontinuities during the years of Porfirian rule. Using the Sierra Zapoteca as a long-term reference point, I have argued that popular classes initially supported Díaz and personally identified with the patriarchal imagery and paternalistic policies of his administration. Support for the government, however, did not come freely or easily. Oftentimes challenging and constantly negotiating with the president and his local representatives, Zapotec peasants were driven by their own sense of rights and responsibilities as loyal citizens of the nation.

As I have repeated throughout this story, fighting in the civil wars of the mid-nineteenth century had created new opportunities for building lasting relationships between ordinary soldiers and the military leaders who went on to influence statewide and national politics. In particular, the reciprocal ties between Porfirio Díaz and the Zapotec peasants who had fought for him were forged on the battlefield and reestablished through personal and communal correspondence over two generations. Díaz rose to power with the support and aid of countless ordinary Mexicans who expected respect, recognition, and reward for their efforts. Conscious of their role in protecting the nation and installing the Porfirian regime in Mexico City, Zapotecs emphasized their own role in nation-state formation during the Porfiriato. As they repeated in stories they told to their children and in letters they wrote to Díaz and his local representatives, the Sons of the Sierra had sacrificed for their own communities and nation, both of which were tied together in a symbiotic relationship.

As told from "below," that is, from the perspective of local actors, the period we now call the Porfiriato did not begin as an authoritarian dictatorship for people in the Sierra Zapoteca. In terms of revising the post-Revolutionary interpretation of the Díaz regime, a major goal of this study has been to identify distinct moments of cooperation and confrontation between the popular classes and the Mexican state. From 1876 to 1890, peasant communities in the Sierra Zapoteca expected and received tangible benefits for their years of service to the nation. In exchange for loyalty and support, basic infrastructural improvements and new industrial jobs demonstrated a tacit agreement between Díaz, his mestizo allies, and Zapotec peasants. After 1890, as men who had fought in the civil wars began to die in greater numbers, the terms of this pact were called into question by a new generation of mestizo elites. Conflicts increased as peasant communities tried to maintain their rights to elect village leaders, work in the industrial wage economy, and receive recognition for having defended the nation. Finally, after 1906, the local political establishment, along with the Porfirian regime in Mexico City, came under increasing criticism. An economic downturn combined with antidemocratic and repressive measures ended the period of consensual politics that Díaz had established as far back as 1876. In short, I have tried to reveal a more nuanced and complex interpretation of Porfirian politics, rejecting a view of the dictator as always brutal and repressive. But my purpose has not been to restore a nostalgic or naive view of Díaz or his willingness to use force. Rather, I have tried to recover the voices and actions of rural popular classes as they dealt with government officials. Acting with their own specific economic and political goals in mind, Zapotecs found multiple ways to confront and cooperate with Díaz and his local representatives.

As I have followed the road that leads through Ixtlán district, there have been other, more specific issues of Porfirian historiography that I have reconsidered as well. When Díaz moved to Mexico City, local elites in Oaxaca assumed the responsibilities of honoring the promises made in the Tuxtepec rebellion. More than any other individual, Francisco Meijueiro negotiated the unwritten but mutually recognized pact between the Porfirian state and Zapotec peasants. Through economic development projects and an expanded set of political rights, peasants and local elites like Meijueiro sought cooperation rather than confrontation during the early years of the Porfiriato. After Francisco Meijueiro's death in 1890, a new generation of men who had not fought in the earlier civil wars inherited the patriarchal challenges of overseeing the regional economy and politics. But these men did not understand or concern themselves with living up to the earlier promises of greater communal autonomy. The most important generational conflict of the Porfiriato was created by relatively young men in local districts and not the group of octogenarians hovering around Díaz in Mexico City. Still, Zapotec peasants could impose their own limits on local abuse. In particular, they found ways to effectively limit the authority of the district jefe político—they appealed to Díaz, filed lawsuits, and refused to abide by unjust and unfair decisions.

Finally, a new political culture engendered symbols of patriarchal authority and legitimacy within local communities and the national community. Elites and popular classes looked to Mexico's three great heroes of the nineteenth century—Hidalgo, Juárez, and Díaz—and found their own historical justifications for thinking about politics. Still, the unifying accomplishment of the nineteenth century—the defense of *Libertad*—meant one thing for elites and another for popular classes. Porfirian elites sought the centralization of a fragmented nation, while popular classes fought for more meaningful local autonomy. Commemorative events intended to celebrate local and national heroes became contingent moments where the intersection of the past and the present brought to light this crucial distinction on the purpose and meaning of *Libertad*.

The degree to which people in other regions in Oaxaca and in other parts of Mexico used their participation in struggles over nation-state formation to negotiate with representatives of the government requires more careful consideration. I have asserted throughout this study that the Serranos enjoyed a unique relationship with both Juárez and Díaz, which gave them unparalleled leverage during the civil wars and later during the Porfiriato. No other group in Oaxaca enjoyed such recognition or privileges during these years. This distinctiveness is captured best by historian Francie Chassen-López, who has described the complexity of village-state relations for people throughout the state of Oaxaca. She describes a "view from the south" that demonstrates how ethnicity in particular, or as she puts it "the indigenous face in the mirror of Mexico," shifts our understanding of village-state relations during the Porfiriato. Not all rural or urban populations in Oaxaca supported Díaz or his representatives in state government, but nearly everyone engaged the state apparatus in ways that shaped the history of these years from below.[48]

Beyond Oaxaca, a rough, incomplete, and at times contradictory pattern emerges when we consider this history of nation-state formation from the bottom up. Geography once again becomes one useful way of organizing this pattern. For many people in southern Mexico, Puebla and parts of the Yucatán in particular, memories of past wars created limited opportunities for popular classes to challenge and negotiate successfully with local representatives of the Porfirian regime. The history of the Sierra de Puebla, according to Florencia Mallon and Guy Thomson, provides the best comparative case for the Sierra Zapoteca. Mallon reveals the deep connections between the politics of local communities and struggles over nation-state formation in the civil wars of the mid-nineteenth century. Yet, when she argues that "radical Liberalism would again emerge to inspire the renewed struggles of 1910 and beyond," I have trouble seeing past the thirty-five years of the Porfiriato.[49] Guy Thomson ties this regional history more closely to the Porfiriato, following in particular the long life history of Juan Francisco Lucas. Thomson argues that Díaz carefully courted village leaders throughout the Sierra de Puebla, reassuring them that he would meet their expectations for maintaining the freedom of their municipalities. During Díaz's early career, particularly for the 1871 La Noria revolt, these peasants supported Díaz even more than the Zapotecs of Ixtlán, who refused to rebel against Juárez. As president, however, Díaz eventually reneged on his promises for greater local autonomy in this region, even as he maintained a long personal relationship with Lucas. Allen Wells and Gilbert Joseph have argued that in the Yucatán, memories of the Caste War (1847–52) served as a cautionary tale for local elites who sought more effective ways of working with Indian caciques. Although elements within the planter class eventually "turned back the clock" to establish "a Porfiriato without Don Porfirio," conflicts within the ruling class, as well as popular mobilizations against local corruption and abuse, indicate a more contingent political process than has been previously considered.[50]

For central Mexico, the pattern of state intervention from the top down becomes less clear. In Mexico City, for example, as Charles Hale has argued, behind the "unifying myth" of liberalism, Porfirian intellectuals and policymakers carried on lively debates over the introduction of positivist philosophy and its application to Mexican social policy. Underlying these debates, according to Hale, was a commitment to constitutionalism and the importance of upholding Mexican law. In that sense, the content and the public nature of ideological conflict during the Porfiriato suggest a more open intellectual climate than that portrayed by post-1910 images of a brutal and unwavering dictatorship. In rural parts of central Mexico, however, Porfirian elites often took advantage of legal codes that gave them access to peasant landholdings. Clearly, the most familiar case of the peasants of Morelos, and their struggle against encroaching sugar estates, typifies this experience. As described by John Womack, the revolutionary movement led by Emiliano Zapata was born of frustration with federal officials who refused to acknowledge the legitimate complaints of peasants. A more recent study by Emilio Kourí documents the end of communal holdings in the Papantla region due to increased pressure to cultivate vanilla. Kourí describes the violent process that led to the privatization of landholdings, a shift completed by 1900. In both cases, the loss of communal landholdings precipitated political conflicts at the local and regional levels. Communities in the Sierra Zapoteca, by contrast, never lost their land, which bolstered the authority within communities of village elders and agrarian communities.[51]

Land tenure figured prominently in the ways in which historians have described northern Mexico as well. Here the pattern of top-down state intervention provided popular classes with little room to challenge unfair labor, land, and tax laws. In northern Mexico regional elites and the federal government used force to obtain both land and compliance from the majority population. Many of these conflicts emerged around new ideas and economic trends that touted "modernity" as the goal of state policy. Populations who stood in the way of "progress" met the brutal and unambiguous response of powerful landowners and Díaz's powerful military. Ana María Alonso describes the northern experience best: "Subaltern groups and classes were excluded from any intervention in the 'political process.' Although 'citizens' on paper, in practice they became the personal subjects of sultanistic caciques."[52] Alienated from the Porfirian state and its allies for most of Díaz's thirty-five years in office, popular classes had a deeper sense of resentment and hostility than anything found among disgruntled Zapotecs in the Sierra Juárez.

In addition to these rather specific issues of Mexican historiography, I have also tried to locate the history of the Sons of the Sierra according to broader theoretical and comparative questions. Three primary issues have concerned me throughout this study: peasant consciousness, popular nationalism, and regional history. The challenge of writing history from "below," from the perspective of illiterate, poor, and indigenous peasants, begins with somehow trying to document the motivation behind peasant actions. Even when the historian can locate sources written by peasants, the context within which those documents were produced may obscure the true goals and aspirations of those who wrote. I have had to acknowledge these obstacles as I tried to make sense of the letters Zapotec peasants sent to Díaz. Quite obviously, I have concluded that careful reading and contextual analysis of these documents can provide key insight into explaining peasant actions and ideas. Underlying this conclusion is my emphasis on communal literacy, which also addresses broader issues of peasant consciousness. Communal literacy, I have argued, made it possible for every member of a community to address officials with personal and political concerns. More important, Zapotec peasants took risks when they wrote; they challenged officials, demanded that promises be kept, and complained about corruption and abuse. Women took an especially active role in maintaining a family's archive and in establishing a written record with local and state officials. Ultimately, it is the volume of letters and documents that corroborate their content and make it possible to read peasant consciousness. Communal literacy created a writing-based society where words on sheets of paper mattered—even to people who could not independently read those words.

In addition to a reconsideration of peasant consciousness, my research explores questions involving the role of subaltern classes and nation-state formation for postcolonial societies more broadly. I have examined the ways in which local power relations, in particular the patriarchal claims of male authority, influenced the construction and legitimization of a national regime. Within this process, rural popular classes simultaneously forged alliances with and challenged regional and national elites over issues of political and economic rights. In terms of political culture, I have also explored the ways in which popular histories and popular images of national unity both created and confronted the possibilities of the hegemonic project of ruling elites. In short, I have analyzed the tension and cooperation within specific local communities and within the national community as a whole. Thus, the notion of an "imagined community" as described by Benedict Anderson fails to acknowledge the conflictual process of building a community or a nation. In Mexico, as in most places I would argue, gender, generational, class, and ethnic differences infused the reproduction of all communities, real and imagined.[53]

Finally, I have intentionally set out to rewrite a history of the Porfiriato from the margins of national power, from the perspective of men and women who had to live with the implications of the policies Díaz enacted in Mexico City. Although I have written mostly about the Sierra Zapoteca, my purpose has not been to write a regional history of Oaxaca. By emphasizing the connections between local and national power, and by seeing geographic space as a product of material and ideological transformations, I have tried to write beyond Oaxaca. To decenter our understanding of what constitutes national history allows us to see that Porfirian economic and political policies were in their first and final analysis issues of local concern. To understand the full impact of Porfirian economic policies—the imposition of new taxes, the disentailment of communal property, the construction of new railroads, schools, and bridges—we must focus on local communities. To grasp the political changes and continuities of the Porfirian era—the connections to National Guard members, the abuses of and limitations on jefes políticos, the controversies surrounding state governors, the myths and symbols about patriotic heroes—we must begin in local communities. For all of these reasons, regional history is not an addendum to national history or a subtle variation to a metanarrative; regional history is national history. For these reasons, we should remember that while the road to Ixtlán first connects the Sierra Zapoteca to Oaxaca City, it also joins other roads that lead to Puebla, Mexico City, and beyond.

Notes

ABBREVIATIONS

AGEO Archivo General del Estado de Oaxaca, Oaxaca City

AGN Archivo General de la Nación, Mexico City

AHDN Archivo Histórico de la Defensa Nacional, Mexico City

AMG Archivo Manual González, Universidad Iberoamericana, Mexico City

AMI Archivo Municipal de Ixtlán de Juárez

APD Archivo Porfirio Díaz (Alberto María Carreño, ed., *Archivo del General Porfirio Díaz, Memorias y Documentos*. 22 vols. Mexico: Editorial "Elede," 1947–56.)

BN Biblioteca Nacional, Mexico City

BN-AJ Biblioteca Nacional, Archivo Juárez

BN-RCH Biblioteca Nacional, Fondo de Rafael Chousal

CEHM Centro de Estudios de Historia de México CONDUMEX, Mexico City

CPD Colección Porfirio Díaz, Universidad Iberoamericana, Mexico City

INTRODUCTION

1. This account comes from APD, 1:51–55. See also Pérez García, *Sierra Juárez*, 2:15–20.

2. The Zapotec army occupied Oaxaca City several days later to ensure compliance with the agreement to keep the state government in liberal hands.

3. Perry, *Juárez and Díaz*, provides an important starting point for understanding the complicated relationship between Juárez and Díaz during the Restored Republic. Perry's study concentrates on the political struggle that ended with Juárez's death in 1872. As I argue, the relationship between these two Oaxacans continued well into the Porfiriato, once Díaz had decided to remake Juárez into a national icon. Similarly, Juárez and Díaz were linked through their ties to the people of Ixtlán district. Krauze, *Siglo de Caudillos*, offers an important, though top-down, analysis of the similarities and differences between Juárez and Diaz. Read together, Hamnett, *Juárez*, and Garner, *Porfirio Díaz*, provide a useful comparative analysis of the two Oaxacans.

4. I am grateful to Dr. Víctor Raúl Martínez Vásquez for inviting me to join a small

research team from the Instituto de Investigaciones Sociológicas of the Universidad Autónoma Benito Juárez de Oaxaca.

5. See Federico H. Toro, "Leyenda Zapoteca de Ixtlán de Juárez, Oaxaca, tradición del año 1468" [ca. 1908], in Pérez García, *Sierra Juárez*, 1:159–65. The literal translation of "Zapotecatl" would be "people of the zapote [sapote] river." Sapote fruit trees grow wild in the Sierra Zapoteca; see ibid., 1:349.

6. Ibid., 1:134–45.

7. Chance, *Conquest of the Sierra*, 16.

8. Ibid., 89–90. See also Barabas, "Rebeliones e insurrecciones indígenas en Oaxaca"; Hamnett, *Juárez*, 20; Stern, *Secret History of Gender*, 31; and Baskes, "Coerced or Voluntary?"

9. For more on the complexity of using "peasant" as a translation of *"campesino,"* see Gould, *To Lead as Equals*, 7–8.

10. The agricultural history of the Sierra Zapoteca is limited in comparison to other parts of the state. The best source for the entire state is Chassen-López, *From Liberal to Revolutionary Oaxaca*, 173–86. Speculation in the corn market became a major problem during a recession that began in 1907; see chapter 6 herein.

11. For place-names see Pérez García, *Sierra Juárez*, 1:158–65, 196–202. The cultural and ideological importance of indigenous place-names is beautifully explained in Basso, *Wisdom Sits in Places*.

12. Córdoba quotation in Pérez García, *Sierra Juárez*, 1:349–50; other Zapoteco words are explained in ibid., 1:356.

13. Ibid., 2:18. Biographies of Juárez abound; the most recent biography by a professional historian is Hamnett, *Juárez*.

14. In 1855 some fifteen thousand Zapotecs lived throughout the district in forty-five different communities, most of which had only a few hundred inhabitants. The largest town, Ixtepeji, had nearly two thousand residents in 1855, while the *cabecera* or head town of Ixtlán had half that many. See Pérez García, *Sierra Juárez*, 2:371–75.

15. In addition to capturing key notions of Zapotec identity, I have consciously chosen the title *Sons of the Sierra* to draw comparisons with Wolf, *Sons of the Shaking Earth*. Although other scholars have revised many of his conclusions, Wolf's major themes of geography, peasant communities, and revolution continue to be crucially important for understanding Mexican history.

16. Hunt, *Politics, Culture, and Class in the French Revolution*, 10, defines political culture as "the values, expectations, and implicit rules that expressed and shaped collective intentions and actions." Guardino, *Time of Liberty*, 1–18, emphasizes the tenuous, changing quality of political culture as people share ideas and references over time.

17. Turner, *Barbarous Mexico*. For background on the Partido Liberal Mexicano (PLM) and the precursor movement, see especially Cockcroft, *Intellectual Precursors of the Mexican Revolution*; and Cockcroft, *Mexico*. See also Cumberland, "Precursors of the Mexican Revolution of 1910." Blaisdell, *Desert Revolution*, offers an account of the unsuccessful PLM rebellion that predated Madero's revolt. Gomez-Quiñones, *Sembra-*

dores, argues that the PLM united Chicanos with their native Mexico. For an account of the repressive measures that U.S. and Mexican authorities used to put down the PLM, see Raat, *Revoltosos*. Walker, "Porfirian Labor Politics," argues that the brutalities of 1906 and 1907 were an aberration rather than the rule of Porfirian labor policy.

18. Gould, *To Lead as Equals*, 15. For a similar view on Somoza see Walter, *Regime of Anastasio Somoza*. For one of the first books to examine the Porfiriato "from the perspective of popular classes," see Wells and Joseph, *Summer of Discontent, Seasons of Upheaval*, 5.

19. "The Other Mexico" [1969], in Paz, *Labyrinth of Solitude*, 293.

20. Knight, "Revolutionary Project, Recalcitrant People"; Knight, *Mexican Revolution*, 1:2. The classic assessment of Mexico's diverse political and cultural features is Simpson, *Many Mexicos*. For an original reevaluation of Simpson's thesis, see Stern, *Secret History of Gender*, 217–21.

21. González y González, *San José de Gracia*, coined the phrase "*microhistoria* [microhistory]" to describe this perspective. Simpson, *Many Mexicos*, argues for the existence of multiple Mexicos within the nation. For the notion of "closed corporate communities" see Wolf, "Closed Corporate Peasant Communities in Mesoamerica and Central Java"; and Wolf, *Peasants*. For studies that stress the predominance of the "*patria chica*" in shaping local identity, see Tutino, *From Insurrection to Revolution*; Knight, *Mexican Revolution*; and González y González, "Patriotismo y matriotismo, cara y cruz de México." Most recently, Eric Van Young has argued that peasants focused exclusively on events going on within the radius of their view from the church tower bell. See Van Young, *Other Rebellion*, 483.

22. Lomnitz-Adler, "Concepts for the Study of Regional Culture." For a review of regional studies see Fowler-Salamini, "Boom in Regional Studies of the Mexican Revolution." See also the essays in Benjamin and Wasserman, *Provinces of the Revolution*; in Van Young, *Mexico's Regions*; and finally, in Katz, *Riot, Rebellion, and Revolution*.

23. Feierman, *Peasant Intellectuals*, 36, makes a similar argument about Shambaai communities in Tanzania: "The wider world is not external to the local community; it is at the heart of the community's internal processes of differentiation."

24. Lefebvre, *Everyday Life in the Modern World*, 68. For his earlier work see Lefebvre, *Critique de la vie quotidienne*.

25. Braudel, *La Méditerranée et le monde méditerranéen à l'époque de Philippe II*.

26. Soja, *Postmodern Geographies*; Soja, *Thirdspace*. See also Mignolo, *Local Histories/Global Designs*. Soja and Mignolo attribute much of their thinking about the social construction of space along border communities to Anzaldua, *Borderlands/La Frontera*. See also Sommer, *Places of History*.

27. Rubin, *Decentering the Regime*, uses this approach to reevaluate the history of post-Revolutionary Oaxaca and Mexico. Wasserman emphasized this same point two decades ago: "The history of Mexico from independence (1821) to the Revolution (1910–20) is the history of its regions and localities." Wasserman, *Capitalists, Caciques, and Revolution*, 3. More recently, Reséndez, *Changing National Identities at the Frontier*,

carefully analyzes the spatial relationships that contributed to the formation of both "market" identities and nationalist loyalties; see especially chap. 1, "Carved Spaces," 15–55.

28. For the now-classic association of poverty and ethnic identity see Friedlander, *Being Indian in Hueyapan.*

29. Bernstein, *Mexican Mining Industry*, 6; Mexico, Secretaría de Hacienda, *Mexican Year Book*, 72.

30. Cosío Villegas, *Historia moderna de México, el Porfiriato*, 2:1134. Mexico's Federal District had more than 60 percent of foreign investment itself, followed by Coahuila (10 percent), Sonora (7 percent), Chihuahua (6 percent), and Oaxaca (2 percent). Foreign investments in Oaxaca were primarily in mining operations. From 1902 to 1907, the last five years of a national mining boom, North Americans invested some $10 million in Oaxacan mines. See also Bernstein, *Mexican Mining Industry*, 73.

31. On the usefulness of "generation" as an analytical category, see especially Spitzer, *French Generation of 1820*; and Spitzer, "Historical Problem of Generations."

32. Mallon, *Peasant and Nation*, 6–7. For more on hegemony as contestation see Roseberry, "Hegemony and the Language of Contention."

33. I compare the history of the Sierra Zapoteca during the Porfiriato with other parts of Oaxaca and other regions in Mexico in the conclusion.

34. Connerton, *How Societies Remember*, 70.

35. Although I am interested in the origins and changes over time within rituals, I find Connerton's emphasis on the connection between performativity and collective memory more useful for explaining the importance of patriotic rituals in the Sierra Zapoteca. See Connerton, *How Societies Remember*, 103. For histories dealing with the origins of rituals and traditions, see especially Hobsbawm and Ranger, *Invention of Tradition.*

36. Nora, *Realms of Memory*, 14–15.

37. Village leaders officially changed the district name on July 30, 1857; see Pérez García, *Sierra Juárez*, 2:13.

38. Anderson, *Imagined Communities*, xiii.

39. Ibid., 187.

40. Chatterjee, *Nationalism and the Colonial World*, 19–22. For an excellent assessment of both the strengths and weakness of Anderson's formulation as it applies to Mexican nationalism, see Lomnitz, *Deep Mexico, Silent Mexico*, 3–34. For a more complex understanding of nation-state formation, organized in part by projects of racial identification and exclusion within nations, see Appelbaum, Macpherson, and Rosemblatt, *Race and Nation in Modern Latin America.*

41. Anderson, *Imagined Communities*, 7 (emphasis added).

42. Confino, *Nation as a Local Metaphor*. Ducey, *Nation of Villages*, convincingly argues for the same idea during an earlier period of nation-state formation in the Huasteca region of Mexico. For a compelling comparative case with Austria see Stauter-Halsted, *Nation in the Village.*

43. My concept of "communal literacy" borrows from the "social practices" approach to literacy, as explained in Olson and Torrance, *Making of Literate Societies*; and Prinsloo and Breier, *Social Uses of Literacy*. For a critique of "exclusionary" literacy models and a reconsideration of literacy as critical representation, see Mitchell and Weiler, *Rewriting Literacy*. For problems directly related to issues of women's literacy, see Horsman, *Something in My Mind Besides the Everyday*.

44. Pérez García, *Sierra Juárez*, 1:356.

45. While James C. Scott, in *Domination and the Arts of Resistance* and *Weapons of the Weak*, argues that popular resistance most often takes place "offstage," precisely in a discursive field inaccessible to historians working in official archives, the letters written by Zapotec peasants indicate otherwise.

46. Feierman, *Peasant Intellectuals*, 42–44, describes a similar "onstage" discourse of resistance for peasants in Tanzania. In addition, Connerton, *How Societies Remember*, 44, provides an alternative way of reading peasant consciousness through public rituals and communal memory. Historians of the United States have also made use of letters and petitions to explain subaltern consciousness. For example, Child, *Boarding School Seasons*, uses letters written by North American Indian students and families to retell the history of government boarding schools. Zaeske, *Signatures of Citizenship*, examines antislavery petitions signed by women to reveal changes in women's political consciousness.

47. The most thorough treatment of the subaltern studies debate for Latin American history is Mallon, "Promise and Dilemma of Subaltern Studies." A short list of the subaltern studies work that I have found most useful includes Guha, "On Some Aspects of the Historiography of Colonial India"; Spivak, "Can the Subaltern Speak?"; and Skaria, "Writing, Orality, and Power in the Dangs."

48. Beverley, *Subalternity and Representation*, 42–43.

49. For Morelos see especially Womack, *Zapata and the Mexican Revolution*; Hernández Chávez, *Anenecuilco*; Sotelo Inclán, *Raíz y razón de Zapata*; and Brunk, *Emiliano Zapata*.

50. Iturribarría, "Oaxaqueños notables"; Brioso y Candiani, "D. Manuel Martínez Gracida."

51. Quoted in Simpson, *Many Mexicos*, 297.

CHAPTER 1

1. For background on the stages of occupation and settlement at Monte Albán and central Oaxaca, see Whitecotton, *Zapotecs*, 23–80. See also Flannery and Marcus, *Cloud People*; Caso, "Monte Alban"; and Iturribarría, *Las viejas culturas de Oaxaca*.

2. Federico H. Toro, "Leyenda Zapoteca de Ixtlán de Juárez, Oaxaca, tradición del año 1468" [ca. 1908], in Pérez García, *Sierra Juárez*, 1:159–65; Chance, *Conquest of the Sierra*, 16.

3. Historians have emphasized for too long only the desire of native communities

to retain or regain administrative autonomy from state and federal governments. As will become clear, political autonomy of indigenous communities had advantages for nonnative communities as well.

4. In addition to ideology, class distinguished the differences between liberals. Unlike the majority of radical liberals, the "*borlados*" or "tassled ones" were mostly lawyers and doctors with academic degrees. Pérez García, *Sierra Juárez*, 1:39; Iturribarría, *Oaxaca en la historia*, 193.

5. See Díaz's account of the circumstances surrounding his appointment in APD, 1:51–55. Díaz's autobiography should be read with caution as he omitted some events and offered a rather one-sided view of others. For an excellent review of Díaz biographies and the problems surrounding Díaz's autobiography, see Garner, *Porfirio Díaz*, 5–17. See also Iturribarría, *Historia de Oaxaca*, 2:30–32.

6. Significantly, no one accused Díaz of personal corruption during his short tenure as jefe político. For background on jefes políticos in other states, see Falcón, "Force and the Search for Consent"; Vanderwood, *Disorder and Progress*; and Mecham, "Jefe Político in Mexico."

7. Population estimates come from González Navarro, "Indio y propiedad en Oaxaca." See also Reina, "De las reformas borbónicas," 1:192, 224.

8. See Chassen-López, *From Liberal to Revolutionary Oaxaca*, 315–47. There are seven distinct Zapotec groups in Oaxaca, each with their own history. The Zapotecs of Ixtlán district, the Serranos, did not represent the political or economic interests of the other groups and vice versa. The Zapotecs of the Isthmus of Tehuantepec have received much scholarly attention, in part because of the region's reputation as the home of strong women. For accounts by anthropologists and travelers, see Starr, *In Indian Mexico*; Franck, *Tramping through Mexico*; and Covarrubias, *Mexico South*. More recent scholarly work on the Isthmus Zapotecs includes Chiñas, *Isthmus Zapotecs*; Campbell, *Zapotec Renaissance*; Campbell, Binford, Bartolomé, and Barabas, *Zapotec Struggles*; Rubin, *Decentering the Regime*; and Campbell, *Mexican Memoir*.

9. For more on the Oaxacan rebellions see Barabas, "Rebeliones e insurrecciones indígenas en Oaxaca." For the Yucatán see Rugeley, *Yucatán's Maya Peasantry*; and Reed, *Caste War of Yucatan*.

10. Stern, *Secret History of Gender*, 31.

11. For an analysis of the dynamic cochineal trade see Baskes, *Indians, Merchants, and Markets*; Sánchez Silva, *Indios, comerciantes y burocracia*; and Baskes, "Coerced or Voluntary?"

12. Carmagnani, *El regreso de los dioses*, 229–32.

13. In *Apuntes para mis hijos*, Juárez mentioned the anguish he felt upon leaving his village in 1818. His real remorse, however, was that the region did not have adequate schools for teaching children how to read, write, and think in Spanish. Apart from this brief reference to his Indian past, Juárez rarely made public his feelings about Guelatao. See also Hamnett, *Juárez*, 34–35.

14. Mallon, *Peasant and Nation*, discusses the intense anti-Juárez sentiment in the Sierra de Puebla. Weeks, *Juárez Myth*, argues that Juárez had always faced intense opposition both before and after the French Intervention. For Juárez's status in Ixtlán district see McNamara, "Felipe García and the Real Heroes of Guelatao."

15. "Exposición al Soberano Congreso de Oaxaca, 1849," in Juárez, *Documentos*, 1:659; "Exposición al Soberano Congreso de Oaxaca, 1848," in ibid., 1:579. See also Carmagnani, *El regreso de los dioses*, 233.

16. Hamnett, *Juárez*, 37–38; Carmagnani, *El regreso de los dioses*, 234.

17. "Exposición 1852," in Juárez, *Documentos*, 1:781.

18. Rugeley, *Yucatán's Maya Peasantry*, 52–53, 173–74, discusses a similar wave of new taxes in the Yucatán that led to popular tax revolts in 1814 and 1847. Guardino, *Peasants, Politics, and the Formation of Mexico's National State*, discusses the connection between taxes and popular revolts in the state of Guerrero.

19. For persuasive arguments that the "second conquest" described by Carmagnani ultimately failed, see Chassen-López, *From Liberal to Revolutionary Oaxaca*; and Sánchez Silva, *Indios, comerciantes y burocracia*.

20. For example, during the Porfiriato, the Serranos preferred to call Díaz "General" rather than "Presidente" because it marked their status as his former subordinates and emphasized their common history with Díaz.

21. My assessment of the recruitment process comes from APD, 1:51–52; and from letters describing cooperation between Díaz and the Serranos found in CPD.

22. This was El Estatuo Orgánico of September 13, 1855.

23. AGEO Gobernación, sin clasificación, Paquete #1, Villa Juárez, 1855. The document was signed first by Porfirio Díaz and then Sixto M. Pérez, the leader of the largest town in the district. Other prominent signers included Cenobio Luis of Ixtepeji and Felipe García of Guelatao.

24. For Oaxaca during the Reform see Berry, *Reform in Oaxaca*.

25. Pérez García, *Sierra Juárez*, 2:45.

26. More specific examples involving women and war will be discussed below. For the Sierra Norte de Puebla see Mallon, *Peasant and Nation*, 74–79. For a broader history of Mexican women and war see Salas, *Soldaderas*.

27. Memories of war are discussed in subsequent chapters. For war as discourse see Huston, "Tales of War and Tears of Women"; and Huston, "Matrix of War."

28. For cargo systems in Oaxaca see especially Guardino, "Community Service, Liberal Law, and Local Custom in Indigenous Villages"; and Chassen-López, *From Liberal to Revolutionary Oaxaca*, 286–91. See also Chance and Taylor, "Cofradías and Cargos"; Rus and Wasserstrom, "Civil-Religious Hierarchies in Central Chiapas"; and Friedlander, "Secularization of the Cargo System." For the influence of *pasados* in other parts of Mexico, see Mallon, *Peasant and Nation*, 66–74.

29. CPD 27-12 4583–4586, Miguel Bolaños Cacho to Porfirio Díaz, April 23, 1902. See also McNamara, "Felipe García and the Real Heroes of Guelatao." For a similar case

see the promotion of soldiers under Captain Cenobio "El Gallo" Pérez discussed in AGEO Gobernación, sin clasificación, Paquete #1, Mariano Castellanos to Ministro de Guerra, May 14, 1859.

30. Pérez García, *Sierra Juárez*, 1:221, discusses the spatial distinctiveness of neighborhoods within the town of Ixtlán.

31. Francisco Meijueiro's military service record can be found at AHDN Cancelados XI/111/3-1084. Fidencio Hernández's service record is AHDN Cancelados XI/111/2-356. The Meijueiro family eventually changed the spelling of its name to Meixueiro. As much as possible I have tried to keep the spelling consistent with those changes. Thus, Francisco Meijueiro was the father of Guillermo Meixueiro.

32. Mallon, *Peasant and Nation*, 74-84. For more on the tensions within practices of "democratic patriarchy," see Stacey, *Patriarchy and Socialist Revolution in China*.

33. Mallon, *Peasant and Nation*, 117-18. Thomson, *Patriotism, Politics, and Popular Liberalism*, 38-39, credits the patriarchal influence of *principales* with maintaining authority and obedience in Indian towns.

34. APD, 1:55. Díaz initially sought a position as a lieutenant, which paid only forty pesos per month. See Díaz's letter accepting the commission in Tehuantepec in AGEO Gobernación, sin clasificación, Paquete #1, Porfirio Díaz to Gobernación, April 9, 1856.

35. Pérez García, *Sierra Juárez*, 2:13.

36. Liberal preparations for war can be found in AHDN Operaciones Militares XI/481.3-7355, "Partes de D. Miguel Castro, Gobernador del Edo. de Oaxaca," June 7, 1859. See also Berry, *Reform in Oaxaca*, 45-46, 67-70; and Iturribarría, *Historia de Oaxaca*, 2:216-18. Iturribarría is especially attentive to the intraparty struggle of the liberals.

37. Berry, *Reform in Oaxaca*, 68; Pérez García, *Sierra Juárez*, 2:27.

38. CPD 24-19 9325, Adolfo Martínez [José Martínez's son] to Porfirio Díaz, July 3, 1899; the stories of military service had been passed from father to son. For the exiled liberal government in Ixtlán see Pérez García, *Sierra Juárez*, 2:27. See also CPD 14-22 10915-10916, Monica Cruz et al. to Porfirio Díaz, October 8, 1889; CPD 14-28 13507, Fernando Pérez to Porfirio Díaz, December 6, 1889; and CPD 35-29 14151-14155, Tiburcio Pérez to Porfirio Díaz, May 29, 1910.

39. AHDN Operaciones Militares XI/481.3-4340, "Armamentos y municiones para las fuerzas liberals situadas en los Estados de Campeche, Oaxaca, Puebla, Tamaulipas y Zacatecas," José María Díaz Ordaz to Ministro de Guerra, January 3, 1860. National liberal leaders had placed Cristobal Salinas in command of the Ixtlán army, which would prove problematic; see AHDN Operaciones Militares XI/481.3-7534, "Nombramiento en favor del Coronel Cristobal Salinas para ocupar el mando de la Brigada de la Sierra de la Villa Juárez," November 12, 1859. For Salinas's military records see AHDN Cancelados XI/111/2-883.

40. Interestingly, the defense archives dealing with this conflict in Oaxaca contain reports from both liberal and conservative armies. The following analysis comes from reading both accounts.

41. See "Noticia de las personas que no han satisfecho sus notas en esta tesorería," February 1, 1860; *El Boletín*, February 11, 1860 (conservative newspaper in Oaxaca); *El Boletín*, February 21, 1860; and the lists of names of men conscripted into the conservative army from Octolan, Tlacolula, and Ejutla. These documents can be found in Martínez Gracida, "Gobierno reaccionario, conservador o mocho." I have not found forced conscription lists for the liberals for 1860.

42. AHDN Operaciones Militares XI/481.3-4340, "Armamentos y municiones para las fuerzas liberales," January 3, 1860; AHDN Operaciones Militares XI/481.3-4341, "Envio de armamentos y municiones con destino a las fuerzas liberales," Vicente Rosas Landa to Ministro de Guerra, February 7, 1860, Marcos Pérez to Ministro de Guerra, February 11, 1860, and Vicente Rosas Landa to Ministro de Guerra, March 21, 1860; AHDN Operaciones Militares XI/481.3-8054, Vicente Rosas Landa to Ensemo. Señor [Ministro de Guerra], February 21, 1860.

43. AHDN Operaciones Militares XI/481.3-4268, "Parte del Col. Cristobal Salinas, dando cuenta de la acción desarrollado en Santo Domingo del Valle, Oaxaca," José María Cobos to Ministro de Guerra, February 1, 1860.

44. AHDN Operaciones Militares XI/481.3-4268, "Parte del Col. Cristobal Salinas, dando cuenta de la acción desarrollado en Santo Domingo del Valle, Oaxaca," José María Cobos to Ministro de Guerra, February 1, 1860; see also Miguel Castro's letter to the liberal Ministro de Guerra y Marina, January 25, 1860. Castro described both Díaz's defeat at Mitla and the Zapotec victory at Santo Domingo in ways similar to Cobos.

45. Iturribarría, *Oaxaca en la historia*, 197, argues that Díaz Ordaz was actually murdered in a *borlado* plot to take control of the Oaxacan liberal government. Iturribarría credits this theory to Díaz Ordaz's family and notes that it has not been satisfactorily "disproven." I have found no evidence of this plot in archival sources in either the AHDN or the Benito Juárez Papers, BN-AJ. The place of his death was renamed Villa Díaz Ordaz.

46. Statement by Díaz in Reyes, *El General Porfirio Díaz*, 13–14.

47. Ibid., 60–62.

48. Rosas Landa describes his plan in AHDN Operaciones Militares XI/481.3-8054, Vicente Rosas Landa to Ministro de Guerra, February 23, 1860. See also AHDN Operaciones Militares XI/481.3-4341, Vicente Rosas Landa to Ministro de Guerra, February 7, 1860, February 11, 1860, March 21, 1860; and Marcos Pérez to Ministro de Guerra, February 11, 1860; and AHDN Operaciones Militares XI/481.3-7764, Vicente Rosas Landa to Ministro de Guerra, February 14, 1860.

49. AHDN Operaciones Militares XI/481.3-7764, Marcos Pérez to Ministro de Guerra, February 12, 1860.

50. AHDN Operaciones Militares XI/481.3-8054, Vicente Rosas Landa to Ministro de Guerra, March 24, 1860, April 17, 1860. See also Cobos's reports on the fighting around Oaxaca City in the same file: José María Cobos to Ministro de Guerra, February 7, 1860, March 14, 1860. In the March report Cobos claimed his men were "in good shape."

51. Reyes, *El General Porfirio Díaz*, 62. See also AHDN Operaciones Militares XI/481.3-8054, Vicente Rosas Landa to Ministro de Guerra, February 23, 1860, March 24, 1860, April 17, 1860. Thomson, *Patriotism, Politics, and Popular Liberalism*, 66–67, highlights similar doubts surrounding the effectiveness of the National Guard troops in Puebla.

52. *El Boletín*, February 21, 1860, in Martínez Gracida, "Gobierno reaccionario." See also *El Boletín*, February 11, 1860.

53. See the specific case files in Martínez Gracida, "Gobierno reaccionario": "Contiene este tomo 9 causas instruidos contra liberales y Señoras y Señoritas de familias liberales." These incidents are also discussed in Iturribarría, *Historia de Oaxaca*, 2:219, though his account goes beyond the documents preserved by Martínez Gracida. Iturribarría claims that Teresa Agüero, Pila Casorla, Susana Ortega, Juana Mejía, and Josefa and Manuela Solís were jailed and/or punished for contacting the liberals in Ixtlán. The Solís sisters, according to Iturribarría, were handed over to conservative troops who repeatedly raped them. Other women had their hair cut or were stripped naked in public in order to humiliate them for supporting the liberals. Iturribarría does not provide a source for his information, and I have been unable to corroborate these allegations in military reports or the documents preserved by Martínez Gracida.

54. Martínez Gracida, "Gobierno reaccionario," Sumaria instruida contra Manuel José Ramírez, various dates. Félix Romero wrote his wife on March 2, 1860.

55. AHDN Operaciones Militares XI/481.3-4303, "Lista de viudas de los que fallecieron . . . ," José María Cobos to Ministro de Guerra, March 1, 1860. For a similar list of widows, mothers, and "orphans" see AHDN Operanciones Militares XI/481.3-8048, "Ordenes . . . para formular una relación durante viudas, madres, e hijos del personal que falleció durante las acciones que dieron por resultado la toma de la plaza de Oaxaca," August 22, 1860.

56. AHDN Operaciones Militares XI/481.3-8054, Vicente Rosas Landa to Ministro de Guerra, April 17, 1860; AHDN Operaciones Militares XI/481.3-8060, José María Cobos to Ministro de Guerra, May 11, 1860.

57. See CPD 33-33 13089–13090, Onofre Jiménez et al. to Porfirio Díaz, September 22, 1908; see also CPD 33-33 13089–13090, Emilio Pimentel to Porfirio Díaz, October 26, 1908; and CPD 33-37 14616, Onofre Jiménez et al. to Porfirio Díaz, November 7, 1908. I had planned on sharing this story with people in Ixtlán, but they already knew it and provided me with details not included in official reports.

58. Díaz bragged about his success as one of the real highlights of his career in Reyes, *El General Porfirio Díaz*, 62: "Since I knew the region better than [conservative Anastasio] Trejo, I ordered his column of some 700 men to be destroyed; fewer than 100 arrived back to the city." See also the drawing in Reyes, "El enemigo es cortado en la retirada de Ixtepeji." Most likely, Pérez García relied on this book for *Sierra Juárez*, which explains why this rare book is in the Biblioteca Pública de Guelatao. See also "Relación de los muertos, heridos y disperses havidos en la acción de hoy [May 16, 1860] en el pueblo de Ixtepeji," in Martínez Gracida, "Gobierno reaccionario."

59. AHDN Operaciones Militares XI/481.3-8054, José Maria Cobos to Ministro de Guerra, May 31 and June 1, 1860.

60. AHDN Operaciones Militares XI/481.3-4283, Cristobal Salinas to Ministro de Guerra, August 5, 1860.

61. AHDN Operaciones Militares XI/481.3-4286, Anastasio Trejo to Ministro de Guerra, August 11, 1860. For criticism of Cobos and commentary on how conservatives believed they had lost Oaxaca, see various reports in AHDN Operaciones Militares, XI/481.3-4282, Antonio Ayestaran to Ministro de Guerra, August 13, 1860.

62. Díaz led a key attack against a conservative command post inside a church; he set fire to the church and then attacked the soldiers as they fled through the surrounding cemetery. According to the field report, numerous Oaxacan soldiers were killed in the fighting. See AHDN Operaciones Militares XI/481.3-8348, General G. Ortega to Ministro de Guerra, August 22, 1860.

63. AHDN Operaciones Militares XI/481.3-8048, "Ordenes al Gral. Cristobal Salinas ... para formular una relación de viudas, madres e hijos del personal que falleció durante las acciones que dieron por resultado la toma de la plaza de Oaxaca," August 22, 1860.

64. AHDN Operaciones Militares XI/481.3-7758, Cristobal Salinas to Ministro de Guerra, October 9, 1860. In this letter Salinas claimed, "the forces under my command have not taken part in and will not take part in any political questions."

65. Pérez García, *Sierra Juárez*, 1:39. Several months later Francisco Meijueiro resigned his military commission in order to participate more openly in politics and business; see AGEO Gobernación, sin clasificación, Paquete #1, Francisco Meijueiro to Ministro de Guerra, March 13, 1861.

CHAPTER 2

1. Louis Napoleon Bonaparte, the nephew of Napoleon I, became president of the French Republic in 1848. Four years later he won a plebiscite, which granted him the title of Emperor Napoleon III. He embarked on an aggressive foreign policy in the name of the Second French Republic. He claimed parts of Algeria, established a protectorate in Indochina, landed troops in Lebanon, founded French colonies on the west coast of Africa, and helped defeat Russian troops in the Crimean War. He also wanted to replant the French flag somewhere in the Americas; Mexican conservatives presented him with that opportunity in 1862.

2. The current toll highway runs about ten kilometers from Ciudad Serdán today, which gives the mistaken impression that the town has always been bypassed by travelers going from Veracruz to Puebla. In fact, the region was even an important pre-Columbian destination for Nahau royalty due to its sacred mountain peaks and cool summer climate.

3. Iturribarría, *Historia de Oaxaca*, 3:23–29; Iturribarría, *Oaxaca en la historia*, 205–6. See AHDN Operaciones Militares XI/481.4-8771, "Acuerdo del H. Congreso de la

Unión de 16 de abril de 1862 . . . la voladura del edificio de la colecturía en el pueblo San Andres Chalchicomula, Puebla." On March 10, 1862, the Oaxacan newspaper *El Siglo XIX* reported only that the division had been sent to San Andres Chalchicomula.

4. Doctors saved only 190 men, 25 women, and 9 children. See the full report by the commanding officer at Chalchicomula, Antonio Alvarez, reprinted in Santibañez, *Reseña historica*, 1:46–52. For a brief reference to this accident see Berry, *Reform in Oaxaca*, 81.

5. AHDN Operaciones Militares XI/481.4-8771 37–41, Médico cirujano de ejercito C. Manuel Burguichani to Ministro de Guerra, March 14–25, 1862.

6. Santibañez, *Reseña historica*, 1:50. See also AHDN Operaciones Militares XI/481.4-8771 32, Ignacio Mejia to Ministro de Guerra, March 7, 1862.

7. Zaragoza, the commanding officer over the entire liberal army, initially contacted the Ministry of War and President Juárez about the accident on March 8, 1862. All of his reports were collected for a special, closed session of Congress on April 18, 1862. See AHDN Operaciones Militares XI/481.4-8771 28–30, 45, 47.

8. AHDN Operaciones Militares XI/481.4-8843, "Ejecución del Gral. Manuel Robles Pezuela," March 21, 1862. Independently, Robles Pezuela had been in the area around Chalchicomula before the accident. See also Ridley, *Maximilian and Juárez*, 86–88.

9. The tragedy of Chalchicomula has been compounded over the years by a failure to recognize the impact of this event. Eventually, liberals asserted a glorious, "predestined" interpretation of their efforts against the French. Chalchicomula and the deaths of more than 1,500 people did not fit that narrative. A filtered view of the French Intervention was the product of the Pax Porfiriana, however, and did not represent the memories of war for those who had survived. A year after the war ended, Juan A. Mateos published *El sol de mayo*, a "novel" in which he told the entire story of the French invasion, including the explosion at Chalchicomula. I traveled to Ciudad Serdán in 2002 and met local historians and townspeople who are actively working to keep this story alive. The ruins of the explosion are still visible. For help in Ciudad Serdán I am grateful to Virgilio González Flores and María Elena Hernández Solares.

10. Ridley, *Maximilian and Juárez*, 86–87.

11. For details about the battle at Puebla based on eyewitness accounts see Santibañez, *Reseña historica*, 1:93–101.

12. CEHM Fondo CXIX-1, Carpeta 1, Legajo 4, Porfirio Díaz to Nicolasa Díaz, May 10, 1862. Díaz's use of the word *"mamelucos"* pokes fun at the uniforms worn by some of the Algerian units in the French army. It also means "fool" in Spanish. I am grateful to an anonymous reader for the University of North Carolina Press for this clarification.

13. These memories were recorded in hundreds of letters to President Porfirio Díaz and are discussed in subsequent chapters. Thomson, *Patriotism, Politics, and Popular Liberalism*, 73–78, remarks on the difference between the ragtag, desperate situation of the soldiers from the Sierra de Puebla and the historical reimagination of "indomitable" National Guard troops from Zacapoaxtla.

14. AHDN Operaciones Militares XI/481.4-8771 19, October 16, 1862. Porfirio Díaz had actually led a squadron to Chalchicomula in September but failed to eliminate the French threat. In letters to his sister, Díaz complained that the French still did not respect the Mexican army; see CEHM Fondo CXIX-1, Porfirio Díaz to Nicolasa Díaz, September 4, 1862, and September 13, 1862.

15. Ridley, *Maximilian and Juárez*, 130–31; Iturribarría, *Oaxaca en la historia*, 207.

16. CEHM Fondo IX-1, Carpeta 1–8, Documento 23, F. Arrangoiz to Ignacio Aguilar, February 3, 1864. Maximilian's request for an expression of popular support bolsters Erika Pani's argument that the Second Empire should be understood in the context of Mexican history and not as a foreign interlude; see Pani, *Para mexicanizar el Segundo Imperio*.

17. For a highly readable history of the French Intervention, see Ridley, *Maximilian and Juárez*.

18. AGEO Gobernación, sin clasificación, Paquete #1, Felipe García et al., July 10, 1864.

19. CEHM Fondo IX-1, Carpeta 2–8, Documento 177, L. [Leonardo] Márquez to Ignacio Aguilar, August 29, 1864, and Documento 184, Angel Iglesias to Ignacio Aguilar, September 7, 1864. See also Duncan, "Embracing a Suitable Past."

20. For conservative complaints and criticism of both Maximilian and Carlota, see CEHM Fondo IX-1, Carpeta 2–8, Documento 264, J. I. de Anievas to Ignacio Aguilar, November 11, 1864; CEHM Fondo IX-1, Carpeta 3–8, Documento 311, Joaquín Velázquez de León to Ignacio Aguilar, December 26, 1864; CEHM Fondo IX-1, Carpeta 3–8, Documento 315, Pablo Vergapa et al. to Ignacio Aguilar, December 28, 1864; CEHM Fondo IX-1, Carpeta 3–8, Documento 316, José F. Ramírez to Ignacio Aguilar, December 28, 1864; CEHM Fondo IX-1, Carpeta 4–8, Documento 404, F. de Arrangoiz to Ignacio Aguilar, April 5, 1865; and CEHM Fondo IX-1, Carpeta 4–8, Documento 478, F. de Arrangoiz to Ignacio Aguilar, July 23, 1865.

21. CEHM Fondo IX-1, Carpeta 3–8, Documento 312, Teodosto (Pelagio Antonio de) Lares to Ignacio Aguilar, December 26, 1864.

22. CEHM Fondo IX-1, Carpeta 3–8, Documento 318, Ana Aguilar de Solórzano to Josefa Aguierre de Aguilar, December 28, 1864.

23. CEHM Fondo IX-1, Carpeta 3–8, Documento 315, Pablo Vergapa to Ignacio Aguilar, December 28, 1864. See also CEHM Fondo IX-1, Carpeta 3–8, Documento 309, Isidro Díaz to Ignacio Aguilar, December 26, 1864.

24. CEHM Fondo IX-1, Carpeta 4–8, Documento 424, Isidro Díaz to Ignacio Aguilar, May 9, 1865.

25. CEHM Fondo IX-1, Carpeta 4–8, Documento 478, F. de Arrangoiz to Ignacio Aguilar, July 23, 1865; see also CEHM Fondo IX-1, Carpeta 4–8, Documento 404, F. de Arrangoiz to Ignacio Aguilar, April 5, 1865.

26. CEHM Fondo IX-1, Carpeta 4–8, Documento 517, Isidro Díaz to Ignacio Aguilar, September 26, 1865.

27. Plans to attack Díaz in Oaxaca were prepared as early as July. See CEHM Fondo IX-1, Carpeta 2-8, Documento 143, Francisco J. Bermúdez to Ignacio Aguilar, July 27, 1864.

28. Iturribarría, *Historia de Oaxaca*, 3:112-15; Iturribarría, *Oaxaca en la historia*, 205-9.

29. See various letters and reports from Francisco Meijueiro during this time in AGEO Gobernación, sin clasificación, Paquete #1, various dates. See also Berry, *Reform in Oaxaca*, 204-6.

30. See his military file in AHDN Cancelados XI/111/2-883.

31. For a full account of Franco's policies in Oaxaca, see Berry, *Reform in Oaxaca*, 92-105. For an insightful discussion on the problem of explaining collaboration, see "Appendix C, Collaboration and Historiography," in ibid., 204-6.

32. Santibañez, *Reseña historica*, 2:277-82.

33. See Manuel Martínez Gracida, Libro No. 57, "Documentos para la historia de Oaxaca," unedited manuscript and notes, Biblioteca Pública, Oaxaca City, including "Asalto del Capitan imperial Bentio Arrango sobre los jefes Vicente Bolaños y Cenobio Pérez (a) el Gallo en el pueblo de Yolox," September 20, 1865; and "Batalla del 'Rio Grande' por el capitan Cenobio Pérez," October 21, 1865.

34. For a copy of the decree and the long-term importance liberals attached to it, see Santibañez, *Reseña historica*, 2:284.

35. See Manuel Martínez Gracida, Libro No. 57, "Documentos para la historia de Oaxaca," unedited manuscript and notes, Biblioteca Pública, Oaxaca City, "Fue asaltado el Capitan Cenobio Pérez (a) el Gallo del pueblo de Ixtepeji en su casa por un troso de caballeria imperial, y al conducirlo como prisionero para la capital, fue asesinado cobardemente en el trayecta," August 18, 1866.

36. CPD 25-39 15477, Jacinta R. de Perzabal to Porfirio Díaz, December 21, 1900.

37. Taken from Díaz's field report of October 20, 1866, to the minister of war, reprinted in [Díaz et al.], *Batalla de la Carbonera*. Also see Pérez García, *Sierra Juárez*, 2:49-51.

38. For reports on Díaz's victory see BN-AJ 1561, Alejandro García to Benito Juárez, October 27, 1866; and BN-AJ 1842, Matías Romero to Benito Juárez, November 18, 1866. For details of the medal Díaz wanted, including a drawing, see BN-AJ 1505, Porfirio Díaz to Benito Juárez, November 1, 1866. The medal consisted of a red ribbon hanging from a gold coin with the names of the four major battles in Oaxaca—Soyaltepec, Juchitán, Miahuatlán, and Carbonera—raised in bold letters on one side, and the eagle from the Mexican flag on the other side.

39. Pérez García, *Sierra Juárez*, 2:54-55. The wounds were serious. See, for example, the account of Luz López, wife of wounded soldier Mariano Paz, in CPD 34-26 12876, August 5, 1909. There were at least two contingents from Ixtepeji, La Compañía de Cazadores de Ixtepeji and the Fifth Company, both made up of 54 men each; another 34 men from Ixtepeji served in other units. Altogether, then, at least 142 men from Ixtepeji served at Carbonera.

40. Félix Díaz to "Serranos," November 2, 1866, reprinted in Pérez García, *Sierra Juárez*, 2:59.

41. APD, 2:191–92.

42. APD, 2:341–52; Iturribarría, *Historia de Oaxaca*, 3:223–25, which includes a condolence letter from Maximilian to Franco's widow.

43. APD, 2:341, Juan Pablo Franco to his wife, January 27, 1867. Díaz read Franco's letter and included a copy in his papers, which were later published together. Ironically, at roughly the same time as Franco was saying goodbye to his family, Díaz began to more seriously consider starting his own. Two months after Franco's execution, Díaz wrote a love letter to his niece Delfina, in which he stated, "in my heart you have no rival." They were married one month later, after securing the necessary dispensations because of their blood ties. See CEHM Fondo CXIX-1, Porfirio Díaz to Delfina Ortega, March 18, 1867.

44. Pani, "Apéndice 2: Los Imperialists, antes y después," *Para mexicanizar el Segundo Imperio*, 375–402.

45. In 1902 Alfonso Cicero, a former soldier, wrote an epic account of the tragedy surrounding Maximilian's intervention and the need for his execution. Cicero placed the blame for Maximilian's death on Napoleon III and on the October 1865 decree. See CPD 27-20 7694–7703, Alfonso Cicero to Porfirio Díaz, no date [1902]. Cicero may have been responding to other expressions of sympathy for Maximilian; see, for example, Juan de Dios Peza's brief treatment of Maximilian's execution, "Los valientes mueren en su puesto," *Memorias, reliquias y retratos*, 14–16. Significantly, Dios Peza's father had served in Maximilian's cabinet. A nostalgic romanticism about the Second Empire has always had an audience in Mexico. For example Fernando del Paso's novel, *Noticias del Imperio*, paints Juárez as a bloodthirsty villain and Maximilian as the misunderstood victim.

CHAPTER 3

1. See especially Hale, *Mexican Liberalism in the Age of Mora*; and Hale, *Transformation of Liberalism*.

2. Falcone, "Federal-State Relations during Mexico's Restored Republic"; Falcone, "Benito Juárez versus the Díaz Brothers." See also Iturribarría, *Historia de Oaxaca*, 3:245–61.

3. Mallon, *Peasant and Nation*, 248–56.

4. BN-AJ 3795, Joaquín Rangel to Benito Juárez, Oaxaca, February 12, 1867; see also Cosío Villegas, *Historia moderna de México, la república restaurada*, 138.

5. Perry, *Juárez and Díaz*; Falcone, "Benito Juárez versus the Díaz Brothers."

6. APD, 5:73–76, Porfirio Díaz to Miguel Castro, September 25, 1867. On historians critical of Díaz's actions as a young man, see especially Cosío Villegas, *Porfirio Díaz en la revuelta de la Noria*. For insightful analysis on Cosío Villegas's influence regarding the interpretation of Díaz and the Porfiriato, see Hale, "Liberal Impulse."

7. Mallon, *Peasant and Nation*, sees the *Convocatoria* as a major sign of Juárez's increasing authoritarianism. Perry, *Juárez and Díaz*, argues that it was either a blunder or a misguided coup d'état. Hamnett, *Juárez*, 207, considers the *Convocatoria* "a response to the porfirista challenge, an attempt to preempt its populist appeal."

8. Berry, *Reform in Oaxaca*, 110–20.

9. BN-AJ 3732, General Luis Pérez Figueroa to Benito Juárez, August 31, 1867.

10. BN-AJ 2444, Miguel Castro to Benito Juárez, September 28, 1867. Castro also advised Juárez to name a new governor who could then appoint new jefes políticos.

11. BN-AJ 2443, Miguel Castro to Benito Juárez, September 25, 1867.

12. Ibid. (Juárez's reply was written on the bottom of Castro's original letter).

13. BN-AJ 4055, José V. Silva to Benito Juárez, September 25, 1867.

14. BN-AJ 2444, Miguel Castro to Benito Juárez, September 28, 1867.

15. BN-AJ 3373, José López Viascán to Benito Juárez, September 30, 1867. Miguel Castro had asked for Díaz's advice about reorganizing the National Guard in Oaxaca; APD, 5:1–11, Miguel Castro to Porfirio Díaz, September 4, 1867.

16. Fidencio Hernández actually played both sides of the partisan struggle. He professed his loyalty to Juárez but provided Díaz with sensitive information about preparations for the electoral process in Ixtlán district. At one point, Hernández complained that "Félix Romero, Manuel Toro, and Castro . . . have waged a terrible war that I will have to wait to tell you about." APD, 5:213–14, Fidencio Hernández to Porfirio Díaz, October 15, 1867; see also APD, 4:206–7, Fidencio Hernández to Porfirio Díaz, August 18, 1867.

17. The Díaz brothers anticipated that Ixtlán would support Juárez since Castro would be counting the votes. See APD, 5:126–27, Félix Díaz to Porfirio Díaz, October 3, 1867; and APD, 5:167–68, Félix Díaz to Porfirio Díaz, October 9, 1867. See also APD, 5:142–43, José F. Valverde to Porfirio Díaz, October 5, 1867.

18. Each electoral vote represented five hundred inhabitants. For electoral results see Iturribarría, *Historia de Oaxaca*, vol. 4: *La restauración*, 26–27.

19. BN-AJ 2451, Miguel Castro to Benito Juárez, October 23, 1867. See also BN-AJ 2415, Agustín Castañeda to Benito Juárez, October 24, 1867. Complaints about interference with the mail service continued for the next four years. See U.S. Department of State, *Despatches from United States Consuls in Oaxaca*, No. 21, L. L. Laurence to Hamilton Fish, February 3, 1872.

20. BN-AJ 2455, Miguel Castro to Benito Juárez, November 6, 1867.

21. BN-AJ 5936, Joaquín Mauleón to Benito Juárez, February 29, 1868. Significantly, the Díaz brothers themselves began to disagree. Porfirio tried to influence Félix's decisions on key cabinet positions, while the governor resented his older brother's interference. See BN-AJ 5948, Joaquín Mauleón to Benito Juárez, October 7, 1868; and APD, 5:345–46, José Francisco Valverde to Porfirio Díaz, November 23, 1867.

22. For the view that Juárez mistrusted the regular army more than the National Guard, see the memoirs of General Eduardo Paz in Hernández Chávez, "Origen y ocaso del ejército porfiriano."

23. BN-AJ 4020, Ramón Sarmiento to General Luis Pérez Figueroa, November 30, 1867.

24. For Juárez's efforts to disarm National Guard battalions in Puebla, see Mallon, *Peasant and Nation*, 166.

25. BN-AJ 4965, Porfirio Díaz to Benito Juárez, January 2, 1868.

26. BN-AJ 4316, "Informes dados por un comerciante extranjero residente in Acapulco," November 26, 1868. Other reports of the arms shipments are in BN-AJ 4314, Diego Alvarez to Benito Juárez, November 20, 1868. See also BN-AJ 4254, Ignacio Alatorre to Benito Juárez, December 4, 1868; and BN-AJ 4994, José Pantaleón Dominguez to Benito Juárez, December 4, 1868.

27. For the rift between Porfirio and Félix Díaz see APD, 5:345–46, José Francisco Valverde to Porfirio Díaz, November 23, 1867; APD, 5:361–62, I. Muñoz to Porfirio Díaz, November 30, 1867; and APD, 5:365–66, Enrique Canseco to Porfirio Díaz, December 1, 1867. The brothers had reconciled by February 1869. For Castro's anger regarding the office of jefe político, see APD, 5:386–87, Miguel Castro to Porfirio Díaz, December 7, 1867, and Díaz's reply on December 10, 1867.

28. Many of these benefits were acknowledged even thirty-five years later, when the people of Ixtepeji endorsed the gubernatorial campaign of Félix Díaz's son. Elders in Ixtepeji wrote that Governor Félix Díaz "did not allow the ignorant Indian to be viciously exploited or forced to work on roads that benefited only particular businesses." See CPD 31-18 7187–7188, Isidoro Zuñiga et al. (more than 320 men from Ixtepeji) to Porfirio Díaz, June 1, 1906.

29. For the case against the local priest see AGEO Juzgados 42-704, "Criminal contra el ministro católico Antonio Avella por sedición [Ixtlán district]," 1870. The state government had previously brought charges against priests in at least two other districts: AGEO Juzgados 39-649, "Criminal contra el cura de San Miguel Sola [Huayapam district] Pedro García por haber predicado un sermón sedicioso," 1868; and AGEO Juzgados 39-657, "Criminal contra el cura Angel M. Cruz por abusos de su ministerio [Ocotlán district]," 1868. The case against the jefe político will be discussed in more detail below.

30. For background on criticism aimed at Juárez, see Weeks, *Juárez Myth*; and Perry, *Juárez and Díaz*.

31. AGEO Gobernación, sin clasificación, Paquete #1, Mauro Vazques report, January 27, 1871.

32. BN-RCH 1-3 16, Porfirio Díaz (Ixtlán) to Delfina, August 19, 1871.

33. APD, 9:263, Fidencio Hernández to Porfirio Díaz, August 26, 1871; APD, 9:271–72, Hernández to Díaz, August 31, 1871; APD, 9:275, Hernández to Díaz, September 3, 1871; APD, 9:285–86, Hernández to Díaz, September 8, 1871; APD, 9:294–96, Hernández to Díaz, September 12, 1871.

34. CPD 6-3 1015, Celestino Pérez to Porfirio Díaz, May 27, 1881.

35. According to Vanderwood, *Disorder and Progress*, 66, Juárez saw Díaz's rebellion as a way to eliminate brigands as well.

36. U.S. Department of State, *Despatches from United States Consuls in Oaxaca*, No. 21, L. L. Laurence to Hamilton Fish, February 3, 1872.

37. AGN Gobernación, Caja 2 (1871), Exp. 4, Legajo 3, "Sobre el pago de derechos que causaron unas rifles consignados al Gobierno de Oajaca [*sic*]." Herein are a series of letters between Matías Romero and Félix Díaz.

38. Mallon, *Peasant and Nation*, 131; Cosío Villegas, *Historia moderna de México, la república restaurada*, 604-21.

39. See the last sentence in the Plan of La Noria (1871): "*Que ningún ciudadano se imponga y perpetúe en el ejercico del poder, y esta será la última revolución.*" For the text of the Plan of La Noria, see Davis and Ricón Virulegio, *Political Plans of Mexico*, 549-51. For more commentary on this passage see Mallon, *Peasant and Nation*, 129-33.

40. See the various plans and pronouncements reprinted in Davis and Ricón Virulegio, *Political Plans of Mexico*.

41. Davis and Ricón Virulegio, *Political Plans of Mexico*, 549-51.

42. CPD 2-3 1082, Concepción Prieto to Porfirio Díaz, November 8, 1877.

43. CPD 28-9 3428-3432, Trinidad Gamboa to Porfirio Díaz, March 20, 1903. For letters from other La Noria veterans see CPD 2-3 1095-1096, Martín Maldonado to Porfirio Díaz, December 17, 1877; CPD 2-3 1005, Jesús E. Cervantes to Porfirio Díaz, July 16, 1877; CPD 24-11 5124-5125, Vicente Garcés to Porfirio Díaz, April 8, 1899; CPD 36-6 2836, Marino Salinas to Porfirio Díaz, February 14, 1911; and CPD 28-17 6569, Tomás Abúndi to Porfirio Díaz, May 5, 1903.

44. For the view that Juárez's death ended the rebellion see Perry, *Juárez and Díaz*, 173; and Mallon, *Peasant and Nation*, 129.

45. According to one observer, Félix Díaz had so angered the people of the isthmus that they had uncharacteristically set aside their own local conflicts in order to challenge the governor; see AGN Juárez 2:53-2, Máximo Toledo to Benito Juárez, June 26, 1872. See also CPD 29-29 11353-11355, Manuel Canseco to Porfirio Díaz, September 14, 1904.

46. CPD 27-6 2251, Ramón A. Alor to Porfirio Díaz, February 10, 1902.

47. CPD 13-21 10184-10187, Adolfo Rivi to Porfirio Díaz, September 25, 1888.

48. Some people questioned whether Díaz had initiated the revisions of the Plan of La Noria since he was not at Ameca when the revised document was circulated on April 3, 1872. It was later confirmed that Díaz had met with supporters in late March and had sanctioned the changes. Cosío Villegas, *Historia moderna de México, la república restaurada*, 722-26, discusses the articles of the original Plan of La Noria that were modified at Ameca. For the revised plan see Davis and Ricón Virulegio, *Political Plans of Mexico*, 551-53.

49. Cosío Villegas, *Historia moderna de México, la república restaurada*, 722-26. See also Mallon, *Peasant and Nation*, 132-33.

50. CPD 24-2 685-687, José Rosas Landa to Porfirio Díaz, January 9, 1899; CPD 24-2 707-708, José Rosas Landa to Porfirio Díaz, January 28, 1899; and CPD 25-39 15548-15554, José Rosas Landa to Porfirio Díaz, September 7, 1900. Rosas's account provides

the most complete written record from the perspective of an ordinary soldier fighting during the La Noria rebellion. His purpose for writing was simple; he wanted to convince President Díaz that he had in fact fought for the rebellion in 1871 and should therefore receive a pension. For another view of the challenges faced by the rebels in Jalisco see CPD 5-7 3062, Brígido Rosales to Porfirio Díaz, September 1880.

51. CPD 25-39 15548–15554, José Rosas Landa to Porfirio Díaz, September 7, 1900.

52. Ibid.

53. For the view that Díaz modified the Plan of La Noria at Ameca because he believed he was about to gain power and wanted to soften his populist appeal so that lerdista Liberals would join him in Mexico City, see Mallon, *Peasant and Nation*, 132–33.

54. AGN Gobernación 2-872 8-12, "Comunicación sobre la muerte del presidente Benito Juárez," July 19, 1872, signed by Cayetano Gómez y Pérez.

55. Weeks, *Juárez Myth*, 12–25.

56. AGN Gobernación 2-872 8-12, Governor Miguel Castro to Secretaría de Gobernación, July 20, 1872. Castro was named provisional governor in the wake of Díaz's failed revolt at La Noria; Hamnett, *Juárez*, 230–34. Reaction to Juárez's death came quickly from around the country. See AGN Gobernación 2-872 8-12, "Muerte de Juárez. Relativo a su muerte y funerales," July 20, 1872.

57. BN-AJ Supl. 527, letter to Juárez's cabinet from Miguel Castro and 155 other signers, July 20, 1872.

58. See Celada, *Bronces*, 27; and the undated composition read at the tomb of Benito Juárez by Manuel H. San Juan, reprinted in Ramírez, *Florilegio de poetas y escritores de Oaxaca*, 116–19.

59. For background on Carvajal, see Hamnett, *Juárez*, 36, 101.

60. Bernardino Carvajal, "A Juárez" [1872], in Ramírez, *Florilegio*, 51–53. The translation of this poem is my own.

61. The Hemíciclo, Juárez's tomb, sits in the Alameda Park in Mexico City. It was dedicated in 1910 during the month of celebrations commemorating Mexico's centennial anniversary of independence from Spain. Designed by architect Guillermo Heredia, the mammoth Hemíciclo was built with some 1,400 tons of marble. Above the center of the monument sits a statue of Juárez, depicted as the Lawgiver. Standing behind him are female figures representing Glory and the Republic. According to Weeks, *Juárez Myth*, 2, "Like many other such monuments it is the embodiment of myth." For more information on the Hemíciclo see Weeks, *Juárez Myth*, 1–6; and Escobedo, *Mexican Monuments*, 70–71.

62. See CPD 14-8 3903–3905, February 19, 1889, regarding Díaz's concern about building a monument to Hidalgo before one to Juárez. CPD 12-13 6259–6262, speech by Manuel Dublán for July 18, 1887, sent to Porfirio Díaz. Dublán was secretary of finance and a Oaxacan. See also Hamnett, *Juárez*, 271; and Chassen-López, "Orígenes de la revolución en Oaxaca."

63. CPD 34-25 12437, Juan A. Hernández to Porfirio Díaz, July 18, 1909. Hernández wrote on the thirty-seventh anniversary of that day.

64. Hamnett, *Juárez*, 205. Ignacio Mejía had an interesting military career. Originally from Zimatlán, Oaxaca, he joined the military in 1829. In 1863 he was taken prisoner by the French and exiled to France. In October 1867 he moved to El Paso, Texas, until the war with France had ended. Félix Díaz filed a formal protest against Mejía in 1868, claiming he had betrayed Mexico by agreeing to exile during the war. Thus, there was no love lost between the Díaz brothers and Mejía. Mejía's full military report is made up of 414 folders in AHDN Cancelados XI/111/1-277.1-18.

65. Díaz did not participate in a single battle during the rebellion. See his official military records in "Campañas y acciones de guerra en que se ha hallado," in Díaz, *Memorias de Porfirio Díaz*, 2:199–200.

66. AGEO Juzgados 42-694, "Testimonio de las diligencias practicadas en el secuestro de los bienes de Porfirio Díaz," February 20, 1872; AGEO Juzgados 48-792, "Doña Rafaela Varela de Díaz pide se levante el secuestro de los bienes de su finado marido don Félix Díaz y se le devuelvan," February 16, 1872; AGEO Juzgados 46-754, "Averiguación instruída en contra de Sebastián Luengas, José María Irigoyen y otros por rebelión," November 9, 1871; AGEO Juzgados 48-784, "Primeras diligencias en contra de Tiburcio Guzmán por conatos de rebelión contra las autoridades constituídas en el Distrito de Juquila," June 7, 1872. Foreigners who aided Díaz were also expelled. See AGEO Juzgados 47-763, "Contra el extranjero Alonso Harper por complicidad en el delito de rebelión," [1872].

67. APD, 11:185–87, José Esperón to Porfirio Díaz, August 11, 1874.

68. For José Esperón's rise to power see AGN Gobernación 2-874-4-1 9–21, letters from Miguel Castro informing Gobernación of changes in the state government, October–November 1874. Iturribarría describes these events in detail in *Historia de Oaxaca*, vol. 4: *La restauración*, 132–37.

69. "Radical" liberals claimed that the "moderates" had betrayed the accomplishments of the Reform, the example of Juárez, and the promises of the 1857 Constitution. In particular, "radicals" argued that Lerdo had violated the "no reelection" clause of the constitution. Of course, Díaz's supporters in Oaxaca had to ignore Juárez's reelection in 1871 to make this argument. For the challenge to Lerdo's presidency see Hale, *Transformation of Liberalism*, 87–88, 91–92. For background on Lerdo's attempt to control Oaxacan politics, see Perry, *Juárez and Díaz*, 191–92.

70. Pérez García, *Sierra Juárez*, 2:65–91.

71. For background on these veterans see CPD 28-23 9087–9088, Agustín Robles Arenas to Porfirio Díaz, June 30, 1903; CPD 28-33 12955–12957, Mariano Ibarra to Porfirio Díaz, September 12, 1903; CPD 30-19 7202, Dionisio Santiago to Porfirio Díaz, May 31, 1905; CPD 32-28 10835–10836, Rosalino Santiago to Porfirio Díaz, August 31, 1907; CPD 33-33 13132–13138, José Pacheco to Porfirio Díaz, October 1, 1908.

72. AGN Gobernación 2-874-1-1 67–94, and 102–139, telegram from Miguel Castro to Secretaría de Gobernación, October 27, 1874.

73. Pérez García, *Sierra Juárez*, 2:71–72.

74. Quoted in ibid., 2:72.

75. National Guard officers made frequent references to the historic role of the Sierra Zapoteca in protecting their ancestral homes; see ibid., 2:71–72.

76. CPD 32-28 10835–10836, Rosalino Santiago to Porfirio Díaz, August 31, 1907. Santiago returned a copy of Díaz's 1876 handbill.

77. See CPD 32-28 10835–10836, Rosalino Santiago to Porfirio Díaz, August 31, 1907; also see CPD 32-37 14476–14478, Miguel López to Porfirio Díaz, December 20, 1907. López was from Santiago Comaltepec, Oaxaca. Fidencio Hernández distributed his own handbill to rally the Ixtlán National Guard in February 1876: "I know full well that when the sons of a heroic people fight for their liberty they are invincible." López returned a copy of this handbill to Díaz in 1907.

78. See CPD 30-19 7202–7204, Dionisio Santiago to Porfirio Díaz, May 31, 1905. See also CPD 30-26 10115, Dionisio Santiago to Porfirio Díaz, August 8, 1905. Santiago was from Xiacui, Ixtlán district. The handbill was distributed on September 10, 1876. See also CPD 24-11 5294, Luis Colmenares to Porfirio Díaz, April 15, 1899.

79. APD, 12:104, Porfirio Díaz to Fidencio Hernández, March 23, 1876.

80. Ibid.

81. Díaz spoke to the Ixtlán National Guard troops on July 25, 1876; comments reprinted in Pérez García, *Sierra Juárez*, 2:83.

82. Rojas's statement reprinted in Pérez García, *Sierra Juárez*, 2:85. Juan N. Méndez complained that Hernández had not followed orders. Manuel González suspected Hernández had been plotting to switch sides. Díaz did not express an opinion, though Hernández largely retired from politics after the Tuxtepec rebellion. See AMG Caja 3, Doc. 369–70, Juan N. Méndez to Manuel González, August 3, 1876; AMG Caja 3, Doc. 407, Manuel González to Porfirio Díaz, August 8, 1876; and AMG Caja 3, Doc. 421, Manuel González to Juan N. Méndez, August 14, 1876.

CHAPTER 4

1. The details of this banquet were recalled nearly twenty-five years after they occurred. See CPD 16-2 510, Francisco García to Porfirio Díaz, January 9, 1891. Even after assuming the presidency in Mexico City, Díaz continued to favor the regional cuisine of Oaxaca; see CPD 11-6 2722, Francisco Meijueiro to Porfirio Díaz, March 17, 1886; CPD 11-6 2641, Porfirio Díaz to Francisco Meijueiro, March 26, 1886; CPD 28-20 7768, jefe político of Ixtlán to Porfirio Díaz, May 26, 1903; CPD 28-24 89296–89297, Porfirio Díaz to jefe político of Ixtlán, July 23, 1903; and AGEO Secretaría de Gobierno 117-5, Porfirio Díaz to jefe político of Ixtlán, 1905.

2. CPD 14-22 10915–10916, Fernando Pérez to Porfirio Díaz, October 8, 1899; CPD 30-19 7202, Dionisio Santiago to Porfirio Díaz, May 31, 1905; CPD 30-26 10115, Dionisio Santiago to Porfirio Díaz, August 8, 1905; CPD 28-33 12955–129577, Mariano Ibarra to Porfirio Díaz, September 12, 1903; CPD 26-2 573–574, Felipe García and Anastasio García to Porfirio Díaz, January 4, 1901; CPD 27-12 4586, Salvador Bolaños Cacho, jefe político of Ixtlán to Porfirio Díaz, April 23, 1902.

3. CPD 34-26 12876, Luz López to Porfirio Díaz, August 5, 1909; CPD 29-9 3498, Ignacia Ceballos, widow of Julián Medina, to Porfirio Díaz, March 16, 1904; CPD 24-4 1652, Rosalia García to Porfirio Díaz (written by scribe L. Pérez), February 25, 1899; CPD 33-33 13132–13138, José Pacheco to Porfirio Díaz, October 1, 1908. See also CPD 27-26 10348 Mercedes García, widow of Liro Mori Cervantes, to Porfirio Díaz, August 29, 1902.

4. There exists a certain irony to the notion that the Porfirian regime became less responsive to the needs of popular classes "as it aged" since it was actually the actions and arrogance of a younger generation of Porfirian allies who failed to reproduce a working consensus with the popular classes. See chapter 5.

5. Meijueiro's brother-in-law, Fidencio Hernández, focused most of his energy on business, purchasing extensive land holdings in Veracruz and building new factories to make soap, candles, and bread. When called on, Hernández would serve as a representative in the national legislature, but he did not reclaim a term as governor. He died at the age of forty-nine in 1881. Meijueiro's mentor Miguel Castro had used his friendship with Juárez and ties to the Sierra to dominate statewide politics during the Restored Republic. By 1876, Castro had retired from public office, though he continued to be an influential landholder in Ixtlán district. His retirement served him well; he outlived both Hernández and Meijueiro, dying at the age of seventy-nine in 1892. For background on Hernández and Castro, see Pérez García, *Sierra Juárez*, 3:130–40.

6. Ibid., 2:135.

7. In general, Francisco Meijueiro's importance to Oaxacan history has been slighted by the attention his son Guillermo has received for leading the First Battalion of the Sierra Juarez against the Constitutionalists from 1915 to 1920. For background on Francisco Meijueiro see ibid., 2:134–35. For the emphasis on Guillermo Meixueiro, see the book by his son, Ernesto Meixueiro Hernández, *Guillermo Meixueiro Delgado*; and the essays in Martínez Vásquez, *Revolución en Oaxaca*.

8. In 1878 Ixtepeji had a population of 2,441, more than twice that of Ixtlán. The entire district population in 1878 was 24,527 inhabitants, 10 percent of whom resided in Ixtepeji. For background on Ixtepeji see Pérez García, *Sierra Juárez*, 1:134–46; and Kearney, *Winds of Ixtepeji*.

9. Kearney, *Winds of Ixtepeji*; Ruiz Cervantes, *Revolución en Oaxaca*; Garner, *Revolución en la provincia*. In the previous chapter we saw how Ixtepeji's support for Díaz's Plan of La Noria (1871) threatened to split the Ixtlán National Guard. Throughout the Porfiriato, Ixtepeji town leaders looked for ways to challenge Ixtlán's authority.

10. From 1910 to 1921 Ixtepeji's population fell from 3,168 to 866; Pérez García, *Sierra Juárez*, 1:372. Kearney, *Winds of Ixtepeji*, argues that the people of Ixtepeji were still dealing with the trauma of 1912 two generations later.

11. Ixtepeji had ongoing land disputes with several villages: Tlalixtac, Chicomezuchil, and Xía; see CPD 24-38 18698, Governor Martín González to Porfirio Díaz, Decem-

ber 20, 1899; AGEO Conflictos 62-17, "Ixtepeji y Tlalixtac (Centro) en conflicto por tierras," 1900; and CPD 27-22 8409, Miguel Bolaños Cacho to Porfirio Díaz, July 25, 1902.

12. Although published after Meijueiro had resigned as governor, the negotiations for this agreement were carried out during the previous year. For a copy of the 1877 *Reglamento* see CPD Folletos y Periódicos 40-15 781-B.

13. In alphabetical order, the original Ixtepejano rancheros were Pablo Acebedo, Carlos Acevedo, Liborio Acevedo, José Ambrosio, Francisco Avedaño, Bernardo Carrasco, A. Castellanos, Cipriano Cruz, Pablo Cruz, Tomás Cruz, Félix Gutierrez, Manuel Juárez, Nicolás Juárez, Miguel Laurcano Pérez, Estéban Lázaro, Francisco Lázaro, José María Leon, Silverio Leon, Tiburio Leon, Manuel María Marcos, Santiago Méndez, José de Paz, Carlos Pérez, Eduardo Pérez, Fernando Pérez, Manuel Pérez, Andrés Ramírez, Manuel Ramos, Tomás Ramos, Hermenegildo Rojas, Eligio Santiago, and Antonio Zuñiga.

14. A more complete version of the 1912 Ixtepeji revolt is presented in this book's conclusion.

15. Many of the houses reserved for workers were destroyed in a massive fire; CPD 28-33 12955–129577, Mariano Ibarra to Porfirio Díaz, September 12, 1903.

16. These observations come from oral interviews conducted in the summer of 1991 and from visiting the Xía factory ruins several times.

17. Tensions between Ixtepeji workers and others at the factory resurfaced during negotiations for a new water contract, during a riot in 1911, and finally during the 1912 rebellion. These issues will be discussed in subsequent chapters.

18. See Decree #51 of January 15, 1873, which designated a tract of land in the district of Ixtlán as the site on which the new factory would be built, cited in Pérez García, *Sierra Juárez*, 2:273–75.

19. Vista Hermosa, another factory, opened in the central valley in 1883; see Chassen-López, *From Liberal to Revolutionary Oaxaca*, 220–22, 270–73.

20. Pérez García, *Sierra Juárez*, 2:273–75. According to Pérez García, Spanish explorers changed the name of the river valley to Xía in the sixteenth century.

21. AGEO Fomento 39-4, "La Secretaría de Fomento pide datos ó noticias de las industrias establecidas en el Estado," [1902]; AGEO Fomento 7-4, data collected for the St. Louis International Exposition, 1903; González Navarro, *Las Huelgas textiles en el Porfiriato*, 138–41, 192.

22. See, especially, Coatsworth, *Growth against Development*; and Haber, *Industry and Underdevelopment*.

23. Miller, *Industrialization in Mexico*. For a comparative case in Guatemala, see Nash, *Machine Age Maya*; and Grandin, "Strange Case of 'La Mancha Negra.'"

24. Details regarding these disputes are discussed in chapter 6.

25. Pérez García, *Sierra Juárez*, 2: 273–75.

26. In 1887 the conflict between merchants and manufacturers became so intense that Governor Luis Mier y Terán was forced to intervene; see CPD 12-2 521–525, Luis

Mier y Terán to Porfirio Díaz, January 21, 1887. Years later, in 1922, factory owners in Puebla refused to sell cotton or buy finished cloth from the textile factory in Etla after workers temporarily took control of the factory in a labor dispute. See AGN Trabajo, Legajo 444, Expedientes 13–14; and AGEO Conciliación y Arbitraje, Legajo 34, Expediente 1, August 28, 1922.

27. Newspapers widely debated the pros and cons of the "no reelection" law. See Hale, *Transformation of Liberalism*, 60–62.

28. CPD 4-1 160, Porfirio Díaz to Francisco Meijueiro, October 31, 1879.

29. Hale, *Transformation of Liberalism*, 61.

30. For unknown reasons, the original letter can be found in Díaz's personal archive. Díaz was either given this "confidential" letter by Carbó, or he confiscated it at a later time. See CPD 4-1 270, Manuel González to General José Guillermo Carbó, November 16, 1879.

31. Ibid.

32. As González predicted, Díaz endorsed his candidacy for president, and González easily won the 1880 elections. During his tenure, González consulted frequently with Díaz. In 1882, for example, he asked for Díaz's opinion on the appointment of General Francisco Tolentino as governor of Jalisco. Díaz wrote back that he supported the appointment. Díaz was also directly involved in political appointments in the Yucatán, advising González on which men to name to which positions. See CPD 7-2 450, Manuel González to Porfirio Díaz, April 14, 1882; CPD 7-3 1069, Carlos Pacheco to Porfirio Díaz, May 13, 1882. For background on the González administration see Ponce Alocer, *Elección presidencial de Manuel González*.

33. "*Los bisoños soldados de 1854 eran considerados como una amenaza a los treinta años por el mismo general que les enseño la carrera militar*." Pérez García, *Sierra Juárez*, 2:102–3.

34. Ibid.

35. CPD 10-15 7429–7430, Luis Mier y Terán to Porfirio Díaz, July 3, 1885.

36. See especially CPD 11-6 2629, Francisco Meijueiro to Porfirio Díaz, February 22, 1886.

37. CPD 7-2 458, Manuel Dublán to Porfirio Díaz, April 12, 1882.

38. CEHM Fondo CXIX-1, 1–131, July 27, 1882.

39. Francisco Meijueiro sent Díaz mescal even though he knew the president did not drink alcohol: "*Yo sé bien que U. no usa licos, mas este se sirba [sic] para carnivadas a los chinacos que viciten a U.*" See CPD 11-6 2641, Francisco Meijueiro to Porfirio Díaz, March 21, 1886. See also CPD 11-6 2738, Porfirio Díaz to Francisco Meijueiro, March 26, 1886. For other foods sent to and requested by Díaz, see CPD 11-6 2765, Francisco Meijueiro to Porfirio Díaz, March 11, 1886; CPD 11-6 2722, Porfirio Díaz to Francisco Meijueiro, March 17, 1886; CPD 28-20 7768, jefe político of Ixtlán to Porfirio Díaz, May 26, 1903; CPD 28-24 89296–89297, Porfirio Díaz to jefe político of Ixtlán, July 23, 1903; and AGEO Secretaría de Gobierno 117-5, Porfirio Díaz to jefe político of Ixtlán, 1905.

40. CPD 10-17 8300–8301, Francisco Meijueiro to Porfirio Díaz, August 12, 1885; CPD 10-17 8300-A, Francisco Meijueiro to Porfirio Díaz, August 19, 1885.

41. CPD 10-23 11158–11159, Francisco Meijueiro to Porfirio Díaz, November 27, 1885.

42. CPD 10-19 9457–9458, Juan Rey to Porfirio Díaz, September 18, 1885; CPD 11-2 676, Francisco Meijueiro to Porfirio Díaz, January 22, 1886.

43. For the actual decision as voted on by the board of directors of Natividad see CPD 11-3 1074, Report of the Board of Directors of Natividad, February 15, 1886. See also CPD 11-6 2629, Francisco Meijueiro to Porfirio Díaz, February 22, 1886; and CPD 11-5 2361, Carlos Sodi to Porfirio Díaz, February 26, 1886.

44. CPD 11-6 2629, Francisco Meijueiro to Porfirio Díaz, February 22, 1886.

45. CPD 11-19 9281–9282, Francisco Meijueiro to Porfirio Díaz, August 17, 1886; see also CPD 11-22 10542–10543, Demetrio Sodi to Porfirio Díaz, August 27, 1886.

46. CPD 11-6 2694, Francisco Meijueiro to Porfirio Díaz, March 6, 1886. See also CPD 11-6 2765, Francisco Meijueiro to Porfirio Díaz, March 11, 1886.

47. CPD 10-20 9783, Porfirio Díaz to Francisco Meijueiro, October 30, 1885; CPD 11-26 12778–12779, Francisco Meijueiro to Porfirio Díaz, November 3, 1886; CPD 10-22 10727, N. S. Reneau to Porfirio Díaz, November 26, 1885; CPD 11-18 8820–8822, N. S. Reneau to Porfirio Díaz, August 3, 1886; CPD 11-23 11284, N. S. Reneau to Porfirio Díaz, October 26, 1886; CPD 11-25 12347–12348, N. S. Reneau to Porfirio Díaz, October 30, 1886; CPD 12-10 4844, Juan Butler (associate of N. S. Reneau) to Porfirio Díaz, June 13, 1887.

48. CPD 11-26 12735, Porfirio Díaz to Luis Mier y Terán and a copy sent to Francisco Meijueiro, November 3, 1886.

49. CPD 13-3 1381, N. S. Reneau to Porfirio Díaz, February 23, 1888.

50. CPD 13-4 1512, Francisco Meijueiro to Porfirio Díaz, February 22, 1888.

51. CPD 13-17 8203–8205, N. S. Reneau to Porfirio Díaz, August 17, 1888; Díaz responded on August 20, 1888.

52. CPD 11-29 14269, Francisco Meijueiro to Porfirio Díaz, January 4, 1887; CPD 12-2 544, Porfirio Díaz to Francisco Meijueiro, January 4, 1887.

53. In 1888 Meijueiro sent Díaz a gold nugget and a silver nugget to celebrate Díaz's marriage to Carmen Romero Rubio. CPD 13-20 9936–9937, Francisco Meijueiro to Porfirio Diaz, October 19, 1888.

54. CPD 11-20 9078–9709, Francisco Meijueiro to Porfirio Díaz, August 29, 1886.

55. CPD 13-2 800–803, N. S. Reneau to Porfirio Díaz, January 21, 1888; CPD 13-12 5905, Miguel Castro to Francisco Meijueiro, June 11, 1888.

56. AGN Gobernación 2-877-3-3, Carta de Francisco Meijueiro, March 13, 1877.

57. Iturribarría, *Historia de Oaxaca*, 4:242–44; see also Cosío Villegas, *Historia moderna de México, el Porfiriato*, 2:550–67. Coatsworth writes only that the Mexican Southern Railroad was an important regional line in *Growth against Development*, 216.

58. CPD 11-6 2665, Luis Mier y Terán to Porfirio Díaz, March 4, 1886.

59. CPD 12-9 4070–4071, Luis Mier y Terán to Porfirio Díaz, May 11, 1887. See also Chassen-López, *From Liberal to Revolutionary Oaxaca*, 45–60.

60. Iturribarría, *Historia de Oaxaca*, 4:243–44.

61. CPD 14-22 10559, Francisco González y Cosío to Porfirio Díaz and Díaz's reply, September 29, 1889.

62. CPD 14-23 11275, Porfirio Díaz to Albino Zertuche, October 9, 1889.

63. CPD 14-24 11830, Francisco Meijueiro to Porfirio Díaz, November 19, 1889.

64. CPD 14-24 11830, Francisco Meijueiro to Porfirio Díaz, November 19, 1889 (postscript). See also CPD 14-24 11829, Francisco Meijueiro to Porfirio Díaz, November 20, 1889; and CPD 14-24 11831, Porfirio Díaz to Francisco Meijueiro, November 20, 1889.

65. CPD 14-26 12703, Benjamin Cartas to Porfirio Díaz, December 18, 1889; CPD 14-28 13865–13866, Albino Zertuche to Porfirio Díaz, December 6, 1889; CPD 14-28 13871–13872, Albino Zertuche to Porfirio Díaz, December 12, 1889.

66. Iturribarría, *Historia de Oaxaca*, 4:242–44.

67. CPD 9-3 1149–1150A, Luis Mier y Terán to Porfirio Díaz, December 7, 1884.

68. See Díaz's response to Mier y Terán, attached to CPD 9-3 1150A, December 12, 1884.

69. CPD 13-18 8912–8913, Francisco Meijueiro to Porfirio Díaz, August 24, 1888. As a young boy Meijueiro had not attended school. He learned to read and write from the private instruction of Carlota Laureng, an Englishwoman whose husband was an executive for Natividad.

70. CPD 10-17 8300–8301, Francisco Meijueiro to Porfirio Díaz, August 12, 1885; CPD 10-17 8300-A, Francisco Meijueiro to Porfirio Díaz, August 19, 1885.

71. CPD 14-24 11829–11830, Francisco Meijueiro to Porfirio Díaz, November 20, 1889. See also Díaz's reply in CPD 14-24 11830, Porfirio Díaz to Francisco Meijueiro, November 20, 1889.

72. CPD 15-3 1457–1459, Cruz García et al. to Porfirio Díaz, February 5, 1890. This petition included some forty-seven signatures, although many of the men did not know how to sign their names, including Cruz García. Rosendo Pérez also refers to a promise Díaz had made to build the bridge; see Pérez García, *Sierra Juárez*, 1:283–84.

73. CPD 15-3 1457–1459, Cruz García et al. to Porfirio Díaz, February 5, 1890; and Díaz's attached reply.

74. CPD 10-6 2834–2835, Miguel Meijueiro to Porfirio Díaz, March 13, 1885. Toro eventually forced Miguel Meijueiro to resign as jefe político by accusing him of stealing the payroll for public employees, a clever trick since it may have been Toro who had actually absconded with the money. Toro was quite ruthless in his dealings with potential rivals. In 1867 he confiscated land belonging to Jacinto Juárez, a well-known conservative. Toro claimed he could take the land as compensation for his military service during the civil wars. The Juárez family fought Toro for thirty-two years and finally won the land back in a court victory in 1899. For background on that case see the service record of Colonel Manuel Toro, AHDN Cancelados D/111/4/2970. Toro's son, Federico, would later serve as secretary to the Ixtlán jefe político for more than twenty years.

75. CPD 2-3 985–987, Francisco Meijueiro to Porfirio Díaz, June 5, 1877.

76. CPD 11-13 6139–6140, Francisco Meijueiro to Porfirio Díaz, June 4, 1886.

77. See, for example, CPD 11-2 676, Francisco Meijueiro to Porfirio Díaz, January 22, 1886.

78. CPD 10-23 11273–11274, Francisco Meijueiro to Porfirio Díaz, April 18, 1885; Díaz's response came on April 26, 1885. By January 1, 1886, Carlos Meijueiro was the tax collector; see CPD 11-2 587–588, Francisco Meijueiro to Porfirio Díaz, January 1, 1886.

79. CPD 14-3 1483, Francisco Meijueiro to Porfirio Díaz, February 15, 1889. Significantly, Rafael Pimentel had been the previous *jefatura de hacienda*. The Pimentels were a more established, aristocratic family in Oaxaca than were the Meijueiros. Although the request for Guillermo's appointment did not mention a rivalry between the two families, Guillermo would eventually challenge Emilio Pimentel for the governorship of Oaxaca. The *jefatura de hacienda* was the equivalent of the head of the Public Finance or Treasury office.

80. CPD 14-22 10915–10916, Monica Cruz et al. to Porfirio Díaz, October 8, 1889. Díaz responded on October 14, 1889.

81. CPD 14-22 10717–10718, Francisco Meijueiro to Porfirio Díaz, October 21, 1889. Meijueiro forwarded copies of all of the patents and papers for Monica Cruz. The pensions had been granted by Díaz in 1866.

82. CPD 14-28 13507, Fernando Pérez to Porfirio Díaz, December 6, 1889.

83. CPD 15-4 1635, Francisco Meijueiro to Porfirio Díaz, February 24, 1890. Here Meijueiro defends himself against accusations that he had sold the pensions, but he still did not know all of the facts about the case.

CHAPTER 5

1. For background on these men, see especially Pérez García, *Sierra Juárez*; Chassen-López, *From Liberal to Revolutionary Oaxaca*; Chassen-López, "Orígenes de la revolución en Oaxaca"; Fortson et al., *Gobernantes de Oaxaca*; Henderson, *Félix Díaz*; Meixueiro Hernández, *Guillermo Meixueiro Delgado*; and the letters by and about these individuals in the CPD cited throughout this chapter.

2. Life expectancies in rural Mexico averaged only thirty years during the Porfiriato; see Meyer and Sherman, *Course of Mexican History*, 470.

3. See CPD 29-32 12438–12444, Felipe García et al. to Porfirio Díaz, October 12, 1904.

4. The role of jefe político in Ixtlán district during the Porfiriato has been universally described as oppressive, though a more careful reading of documentary sources suggests that the secretary to the jefe político, Federico Toro, was responsible for most of the abuses committed against peasants. This distinction will be discussed more fully below.

5. Stern, *Secret History of Gender*, 199–204, discusses the difference between "good" patriarchs who recognize the conditional and reciprocal nature of their status within a community and the "parasitism" of patriarchs who abuse their authority. In this

sense, Francisco Meijueiro had been a "good" patriarch, while his son Guillermo took advantage of his influence by extorting the goods and services of Zapotec peasants in the district.

6. See Lerner, *Creation of Patriarchy*, 238–39; and Stern, *Secret History of Gender*, 21–22, for more complete definitions of "patriarchy," though their definitions should be understood in the broader context of their respective studies. Lerner examines the historical creation of patriarchy, which began in the third millennium B.C.E., as men appropriated female symbols of power and asserted instead monotheistic notions of the father-god. Stern analyzes patriarchy as a series of specific, hierarchical, and contested social relationships between men and women, and between men and men, for late colonial Mexico. My use of patriarchy draws on both Lerner and Stern by looking at symbols of patriarchal citizenship and specific social relationships within communities and the region of the Sierra Zapoteca.

7. CPD 11-17 8266, Luis Mier y Terán to Porfirio Díaz, July 6, 1886. Mier y Terán closed his letter thus: "Your brother who loves you."

8. Chassen-López, *From Liberal to Revolutionary Oaxaca*, 370–77 (quotation on p. 371).

9. Iturribarría, *Oaxaca en la historia*, 249.

10. AGEO Conflictos 63-2, April 15, 1896. Miguel E. Torres represented the Ixtlán town councils in negotiations with the state government.

11. Ibid. This file contains twenty-one separate folders dealing with the controversy over the property tax increases.

12. CPD 27-12 4616, Salvador Bolaños Cacho to Porfirio Díaz, April 9, 1902. See also CPD 27-12 4609, Salvador Bolaños Cacho to Porfirio Díaz, April 14, 1902. For more on tax disputes and collective action see CPD 27-22 8445, Zeferino Hernández to Porfirio Díaz, July 11, 1902; CPD 26-14 5318–5319, Martín González to Porfirio Díaz, June 12, 1901; and CPD 26-8 2990–2992, Anastasio Juárez et al. (forty men in total) to Porfirio Díaz, April 15, 1901.

13. In the summer of 1902 interim governor Miguel Bolaños Cacho, Salvador's brother, enacted a new property tax code that provided large landowners a generous tax break. Property owners who made improvements on their lands were exempt from the new property tax for a period of four, eight, or ten years, depending on the value of the property. Farms worth more than ten thousand pesos did not have to pay the new tax for a period of ten years, while farms valued below five thousand pesos enjoyed an exemption for just four years. See CPD 27-22 8440–8441, Miguel Bolaños Cacho to Porfirio Díaz, July 1902.

14. CPD 29-5 1874, Emilio Pimentel to Porfirio Díaz, January 4, 1904.

15. CPD 29-5 1875, Porfirio Díaz to Emilio Pimentel, February 8, 1904.

16. A sampling of studies on water resources would include Enge and Whiteford, *Keepers of Water and Earth*; Lipsett-Rivera, *To Defend Our Water with the Blood of Our Veins*; Lipsett-Rivera, "Water and Bureaucracy in Colonial Puebla de Los Angeles";

Murphy, *Irrigation in the Bajío Region of Colonial Mexico*; and Trawick, *Struggle for Water in Peru*.

17. AGEO Fomento 14-2, "Contrato de arrendamiento de las aguas del arroyo 'Las Vigas,'" January 10, 1901. See also AGEO Fomento 16-5, "Boleto para recoger datos sobre producción de las minas," 1903. Clark never intended to fully assimilate with the local population. He gave his mines English names—Gold Eagle, Silver King, Eureka, even Pocahontas—in stark contrast to most other mine owners throughout the district. Still, Clark's enthusiasm was always high on Oaxaca. In 1907 he was quoted in the *Oaxacan Herald* proclaiming the rich opportunities available in Oaxaca; see Chassen-López, "Oaxaca," 154.

18. AGEO Fomento 14-2, "Contrato de arrendamiento de las aguas del arroyo 'Las Vigas,'" February 2, 1901; AGEO Fomento 14-2, "Contrato de arrendamiento de las aguas del arroyo 'Las Vigas,'" February 16, 1901.

19. AGEO Fomento 14-2, "Contrato de arrendamiento de las aguas del arroyo 'Las Vigas,'" February 23, 1901; AGEO Fomento 14-2, "Contrato de arrendamiento de las aguas del arroyo 'Las Vigas,'" May 2, 1901.

20. For the growing demand for access to water see AGEO Fomento 14-17, "Contrato de arrendamiento de aguas con el Señor William C. Davenport," 1903; AGEO Fomento 24-1, "Solicitudes para concesión usufructo de aguas para riego de terrenos de haciendas," September 13, 1906. For water disputes between villages see AGEO Conflictos 62-17, "Ixtepeji y Tlalixtac (Centro) en conflicto por tierras," 1900; CPD 24-38 18698, Martín González to Porfirio Díaz, December 20, 1899; CPD 15-27 10701–10703, letter to Porfirio Díaz, 1900; and CPD 25-4 1334–1336, letter to Porfirio Díaz, February 16, 1900. See also AGEO Fomento 14-3, "Contratos de arrendamiento de los ríos de 'Las Peñas' y 'San Juan' celebrado entre el municipio de Tlazoyaltpec y el Señor Jacobo L. Grandison," February 17, 1901; and AGEO Fomento 20-12, "El Lic. Fidencio Hernández pide se le concedan las aguas de los arrollos de la 'Trinidad' y 'Yavesía' del dto. de Ixtlán," December 19, 1903.

21. For letters from Ruíz Jiménez to Porfirio Díaz see CPD 28-31 12272–12281, September 11, 1903; CPD 29-17 6670–6677, May 31, 1904; CPD 29-23 8804–8810, June 27, 1904; CPD 31-45 17933–17938, April 19, 1906; CPD 32-6 2199–2204, February 19, 1907; CPD 32-14 5579–5581; CPD 32-21 8111–8117, July 5, 1907; and CPD 32-21 8145–8147, July 21, 1907.

22. Mecham, "Jefe Político in Mexico"; Guerra, *México*. For a view of the jefes políticos as agents of coercion and consent, as intermediaries between those who had power and those who did not, see Falcón, "Force and the Search for Consent."

23. These opportunities were enhanced by working with governors who had strong ties to the Sierra Zapoteca: Benito Juárez, Porfirio Díaz, Félix Díaz, Miguel Castro, Francisco Meijueiro, Fidencio Hernández, Benito Juárez Maza, Félix Díaz (*hijo*), Isaac Ibarra, and Onofre Jiménez.

24. I am unaware of any other case where the secretary in the jefe político's office

obtained as much power, though there must have been others. The history of the jefe político in Ixtlán suggests the need for more detailed analyses of these important officials. For background on Federico Toro (1867–1913), see Pérez García, *Sierra Juárez*, 2:136–37.

25. CPD 24-11 5117–5118, Martín González to Porfirio Díaz, April 13, 1899. Díaz monitored the Ixtlán situation closely, eventually agreeing to Trejo Zerril's appointment. See CPD 24-11 5069–5070, Martín González to Porfirio Díaz, April 24, 1899.

26. CPD 24-14 6536, Martín González to Porfirio Díaz, May 13, 1899. See also CPD 24-38 18690–18693, Martín González to Porfirio Díaz, December 23, 1899.

27. CPD 27-19 7363–7369, letter to Porfirio Díaz from hundreds of men in Ixtlán district, July 29, 1902. There are thirty-four pages of signatures, including sixty-three men from the town of Ixtlán, seventeen from Guelatao, twenty-seven from Ixtepeji, thirty-nine from San Miguel del Río, and so forth. See also AGEO Secretaría de Gobierno 85-12, "Los pueblos piden no sea removido el jefe político," 1902. For the original appointment to Ixtlán, see AGEO Secretaría de Gobierno 70-12, "Nombramiento de jefe político del Distrito de Ixtlán en favor del C. Salvador Bolaños Cacho," 1901.

28. AGEO Secretaría de Gobierno 121-2, "El jefe político participa que el juez pide auxilio de la fuerza armada," April 27–28, 1904.

29. CPD 24-25 12365–12369, José Luciano Zuñiga to Porfirio Díaz, September 6, 1899. In a separate matter, a group of fourteen Zapotec men accused Pablo Meixueiro, a cousin of Guillermo's who was working for the Ixtlán jefe político, of unfairly holding them in prison for crimes they did not commit. See CPD 24-32 15674–15675, Andres Arreola et al. to Porfirio Díaz, November 20, 1899. For the role of jefes políticos in other regions in Oaxaca, see CPD 24-6 2761–2763, a request by villagers in Silacayóapam, Oaxaca, to name their own jefe político, March 8, 1899; and CPD 24-38 18704, regarding a problem with jefe político in Miahuatlán, 1899.

30. See CPD 32-9 3379–3381, a letter from Anacleto Juárez and twenty other peasants from Guelatao to José Ruíz Jiménez, February 21, 1907, a copy of which was sent to Díaz. These men were hopeful that their complaints against state and district officials would be considered fairly since "we know and understand that our affairs are in the hands of Papá Grande and we cannot take another route."

31. As Phelan, *People and the King*, discusses through the phrase "*Viva el rey y muera el mal gobierno* [Long live the king and death to bad government]," these contradictions had also punctuated riots and popular movements at the end of the colonial period.

32. See, for example, CPD 24-35 17383–17384, Antonio Ramírez to Porfirio Díaz, December 30, 1899; CPD 23-3 1398, María Cazorla to Porfirio Díaz, February 13, 1898; CPD 32-22 8479, Vicente Garcés et al. (twenty-five pages of signatures) to Porfirio Díaz, June 9, 1907; and CPD 33-34 13448, Onofre Jiménez et al. to Porfirio Díaz, September 22, 1908.

33. CPD 25-39 15537, Enrique Romero to Porfirio Díaz, December 26, 1900; CPD 24-11 5124–5125, Vicente Garcés to Porfirio Díaz, April 8, 1899; CPD 25-39 15477, Jacinta

R. de Perzabal to Porfirio Díaz, December 21, 1900; CPD 25-39 15555, Manuel Reyes to Porfirio Díaz, December 24, 1900.

34. CPD 14-24 11829, Francisco Meijueiro to Porfirio Díaz, undated [November 1889]: *"De todos modos me afiarse en demostrar a los Oaxaqueños y Serranos que de U. solo debemos experar consideraciones de Padre y que le debemos quedar obligador como si fueramos sus hijos."*

35. CPD 28-7 2762–2763, Tomás Ramos to Porfirio Díaz, March 14, 1903. See also Díaz's draft response, CPD 28-7 2764, Porfirio Díaz to Tomás Ramos.

36. CPD 32-9 3379–3381, Anacleto Juárez and twenty other peasants from Guelatao to José Ruíz Jiménez, February 21, 1907. For a similar view see the letter from four *"principales,"* or elders, from the village of Santiago Huajilotitlán in Huajuapam district, Oaxaca. Asking for Díaz's help in negotiating a land dispute with several large landowners, they noted that *"habian acordado que en esta Capital tenemos un verdadero Padre que es de nosotros todos los Mexicanos* [it has been resolved that in this capital we have a true Father who represents all Mexicans]." CPD 28-32 12640, Agustin Hernández, Francisco Loyola, Tranquilino Hernández, and Ventura Alavez to Porfirio Díaz, September 12, 1903.

37. CPD 31-17 6414–6415, María Manzano to Porfirio Díaz, June 18, 1906.

38. CPD 34-32 15969, Mauricia Jiménez, Josefa Jiménez, and Juana Sabina Santiago to Porfirio Díaz, August 28, 1909. In this letter they list the dates of their previous correspondence with Díaz.

39. For other letters written by women to Porfirio Díaz, see CPD 14-22 10915–10916, Monica Cruz de Pérez, Luisa Ramos, Carmen Sánchez to Porfirio Díaz, October 8, 1889; CPD 24-4 1652, Rosalía García to Porfirio Díaz, February 25, 1899; CPD 27-20 7629, María L. Vela de Ruíz to Porfirio Díaz, July 9, 1902; CPD 34-26 12876, Luz López to Porfirio Díaz, August 5, 1909; and CPD 35-26 12745–12746, Señora de Hernández to Porfirio Díaz, August 20, 1910.

40. For the legislative debates regarding the Colonization Law of 1883, see Hale, *Transformation of Liberalism*, 234–38. For estimates on the amount of land transferred to survey companies see González Navarro, *Colonización en México*, 12–14, 36, 123; and González Navarro, *Historia moderna de México, el Porfiriato*, 195–96.

41. AGEO Repartos 13-28, "Expediente sobre reparto de terrenos comunales," September 20, 1890.

42. No hacienda over one thousand hectares existed in Ixtlán district in 1899; see AGN Fomento: Exposiciones 53-44, "Comisión Mexicana para la Exposición de París, Grupo VII, Estadística Agrícola," various dates, 1899.

43. AGEO Juzgados 120-2045, "Jacobo Grandison denuncia como baldíos unos terrenos en Tecotpec, Choapam," June 23, 1891. Located east of Ixtlán district, Choapam district borders the state of Veracruz. AGEO Repartos 2-5, "Contrato para colonización de terrenos entre Jacobo Grandison y la Secretaría de Fomento," August 7, 1894.

44. AGEO Conflictos 55-40, "Queja de que Jacobo Grandison se extralimita de su

adjudicación y siembra café en terrenos del municipio Jocotepec," March 15, 1894. Grandison responded to the charge on April 16, 1894.

45. CPD 23-36 17906, José Alatamirano to Porfirio Díaz, December 8, 1898.

46. AGEO Repartos 7-16, "Relativo a la venta de terrenos que hace la Companía Limitada de Río Manzo en liquidación a Jacobo Grandison," 1901; CPD 27-35 14036, Jacobo Grandison to Porfirio Díaz, September 13, 1902.

47. For a listing of these disputes and a concern among peasants that nothing was being done to settle these conflicts, see CPD 31-38 14898, Antonio Hernández to Porfirio Díaz, November 14, 1906.

48. The documents consulted for this dispute can be found in AGEO Conflictos 63-9, "Los de Abejones invaden terrenos de Maninaltepec," "Los de Abejones dicen que Maninaltepec trajeron arrendatarios de Comaltepec a esos terrenos," and "De Abejones desconoce a la autoridad del jefe político"; and AGEO Conflictos 62-1, "Abejones solicita aprobación del convenio con Maninaltepec." See the individual correspondence within these files, including, Nestor Bautista, municipal president of Abejones to Governor Martín González, August 27, 1896; notes of the Secretaría de Gobierno in Oaxaca, September 5, September 10, and September 15, 1896; Ramón González, jefe político of Ixtlán, to Juez de 1ª Instancia, September 6 and September 10, 1896; José Anacleto Durán, municipal agent of Maninaltepec to Governor Martín González, October 13, 1896; Mauricio Bautista, municipal president of Abejones to Governor Martín González, December 2, 1896; Nestor Bautista, municipal president of Abejones to Governor Martín González, December 15, 1896; Enrique León, Secretaría de Gobierno of Oaxaca to Governor Martín González, December 16, 1896; Ramón González, jefe político of Ixtlán, to Governor Martín González, December 21, 1896; Miguel López, municipal agent of Maninaltepec, to jefe político of Ixtlán, January 2, 1897; José Domingo Bautista, municipal president of Abejones, to Governor Martín González, January 15, 1897; José Domingo Bautista, municipal president of Abejones, to jefe político of Ixtlán, February 6, 1897; Victoriano Salinas, municipal agent of Maninaltepec, to jefe político of Ixtlán, February 10, 1897; Ramón González, jefe político of Ixtlán, to secretary general of Oaxaca, February 16, 1897; and Enrique León to Governor Martín González, November 1, 1898. See also CPD 24-31 15184, Martín González to Porfirio Díaz, October 28, 1899.

49. Cerrilo López, José Domingo López, Manuel Hernández, Aúreo Luis López, and Pedro López, all from Comaltepec, rented the land from Maninaltepec. AGEO Conflictos 63-9, José Domingo Bautista to Governor Martín González, January 15, 1897.

50. AGEO Conflictos 62-1, Ramón González et al., minutes of meeting on July 23, 1896.

51. AGEO Conflictos 63-9, "Los de Abejones invaden terrenos de Maninaltepec," August 5, 1896.

52. Ibid., December 15, 1896.

53. Ibid., August 14, 1896; AGEO Conflictos 62-1, Ramón González, jefe político of Ixtlán, to Governor Martín González, December 21, 1896.

54. AGEO Conflictos 63-9, "Los de Abejones invaden terrenos de Maninaltepec," January 15, 1897.

55. AGEO Conflictos 62-1, Ramón González to secretary general of Oaxaca, February 16, 1897.

56. Ibid.

57. AGEO Conflictos 62-1, minutes of Abejones town meeting, October 15, 1898. See also Enrique León to Governor Martín González, November 1, 1898.

58. AGEO Secretaría de Gobierno 125-23, "El president municipal de San Miguel Abejones se queja contra actos de le autoridad municipal del pueblo Maninaltepec de aquel distrito," August 12, 1912; AGEO Conflictos, "El pueblo de Maninaltepec se queja de invasiones de terranos por vecinos del pueble de Abejones," June 22, 1900. See also AGN Gobernación: Período Revolucionario 98-34, Pedro Pérez to Secretaría de Gobernación, August 20, 1912. Other historians have taken Abejones's complaints at face value; see, for example, Sánchez Silva, *Crisis política y contrarevolución en Oaxaca*, 130–34.

59. CPD 24-28 13658–13659, Martín González to Porfirio Díaz, August 28, 1899.

60. Ibid.

61. On the effectiveness of pluralizing patriarchs as a strategy of resistance, see Stern, *Secret History of Gender*, 99–106.

62. According to Chassen-López, *From Liberal to Revolutionary Oaxaca*, 241, Ixtlán's population grew from nearly 25,895 in 1877 to 32,224 in 1910. Growth was uneven across the district. Ixtepeji's population grew over the same period from 2,460 to 3,168, nearly a 30 percent increase. The impact of this rapid growth for Ixtepeji will be discussed below. For district population figures see Pérez García, *Sierra Juárez*, 1:134–46.

63. Quoted in Bernstein, *Mexican Mining Industry*, 6. Chassen-López, *From Liberal to Revolutionary Oaxaca*, 189–95, demonstrates the short-term nature of this boom, arguing that success in the mining industry was more illusory than real. In a report produced during the early years of the Porfiriato, the potential of Oaxacan mineral deposits received unparalleled attention. See Busto, *Estadistica de la República Mexicana*, 206–7.

64. Henry "Guillermo" Trinker, Jacobo Grandison's brother-in-law and treasurer of the board of directors at Natividad, sent Díaz a dividend check for 225 pesos in September 1898. One month later, Fidencio Hernández sent Díaz another check for 300 pesos. CPD 23-24 11731, Guillermo Trinker to Porfirio Díaz, September 27, 1898; CPD 23-28 13568, Fidencio Hernández to Porfirio Díaz, October 20, 1898.

65. CPD 25-18 6953, Manuel Muñoz Gómez to Porfirio Díaz, June 13, 1900; CPD 28-24 9380, Emilio Pimentel to Porfirio Díaz, July 13, 1903.

66. CPD 25-18 6953, Manuel Muñoz Gómez to Porfirio Díaz, June 13, 1900.

67. AGEO Fomento 16-02, "Boleta para recoger datos sobre la industría mineria," April 13, 1900; AGEO Fomento 16-05, "Boleta para recoger datos sobre producción de la minas," 1903. For a fascinating look at the interwoven connections between Oaxa-

can elites, see AGEO Fomento 17-1, "Testimonio original de la escritura en que se hizo constar el acuerdo de los representantes de la Sociedad Minera 'La Unión,' por virtud del cual se nombró Gerente de la misma sociedad al Señor Jacobo Grandison," September 19, 1907.

68. I have counted Jacobo Grandison as a Oaxacan owner since he lived most of his life in the state. The Meixueiro family had also expanded their mining investments, owning a total of seventeen mines in 1903 as opposed to just nine in 1900.

69. AGEO Fomento 16-02, "Boleta para recoger datos sobre la industría mineria," April 13, 1900.

70. See Bernstein, *Mexican Mining Industry*, 86.

71. See CPD 31-23 9069–9081, "Report of A. B. Adams, President to the Board of Directors of A. B. Adams, Incorporated," New York, August 21, 1906. As the report noted in describing the company's plans for developing a coal mine in Oaxaca, "The labor supply, especially in western Oaxaca, is very abundant and receives a rate of wage averaging much below most other parts of the Republic. This is due to the fact that they are mainly Mexteca [*sic*] Indians." For background on the state's intervention in behalf of A. B. Adams, Inc., see CPD 32-18 7191, Emilio Pimentel to Porfirio Díaz, July 13, 1907.

72. Pérez García, *Sierra Juárez*, 1:268–69.

73. CPD 29-23 8867, Manuel, Andres, and Pedro Arreortúa to Porfirio Díaz, July 26, 1904; CPD 30-28 10931–10932, Andres and Pedro Arreortúa to Porfirio Díaz, August 4, 1905; CPD 30-27 10500, Governor Emilio Pimentel to Porfirio Díaz, August 10, 1905; CPD 31-23 8841–8843, Manuel, Pedro, and Andres Arreortúa to Porfirio Díaz, July 16, 1906. See also AGEO Fomento 20-2, September 18, 1906.

74. The original contract was included in a series of documents forwarded to state and federal officials after the contract expired. See AGEO Fomento 21-6, "Contrato celebrado entre los Señores Mowat y Grandison y hijos y el municipio de Ixtepeji para el uso de las aguas del río 'Grillo,'" October 4, 1906.

75. CPD 27-22 8592, Rito Cruz and Margarito Santiago to Porfirio Díaz, 1902.

76. While Ixtepeji's population grew by 30 percent, the ranchero population, those families who had rights to farm on separate plots, doubled over the same period. See Pérez García, *Sierra Juárez*, 1:134–46.

77. AGEO Fomento 14-9, "Sobre aprobación de un contrato que pretende celebrar el Municipio de Ixtepeji con los dueños de la Fábrica de Xía para el arrendamiento de las aguas del río que se sirve dicha Fábrica," May 9, 1902. See also AGEO Fomento 21-6, September 10, 1903. The meeting took place on May 8, 1902.

78. AGEO Fomento 14-9, "Sobre aprobación de un contrato que pretende celebrar el Municipio de Ixtepeji con los dueños de la Fábrica de Xía para el arrendamiento de las aguas del río que se sirve dicha Fábrica," May 9, 1902.

79. See CPD 27-22 8409, Miguel Bolaños Cacho to Porfirio Díaz, July 15, 1902, in which the jefe político accused the town's hired representative José Ruíz Jiménez of instigating the emerging conflict between Ixtepeji and the factory.

80. The new contract was signed the day before Christmas, December 24, 1903. Fiburcio Hernández, Ixtepeji municipal president Manuel de Paz, and town council representatives Francisco and Mauricio Pérez, along with *"principales"* Florencio Cruz, Agapito Chávez, Serapio Avendaño, Ignacio Castellanos, and José Cruz Castellanos, signed the agreement with Guillermo Trinker. See AGEO Fomento 21-6, "Contrato celebrado entre los Señores Mowat y Grandison y hijos y el municipio de Ixtepeji para el uso de las aguas del río 'Grillo,'" September 1, 1903, and December 24, 1903.

81. See CPD 30-14 5259, Margarito Santiago to Porfirio Díaz, April 2, 1905; see also AGEO Fomento 21-6, "Contrato celebrado entre los Señores Mowat y Grandison y hijos y el municipio de Ixtepeji para el uso de las aguas del río 'Grillo,'" October 4, 1906.

82. CPD 23-24 11968–11969, Margarito Hernández to Porfirio Díaz, September 9, 1898; CPD 23-33 16414, Pánfilo Méndez et al. to Porfirio Díaz, December 26, 1898. Hernández prodded Díaz by stating, "We hear, Señor Presidente, that you no longer love the Serranos."

83. CPD 24-03 1438, Agapito Chávez et al. to Porfirio Díaz, February 15, 1899: *"Los importantes y leales servicios que nuestros finados padres y algunos de los presentes hemos prestado a la causa de la República."*

84. CPD 26-09 3496, Sebastián Trejo Zerril to Porfirio Díaz, April 20, 1901. Meixueiro intervened in the affairs of other towns as well. For a summation of many of the problems faced by other communities, see CPD 29-32 12439–12442, Felipe García et al. to Porfirio Díaz, October 12, 1904.

85. CPD 23-30 14865–14866, letters to Porfirio Díaz and Governor González, November 23, 1898. For another plea to end forced conscription see CPD 28-17 6538, María Antonia Arellanos to Porfirio Díaz, regarding the case of her son Tranquilino Barrios, May 12, 1903.

86. CPD 31-38 14917 and 14898, Antonio Hernández to Porfirio Díaz, November 14, 1906. Antonio Hernández explained his reasons for turning to Ruíz Jiménez: "My misfortune is doubly sad because I don't know how to speak Spanish, which is why I went to Don José Ruíz Jiménez, so that I could relate to him my sad situation in Zapoteco."

87. CPD 31-38 14898, Antonio Hernández to Porfirio Díaz, November 14, 1906.

88. Fortson et al., *Gobernantes de Oaxaca*, 166–69.

89. See, for example, the discussion in CPD 23-11 5219–5220, Manuel Olivera Toro to Porfirio Díaz, April 14, 1898.

90. CPD 24-18 8564–8566, Martín González to Porfirio Díaz, June 12, 1899.

91. Political repression also grew as González ordered his police forces to jail his opponents. For example, Fermin Díaz (no relation to Porfirio Díaz) was jailed for simply carrying a poster of Félix Díaz through the streets of Oaxaca. See CPD 27-11 4113, Melchora Lascares (Fermin Díaz's mother) to Porfirio Díaz, April 25, 1902.

92. Henderson, *Félix Díaz*, 7.

93. For letters supporting Félix Díaz for governor see CPD 27-7 2544–2546, Manuel Pérez et al. to Porfirio Díaz, March 14, 1902; CPD 27-11 4113, Melchora Lascares to

Porfirio Díaz, April 25, 1902; CPD 31-11 4197, "Los Felixistas y los Serranos" to Porfirio Díaz, April 30, 1906 (discussed in detail below); CPD 31-18 7187–88, Men of Ixtepeji to Porfirio Díaz, June 1, 1906; CPD 31-26 10085–10087, Apolinar Bautista et al. to Porfirio Díaz, August 10, 1906; and CPD 34-17 8205–8207, Rosendo Jiménez to Porfirio Díaz, May 7, 1909.

94. For biographical information on Pimentel see Fortson et al., *Gobernantes de Oaxaca*, 170–73.

95. Hale, *Transformation of Liberalism*, 230–31; Chassen-López, *From Liberal to Revolutionary Oaxaca*, 383, 256–58.

96. Indeed, Díaz's unwavering support for Pimentel frustrated Guillermo Meixueiro, who briefly joined the opposition in the Asociación Juárez. See Chassen-López, *From Liberal to Revolutionary Oaxaca*, 460–66. For the article, see CPD 27-22 8482–8484, Governor Bolaños Cacho to Porfirio Díaz, June 28, 1902; see also CPD 27-22 8491–8493, Bolaños Cacho to Porfirio Díaz, June 24, 1902.

97. CPD 27-21 8294–8298, Guillermo Meixueiro to Porfirio Díaz, July 6, 1902.

98. Díaz asked Romulado Zárate to form a pro-Pimentel club in Ixtlán. See CPD 27-16 6079, Porfirio Díaz to Romulado Zárate, June 9, 1902.

99. CPD 27-22 844, Miguel Bolaños Cacho to Porfirio Díaz, July 12, 1902. See also CPD 27-18 7170, Miguel Bolaños Cacho to Porfirio Díaz, June 11, 1902. State officials temporarily considered moving the Ixtlán electoral stations to Etla district in order to "guarantee" a fair election. See AGEO Secretaría de Gobierno 85-9, "Los pueblos de distrito de Ixtlán suplican se les conceda que sus electores no vayan al distrito de Etla . . . ," June 30, 1902.

100. CPD 29-17 6623, Federico H. Toro to Porfirio Díaz, May 20, 1904. See also AGEO Secretaría de Gobierno 116-12, April 6, 1906. Fidencio Hernández also organized the Club Democratico Electoral to support Pimentel's reelection in 1906 in Ixtlán.

101. Guerra, *México*, 1:182–245. Chassen-López, *From Liberal to Revolutionary Oaxaca*, 437–38, critiques Guerra for the same reasons.

CHAPTER 6

1. Creelman, "President Diaz," 245. Aguilar Camín and Meyer, *In the Shadow of the Mexican Revolution*, 12–13, note that Díaz's sentimentality increased as he grew older.

2. Romero had also served briefly as governor of Oaxaca, ironically during the first three months of Porfirio Díaz's rebellion against Juárez in 1871.

3. Weeks, *Juárez Myth*, 46.

4. García and others expected volunteer organizations, along with the new administrative channels as an autonomous municipality, to play a fundamental role in improving living conditions in Guelatao. CPD 26-2 573–574, Felipe García and Anastasio García to Porfirio Díaz, January 4, 1901. See also CPD 26-3 1027, Juan Juárez, municipal president of Guelatao, to Porfirio Díaz, January 4, 1901. For military background on Felipe García see CPD 27-12 4586, Salvador Bolaños Cacho, jefe político of Ixtlán, to

Porfirio Díaz, April 23, 1902. Bolaños Cacho also included a list of the soldiers García led as captain.

5. AGEO Secretaría de Gobierno 116-9, "Relativo establecimiento de la junta 'Juárez y Progreso,'" May 5, 1903; see also the resolution in CPD 28-19 7258, Mesa Directiva de la Junta "Juárez y Progreso" to Porfirio Díaz, June 29, 1903.

6. For the pension granted to García see CPD 27-26 10085, Governor Bolaños Cacho to Porfirio Díaz, September 26, 1902.

7. Other members of the Mesa Directiva in Guelatao included Anselmo García, vice president; Juan B. García, first representative, Esteban Pérez, second representative, and Mauricio Pérez, second secretary. CPD 28-19 7258, Mesa Directiva de la Junta "Juárez y Progreso" to Porfirio Díaz, June 29, 1903.

8. AGEO Secretaría de Gobierno 116-9, "Relativo establecimiento de la junta 'Juárez y Progreso,'" May 5, 1903, copies of various letters sent to the Mesa Directiva, "Juárez y Progreso," and forwarded to Porfirio Díaz. At the same time, the Comisión Nacional del Centenario de Juárez was also collecting funds for a statue to Juárez in Mexico City. The widely acclaimed engineer Gabriel Mancera was in charge of designing the monument. State governments from throughout the country donated various amounts: Yucatán, five thousand pesos; San Luis Potosí, three thousand pesos; Veracruz, ten thousand pesos. Individuals also donated money; for example, José Ives Limantour gave one hundred pesos. See AGN Gobernación 1-906-4-2, "Expediente relativo a la erección del monumento destinado a perpetuar la memoria del C. Benito Juárez," March 20, 1906.

9. Hale, *Transformation of Liberalism*, 230–31. For more on Pimentel's policy of Indian education, see Chassen-López, *From Liberal to Revolutionary Oaxaca*, 415–18.

10. See the letters from Emilio Pimentel to Porfirio Díaz in CPD 28-21 8039, June 17, 1903; CPD 28-24 9296–9297, July 23, 1903; and CPD 31-24 9400, July 31, 1906. See also the various letters sent to Porfirio Díaz from villagers of Guelatao and Ixtlán: CPD 30-32 12450–12479, Espirón Hernández et al. to Porfirio Díaz, September 22, 1905; and CPD 31-7 2698–2700, various villagers of Ixtlán to Porfirio Díaz, January 19, 1906. See also AGEO Conflictos 37-5, villagers of Guelatao to Emilio Pimentel, 1905; and AGEO Conflictos 62-11, municipal president of Ixtlán to Emilio Pimentel, 1905.

11. Pimentel relied on the engineer's report and on the advice of the jefe político of Ixtlán. See CPD 28-24 9411–9416, Emilio Pimentel to Porfirio Díaz, June 25, 1903; and CPD 28-24 9379–9380, Emilio Pimentel to Porfirio Díaz, July 14, 1903; see attached map with school plans and layout.

12. In fact, arable land had become an even more precious commodity after the turn of the century because the district's population had increased from 26,430 in 1883 to 32,224 by 1911. AGEO Memorias Administrativas, 1883, 1911. See also Garner, *Regional Development in Oaxaca*, 36.

13. CPD 29-32 12589, Martín Ramirez et al. to Porfirio Díaz, October 15, 1904. These leaders from Guelatao were notified of the rent increase as they were paying for the upcoming year.

14. *Xoo vetó*, also known as the Río de Jaltianguis, flowed eventually into the district's Río Grande. See Pérez García, *Sierra Juárez*, 1:237–38.

15. CPD 30-24 9315–9316, Emilio Pimentel to Porfirio Díaz, July 8, 1905. Originally, Ixtlán also requested a tax of twenty-five centavos per month on individuals who leased municipal land, but that provision was dropped in subsequent deliberations.

16. CPD 29-32 12589, Guelatao villagers Martín Ramírez, Estéban Pérez, Pánfilo Pérez, and Tomás Martínez to Porfirio Díaz, October 15, 1904.

17. For example, Anacleto Juárez, Felipe García (*hijo*), and Juan Bautista García told Díaz that Toro "intends to turn us against [*enemistarnos*] our brothers in Ixtlán"; CPD 30-20 7989–7990, Anacleto Juárez et al. to Porfirio Díaz, May 30, 1905.

18. CPD 29-32 12438–12442, Felipe García et al. to Porfirio Díaz, October 12, 1904.

19. CPD 30-24 9315–9316, Emilio Pimentel to Porfirio Díaz, July 8, 1905.

20. CPD 30-38 15194–15197, Emilio Pimentel to Porfirio Díaz, October 28, 1905.

21. CPD 30-32 12464, copy of telegram sent to Ezequiel Muñozcano, jefe político of Ixtlán, by Tomás Soto, municipal president of Guelatao, February 26, 1905.

22. Ibid.

23. CPD 30-38 15194–15197, Emilio Pimentel to Porfirio Díaz, October 28, 1905. Pimentel sent the notarized copy of the 1636 meeting to Díaz.

24. CPD 30-26 10268, Emilio Pimentel to Porfirio Díaz, July 13, 1905.

25. CPD 30-31 12109–12112, Tomás Soto et al. to Porfirio Díaz, August 30, 1905. A copy of this letter was also sent to Governor Emilio Pimentel.

26. CPD 30-38 15194–15195, Emilio Pimentel to Porfirio Díaz, October 28, 1905. See also CPD 30-37 14502, villagers of Guelatao to Porfirio Díaz, October 19, 1905, in which they state, "we will live eternally grateful to you, our General, for your mediation in this matter."

27. CPD 30-24 13274–13275, Ixtlán town council to Porfirio Díaz, September 28, 1905. See also CPD 30-39 15247, Emilio Pimentel to Porfirio Díaz, November 22, 1905; and AGEO Conflictos 62-11 391, Ezequiel Muñozcano, jefe político in Ixtlán, to Emilio Pimentel, September 12, 1905; AGEO Conflictos 62-11 400, Ezequiel Muñozcano to Emilio Pimentel, September 23, 1905; AGEO Conflictos 62-11 s/n, Ixtlán municipal president to Emilio Pimentel, September 11 and September 12, 1905; and AGEO Conflictos 62-11 s/n, Tomás Soto et al. to Emilio Pimentel, August 30, 1905.

28. CPD 31-1 239, Felipe García (*hijo*), municipal president of Guelatao, and his cabinet to Porfirio Díaz, January 23, 1906.

29. See the reference to the conflict in CPD 35-2 889, Tomás Soto, municipal president of Guelatao, et al. to Porfirio Díaz, January 21, 1910. The villagers of Guelatao never forgot the incident, but the intensity of their conflict with Ixtlán subsided, especially after the dislocations caused by the 1912 Ixtepeji revolt and the battles with the Constitutionalists after 1915 (see below). No doubt it contributes to the unspecified tension that occasional resurfaces between the two towns today.

30. The notarized copies of original land agreements are of particular importance

since both villages lost most of their archives in fighting against the Constitutionalist army in 1916. In many cases, these copies are the only remaining texts of crucial historical documents.

31. See Pérez García, *Sierra Juárez*, 2:196–202. Like the new school, other manifestations of economic development came only slowly to Guelatao. A potable water system was built in 1941, and the village did not receive access to electricity until 1946. The people of Guelatao never abandoned their hope for a school to honor Juárez. In the late 1930s leaders from Guelatao requested and received the honor of becoming one of only eight sites around the country with a new Indian boarding school. In effect, President Lázaro Cárdenas completed Porfirio Díaz's plan to recognize Guelatao as the birthplace of Benito Juárez.

32. CPD 31-10 3719, *ayuntamiento* of Guelatao to Porfirio Díaz, March 10, 1906.

33. Villagers requested new instruments on March 10, 1902. By June 7, 1902, the new instruments had already arrived. See CPD 27-11 4190, Cirilo Santiago et al. to Porfirio Díaz, March 10, 1902; and CPD 27-17 6777, Cirilo Santiago et al. to Porfirio Díaz, June 7, 1902. See also CPD 28-38 15076–15077, Cirilo Santiago et al. to Porfirio Díaz, October 2, 1903. The group formed two main bands, the "Luis Mier y Terán" and the "Félix Díaz."

34. Thomson, "Bulwarks of Patriotic Liberalism"; Thomson, "Ceremonial and Political Roles of Village Bands." Music and the National Guard battalions were clearly linked in the minds of most Mexicans. "*Los Soldados Leales* [The Loyal Soldiers]," an original poem sent to President Díaz in 1904, echoed this sentiment, by describing soldiers marching to the beat of drums, flutes, and whistles: "*No tienen buestras ropas / Ribetes de color / Ni areys bonitas tropas / Marchando con tambor. Con flautas y con pitos / Sin gritos de Escuadrón / Marchando en alajilos / Lire es linda formación.*" CPD 29-16 6041–6042, J.M.O. to Porfirio Díaz, January 25, 1904. Few veterans actually mentioned that they had been members of philharmonic corps. One exception, Francisco Valdez, noted with pride that he had enlisted in the musical company of the Third Battalion. See CPD 29-35 13649–13650, Francisco Valdez to Porfirio Díaz, October 24, 1904.

35. Chassen-López, *From Liberal to Revolutionary Oaxaca*, 460–66. For a brief summary of Juárez centennial celebrations in other parts of Mexico, see Weeks, *Juárez Myth*, 49. Even as militias rebelled against the Díaz regime in 1910, the importance of musical instruments remained uppermost for some village leaders. Whether they intended to defend the regime or not, village leaders from the Zapotec town of Yatuni requested aid for buying musical instruments, which, as they pointed out, were a key part of mobilizing soldiers. See CPD 3-2 646–648, Margarito Jiménez et al. to Porfirio Díaz, January 25, 1910. Villagers from the Sierra Zapoteca tried to revive the musical tradition of forming philharmonic corps after the Revolution had ended, but they no longer had the support of the president, and their requests were usually denied. See AGN Obregón y Calles 241-E-I-5, May 13, 1922, letter from Francisco Ruiz, Ixtlán municipal president, to President Obregón: "*Suma pobreza por la revolución. Perdidos*

instrumentos musicales en época anterior. Piden al Sr. Pdte. les done unos instrumentos musicales esp. para celebrar sus fiestas patrias." Obregón forwarded the letter to the Department of Education. The secretary of education wrote back on June 20, 1922, saying he could not fulfill the request as he did not have a budget for instruments.

36. CPD 30-30 11621, Emilio Pimentel to Porfirio Díaz, September 21, 1905.

37. CPD 30-34 13367–13368, Emilio Pimentel to Porfirio Díaz, October 21, 1905.

38. Building this huge statue had been somewhat problematic for Pimentel. The owner of the land, Anastasia Martínez, forced the state into complicated negotiations over access to her property. She eventually received only twenty pesos for allowing the government to build a road through her property up to the Cerro de Fortín. See AGEO Conflictos 51-1, series of letters between Anastasia Martínez and Oaxacan state officials, 1905.

39. CPD 31-7 2420–2421, Emilio Pimentel to Porfirio Díaz, March 13, 1906. Chassen-López, *From Liberal to Revolutionary Oaxaca*, 457–60, 472–73, analyzes the connections between Oaxacans and the Flores Magón brothers.

40. For the best explanation of the role of the Asociación Juárez in Oaxacan politics, see Chassen-López, *From Liberal to Revolutionary Oaxaca*, 460–63. See also Chassen-López, "Orígenes de la revolución," 122–31.

41. According to Chassen-López, "Orígenes de la revolución," 124, elite members of the Asociación Juárez did not approve of the candidate for municipal president in Oaxaca City. Bulnes called into question Juárez's leadership during the Reform, arguing that Porfirio Díaz had been much more faithful to liberal ideals; see Weeks, *Juárez Myth*, 54–70; and Hale, *Transformation of Liberalism*, 11.

42. Chassen-López, "Orígenes de la revolución," 125–26.

43. CPD 31-46 18054–18057, Rosendo Robles, Manuel Vásquez, Emilio Cruz et al., to Porfirio Díaz, April 7, 1906.

44. CPD 31-46 18088–18091, Anselmo García et al. (140 signatories) to Porfirio Díaz, December 18, 1905.

45. Ibid.

46. CPD 31-46 18092–18908, letters and petitions to Porfirio Díaz from peasants of Ixtlán district, various dates. The signers from Yolox listed their names according to rank, claiming their legitimacy as members of the Fifth Battalion of the Sierra Juárez. Felix Díaz did not promote himself for governor in 1906, fully realizing that the only vote that counted was his uncle's. See Henderson, *Félix Díaz*.

47. CPD 31-11 4197, "Los Felixistas y los Serranos" to Porfirio Díaz, April 30, 1906. Emphasis and spacing of the letter are in the original. Indirect evidence suggests Onofre Jiménez may have been the person who drafted this letter. Jiménez, a schoolteacher in 1906, later became municipal president, rebel general during the Revolution, and state governor in 1924. He publicly challenged Pimentel after the 1906 elections.

See also CPD 31-18 7172–7178, letter to Porfirio Díaz, June 12, 1906, complaining of Pimentel's candidacy for governor. The writers warned Díaz that peace was not possible as long as Pimentel remained governor. His regime was "unacceptable and insufferable for those of us born in this free nation, raised on the principles of democracy that you yourself have inculcated." Pimentel, they claimed, listened only to rich businessmen who protected him; "they all treat the reelection as if it were a business deal and in no way are they serving the country." See also CPD 30-27 10458–10461, Gonzalo S. Camacho, Sabino Pérez et al., Zaachila, Oaxaca, to Porfirio Díaz, July 23, 1905.

48. According to Womack, *Zapata and the Mexican Revolution*, 20–36, the 1909 election for governor in Morelos also raised popular expectations for a more open process. As the opposition movement supporting Francisco Leyva gained strength, old grievances against sugar planters rose to the surface, and the call for land and justice reflected the influences of popular demands. When Díaz's official candidate, Pablo Escandón, was handed the victory, his regime bore the scars of an illegitimate election orchestrated by Mexico City: "however long he lasted, he would never be respected. His election was an insult imprinted in the annals of the state's history—and branded in the minds of its people." Ibid., 36.

49. The lessons taken from analyzing aggregate statistical data on the 1907 recession remain unclear. For a critique of the notion that relative deprivation led to revolution, see Coatsworth, "Anotaciones sobre la producción de alimentos durante el Porfiriato"; and Knight, *Mexican Revolution*, 1:130.

50. Chassen-López, *From Liberal to Revolutionary Oaxaca*, 213–19.

51. Ibid.

52. AGEO Fomento 20-2, September 18, 1906; CPD 29-23 8867, Andres and Pedro Arreortúa to Porfirio Díaz, July 26, 1904; CPD 30-28 10931–10932, Andres and Pedro Arreortúa to Porfirio Díaz, August 4, 1905; CPD 30-27 10500, Governor Emilio Pimentel to Porfirio Díaz, August 10, 1905; CPD 31-23 8841–8843, Manuel, Pedro, and Andres Arreortúa to Porfirio Díaz, July 16, 1906; CPD 31-23 8843, Porfirio Díaz to Manuel Arreortúa, July 23, 1906. See also other requests for water concessions opposed by Natividad by L. N. Forman of the Canadian Oaxaca Mining Company, AGEO Fomento 24-2, 1906; and by Mauricio Clark, AGEO Fomento 25-2, 1906.

53. See AGEO Período Revolucionario 1b-142, telegram from Fidencio Hernández to Félix Díaz, May 24, 1911.

54. Pérez García, *Sierra Juárez*, 1:268.

55. This comparison is based on Mexico, Dirrección General de Estadística, *Anuario estadístico* (1907), 359.

56. CPD 34-32 15507–15508, Emilio Pimentel to Porfirio Díaz, September 22, 1909.

57. CPD 34-39 19090, Juan B. García to Porfirio Díaz, December 15, 1909.

58. CPD 34-39 19176–19177, Emilio Pimentel to Porfirio Díaz, December 21, 1909. Significantly, Pimentel accused Constantino Chapital for the problems: "unfortunately, he [Chapital] is a member of the Board of Directors; his attitude is essentially imprudent and undisciplined and he is a critic of the state government."

59. CPD 34-37 18398, copy of Aguirre Cinta's report, November 30, 1909.

60. AGEO Período Revolucionario 1a-75 3, January 18, 1910. Peasants feared that the Natividad River was polluted and that they, their livestock, and their crops would be harmed.

61. CPD 35-6 2830–2833, Emilio Pimentel to Porfirio Díaz, includes a copy of the report from Huntington Adams, February 15, 1910.

62. CPD 35-6 2830–2832, Emilio Pimentel to Porfirio Díaz, February 15, 1910. Adams's top executives also faced the hostility of the villagers. Howell MacKinlay and F. F. Siefert, administrators for the mine, were detained and harassed by local policemen for being on the streets past 9 P.M. The policemen had been drinking and had forgotten their inhibitions about dealing with these important men. They arrested Siefert and MacKinlay and began escorting them to the local jail. MacKinlay managed to escape, but Siefert was detained until Miguel Meixueiro bailed him out of jail. CPD 35-6 2833, F. F. Siefert to Huntington Adams (copy sent to Porfirio Díaz), February 28, 1910.

63. CPD 35-6 2829–2833, Emilio Pimentel to Porfirio Díaz, March 30, 1910. Pimentel relied on reports by Vicente García, Rafael Aguirre Cinta, and Maximiliano Ramírez. García concluded that the fire was probably an accident since the fence appeared to be impenetrable, though mine administrators strongly disagreed. See AGEO Período Revolucionario 1a-46, Vicente García to Emilio Pimentel, February 14, 1910.

64. CPD 35-36 17933–17938, Antonio Allende to Porfirio Díaz, November 3, 1910.

65. Adams's plan was to issue 36,000 more shares of stock at fifty pesos each, in order to raise 1.8 million pesos.

66. CPD 31-38 14898, Antonio Hernández to Porfirio Díaz, November 14, 1906. Hernández's specific complaint was that one of his sons had been unjustly imprisoned for failing to pay a head tax. On the advice of José Ruíz Jiménez, Hernández wrote directly to Porfirio Díaz.

67. CPD 33-9 3266–3268, Enrique Martínez, municipal president of Chicomezuchil, et al. to Porfirio Díaz, February 20, 1908. See also CPD 33-9 3269–3274, Enrique Martínez et al. to Porfirio Díaz, February 18, 1908.

68. CPD 33-9 3266–3268, Enrique Martínez et al. to Porfirio Díaz, February 20, 1908.

69. CPD 34-19 9271–9272, Juan Ramírez et al. to Porfirio Díaz, June 11, 1909.

70. CPD 34-32 15969, Mauricia Jiménez, Josefa Jiménez, and Juana Sabina Santiago to Porfirio Díaz, August 28, 1909; CPD 35-2 889, Tomás Soto et al., *ayuntamiento* of Guelatao, to Porfirio Díaz, January 21, 1910.

71. See, for example, the report on the 1906 Independence Day celebration in the village of Yatuni, Ixtlán district, Oaxaca in CPD 31-29 11587–11588, Rosalino Santiago to Porfirio Díaz, September 20, 1906.

72. I am currently researching the history of the 1910 Centennial throughout rural Mexico.

73. CPD 35-17 8001–8003, "Club Cuahutémoc de Ixtlán de Juárez" to Porfirio Díaz, June 7, 1910. The political clubs also supported Porfirio Díaz for president and his nephew Félix Díaz for vice president.

74. Jiménez, "Mi actuación revolucionario en la Sierra Juárez," 2–4.

75. A copy of this open letter appears in CPD 40 9156, Guillermo Meixueiro and Fidencio Hernández to Federico Toro, June 1, 1910. Three days later, Meixueiro reprinted the same letter to "Los Presidentes, Agentes Municipales y principales de la Sierra de Juárez," June 4, 1910.

76. Ibid.

77. Juárez Maza made only a brief campaign swing through the state; see Chassen-López, *From Liberal to Revolutionary Oaxaca*, 501–9.

78. Jiménez, "Mi actuación revolucionario en la Sierra Juárez," 4, argued that Pimentel "had been imposed a third time" on the state. Jiménez was especially angry because official results in the town of Ixtlán gave Pimentel 118 votes and Juárez Maza only 90. Given the broad support for Juárez Maza throughout the district of Ixtlán, Jiménez probably had grounds for claiming fraud. Several days of drinking and rioting continued in the town of Ixtlán until July 1. See CPD 35-22 10646–10650, Onofre Jiménez to Porfirio Díaz, July 11, 1910; CPD 35-26 12701–12704, S. Garcés to Porfirio Díaz, July 27, 1910; CPD 35-26 12697–12699, Vicente Garcés to Porfirio Díaz, July 29, 1910; and CPD 35-26 12691–12695, Emilio Pimentel to Porfirio Díaz, August 1, 1910.

79. CPD 35-19 9152–9154, Club Cuahutémoc de Ixtlán de Juárez, Club Cuna de Juárez de Guelatao, Club Benemerito de las Americas Lic. Benito Juárez de la Villa de Ixtepeji, Club Melchor Ocampo de Chicomezuchil, Club 18 de Octubre de 1866 de Jaltianguis, Onofre Jiménez et al. (543 signatories) to Porfirio Díaz, June 28, 1910.

80. Ibid.

81. For other moments of ritual resistance see the essays in Beezley, Martin, and French, *Rituals of Rule, Rituals of Resistance*. For a more complete analysis of the importance of ritual to memory see Connerton, *How Societies Remember*, 70–71.

82. See Scott, *Weapons of the Weak*, esp. chap. 8. See also Scott, *Domination and the Arts of Resistance*. For a useful critique of Scott's onstage/offstage distinction, see Feierman, *Peasant Intellectuals*.

83. In a similar way, the essays in Joseph and Nugent, *Everyday Forms of State Formation*, make careful use of documentary evidence from "below."

84. CPD 30-42 16672–16679, villagers of Guelatao to Porfirio Díaz, November 26, 1905.

85. The practice of multiplying patriarchs is discussed in Stern, *Secret History of Gender*.

86. Foucault, *Discipline and Punish*, 176–77.

87. Anti-Pimentel protests increased throughout Ixtlán district during July and August. See CPD 35-23 11360, Juan C. Carbajal to Porfirio Díaz, August 16, 1910; CPD 35-22 10861, Guillermo Meixueiro to Porfirio Díaz, August 20, 1910; CPD 35-26 12745–12746, Santos Delgado to Porfirio Díaz, August 20, 1910; CPD 35-24 11663–1163A, Onofre Jiménez to Porfirio Díaz, August 27, 1910; CPD 35-25 12337–12342, José Ruíz Jiménez to Porfirio Díaz, August 27, 1910; and CPD 35-24 11693–11694, "Varios Porfiristas" to Porfirio Díaz, September 2, 1910.

1. Much of the historiography on the revolution in Oaxaca has been aimed at revising Waterbury, "Non-Revolutionary Peasants." The essays in Martínez Vásquez, *Revolución en Oaxaca*, demonstrated the complexity and depth of revolutionary events in Oaxaca. Later studies solidified the rich history of revolutionary events in Oaxaca; see Chassen-López, "Orígenes de la revolución"; Ruiz Cervantes, *Revolución en Oaxaca*; Sánchez Silva, *Crisis política y contrarevolución en Oaxaca*; and Garner, *Revolución en la provincia*.

2. "Land of Tomorrow" comes from promotional literature around mining; "Land of Yesterday" reflects the post-1910 focus on Oaxaca's native ruins and ancient past.

3. Hall, *Alvaro Obregón*, 38, calls Carranza (fifty-one, born December 29, 1859) "the elder statesman and father figure of the revolutionary movement." Zapata's date of birth remains a minor contested issue, but Womack, *Zapata and the Mexican Revolution*, 5 n. 5, uses 1879. The Sierra de Puebla, as Thomson, *Patriotism, Politics, and Popular Liberalism*, and Mallon, *Peasant and Nation*, point out, offers an especially interesting case where a longtime ally of Díaz's, Juan Francisco Lucas, led the opposition movement against the regime in 1910.

4. Tannenbaum, *Peace by Revolution*, 133.

5. For an analysis of the ways in which the Revolutionary state created its own heroes and myths, see O'Malley, *Myth of the Revolution*. Anti-Díaz and anti-*científico* sentiment formed an integral part of the discourse of legitimacy for the Revolutionary state. Given the widespread political repression and economic hardship suffered by so many Mexicans during the final years of the Porfiriato, it was fairly easy to define Díaz and his regime rather narrowly.

6. AGEO Período Revolucionario 2a-212, "Relativo al movimiento sediciosas de esta capital," February 1, 1911. A group of two hundred men met to discuss plans to rebel against the Díaz regime, including Roberto Olguín, Valentín López, Luís Jiménez Figueroa, and Angel Barrios. See also the report in the same file on the arrest of José Ruíz Jiménez; and AGN Madero 15-366, 11827–11828, Miguel Hernández to Juan Sánchez Azcona, Jesús Munguis Santoyo, and José Vasconcelos, January 24, 1912, for a detailed account of Hernández's pro-Madero activities in the district of Ixtlán. For maderistas in Ixtlán district see CPD 35-42 20633–20641, Fidencio Hernández to Porfirio Díaz, December 13, 1910. For more on the maderista revolt in Oaxaca see especially Martínez Medina, "Génesis y desarrollo del maderismo en Oaxaca."

7. CPD 35-38 18839, Fidencio Hernández and Guillermo Meixueiro to Emilio Pimentel, November 27, 1910; CPD 35-33 16364–16374, Fidencio Hernández to Porfirio Díaz, November 27, 1910; CPD 35-38 18838, Fidencio Hernández and Guillermo Meixueiro to Porfirio Díaz, November 28, 1910; CPD 35-40 19641, Emilio Pimentel to Porfirio Díaz, November 28, 1910.

8. See the letter of support for Díaz from more than two hundred signers in CPD 35-

33 16389–16396, Francisco Ruiz et al. to Porfirio Díaz, November 25, 1910; and Díaz's response on November 26, 1910. See also CPD 35-33 16224, Federico H. Toro to Porfirio Díaz, November 26, 1910. Oaxacans living in Mexico City also wrote Díaz of their support; CPD 35-36 17551–17553, Luis López et al. to Porfirio Díaz, November 26, 1910. For unrest throughout Ixtlán district see CPD 35-34 16790–16793, José Ruíz Jiménez to Porfirio Díaz, November 23, 1910.

9. Meixueiro never fully gave up on his hope of becoming governor of Oaxaca.

10. For the recommendation to remove Garcés, see CPD 35-41 20348, Fidencio Hernández and Guillermo Meixueiro to Emilio Pimentel [copy sent to Porfirio Díaz], December 7, 1910.

11. For the officer appointments of Luis Meixueiro and Aureliano Hernández see CPD 35-42 20639–20641, Fidencio Hernández and Guillermo Meixueiro to Porfirio Díaz, December 6, 1910.

12. Ibid.

13. CPD 35-42 20633–20641, Fidencio Hernández to Porfirio Díaz, December 13, 1910; CPD 35-41 20324–20338, Fidencio Hernández and Guillermo Meixueiro to Porfirio Díaz, December 17, 1910; AGN Gobernación: Período Revolucionario 98-34, Pedro Pérez to Secretaría de Gobernación, August 20, 1912. For a later but related case of forced inscription see AGEO Período Revolucionario 3b-823, "Pedro González se queja contra el jefe político del Dto. por consignado al servicio de armas," January 21, 1913.

14. An account of the lingering tensions within the First Battalion of the Sierra Juárez is provided in AGN Madero 5-118, Manuel Jiménez to Francisco Madero, March 14, 1912.

15. Félix Díaz assumed the governorship for the interim period, so there was at least the semblance of continuity.

16. López, much to Hernández's embarrassment, was actually the local police chief for Xía, but he obviously bore serious resentment against his employers. Rodolfo Romero from Tuxtlahuaca and Fidel Pimentel from Tlaxiaco were also implicated in the disturbance. Their arrests were ordered on May 27, 1911. José Castellanos, José Domingo Pérez, and Ignacio Ramírez were later added to the list of individuals involved.

17. See the collection of telegrams, letters, and reports on the May 21, 1911, riot at Xía in AGEO Período Revolucionario 01b-142, including Fidencio Hernández's telegram to Governor Félix Díaz, May 22, 1911.

18. See AGEO Período Revolucionario 1b-142, "Relación de los desórdenas registrados en la fábrica de Xía," Fidencio Hernández telegram to Porfirio Díaz, May 23, 1911; AGEO Secretaría de Gobierno 110-11, "Pueblos de ambos distritos solicitan la permanencia de destacamento de policía rural para cuidar el orden público," August 5, 1911; AGEO Secretaría de Gobierno 126-25, "Se pide se redoble la vigilancia en los caminos nacionales," September 6, 1911; AGEO Secretaría de Gobierno 125-7, "El

agente municipal de el pueblo de las Llagas denuncia hechos delectuosos en contra del C. Federico H. Toro de Ixtlán," October 30, 1911; and AGEO Secretaría de Gobierno 48-12, "Invadieron los vecinos de la cabecera de Ixtlán," October 31, 1911.

19. For a participant's account of the 1911 mobilization, see Jiménez, "Mi actuación revolucionario en la Sierra Juárez," 9–12.

20. See AGEO Secretaría de Gobierno 125-25, "Los señores agentes consular americano y vice-consul Britanico en esta ciudad se quejan contra los C. C. Isaac Ibarra y socios de Lachatao, Ixtlán," April 11, 1912.

21. The total population of Ixtepeji grew from 2,441 in 1878 to 3,168 in 1910, nearly a 30 percent increase. The ranchero population, those men who had rights to farm on separate plots, doubled over the same period. See Pérez García, *Sierra Juárez*, 1:134–46.

22. CPD 32-03 835, Julian García and Donanciano García et al. (fifty-six total signatures) to Porfirio Díaz, December 29, 1906; CPD 32-15 5671–5675, Donanciano García and Julian García et al. to Porfirio Díaz, April 30, 1907; CPD 32-18 7183–7184, Emilio Pimentel to Porfirio Díaz, July 8, 1907; CPD 32-24 9416, Pedro Juárez and José M. León to Porfirio Díaz, August 14, 1907; CPD 32-22 8747, María de León to Porfirio Díaz, August 22, 1907; CPD 33-32 12418, Emilio Pimentel to Porfirio Díaz, September 23, 1908; CPD 34-03 1295, Felipe Bartolo León to Porfirio Díaz, February 2, 1909; CPD 34-03 1396, Clemente Marcos to Porfirio Díaz, February 11, 1909; CPD 34-08 3677–3792, Felipe Bartolo León, Teófilo B. León, and Clemente Marcos to Porfirio Díaz, May 19, 1909.

23. CPD 34-20 9739, Luciano Juárez for Francisco Santiago to Porfirio Díaz, June 3, 1909; CPD 34-20 9740, Tomás Juárez for Francisco Santiago to Porfirio Díaz, June 7, 1909; CPD 34-20 9743, Teófilo León for Juana Sabina Santiago to Porfirio Díaz, June 19, 1909; CPD 34-32 15969, Mauricia Jiménez to Porfirio Díaz, August 28, 1909.

24. AGEO Secretaría de Gobierno 45-17, "Los habitantes de las rancherias 'El Estudiante,' 'Yovaneli,' 'La Palma,' and 'Lubila' se quejan contra actos del Lic. Guillermo Meixueiro," February 10, 1912; for Ixtepeji residents who fled the rebellion see AGN Gobernación [sin clasificación], 1912, Caja 12, Reginaldo Pérez et al. to Francisco Madero, August 17, 1912. See also AGEO Secretaría de Gobierno 125-23, "El presidente municipal de San Miguel Abejones se queja contra actos de la autoridad municipal del pueblo de Manialtepec de aquel distrito," April 26, 1912.

25. Jiménez, "Mi actuación revolucionario en la Sierra Juárez," 20. Several towns remained neutral though adamantly opposed to aiding Ixtlán; for Abejones see AGN Gobernación: Período Revolucionario 98-34, Pedro Pérez to Secretaría de Gobernación, August 20, 1912; for Yatuní see AGEO Período Revolucionario 4b-982, "Adolfo Tamayo (jefe político de Ixtlán) a Secretario general del Despacho del Superior Gobierno del Estado," January 24, 1913; and AGEO Período Revolucionario 4b-982, Isaac Ibarra to Adolfo Tamayo, January 21, 1913.

26. The Ixtlán jefe político, Daniel García, his secretary, Alejandro Martínez, and Anastasio Juárez were killed at Xía; see Pérez García, *Sierra Juárez*, 2:274.

27. For reports on the Ixtepeji revolt sent to Madero, see AGN Madero 5-118, Manuel Jiménez to Francisco Madero, May 27, 1912, May 30, 1912, June 3, 1912, June 6, 1912, and June 8, 1912. Madero appears completely uninformed about events in Oaxaca in his November 7 reply to Miguel Hernández; see AGN Madero 15-365, 11811–11813, Miguel Hernández to Francisco Madero, October 30, 1912.

28. Jiménez, "Mi actuación revolucionario en la Sierra Juárez," 31, 46.

29. See Kearney, *Winds of Ixtepeji*, 30–42. Tragically, nearly one hundred Ixtepejanos perished in a train accident in Chihuahua in 1915; see Pérez García, *Sierra Juarez*, 1:146. For refugees see AGEO Período Revolucionario 04a-836, "Trata sobre terrenos y falta de agua para siembra," April 8, 1913; and AGEO Período Revolucionario 3a-484-16, "Los C. C. Manuel Chavéz y Socios de Macuiltianguis se quejan contra el jefe político de ese Dto.," May 10, 1913.

30. See AMI Presidencia 23-1, "Sobre regreso de los vecinos de Guelatao a arrendar," January 9, 1914; AMI Presidencia 23-2, "Acta levantada con motivo de los gestiones de los vecinos de Guelatao para su regreso," May 20, 1914; and AMI Presidencia 26, "Acuerdo entre pueblos serranos," April 17, 1915. For another example of the extent to which Ixtlán town leaders sought control over affairs in the district, see the case of Ixtlán elders expelling a priest accused of raping a girl. Elders determined the priest had two hours to leave town; AMI Justicia 7, "Violación contra el socio Benjamin Cuevas," March 4, 1918.

31. AGN Revolución 3-853, sin clasificación, "El Ejército Libertador y la División de Oriente al pueblo Mexicano," February 26, 1915. The Oaxacan view of the Constitutionalists was hardly unique; see, for example, CEHM Fondo XXI, Carpeta 85, Legajo 9535, letter to "publico general" from Guadalajara (letter includes nine pages of signatures), June 23, 1916. See also AGN Revolución 3-781, sin clasificación, unsigned, undated statement addressed to "El Pueblo": "Now that this hoard of thieves and assassins that call themselves Carrancistas have forced you to choose a side, unite with Zapatismo. Zapatismo is the revolution of the Indian."

32. For attempts to form an alliance with the Zapatistas see AGN Zapata 8-4-60, "El general jefe de la división de oriente Higinio Aguilar le comunica a Emiliano Zapata haber firmado un pacto de alianza con el gobierno de Oaxaca, a través del licenciado Guillermo Meixueiro como representante . . . ," June 4, 1915; AGN Zapata 10-8-40, Guillermo Meixueiro to Emiliano Zapata, November 18, 1915; and AGN Revolución 3-855, sin clasificación, "Informe del Gral Higinio Aguilar al Gral Emiliano Zapata, sobre el recorriendo que hizo por algunas regiones de los Estados de Veracruz, Puebla y Oaxaca, con el objeto de dar a conocer al pueblo el Plan de Ayala," April 13, 1915; for potential ties to the Villistas see CEHM Fondo XXI, Carpeta 67, Legajo 7392, Adolfo Carrillo to Venustiano Carranza, February 9, 1916.

33. See CEHM Fondo MIX-3 20-03-11, Rafael Fernández to Pablo González, March 11, 1920; see also AGEO Período Revolucionario 15a-65, "El C. Onofre Jiménez, jefe del Edo. mayor de las fuerzas serranas en Ixtlán comunica a este gobierno que el orden se ha conservado inalterable en esa region," July 2, 1920. For details of the negotiations

see CEHM Fondo MIX-3 19-09-09, G. A. Elizonado to Pablo González, September 19, 1919; CEHM Fondo MIX-3, Num. 5553, 19-09-17, Gustavo A. Elizondo to P. González, September 17, 1919.

34. CEHM Fondo MIX-3, Num. 6822, 19-10-28, José O. Flores to P. González, October 28, 1919.

35. See Ibarra's telegram in CEHM Fondo MIX-3, Num. 6417, 19-10-16, José O. Flores to P. González, October 16, 1919; see also CEHM Fondo MIX-3, 19-10-01, G. A. Elizondo to P. González, October 1, 1919; CEHM Fondo MIX-3, Num. G-1695, 19-10-30, P. González to José O. Flores, October 30, 1919; CEHM Fondo MIX-3, Num. 7066, 19-11-05, José O. Flores to P. González, November 5, 1919; and CEHM Fondo MIX-3, Num. G-209, 19-11-06, P. González to José O. Flores, November 6, 1919.

36. AGEO Período Revolucionario 15a-65, "El C. Onofre Jiménez jefe del Edo mayo de las fuerzas serranas en Ixtlán comunica a este gobierno que el orden se ha conservado inalterable en esa region," July 2, 1920.

37. See Ruiz Cervantes, *Revolución en Oaxaca*, 132–35; and Garner, *Revolución en la provincia*, 198–99, for copies of the peace treaty recognizing the 1857 Constitution and the official documents that recorded the Oaxacan transition to the 1917 Constitution.

38. See Weeks, *Juárez Myth*, 100–103.

39. AGN Obregón y Calles 816-J-1, Natalio Ramírez et al. to Alvaro Obregón, December 20, 1920. Other documents in the same folder address the Guelatao request, including Amado Aguirre telegram to Alvaro Obregón, April 21, 1923. See also AGN Obregón y Calles 805-I-4, Natalio Ramírez et al. to Manuel Vargas, February 8, 1921; AGEO Período Revolucionario 21a-72, "El Presidente y miembro del Ayuntamiento de Guelatao felicitan al C. Gobernador del Edo," February 1, 1923; and AGN Obregón y Calles 816-J-13, Isaac Ibarra to Alvaro Obregón, April 6, 1923.

40. AGEO Período Revolucionario 21a-68, "El Agente municipal de Guelatao invita al gobierno para la ceremonia que tendrá . . . con motivo del natalico del Benemerito de las Americas," March 3, 1923; AGEO Período Revolucionario 25a-20, "Asuntos relacionados con las fiestas patrias celebrados en el ex-Dto Ixtlán," 1924; and AGEO Período Revolucionario 25a-105, "Relativo a la conmemoración del LII Aniversario de la muerte del ilustre reformador Lic. Benito Juárez," 1924.

41. See AGN Obregón y Calles 805-I-19, Alvaro Obregón to B. Flores, director of "Junta Protectora del Indio," state of Mexico, May 10, 1922.

42. AGN Obregón y Calles 805-I-3, "Junta Protectora de Enseñaza" de Ixtlán, Ezequiel Santillán et al. to Alvaro Obregón, January 15, 1921.

43. AGN Obregón y Calles 805-I-19, Alvaro Obregón to B. Flores, director of "Junta Protectora del Indio," state of Mexico, May 10, 1922.

44. See, for example, AGN Abelardo Rodríguez 328-38, "Amado Pérez y otros solicitan ayuda pecuniaria para la celebración del CXXVIII aniversario del natalico del Lic. Benito Juárez," March 13, 1934.

45. See O'Malley, *Myth of the Revolution*; Weeks, *Juárez Myth*; and Brunk, "Remembering Emiliano Zapata."

46. Pérez García, *Sierra Juárez*, 2:196–202.

47. See, especially, Reyes Heroles, *Liberalismo mexicano*.

48. Chassen-López, *From Liberal to Revolutionary Oaxaca*, 539.

49. Mallon, *Peasant and Nation*, 323.

50. Thomson, *Patriotism, Politics, and Popular Liberalism*; Wells and Joseph, *Summer of Discontent, Seasons of Upheaval*, 252.

51. Hale, *Transformation of Liberalism*; Womack, *Zapata and the Mexican Revolution*; Kourí, *Pueblo Divided*.

52. Alonso, *Thread of Blood*, 127. A sampling of studies just in English largely supports this view as well. See, especially, Wasserman, *Capitalists, Caciques, and Revolution*; Nugent, *Spent Cartridges of Revolution*; French, *Peaceful and Working People*; Vanderwood, *Power of God against the Guns of Government*; and most recently, Young, *Catarino Garza's Revolution*.

53. Anderson, *Imagined Communities*, 7.

Bibliography

ARCHIVAL SOURCES

Archivo del Poder Judicial de Oaxaca—Oaxaca City
  Historico Civil
  Historico Penal
Archivo General de la Nación—Mexico City
  Cárdenas del Rio, Lázaro
  Dirección General del Gobierno
  Fomento (Agricultura, Bosques, Industrias Nuevas, Exposiciones,
    Minas y Petróleo)
  Gobernación
  Gobernación: Período Revolucionario
  Juárez, Benito
  Madero, Francisco I.
  Nacionalización y Desamortación de Bienes
  Obregón, Alvaro (Obregón y Calles)
  Ortiz Rubio, Pascual
  Portes Gil, Emilio
  Propiedad Artistica
  Revolución
  Rodríguez, Abelardo L.
  Suprema Corte de Justicia
  Terrenos Baldíos
  Trabajo
  Zapata, Emiliano
Archivo General del Estado de Oaxaca—Oaxaca City
  Catastro
  Censos y Padrones
  Conciliación y Arbitraje
  Conflictos por Limites de Tierras
  Fomento
  Gobernación
  Juzgados
  Memorias Administrativas

Período Revolucionario

Repartos y Adjudicaciones

Secretaría de Gobierno

Archivo Histórico de la Defensa Nacional—Mexico City

Cancelados

Operaciones Militares

Archivo Manual González, Universidad Iberoamericana—Mexico City

Archivo Municipal de Guelatao/Fundación Comunidad de Guelatao

Archivo Municipal de Ixtlán de Juárez

Asuntos Varios

Justicia

Presidencia

Tesorería

Biblioteca Nacional—Mexico City

Archivo Juárez

Fondo de Rafael Chousal

Hemeroteca Nacional

Biblioteca Pública de Guelatao

Biblioteca Pública de Oaxaca, Sala Genaro Vásquez—Oaxaca City

Centro de Estudios de Historia de México CONDUMEX—Mexico City

Fondo IX-1, Manuscritos de Ignacio Aguilar y Marocho

Fondo XXI, Carranza

Fondo CXIII-2, Convención Nacional

Fondo CXIX-1, Cartas de Porfirio Díaz

Fondo CXC, Díaz contra Lerdo

Fondo CMXV, Archivo de Lic. Federico González Garza

Fondo DLI, Archivo de General Bernardo Reyes

Fondo MIX-3, Telegramas

Colección Porfirio Díaz, Universidad Iberoamericana—Mexico City

Cartas, 1876–1911

Folletos y Periódicos

Copiadores

Hemeroteca Pública de Oaxaca—Oaxaca City

PRIMARY MATERIAL

Aznar, Marcial. *Observaciones histórico-políticas sobre Juárez y su época*. Mexico: Tip. El Gran Libro, 1887.

Basch, Samuel. *Recollections of Mexico: The Last Ten Months of Maximilian's Empire*. Originally published as *Erinnerungen aus Mexico* [1868]. Edited and translated by Fred D. Ullman. Wilmington, Del.: Scholarly Resources, Inc., 2001.

Batres, Leopoldo. *Exploraciones de Monte Albán*. Mexico: Casa Editorial Gante, 1902.

Brioso y Candiani, Manuel. "D. Manuel Martínez Gracida." Reseña biográfica formado por Lic. Manuel Brioso y Candiani y leida en la Sociedad Mexicana de Geografía y Estadística, Tacubaya, D.F., junio de 1910. Unpublished manuscript. Later published in *El Centenario* [Oaxaca], October 15, 1910.

Bulnes, Francisco. *El verdadero Juárez y la verdad sobre la Intervención y el Imperio.* Mexico City: La Viuda de Bouret, 1904.

Busto, Emiliano. *Estadistica de la República Mexicana. Estado que guardan la agricultura, industria mineria y comercio. Resúmen y análisis de los Informes Rendidos a la Secretaría de Hacienda por los agricultores, mineros, industriales y comerciantes de la República y los agentes de México en el exterior.* Mexico: Imprenta de Ignacio Cumplido, 1880.

Caballero, Manuel. *Juárez épico.* Mexico: Impreso por A. Carranza y Comp., 1906.

Carreño, Alberto María, ed. *Archivo del General Porfirio Díaz, Memorias y Documentos.* 22 vols. Mexico: Editorial "Elede," 1947–56.

Celada, Fernando. *Bronces. Cantos épicos a Juárez.* Mexico: F. Mata, 1904.

Cleland, Robert G., ed. *The Mexican Year Book.* Los Angeles: Mexican Year Book Publishing Company, 1920–21.

Creelman, James. "Porfirio Díaz: Hero of the Americas." *Pearson's Magazine* 19 (1908): 231–77.

Díaz, Porfirio. *Memorias de Porfirio Díaz.* 2 vols. Mexico: Consejo Nacional para la Cultura y las Artes, 1994.

[Díaz, Porfirio, et al.] *Batalla de la Carbonera. Obsequi del General Luis P. Figueroa al Ejercito Mexicano.* Mexico: El Siglo Diez y Nueve, 1896.

Dios Peza, Juan de. *Memorias, reliquias y retratos.* Paris: Librería de la Vda. de Ch. Bouret, 1900.

Franck, Harry A. *Tramping through Mexico, Guatemala, and Honduras.* New York: Century Company, 1916.

Jiménez, Onofre. "Mi actuación revolucionario en la Sierra Juárez de 1910 a 1920." Unpublished manuscript [undated]. In author's possession.

Juárez, Benito. *Apuntes para mis hijos.* Mexico: Instituto Nacional de la Juventud Mexicana, 1972.

———. *Documentos, discursos y correspondencia.* Edited by Jorge L. Tamayo. 16 vols. Mexico: Secretaría del Patrimonio Nacional, 1964–72.

Martínez Gracida, Manuel. "Gobierno reaccionario, conservador o mocho." Unpublished manuscript and collection of original documents. Biblioteca Pública de Oaxaca, Sala Genaro Vásquez, Oaxaca City.

Mateos, Juan A. *El sol de mayo. Memorias de la intervención.* 1868; Mexico: Editorial Porrúa, 1978.

Meixueiro Hernández, Ernesto. *Guillermo Meixueiro Delgado. Un caudillo de la Soberanía de Oaxaca.* Oaxaca: Lásser Plus, 1989.

Mexico, Dirección General de Estadística. *Anuario estadístico.* Mexico City, 1893–1907.

———. *Censo general de la República Mexicana.* Mexico City, 1897.

———. *Estadística de la República Mexicana.* Edited by J. M. Pérez y Hernández. Guadalajara, 1862.

———. *Estadística de la República Mexicana de 1877 a 1878.* Edited by Emiliano Busto. Mexico City, 1880.

———. *Estadísticas sociales del Porfiriato, 1877–1910.* Mexico: Telleres Graficos de la Nación, 1956.

Mexico, Secretaría de la Defensa Nacional. *Historia documental militar de la intervención Francesa en México y el Denominado Segundo Imperio.* Mexico, 1967.

Mexico, Secretaría de Fomento. *Cuadro sinoptico informativo de la administración del Señor General Don Porfirio Díaz, Presidente de la república. Hasta 1909.* Mexico: Secretaría de Fomento, 1910.

———. *Dirección General de Estadística. Resúmen general del censo de la República Mexicana.* Mexico: Secretaría de Fomento, 1905.

———. *Movimiento de sociedades mineras y mercantiles. Durante los años de 1886–1907.* Mexico: Secretaría de Fomento, 1908.

Mexico, Secretaría de Fomento, Colonizacíon e Industria. *Cuadro sinóptico y estadístico de la República Mexicana.* Mexico: Secretaría de Fomento, 1901.

Mexico, Secretaría de Hacienda. *The Mexican Year Book.* London: McCorquodale and Company, Ltd., 1911.

Middleton, P. Harvey. *Industrial Mexico: 1919 Facts and Figures.* New York: Dodd, Mead and Company, 1919.

Molina Enriquez, Andres. *Los grandes problemas nacionales.* Mexico: Imprenta de Carranza e Hijos, 1909.

Pascual García, Francisco. *Razas del estado de Oaxaca, sus idiomas primitivos y su capacidad para la civilización.* Mexico: El Progreso Mercantil, 1904.

[Oaxaca], Instituto de Ciencias y Artes del Estado Oaxaca. *Tercer concurso científico-literario en honor de Juárez.* Oaxaca: Imprenta del Estado, 1903.

Ramírez, Alfonso Francisco. *Florílegio de poetas y escritores de Oaxaca.* Mexico: Antigua Imprenta de Murguía, 1927.

Ramírez Varela, Manuel. *Recuerdo de la colonia Oaxaqueña a al ilústre memoria del ciudadano Benito Juárez.* Mexico: Imprenta de M. Guerra, 1887.

Reglamento aprobado por el Pueblo de Ixtepeji en 22 de Noviembre de 1877. Villa Juárez: Impresa por Nicolás Mariscal, 1878.

Reyes, Bernardo. *El General Porfirio Díaz.* Mexico: J. Ballescá y Companía, 1903.

Romero, Matias. *El estado de Oaxaca.* Barcelona: Tipo-Litographica de Espasa y Comp., 1886.

———. *Geographical and Statistical Notes on Mexico.* New York: G. P. Putnam's Sons, 1898.

Salazar, Rosendo, and José G. Escobedo. *Las pugnas de la gleba, 1907–1922.* 2 vols. Mexico: Editorial Avante, 1923.

Santibañez, Manuel. *Reseña historica del cuerpo de Ejercito de Oriente.* 2 vols. Mexico: Tipografia de la oficina impresora del timbre, 1892.

Sierra, Justo. *Obras completas. Evolución política del pueblo mexicano.* Mexico: UNAM, 1977.

Starr, Frederick. *In Indian Mexico: A Narrative of Travel and Labor.* Chicago: Forbes and Company, 1908.

———. *The Indians of Southern Mexico.* Chicago: [The Author], 1899.

———. *Notes upon the Ethnography of Southern Mexico.* Reprinted from Vols. 8 and 9, *Proceedings of Davenport Academy of Natural Science.* [Davenport, Iowa]: Putnam Memorial Publication Fund, 1900, 1902.

U.S. Bureau of the Census. *Thirteenth Census of the United States Taken in the Year 1910.* Vol. 3. Washington, D.C.: Government Printing Office, 1913.

Warnes, Vicente. *Album patriotico en honor del Benémerito de las Americas.* Pachuca, Mexico: Tip. Económica, 1889.

SECONDARY SOURCES

Aguilar Camín, Héctor, and Lorenzo Meyer. *In the Shadow of the Mexican Revolution: Contemporary Mexican History, 1910–1989.* Translated by Luis Alberto Fierro. Austin: University of Texas Press, 1993.

Alexius, Robert. "The Army and Politics in Porfirian Mexico." Ph.D. diss., University of Texas at Austin, 1976.

Alonso, Ana María. *Thread of Blood: Colonialism, Revolution, and Gender on Mexico's Northern Frontier.* Tucson: University of Arizona Press, 1995.

Amin, Shahid. *Event, Metaphor, Memory: Chauri Chaura, 1922–1992.* Berkeley: University of California Press, 1995.

Anderson, Benedict. *Imagined Communities: Reflections on the Origin and Spread of Nationalism.* Rev. ed. London: Verso, 1991.

Anderson, Rodney. *Outcasts in Their Own Land: Mexican Industrial Workers, 1906–1911.* DeKalb: Northern Illinois University Press, 1976.

Anzaldua, Gloria. *Borderlands/La Frontera: The New Mestiza.* San Francisco: Aunt Lute Books, 1987.

Appelbaum, Nancy P., Anne S. Macpherson, and Karin Alejandra Rosemblatt, eds. *Race and Nation in Modern Latin America.* Chapel Hill: University of North Carolina Press, 2003.

Arellanes Meixueiro, Anselmo. *Los trabajos y las Guías Mutualismo y Sindicalismo en Oaxaca, 1870–1930.* Oaxaca: Instituto Tecnológico de Oaxaca, 1990.

Barabas, Alicia M. "Rebeliones e insurrecciones indígenas en Oaxaca: La trayectoria histórica de la resistencia étnica." In *Etnicidad y pluralismo cultural. La dinámica étnica en Oaxaca.* Edited by Alicia M. Barabas and Miguel A. Bartolomé, 213–56. Mexico: Instituto Nacional de Antropología e Historia, 1986.

Bartolomé, Miguel, and Alicia Barabas. "La pluralidad desigual en Oaxaca." In *Etnicidad y pluralismo cultural. La dinámica étnica en Oaxaca*. Edited by Alicia M. Barabas and Miguel A. Bartolomé, 13–96. Mexico: Instituto Nacional de Antropología e Historia, 1986.

Bartra, Roger. *La jaula de la melancolia. Identidad y metamorfosis, del mexicano*. Mexico: Grijalbo, 1987.

Basave Benítez, Agustín. *México mestizo. Análisis de nacionalismo mexicano en torno a la mestizofilia de Andrés Molina Enriquez*. Mexico: Fondo de Cultura Económica, 1992.

Baskes, Jeremy. "Coerced or Voluntary? The *Repartimiento* and Market Participation of Peasants in Late Colonial Oaxaca." *Journal of Latin American Studies* 28 (1996): 1–28.

———. *Indians, Merchants, and Markets: A Reinterpretation of the Repartimiento and Spanish-Indian Economic Relations in Colonial Oaxaca, 1750–1821*. Stanford, Calif.: Stanford University Press, 2000.

Basso, Keith H. *Wisdom Sits in Places: Landscape and Language among the Western Apache*. Albuquerque: University of New Mexico Press, 1996.

Beezley, William H. *Judas at the Jockey Club and Other Episodes of Porfirian Mexico*. Lincoln: University of Nebraska Press, 1987.

Beezley, William H., Cheryl English Martin, and William E. French, eds. *Rituals of Rule, Rituals of Resistance: Public Celebrations and Popular Culture in Mexico*. Wilmington, Del.: Scholarly Resources, Inc., 1994.

Benítez, Fernando. *Un indio zapoteco llamado Benito Juárez*. Mexico: Taurus, 1998.

Benjamin, Thomas, and Mark Wasserman, eds. *Provinces of the Revolution: Essays on Regional Mexican History, 1910–1929*. Albuquerque: University of New Mexico Press, 1990.

Bernstein, Marvin D. *The Mexican Mining Industry, 1880–1950*. Albany: State University of New York, 1964.

Berry, Charles R. *The Reform in Oaxaca, 1856–76: A Microhistory of the Liberal Revolution*. Lincoln: University of Nebraska Press, 1981.

Beverley, John. *Subalternity and Representation: Arguments in Cultural Theory*. Durham, N.C.: Duke University Press, 1999.

Blaisdell, Lowell L. *The Desert Revolution: Baja California, 1911*. Madison: University of Wisconsin Press, 1962.

Brading, D. A. *Caudillo and Peasant in the Mexican Revolution*. Cambridge, U.K.: Cambridge University Press, 1980.

———. *The First America: The Spanish Monarchy, Creole Patriots, and the Liberal State*. Cambridge, U.K.: Cambridge University Press, 1991.

———. *The Origins of Mexican Nationalism*. Cambridge, U.K.: Centre of Latin American Studies, University of Cambridge, 1985.

Braudel, Fernand. *La Méditerranée et le monde méditerranéen à l'époque de Philippe II*. Paris: Colin, 1949.

Brunk, Samuel. *Emiliano Zapata: Revolution and Betrayal in Mexico*. Albuquerque: University of New Mexico Press, 1995.

———. "Remembering Emiliano Zapata: Three Moments in the Posthumous Career of the Martyr of Chinameca." *Hispanic American Historical Review* 78 (1998): 457–90.

Campbell, Howard. *Mexican Memoir: A Personal Account of Anthropology and Radical Politics in Oaxaca*. Westport, Conn.: Bergin and Garvey, 2001.

———. *Zapotec Renaissance: Ethnic Politics and Cultural Revivalism in Southern Mexico*. Albuquerque: University of New Mexico Press, 1994.

Campbell, Howard, Leigh Binford, Miguel Bartolomé, and Alicia Barabas, eds. *Zapotec Struggles: Histories, Politics, and Representations from Juchitán, Oaxaca*. Washington, D.C.: Smithsonian Institution Press, 1993.

Carmagnani, Marcello. *El regreso de los dioses. El proceso de reconstitución de la identidad étnica en Oaxaca. Siglos XVII y XVIII*. Mexico: Fondo de Cultura Económica, 1988.

Caso, Alfonso. *La comunidad indigena*. Mexico: Sep/Setentas, 1971.

———. *Culturas Mixteca y Zapoteca*. Mexico: El Nacional, 1939.

———. "Definición del indio y de lo indio." *America Indigena* 4 (1948): 226–34.

———. "Monte Alban: An Archeological Zone of World-Wide Renown." *Mexican Art and Life* 4 (October 1938): [1–4].

Chance, John. *Conquest of the Sierra: Spaniards and Indians in Colonial Oaxaca*. Norman: University of Oklahoma Press, 1989.

———. *Race and Class in Colonial Oaxaca*. Stanford, Calif.: Stanford University Press, 1982.

Chance, John K., and William B. Taylor. "Cofradías and Cargos: An Historical Perspective on the Mesoamerican Civil-Religious Hierarchy." *American Ethnologist* 12 (1985): 1–26.

Chassen-López, Francie R. "'Cheaper Than Machines': Women and Agriculture in Porfirian Oaxaca, 1880–1911." In *Women of the Mexican Countryside, 1850–1990*, edited by Heather Fowler-Salamini and Mary Kay Vaughan, 27–50. Tucson: University of Arizona Press, 1994.

———. *From Liberal to Revolutionary Oaxaca: The View from the South, Mexico, 1867–1911*. University Park: Pennsylvania State University Press, 2004.

———. "Oaxaca: Del Porfiriato a la Revolución, 1902–1911." Tesis doctorado, UNAM, Facultad de Filosofia y Letres, Mexico, 1986.

———. "Los orígenes de la revolución en Oaxaca. Juarismo y Porfirismo contra precursores y revolucionarios." *Eslabones. La Revolución en el Sur-Sureste de México*, Jan.–June 1993, 118–37.

Chatterjee, Partha. *Nationalism and the Colonial World: A Derivative Discourse*. London: Zed Books, 1986.

Child, Brenda J. *Boarding School Seasons: American Indian Families, 1900–1940*. Lincoln: University of Nebraska Press, 1998.

Chiñas, Beverly Newbold. *The Isthmus Zapotecs: A Matrifocal Culture of Mexico*. 2d ed. New York: Harcourt Brace Jovanovich College Publishers, 1992.

Coatsworth, John H. "Anotaciones sobre la producción de alimentos durante el Porfiriato." *Historia Mexicana* 26 (1976): 167–87.

———. *Growth against Development: The Economic Impact of Railroads in Porfirian Mexico*. DeKalb: Northern Illinois University Press, 1981.

Cockcroft, James D. *Intellectual Precursors of the Mexican Revolution, 1900–1913*. Austin: University of Texas Press, 1968.

———. *Mexico: Class Formation, Capital Accumulation, and the State*. New York: Monthly Review Press, 1983.

El Colegio de México, Seminario de Historia Moderna de México. *Estadisticas economicas del Porfiriato. Fuerza de trabajo y actividad economica por sectores.* Mexico City, 1962.

Confino, Alon. *The Nation as a Local Metaphor*. Chapel Hill: University of North Carolina Press, 1997.

Connerton, Paul. *How Societies Remember*. London: Cambridge University Press, 1989.

Cosío Villegas, Daniel. *Historia moderna de México. El Porfiriato, vida política interior.* 2 vols. Mexico: Editorial Hermes, 1970–72.

———. *Historia moderna de México. Le república restaurada, vida política.* Mexico: Editorial Hermes, 1959.

———. *Porfirio Díaz en la revuelta de la Noria*. Mexico: Editorial Hermes, 1953.

Costeloe, Michael. "The Junta Patriótica and the Celebration of Independence in Mexico City, 1825–1855." *Mexican Studies/Estudios Mexicanos* 13 (1997): 21–53.

Covarrubias, Miguel. *Mexico South: The Isthmus of Tehuantepec*. New York: Alfred A. Knopf, 1946.

Cumberland, Charles C. "Precursors of the Mexican Revolution of 1910." *Hispanic American Historical Review* 22 (1942): 344–56.

Davis, Thomas, and Amado Ricón Virulegio. *The Political Plans of Mexico*. Lanham, Md.: University Press of America, 1987.

De La Fuente, J. *Yalalag. Una villa zapoteca serrana*. Mexico: Museo Nacional de Antropología, 1949.

Dennis, Philip. *Inter-Village Conflict in Oaxaca*. New Brunswick, N.J.: Rutgers University Press, 1987.

Díaz-Polanco, Héctor. "Cuestión étnica, estado y nuevos proyectos nacionales." In *El nacionalismo en México*, edited by Cecilia Noriega Elio, 283–312. Zamora: El Colegio de Michoacán, 1992.

Diskin, Martin. "La economía de la comunidad étnica en Oaxaca." In *Etnicidad y pluralismo cultural. La dinámica étnica en Oaxaca*, edited by Alicia M. Barabas and Miguel A. Bartolomé, 257–97. Mexico: Instituto Nacional de Antropología e Historia, 1986.

Ducey, Michael Thomas. *A Nation of Villages: Riot and Rebellion in the Mexican Huasteca, 1750–1850*. Tucson: University of Arizona Press, 2004.

Duncan, Robert H. "Embracing a Suitable Past: Independence Celebrations under Mexico's Second Empire, 1864-6." *Journal of Latin American Studies* 30 (1998): 249–77.

Enge, Kjell, and Scott Whiteford. *The Keepers of Water and Earth: Mexican Rural Social Organization and Irrigation*. Austin: University of Texas Press, 1989.

Escalante Gonzalbo, Fernando. *Ciudadanos imaginarios*. Mexico City: El Colegio de México, 1992.

Escobedo, Helen, ed. *Mexican Monuments: Strange Encounters*. New York: Abbeville Press, 1989.

Falcón, Romana. "Force and the Search for Consent: The Role of the Jefaturas Políticas of Coahuila in National State Formation." In *Everyday Forms of State Formation: Revolution and the Negotiation of Rule in Modern Mexico*, edited by Gilbert M. Joseph and Daniel Nugent, 107–34. Durham, N.C.: Duke University Press, 1994.

Falcón, Romana, and Raymond Buve, eds. *Don Porfirio presidente . . . Nunca omnipotente. Hallazgos, reflexiones y debates, 1876–1911*. Mexico: Universidad Iberoamericana, 1998.

Falcone, Frank S. "Benito Juárez versus the Díaz Brothers: Politics in Oaxaca, 1867–1871." *The Americas* 33 (1977): 630–51.

———. "Federal-State Relations during Mexico's Restored Republic: Oaxaca, a Case Study, 1867–1872." Ph.D. diss., University of Massachusetts, 1974.

Feierman, Steven. *Peasant Intellectuals: Anthropology and History in Tanzania*. Madison: University of Wisconsin Press, 1990.

Flannery, Kent, and Joyce Marcus. *The Cloud People*. New York: Academic Press, 1983.

Fortson, J. R., et al. *Los Gobernantes de Oaxaca*. Mexico: J. R. Fortson, 1985.

Foucault, Michel. *The Archaeology of Knowledge and the Discourse on Language*. Translated by A. M. Sheridan Smith. New York: Pantheon, 1972.

———. *Discipline and Punish: The Birth of the Prison*. Translated by Alan Sheridan. New York: Vintage Books, 1979.

Fowler-Salamini, Heather. "The Boom in Regional Studies of the Mexican Revolution: Where Is It Leading?" *Latin American Research Review* 28 (1993): 175–90.

Franco, Jean. *Plotting Women: Gender and Representation in Mexico*. New York: Columbia University Press, 1989.

French, William E. *A Peaceful and Working People: Manners, Morals, and Class Formation in Northern Mexico*. Albuquerque: University of New Mexico Press, 1996.

———. "Prostitutes and Guardian Angels: Women, Work, and the Family in Porfirian Mexico." *Hispanic American Historical Review* 72 (1992): 529–53.

Friedlander, Judith. *Being Indian in Hueyapan.* New York: St. Martin's Press, 1975.

———. "The Secularization of the Cargo System: An Example from Postrevolutionary Central Mexico." *Latin American Research Review* 16 (1981): 132–43.

Friedrich, Paul. *Agrarian Revolt in a Mexican Village.* 1970; Chicago: University of Chicago Press, 1977.

García, Clara Guadalupe. *Las mujeres de Ruiz. La participación femenina durante la Intervención francesa en Michoacán, en la obra de don Eduardo Ruiz.* Mexico: Centro de Estudios Históricos del Porfiriato, 1998.

Garner, Paul. "Federalism and Caudillismo in the Mexican Revolution: The Genesis of the Oaxacan Sovereignty Movement (1915–20)." *Journal of Latin American Studies* 17 (1985): 111–33.

———. "Oaxaca: The Rise and Fall of State Sovereignty." In *Provinces of the Revolution,* edited by Thomas Benjamin and Mark Wasserman, 163–83. Albuquerque: University of New Mexico Press, 1990.

———. *Porfirio Díaz.* New York: Longman, 2001.

———. *Regional Development in Oaxaca during the Porfiriato (1876–1911).* Liverpool, U.K.: Institute of Latin American Studies, University of Liverpool, 1995.

———. *La Revolución en la provincia. Soberanía estatal y caudillismo en las montañas de Oaxaca (1910–1920).* Mexico City: Fondo de Cultura Económica, 1988.

Gomez-Quiñones, Juan. *Sembradores. Ricardo Flores Magón y el Partido Liberal Mexicano: A Eulogy and Critique.* Los Angeles: Aztlán Publications, University of California Press, 1973.

González y González, Luis. "Patriotismo y matriotismo, cara y cruz de México." In *El nacionalismo en México,* edited by Cecilia Noriega Elio, 477–95. Zamora: El Colegio de Michoacán, 1992.

———. *San José de Gracia: Mexican Village in Transition.* Translated by John Upton. Austin: University of Texas Press, 1972.

González Navarro, Moisés. *La colonización en México, 1877–1910.* Mexico: Estampillas y Valores, 1960.

———. *Historia moderna de México. El Porfiriato, vida social.* Mexico: Editorial Hermes, 1957.

———. *Las Huelgas textiles en el Porfiriato.* Puebla: Editorial José Cajica, 1971.

———. "Indio y propiedad en Oaxaca." *Historia Mexicana* 8 (1958): 175–91.

———. "Mestizaje in Mexico during the National Period." In *Race and Class in Latin America,* edited by Magnus Mörner, 145–69. New York: Columbia University Press, 1970.

Gould, Jeffrey L. *To Lead as Equals: Rural Protest and Political Consciousness in Chinandega, Nicaragua, 1912–1979.* Chapel Hill: University of North Carolina Press, 1990.

Gramsci, Antonio. *Selections from the Prison Notebooks.* Edited and translated by

Quintin Hoare and Geoffrey Nowell Smith. New York: International Publishers, 1971.

Grandin, Greg. "The Strange Case of 'La Mancha Negra': Maya-State Relations in Nineteenth-Century Guatemala." *Hispanic American Historical Review* 77 (1997): 211–43.

Guardino, Peter F. "Community Service, Liberal Law, and Local Custom in Indigenous Villages: Oaxaca, 1750–1850." In *Honor, Status, and Law in Modern Latin America*, edited by Sueann Caulfield, Sarah C. Chambers, and Lara Putnam, 50–65. Durham, N.C.: Duke University Press, 2005.

———. *Peasants, Politics, and the Formation of Mexico's National State: Guerrero, 1800–1857*. Stanford, Calif.: Stanford University Press, 1996.

———. *The Time of Liberty: Popular Political Culture in Oaxaca, 1750–1850*. Durham, N.C.: Duke University Press, 2005.

Guerra, François-Xavier. *México. Del Antiguo Régimen a la Revolución*. Translated by Sergio Fernández Bravo. 2 vols. Mexico City: Fondo de Cultura Económica, 1988.

Guha, Ranajit. "On Some Aspects of the Historiography of Colonial India." In *Selected Subaltern Studies*, edited by Ranajit Guha and Gayatri Spivak, 37–44. New York: Oxford University Press, 1988.

Haber, Stephen. *Industry and Underdevelopment: The Industrialization of Mexico, 1890–1940*. Stanford, Calif.: Stanford University Press, 1988.

Hale, Charles A. "The Liberal Impulse: Daniel Cosío Villegas and the *Historian Moderna de México*." *Hispanic American Historical Review* 54 (1974): 479–98.

———. *Mexican Liberalism in the Age of Mora, 1821–1853*. New Haven, Conn.: Yale University Press, 1968.

———. *The Transformation of Liberalism in Late Nineteenth-Century Mexico*. Princeton, N.J.: Princeton University Press, 1989.

Hall, Linda B. *Alvaro Obregón: Power and Revolution in Mexico, 1911–1920*. College Station: Texas A&M University Press, 1981.

Hamnett, Brian R. *Juárez*. London: Longman, 1994.

———. *Politics and Trade in Southern Mexico, 1750–1821*. London: Cambridge University Press, 1971.

Hart, John M. *Anarchism and the Mexican Working Class, 1860–1931*. Austin: University of Texas Press, 1978.

———. *Revolutionary Mexico: The Coming and Process of the Mexican Revolution*. Berkeley: University of California Press, 1987.

Harvey, David. "The Geopolitics of Capitalism." In *Social Relations and Spatial Structures*, edited Derek Gregory and John Urry, 128–63. London: Macmillan, 1985.

Henderson, Peter V. *Félix Díaz, the Porfirians, and the Mexican Revolution*. Lincoln: University of Nebraska Press, 1981.

Hernández Chávez, Alicia. *Anenecuilco. Memoria y vida de un pueblo*. Mexico: El Colegio de México, 1991.

———. "Origen y ocaso del ejército porfiriano." *Historia Mexicana* 39 (1989): 257–96.

Hobsbawm, Eric J. *Nations and Nationalism since 1780: Programme, Myth, Reality.* Cambridge, U.K.: Cambridge University Press, 1990.

Hobsbawm, Eric J., and Terence Ranger, eds. *The Invention of Tradition.* New York: Cambridge University Press, 1983.

Horsman, Jennifer. *Something in My Mind Besides the Everyday: Women and Literacy.* Toronto: Women's Press, 1990.

Hunt, Lynn. *Politics, Culture, and Class in the French Revolution.* Berkeley: University of California Press, 1984.

Huston, Nancy. "The Matrix of War: Mothers and Heroes." In *The Female Body in Western Culture: Contemporary Perspectives*, edited by Susan Rubin Suleiman, 119–36. Cambridge, Mass.: Harvard University Press, 1985.

———. "Tales of War and Tears of Women." *Women's Studies International Forum* 5 (1982): 271–82.

Ibarra, Isaac M. *Hombres humildes de Sierra Juárez.* Mexico, 1938.

Iturribarría, Jorge Fernando. *La generación oaxaqueña del 57.* Oaxaca: Instituto de Ciencias y Artes, 1956.

———. *Historia de Oaxaca, 1821–1867.* 3 vols. Mexico: Ediciones E.R.B., 1935.

———. *Historia de Oaxaca.* Vol. 4: *La restauración de la república y las revuelatas de la Noria y Tuxtepec, 1867–1877.* Oaxaca: Gobierno del Estado de Oaxaca, 1956.

———. *Oaxaca en la historia. De la época precolombina a los tiempos actuales.* Mexico: Editorial Stylo, 1955.

———. "Oaxaqueños notables: Manuel Martínez Gracida." *Oaxaca. Nuestra causa común*, September 1982, 12–14.

———. *Porfirio Díaz ante la historia.* Mexico: Carlos Villegas García, 1967.

———. *La viejas culturas de Oaxaca.* Mexico: La Administración de los Ferrocarriles Nacionales de México, 1952.

Joseph, Gilbert M. *Revolution from Without: Yucatán, Mexico, and the United States, 1880–1924.* Cambridge, U.K.: Cambridge University Press, 1982.

Joseph, Gilbert M., and Daniel Nugent, eds. *Everyday Forms of State Formation: Revolution and the Negotiation of Rule in Modern Mexico.* Durham, N.C.: Duke University Press, 1994.

Katz, Friedrich, ed. *Riot, Rebellion, and Revolution: Rural Social Conflict in Mexico.* Princeton, N.J.: Princeton University Press, 1988.

Kearney, Michael. "Mixtec Political Consciousness: From Passive to Active Resistance." In *Rural Revolt in Mexico and U.S. Intervention*, edited by Daniel Nugent, 113–24. San Diego, Calif.: Center for U.S.-Mexican Studies, University of California, 1988.

———. *The Winds of Ixtepeji: World View and Society in a Zapotec Town.* New York: Holt, Rinehart and Winston, 1972.

Knight, Alan. "Interpreting the Mexican Revolution." *Texas Papers on Mexico.* Austin, Tex.: Institute of Latin American Studies, 1988.

———. *The Mexican Revolution.* 2 vols. Cambridge, U.K.: Cambridge University Press, 1986.

———. "Peasant and Caudillo in Revolutionary Mexico, 1910–17." In *Caudillo and Peasant in the Mexican Revolution*, edited by D. A. Brading, 17–58. Cambridge, U.K.: Cambridge University Press, 1980.

———. "Peasants into Patriots: Thoughts on the Making of the Mexican Nation." *Mexican Studies/Estudios Mexicanos* 10 (1994): 135–61.

———. "Revolutionary Project, Recalcitrant People: Mexico, 1910–40." In *Revolutionary Process in Mexico: Essays on Political and Social Change, 1880–1940*, edited by Jaime E. Rodríguez O., 227–64. Los Angeles: Latin American Center Publications, University of California, Los Angeles, 1990.

———. "State and Civil Society in Mexico Since the Revolution." *Texas Papers on Mexico.* Austin, Tex.: Institute of Latin American Studies, 1990.

Kourí, Emilio. *A Pueblo Divided: Business, Property, and Community in Papantla, Mexico.* Stanford, Calif.: Stanford University Press, 2004.

Kowalewski, Stephen A., and Jacqueline J. Saindon. "The Spread of Literacy in a Latin American Peasant Society: Oaxaca, Mexico, 1890 to 1980." *Comparative Studies in Society and History* 34 (1992): 110–40.

Krauze, Enrique. *Siglo de Caudillos. Biografía política de México (1810–1910).* Mexico: Edición Mexicana de Tusquets Editores, 1994.

Laclau, Ernesto. *Politics and Ideology in Marxist Theory: Capitalism-Fascism-Populism.* London: Verso Books, 1979.

Laclau, Ernesto, and Chantal Mouffe. *Hegemony and Socialist Strategy: Towards a Radical Democratic Politics.* London: Verso, 1985.

Lafaye, Jacques. *Quetzalcóatl y Guadalupe. La formación de la conciencia nacional en México.* 1974; Mexico: Fondo de Cultura Económica, 1977.

Lefebvre, Henri. *Critique de la vie quotidienne.* Paris: L'Arche, 1946.

———. *Everyday Life in the Modern World.* Translated by Sacha Rabinovitch. London: Allen Lane/Penguin Press, 1971.

Lerner, Gerda. *The Creation of Patriarchy.* New York: Oxford University Press, 1986.

Leslie, Charles M. *Now We Are Civilized: A Study of the World View of the Zapotec Indians of Mitla, Oaxaca.* Westport, Conn.: Greenwood Press, 1960.

Lipietz, Alain. "The Structuration of Space, the Problem of Land, and Spatial Policy." In *Regions in Crisis: New Perspectives in European Regional Theory*, edited by John Carney, Ray Hudson, and Jim Lewis, 60–75. London: Croom Helm, 1980.

Lipsett-Rivera, Sonya. *To Defend Our Water with the Blood of Our Veins: The Struggle for Resources in Colonial Puebla.* Albuquerque: University of New Mexico Press, 1999.

———. "Water and Bureaucracy in Colonial Puebla de Los Angeles." *Journal of Latin American Studies* 25 (1993): 25–44.

Lomnitz, Claudio. *Deep Mexico, Silent Mexico: An Anthropology of Nationalism.* Minneapolis: University of Minnesota Press, 2001.

Lomnitz-Adler, Claudio. "Concepts for the Study of Regional Culture." *American Ethnologist* 18 (1991): 195–214.

———. *Exits from the Labyrinth: Culture and Ideology in the Mexican National Space.* Berkeley: University of California Press, 1992.

Mallon, Florencia E. "Local Intellectuals, Regional Mythologies, and the Mexican State, 1850–1994: The Many Faces of Zapatismo." *Polygraph* 10 (1998): 39–78.

———. *Peasant and Nation: The Making of Postcolonial Mexico and Peru.* Berkeley: University of California Press, 1995.

———. "Peasants and State Formation in Nineteenth-Century Mexico: Morelos, 1848–1858." *Political Power and Social Theory* 7 (1988): 1–54.

———. "The Promise and Dilemma of Subaltern Studies: Perspectives from Latin American History." *American Historical Review* 99 (1994): 1491–515.

Martin, JoAnn. "Contesting Authenticity: Battles over the Representation of History in Morelos, Mexico." *Ethnohistory* 40 (1993): 438–65.

Martínez Medina, Héctor Gerardo. "Génesis y desarrollo del maderismo en Oaxaca (1909–1912)." In *La revolución en Oaxaca, 1900–1930,* edited by Víctor Raúl Martínez Vásquez, 88–158. Oaxaca: Instituto de Administración Pública de Oaxaca, 1985.

Martínez Vásquez, Víctor Raúl. "Oaxaca." *Eslabones. La Revolución en el Sur-Sureste de México,* Jan.–June 1993, 169–76.

———, ed. *La revolución en Oaxaca, 1900–1930.* Oaxaca: Instituto de Administración Pública de Oaxaca, 1985.

Mathews, Holly F. "'We are Mayordomo': A Reinterpretation of Women's Roles in the Mexican Cargo System." *American Ethnologist* 12 (1985): 285–301.

McNamara, Patrick J. "Felipe García and the Real Heroes of Guelatao." In *The Human Tradition in Mexico,* edited by Jeffrey Pilcher, 75–89. Wilmington, Del.: Scholarly Resources, 2003.

Mecham, J. Lloyd. "The Jefe Político in Mexico." *Southwestern Social Science Quarterly* 13 (1933): 333–52.

Meyer, Michael C., and William L. Sherman. *The Course of Mexican History.* 5th ed. New York: Oxford University Press, 1995.

Mignolo, Walter D. *Local Histories/Global Designs: Coloniality, Subaltern Knowledges, and Border Thinking.* Princeton, N.J.: Princeton University Press, 2000.

Miller, David Lynn. "Porfirio Díaz and the Army of the East." Ph.D. diss., University of Michigan, 1960.

Miller, Frank. *Industrialization in Mexico: Old Villages and a New Town.* Menlo Park, Calif.: Cummings Publishing Company, 1973.

Mitchell, Candace, and Kathleen Weiler, eds. *Rewriting Literacy: Culture and the Discourse of the Other.* New York: Bergin and Garvey, 1991.

Murphy, Michael. *Irrigation in the Bajío Region of Colonial Mexico.* Boulder, Colo.: Westview Press, 1986.

Nader, Laura. *Harmony Ideology: Justice and Control in a Zapotec Mountain Village.* Stanford, Calif.: Stanford University Press, 1990.

Nash, Manning. *Machine Age Maya: The Industrialization of a Guatemalan Community.* Chicago: University of Chicago Press, 1958.

Nora, Pierre, ed. *Realms of Memory: Rethinking the French Past. Volume 1: Conflicts and Divisions.* Translated by Arthur Goldhammer. New York: Columbia University Press, 1996.

Nugent, Daniel. *Spent Cartridges of Revolution: An Anthropological History of Namiquipa, Chihuahua.* Chicago: University of Chicago Press, 1993.

Olson, David R., and Nancy Torrance, eds. *The Making of Literate Societies.* Oxford, U.K.: Blackwell, 2001.

O'Malley, Ilene V. *The Myth of the Revolution: Hero Cults and the Institutionalization of the Mexican State, 1920–1940.* New York: Greenwood Press, 1986.

Ozouf, Mona. *Festivals and the French Revolution.* Translated by Alan Sheridan. Cambridge, Mass.: Harvard University Press, 1988.

Pani, Erika. *Para mexicanizar el Segundo Imperio. El imaginario politico de los imperialistas.* Mexico: Colegio de México, Centro de Estudios Históricos, 2001.

Paso, Fernando del. *Noticias del Imperio.* Mexico: Editorial Diana, 1987.

Pastor, Rodolfo. *Campesinos y reformas. La mixteca, 1700–1856.* Mexico: Colegio de México, 1987.

Paz, Octavio. *The Labyrinth of Solitude.* 1961; New York: Grove Press, 1985.

Pérez García, Rosendo. *La Sierra Juárez.* 2 vols. Mexico: Gráfica Cervantina, 1956.

Perry, Laurens Ballard. *Juárez and Díaz: Machine Politics in Mexico.* DeKalb: Northern Illinois University Press, 1978.

Phelan, John Leddy. *The People and the King: The Comunero Revolution in Colombia, 1781.* Madison: University of Wisconsin Press, 1978.

Plasencia de la Parra, Enrique. *Independencia y nacionalismo a la luz del discurso conmemorativo (1825–1867).* Mexico: Consejo Nacional para la Cultura y las Artes, 1991.

Ponce Alocer, María Eugenia Patricia. *La elección presidencial de Manuel González, 1878–1880. (Preludio de un presidencialismo).* Mexico: Universidad Iberoamericana, 2000.

Porter, Susie. *Working Women in Mexico City: Public Discourses and Material Conditions, 1879–1931.* Tucson: University of Arizona Press, 2003.

Prinsloo, Mastin, and Mignonne Breier, eds. *The Social Uses of Literacy: Theory and Practice in Contemporary South Africa.* Capetown: Sached Books, 1996.

Raat, William Dirk. *Los Revoltosos: Mexico's Rebels in the United States, 1903–1923.* College Station: Texas A&M University Press, 1981.

Ramirez, Alfonso Francisco. *Historia de la Revolución Mexicana en Oaxaca.* Mexico: La Nación, 1970.

Reed, Nelson. *The Caste War of Yucatan*. Stanford, Calif.: Stanford University Press, 1964.

Reina, Leticia. "De las reformas borbónicas a las leyes de Reforma." In *Historia de la cuestión agraria mexicana. Estado de Oaxaca*, edited by Leticia Reina, 1:181–268. 2 vols. Mexico City: Juan Pablos, 1988.

———, ed. *Las Luchas populares en México en el siglo XIX*. Mexico: Cuadernos de la Casa Chata, Centro de Investigaciones y Estudios Superiores en Antropología Social, 1983.

Reséndez, Andrés. *Changing National Identities at the Frontier: Texas and New Mexico, 1800–1850*. Cambridge, U.K.: Cambridge University Press, 2005.

Revueltas, Eugenia. "El nacionalismo: De la abstracción a lo concreto poético." In *El nacionalismo en México*, edited by Cecilia Noriega Elio, 743–50. Zamora: Colegio de Michoacán, 1992.

Reyes, Aurelio de lo. "El escenario del nacionalismo cultural." In *El nacionalismo en México*, edited by Cecilia Noriega Elio, 751–64. Zamora: Colegio de Michoacán, 1992.

Reyes Heroles, Jesús. *El Liberalismo mexicano*. 3 vols. Mexico: UNAM, 1957–61.

Ridley, Jasper. *Maximilian and Juárez*. London: Constable and Company, 1993.

Rodríguez O., Jaime E., ed. *The Revolutionary Process in Mexico: Essays on Political and Social Change, 1880–1940*. Los Angeles: Latin American Center Publications, University of California, Los Angeles, 1990.

Roeder, Ralph. *Juárez and His Mexico*. New York: Viking Press, 1947.

Roseberry, William. "Hegemony and the Language of Contention." In *Everyday Forms of State Formation: Revolution and the Negotiation of Rule in Modern Mexico*, edited by Gilbert M. Joseph and Daniel Nugent, 355–66. Durham, N.C.: Duke University Press, 1994.

Rubin, Jeffrey. *Decentering the Regime: Ethnicity, Radicalism, and Democracy in Juchitán, Mexico*. Durham, N.C.: Duke University Press, 1997.

Rugeley, Terry. *Yucatán's Maya Peasantry and the Origins of the Caste War*. Austin: University of Texas Press, 1996.

Ruiz Cervantes, Francisco José. "El movimiento de la Soberanía en Oaxaca (1915–1920)." In *La revolución en Oaxaca, 1900–1930*, edited by Víctor Raúl Martínez Vásquez, 225–308. Oaxaca: Instituto de Administración Pública de Oaxaca, 1985.

———. "La Revolución mexicana en el sur: El movimiento oaxaqueño de la Soberanía." *Eslabones. La Revolución en el Sur-Sureste de México*, Jan.–June 1993, 138–49.

———. *La Revolución en Oaxaca. El movimiento de la Soberanía (1915–1920)*. Mexico City: Fondo de Cultura Económica, 1986.

Rus, Jan, and Robert Wasserstrom. "Civil-Religious Hierarchies in Central Chiapas: A Critical Perspective." *American Ethnologist* 7 (1989): 466–78.

Salas, Elizabeth. *Soldaderas in the Mexican Military*. Austin: University of Texas Press, 1990.

———. "The Soldadera in the Mexican Revolution: War and Men's Illusions." In *Women of the Mexican Countryside, 1850–1990*, edited by Heather Fowler-Salamini and Mary Kay Vaughan, 93–105. Tucson: University of Arizona Press, 1994.

Sánchez Silva, Carlos. *Crisis política y contrarevolución en Oaxaca (1912–1915)*. Mexico: Instituto Nacional de Estudios Históricos de la Revolución Mexicana Secretaría de Gobernación, 1991.

———. *Indios, comerciantes y burocracia en la Oaxaca poscolonial, 1786–1860*. Oaxaca: Instituto Oaxaqueño de las Culturas, Fondo Estatal para la Cultura y las Artes, and Universidad Autónoma Benito Juárez de Oaxaca, 1998.

Scott, James C. *Domination and the Arts of Resistance: Hidden Transcripts*. New Haven, Conn.: Yale University Press, 1990.

———. *Weapons of the Weak: Everyday Forms of Peasant Resistance*. New Haven, Conn.: Yale University Press, 1985.

Scott, Joan Wallach. *Gender and the Politics of History*. New York: Columbia University Press, 1988.

Selby, Henry A. *Zapotec Deviance: The Convergence of Folk and Modern Sociology*. Austin: University of Texas Press, 1974.

Semenario de Cambios Socioeconomicos en México en el Siglo XIX. *Estadisticas economicas del siglo XIX*. Mexico: Instituto Nacional de Antropología e Historía, 1976.

Sigüenza Orozco, Salvador. *Minería y comunidad indígena. El mineral de Natividad, Ixtlán, Oaxaca (1900–1940)*. Mexico: Centro de Investigaciones y Estudios Superiores en Antropología Social, 1996.

Simpson, Lesley Byrd. *Many Mexicos*. 4th rev. ed. Berkeley: University of California Press, 1966.

Sinkin, Richard N. *The Mexican Reform, 1855–1876: A Study in Liberal Nation-Building*. Austin: University of Texas Press, 1979.

Skaria, Ajay. "Writing, Orality, and Power in the Dangs, Western India, 1800–1920s." In *Subaltern Studies IX: Writings on South Asian History and Society*, edited by Shahid Amin and Dipesh Chakrabarty, 13–58. Oxford, U.K.: Oxford University Press, 1996.

Soja, Edward W. *Postmodern Geographies: The Reassertion of Space in Critical Social Theory*. London: Verso, 1990.

———. *Thirdspace: Journeys to Los Angeles and Other Real-and-Imagined Places*. Oxford, U.K.: Blackwell, 1996.

Sommer, Doris, ed. *The Places of History: Regionalism Revisited in Latin America*. Durham, N.C.: Duke University Press, 1999.

Sotelo Inclán, Jesús. *Raíz y razón de Zapata*. Mexico: Editorial Etnos, 1943.

Spitzer, Alan B. *The French Generation of 1820*. Princeton, N.J.: Princeton University Press, 1987.

———. "The Historical Problem of Generations." *American Historical Review* 78 (1973): 1353–85.

Spivak, Gayatri. "Can the Subaltern Speak?" In *Marxism and the Interpretation of Culture*, edited by Cary Nelson and Lawrence Grossberg, 271–313. Urbana: University of Illinois Press, 1988.

Stacey, Judith. *Patriarchy and Socialist Revolution in China.* Berkeley: University of California Press, 1983.

Stauter-Halsted, Keely. *The Nation in the Village: The Genesis of Peasant National Identity in Austrian Poland, 1848–1914.* Ithaca, N.Y.: Cornell University Press, 2001.

Stephen, Lynn. *Zapotec Women.* Austin: University of Texas Press, 1991.

Stern, Steve J. "New Approaches to the Study of Peasant Rebellion and Consciousness: Implications of the Andean Experience." In *Resistance, Rebellion, and Consciousness in the Andean Peasant World*, edited by Steve J. Stern, 3–25. Madison: University of Wisconsin Press, 1987.

———. *The Secret History of Gender: Power, Patriarchy, and the Color-Class Order in Mexico.* Chapel Hill: University of North Carolina, 1995.

———. "What Comes after Patriarchy? Reflections from Mexico." *Radical History Review* 71 (1998): 55–62.

Tamayo, Jorge L. *La realidad geográfica del Estado de Oaxaca.* Mexico: Ocampo, Hermanos, 1943.

Tannenbaum, Frank. "Agrarismo, indianismo y nacionalismo." *Hispanic American Historical Review* 23 (1943): 394–423.

———. *Mexico: The Struggle for Peace and Bread.* New York: Alfred A. Knopf, 1950.

———. *Peace by Revolution: An Interpretation of Mexico.* New York: Columbia University Press, 1933.

———. *A Philosophy of Labor.* New York: Alfred A. Knopf, 1951.

Taylor, William B. *Landlord and Peasant in Colonial Oaxaca.* Stanford, Calif.: Stanford University Press, 1972.

Tello Díaz, Carlos. *El Exilio. Un relato de familia.* Mexico: Cal y Arena, 1993.

Tenorio-Trillo, Mauricio. "1910 Mexico City: Space and Nation in the City of the Centenario." *Journal of Latin American Studies* 28 (1996): 75–104.

———. *Mexico at the World's Fairs: Crafting a Modern Nation.* Berkeley: University of California Press, 1996.

Thomson, Guy P. C. "Bulwarks of Patriotic Liberalism: The National Guard, Philharmonic Corps, and Patriotic Juntas in Mexico, 1847–1888." *Journal of Latin American Studies* 22 (1990): 31–68.

———. "The Ceremonial and Political Roles of Village Bands, 1846–1974." In *Rituals of Rule, Rituals of Resistance: Public Celebrations and Popular Culture in Mexico*, edited by William H. Beezley, Cheryl English Martin, and William E. French, 307–42. Wilmington, Del.: Scholarly Resources, 1994.

———. "Popular Aspects of Liberalism in Mexico, 1848–1888." *Bulletin of Latin American Research* 10 (1991): 265–92.

Thomson, Guy P. C., with David G. LaFrance. *Patriotism, Politics, and Popular Liberalism in Nineteenth-Century Mexico: Juan Francisco Lucas and the Puebla Sierra.* Wilmington, Del.: Scholarly Resources, 1999.

Toledo, Francisco. *Lo que el viento a Juárez.* Mexico: Ediciones Era, 1986.

Trawick, Paul B. *The Struggle for Water in Peru: Comedy and Tragedy in the Andean Commons.* Stanford, Calif.: Stanford University Press, 2002.

Turner, C. Frederick. *The Dynamic of Mexican Nationalism.* Chapel Hill: University of North Carolina Press, 1968.

Turner, John Kenneth. *Barbarous Mexico.* 1910; Chicago: C. H. Kerr and Company, 1914.

Tutino, John. *From Insurrection to Revolution: Social Bases of Agrarian Violence, 1750–1940.* Princeton, N.J.: Princeton University Press, 1986.

Vanderwood, Paul J. *Disorder and Progress: Bandits, Police, and Mexican Development.* Lincoln: University of Nebraska Press, 1981.

———. *The Power of God against the Guns of Government: Religious Upheaval in Mexico at the Turn of the Nineteenth Century.* Stanford, Calif.: Stanford University Press, 1998.

Van Young, Eric. "Conclusion: The State as Vampire—Hegemonic Projects, Public Ritual, and Popular Culture in Mexico, 1600–1990." In *Rituals of Rule, Rituals of Resistance: Public Celebrations and Popular Culture in Mexico*, edited by William H. Beezley, Cheryl English Martin, and William E. French, 343–74. Wilmington, Del.: Scholarly Resources, 1994.

———. *The Other Rebellion: Popular Violence, Ideology, and the Mexican Struggle for Independence, 1810–1821.* Stanford, Calif.: Stanford University Press, 2001.

———, ed. *Mexico's Regions: Comparative History and Development.* San Diego: Center for U.S.-Mexican Studies, University of California, San Diego, 1992.

Vaughan, Mary Kay. "The Construction of the Patriotic Festival in Tecamachalco, Puebla, 1900–1946." In *Rituals of Rule, Rituals of Resistance: Public Celebrations and Popular Culture in Mexico*, edited by William H. Beezley, Cheryl English Martin, and William E. French, 213–45. Wilmington, Del.: Scholarly Resources, 1994.

———. *The State, Education, and Social Class in Mexico, 1880–1928.* DeKalb: Northern Illinois University Press, 1982.

Voekel, Pamela. *Alone before God: The Religious Origins of Modernity in Mexico.* Durham, N.C.: Duke University Press, 2002.

Walker, David. "Porfirian Labor Politics: Working-Class Organizations in Mexico City and Porfirio Díaz, 1876–1902." *The Americas* 3 (1981): 257–89.

Walter, Knut. *The Regime of Anastasio Somoza, 1936–1956.* Chapel Hill: University of North Carolina Press, 1993.

Wasserman, Mark. *Capitalists, Caciques, and Revolution: The Native Elite and Foreign Enterprise in Chihuahua, Mexico, 1854–1911*. Chapel Hill: University of North Carolina Press, 1984.

Waterbury, Ronald. "Non-Revolutionary Peasants: Oaxaca Compared to Morelos in the Mexican Revolution." *Comparative Studies in Society and History* 17 (1975): 410–42.

Weeks, Charles. *The Juárez Myth in Mexico*. Tuscaloosa: University of Alabama Press, 1987.

Wells, Allen, and Gilbert M. Joseph. *Summer of Discontent, Seasons of Upheaval: Elite Politics and Rural Insurgency in Yucatán, 1876–1915*. Stanford, Calif.: Stanford University Press, 1996.

Whitecotton, Joseph W. *The Zapotecs: Princes, Priests, and Peasants*. Norman: University of Oklahoma Press, 1977.

Wolf, Eric R. "Closed Corporate Peasant Communities in Mesoamerica and Central Java." *Southwestern Journal of Anthropology* 13 (1957): 1–18.

———. *Europe and the People without History*. Berkeley: University of California Press, 1982.

———. *Peasants*. New York: Prentice Hall, 1966.

———. *Sons of the Shaking Earth*. Chicago: University of Chicago Press, 1959.

Womack, John. "The Mexican Economy during the Revolution, 1910–20." *Marxist Perspectives* 1 (1978): 80–123.

———. *Zapata and the Mexican Revolution*. New York: Random House, 1968.

Young, Elliott. *Catarino Garza's Revolution on the Texas-Mexico Border*. Durham, N.C.: Duke University Press, 2004.

Zaeske, Susan. *Signatures of Citizenship: Petitioning, Antislavery, and Women's Political Identity*. Chapel Hill: University of North Carolina Press, 2003.

Zendejas, Adelina. *La mujer en la intervención francesa*. Mexico: Sociedad Mexicana de Geografía y Estadística, 1962.

Zepeda Patterson, Jorge. "La nación vs las regiones." In *El nacionalismo en México*, edited by Cecilia Noriega Elio, 497–518. Zamora: Colegio de Michoacán, 1992.

Index

conflict with Guillermo Meixueiro, 181–84

Choapam, district of, 139–40

Científicos, 122, 152, 169

Cinco de Mayo: as national holiday, 19, 124; battle of, 51, 54–56, 58

Citizenship: popular notions of, 3, 190

Ciudad Serdán. *See* Chalchicomula

Clark, George S., 130

Cobos, José María: as conservative general, 28, 39, 41–43, 46–47. *See also* War of the Reform

Cochineal, 6, 31

Comonfort, Ignacio, 39

Confino, Alon, 21

Connerton, Paul, 19

Conservatives: army, 41–44, 46; conflict with liberals, 50–51; conflict with Maximilian, 58. *See also* Cobos, José María; War of the Reform

Constitutionalists, 196–99

Constitution of 1857, 158, 174, 182, 189; Zapotec views of, 3, 171; as inspiration for fighting, 23, 89, 165, 197; proposed changes to, 70, 222 (n. 7)

Constitution of 1917, 197

Convocatoria, 70. *See also* Constitution of 1857: proposed changes to

Cortes, Hernán, 4–5

Cosío Villegas, Daniel, 78

Creelman, James: interview with Porfirio Díaz, 156

Cruz de Pérez, Monica, 118–20. *See also* Pérez, Cenobio "El Gallo"

Díaz, Delfina, 61, 77, 221 (n. 43)

Díaz, Félix: at Carbonera, 62, 84, 101; during Restored Republic, 71–75, 77–78; death of, 79–80

Díaz, Félix, Jr., 122–23; supporters in Ixtlán district, 150–53, 170–73

Díaz, Nicolasa, 55, 61

Díaz, Porfirio, 3–4, 16–18, 25–27, 143–51, 186–87, 201–4; and political ties to Ixtlán district, 1–2, 11–12, 115–17, 122–29,

131; and Ixtlán National Guard, 29–30; and War of the Reform, 38–43, 46–47, 49; and Cinco de Mayo, 54–55; and French Intervention, 59–66; during Restored Republic, 68–75; and La Noria Rebellion (1871), 76–84, 86–87; and rebellion of Tuxtepec (1876), 88–92; during early years of government, 93–97; as governor in Oaxaca (1880–82), 103–7; and mining in Ixtlán district, 107–11, 144–46, 175–80; and railroad in Oaxaca, 111–14; concern for Ixtlán veterans, 118–21, 156; as "father" of the nation, 134–37; and Oaxaca governors, 151–55, 168–75; and celebrations in honor of Juárez, 158–59, 161–62, 164–67; and intervillage conflicts, 160–66; and Centennial of Independence (1910), 183–84; and the 1910 Revolution, 189–91, 199–201. *See also* Cinco de Mayo; French Intervention; National Guard—Ixtlán; Noria, La, Rebellion of; War of the Reform

Díaz Ordaz, José María, 40–42

Díaz Quintas, Helidoro, 167–68. *See also* Asociación Juárez

Dios Peza, Juan de, 57

Dolores, Guanajuato, 56–57

Dublán, Manuel, 108

Economy: recession of 1907–11, 175–80

Elections: of 1867 (presidential), 68–76; of 1902 (Oaxaca governor) 150–53; of 1906 (Oaxaca governor) 168–75; of 1910 (Oaxaca governor), 184–85

Esperón, José, 87–88

Etla, 62

Ferrat, José, 144

Flores Magón, Ricardo, 189; and anti-Díaz movement, 12–13, 167, 175, 208–9 (n. 17)

Foucault, Michel, 187

Franco, Juan Pablo: during French Intervention, 60, 75; execution of, 63–64

181; conflict with Emilio Pimentel, 170, 172–75, 184–87, 249 (n. 78). *See also* Guelatao; Ixtepeji; Ixtlán (district)

Jalisco: during La Noria Rebellion, 81–83
Jefes políticos: in Oaxaca, 30, 69, 71–72; in Ixtlán district, 36, 76, 124, 132–33, 233 (n. 4); limits on authority of, 141–43
Jiménez, Onofre, 184–85, 191, 194, 246 (n. 47), 249 (n. 78)
Joseph, Gilbert, 202
Juárez, Benito, 25, 108, 168–69, 189; and Ixtlán district, 2–4, 7, 18–19, 95, 114, 135, 174; and Guelatao, 7, 11, 157–61; celebrations of, as hero, 16, 86, 135, 157–68, 186, 197–201, 225 (n. 61); as Oaxaca governor, 30–34, 38–40; and War of the Reform, 41–43, 48; and French Intervention, 51, 55–56, 58, 60, 62, 64–65; and Restored Republic, 67–75; and La Noria Rebellion, 76–83; death of, 83–87. *See also* French Intervention; Noria, La, Rebellion of; War of the Reform
Juárez Maza, Benito, 123, 161, 174, 184, 193–95

Kourí, Emilio, 203

Lachatao, 89, 94, 102, 130, 131, 138–39, 181, 184, 192, 194–96
Land disputes in Ixtlán district, 137–38. *See also* Abejones; Guelatao; Intervillage conflicts; Ixtepeji; Ixtlán (town); Maninaltepec
Lares, Teodosto, 57
Lefebvre, Henri, 14
Lerdo de Tejada, Sebastián, 76, 81, 83, 88, 90–91
Lerner, Gerda, 234 (n. 6)
Ley Lerdo (1856), 34
Liberal Catholicism, 76
Liberals, 28, 33, 50–51
Libertad: popular notions of, 23, 48, 67–

68, 165, 189, 201. *See also* Constitution of 1857
Literacy: communal notion of, 22, 204, 211 (n. 43)
López de Santa Anna, Antonio, 29, 79
Lucas, Juan Francisco, 202

Maderistas, in Oaxaca, 190–91, 250 (n. 6)
Madero, Francisco I., 124–25, 157, 180, 189–90
Mallon, Florencia, 37–38, 78–79, 202
Maninaltepec, 140–43. *See also* Abejones; Intervillage conflicts
Manzano, María, 136
Martínez, Enrique, 182
Martínez, José María, 88
Martínez Gracida, Manuel, 24–25, 44
Mateos, Juan A., 218 (n. 9)
Maximilian (emperor of Mexico), 56–65, 68
Maza de Juárez, Margarita, 40
Meijueiro, María Jacinta, 36
Meijueiro, Miguel, 117, 232 (n. 74)
Meijueiro Pérez, Francisco, 36–37, 40; and French Intervention, 59–62; and Restored Republic, 75, 87–90; as caudillo of the Sierra Zapoteca, 94–96, 113, 115–20, 125, 136, 201, 228 (nn. 5, 7); and Ixtepeji, 98–102, 193; and mining in Ixtlán district, 108–11, 144; death of, 122, 153–54, 157. *See also* Meixueiro, Guillermo
Meixueiro, Guillermo: as caudillo of the Sierra Zapoteca, 37, 122–25, 132–34, 157, 162–63, 165, 171–72, 174, 180–84, 186; and conflicts with Ixtepeji, 99–100, 118–20, 137, 147–51; and Emilio Pimentel, 152–54, 168; and conflicts with Chicomezuchil, 180–82; and Revolution of 1910, 190–96. *See also* Chicomezuchil; Ixtepeji; Meijueiro Pérez, Francisco
Meixueiro, Miguel, 134
Mejía, Ignacio, 87
Mejía, Tomás, 65

CPSIA information can be obtained
at www.ICGtesting.com
Printed in the USA
LVOW08s0847210717

542039LV00005B/349/P